PWN the SAT®
Math Guide
Fifth Edition

ISBN: 978-0692984369

Version: 5.0.22.11.8

"SAT" is a registered trademark of the College Board, which has no affiliation with, and does not endorse, this book. "PSAT/NMSQT" is a registered trademark of the College Board and the National Merit Scholarship Corporation, which also has no affiliation with, and does not endorse, this book.

Volume discounts available for teachers and tutors. Contact mike@pwntestprep.com for details.

To Pythagoras: I wish we could have chilled, bro.

All joking aside, there are some people I need to thank. I am overwhelmingly grateful to the students who've come along on this ride, either listening to me babble in person or reading along with any of the four previous editions of this book while I refined this advice into its current form. You folks are the best—seriously.

Table of Contents

Introduction...1
    How to Use This Book...3
    General Test Strategies...9
    Miscellaneous Things You Must Know...17
Techniques...23
    Plugging in...24
    Backsolving..32
Interlude: Look for Trends...41
Heart of Algebra..43
    Translating between Words and Math...44
    Algebraic Manipulation..52
    Solving Systems of Linear Equations...59
    Lines...73
    Absolute Value...82
Passport to Advanced Math...91
    Functions..92
    Exponents and Exponential Functions..104
    Quadratics..114
    Binomial Squares and Difference of Two Squares...............................123
    Parabolas..128
    Polynomials..142
    Working with Advanced Systems of Equations....................................152
Problem Solving and Data Analysis...160
    Percents and Percent Change..161
    Ratios and Proportionality..171
    Measures of Central Tendency and Variability.....................................182
    Data Analysis 1: Graphs and Tables...195
    Data Analysis 2: Histograms, Box Plots, and Scatterplots...................203
    Designing and Interpreting Experiments and Studies...........................224
Interlude: Be Nimble...233
Additional Topics in Math...235
    Angles, Triangles, and Polygons..236
    Right Triangles and Basic Trigonometry..249
    Circles, Radians, and a Little More Trigonometry...............................258
    Working in Three Dimensions..279
    Complex Numbers..292
Extra Practice..301
Solutions..350
Official Test Breakdown..470
    Test 1..471
    Test 2..472
    Test 3..473
    Test 4..474
    Test 5..475
    Test 6..476
    Test 7..477
    Test 8..478
    Test 9..479
    Test 10..480
    PSAT/NMSQT Test 1...481
    PSAT/NMSQT Test 2...482

Introduction

Although I've got a perfect score and work with students on the entirety of the test, I spend most of my SAT-focused energy thinking about the math section. It's the section about which I've had the most arguments with people in my line of work and far outside of it. Emotions tend to run high on both sides, which I understand completely because my own philosophy on the section has changed so much since I was in high school.

I was a math guy in high school. I looked forward to math class every day. I loved the satisfaction I got from constructing an elegant geometrical proof; I thrived on the sturdy reliability of algebra. I won the award for the best math GPA. I couldn't wait to get to college and take harder, more demanding courses in advanced mathematics.

But of course, like everyone, I still got questions wrong sometimes. I'd subtract incorrectly, or forget to distribute a negative sign, and feel my stomach sink when my teacher handed me back a 95% when I'd been sure a 100% was coming.

Despite mountains of evidence indicating that I was fallible and likely to make a few mistakes under pressure, I brute-forced the math section on the SAT because I knew no other way. It's been too long for me to remember any of the questions and I'm fairly sure I never knew which ones I got wrong, but I do remember that I was devastated when my scores came back that I had only scored a 730 in math. I had done better than that in reading! FFFFFFFUUUU-UUUUUU.

Taking the SAT using only brute force math is like a Little Leaguer insisting on using a wooden bat because that's what the pros use, even though it puts him at a huge disadvantage since all the other kids use metal bats. When that kid then complains that the best kids in Little League are doing it wrong, he's basically asking that the playing field adjust to him because he refuses to adjust to the playing field.

Here's what I wish someone had told me when I was in high school, and one of the first things I tell all my students now: *the SAT is not like other math tests*. The SAT is mostly multiple choice, for one. The math tests you're so used to pwning in school are almost certainly not multiple choice. And then there's the fact that, on the SAT, there's nobody looking at your work and possibly giving you partial credit when you don't get a question all the way right. Not to mention that SAT math sections cover a vast range of content and are written by people who aren't rooting for you at all. Your math teacher in school wants you to do well and probably writes tests that are fair based on what has been covered in class. He or she is happy when nobody fails a test. The people who write the SAT just want you, and everyone else taking the test, to distribute nicely over a normal curve. They want—they *need*, really—most people to be average, some students to be in the very bottom percentiles, and only a few students in the top percentiles. That's the way the test is supposed to work.

If you want to be one of the students at the top, you need to prepare for this test in a different way than you prepare for regular math tests—even big ones like midterms and finals. You need not only to learn the material, but also to learn to identify opportunities to circumvent long-way solutions with either deft calculator skills or non-mathy techniques like plugging in numbers.

If you want to drastically improve your score, you're going to have to drastically change the way you take the test. I'm here to help.

How to Use This Book

I'm willing to guess that, since you're reading these words right now, you're pretty interested in score improvement. What a coincidence! Me too!

I spend a lot of time thinking about the best way to help my students improve without wasting tons of their time and without frustrating them more than is necessary. However, as any good tutor or teacher will tell you, big score gains are possible, but they usually don't come easy. A cursory glance at the practice questions in here—or in any book—will not be sufficient to raise your score. You're going to have to be thorough. (The fact that you're reading this introduction bodes well.) I wrote this book to be read cover-to-cover, and although I'll outline another way to approach things a little later on, I really think that reading every page and doing every drill is the surest way to improve your score.

Here are some things that you should have to help you get the most out of this book.

"Math Guide Owner" account on PWNTestPrep.com

This membership is free for you if you own this book. All you need to do is visit https://verify.pwntestprep.com and follow the instructions. You'll get access to explanatory videos, extra drills, updates to this book if/when new editions are released, etc.

Pencils

You should try to solve every single problem in this book *before you read its explanation*. If you just read my explanations, you'll probably forget what you read as soon as you turn the page. I want this book to work for you, so I want you to write all over it. Practice as you'll play: with a yellow, wooden #2 pencil that you can erase if you make mistakes.

Graphing calculator

I've been tutoring for long enough to know that some teachers, even in this digital age, still discourage their students from using calculators in math class. I understand their reasons, but I disagree. On the SAT, you're going to be at a big disadvantage if you don't really know how to make your calculator sing, so make sure you're becoming well-acclimated to its ins and outs as you're prepping for the big test.

As for what calculator to get, well, I'm partial to my TI-83, which you'll be seeing screenshots from littered through this book, but whatever you already own should be fine. As long as it doesn't have a QWERTY keyboard or an internet connection and as long as it doesn't beep or print, your calculator should be fine on test day.[*] Your calculator can probably do like ten million things, but I've compiled a short list of tasks you should know how to perform on your calculator for the SAT. If you don't know how to do any of these, Google the specific procedure for your calculator.

→ **Graph functions.** Occasionally, you'll be able to solve an SAT problem simply by graphing. We will discuss these opportunities in some detail in this book, but just spotting the opportunities won't help if you don't know how to use your calculator. Once you've graphed, you must also be able to:

⇨ Find the x- and y-intercepts of a function.

⇨ Find the intersections of two functions.

⇨ View a table of values.

⇨ Adjust window dimensions and scale.

→ **Convert a decimal to a fraction.** This is all kinds of useful.

→ **Work with exponents and radicals.** You should not have to fiddle with your calculator to figure out how to take the fifth root of something on test day. Know how to do so in advance.

→ **Use parentheses.** It's not your calculator's fault if you enter 8^{x+4} as 8^X+4 instead of 8^(X+4). That kind of careless mistake can really spoil an otherwise solid outing on test day.

→ **Access other special functions.** Make sure you know how to work with absolute value, trigonometric functions, etc.

---

[*] You can view College Board's calculator policy here:
https://collegereadiness.collegeboard.org/sat/taking-the-test/calculator-policy

Official SAT Practice Tests

Taking full-length, simulated tests is a necessary element of any good SAT prep plan. The test itself is a harrowing and protracted experience, and if you haven't put yourself through rigorous simulations a few times before you sit down for the real thing, you'll be at a real disadvantage. People prep at different speeds, but as a general rule I recommend taking at least four full-length, all-in-one-sitting practice tests before you sit for the real thing.*

Official practice tests are a very precious commodity. There are currently eight official practice tests available online. Tests 1–4 were released before the first administration of the new test (Tests 2 and 4 have been retired); Tests 5–10 are actual test administrations. The Official SAT Study Guide contains the same official practice tests that are available online. The book contains some other practice materials, too, but those are *also* available as free downloads from College Board's site, so it's perfectly reasonable if you choose not to buy the book. Lastly, College Board has also released two free PSAT/NMSQTs online, which are also worth a look even if the PSAT is already behind you. With so few official tests out there, you'll want everything you can get your hands on, even if, in the case of the PSAT/NMSQT, it's not *quite* the same.**

Anyway, once you've got your hands on the practice tests you need, here's how you take one. First, drag your lazy bones out of bed early on a weekend morning. Set your alarm to go off early enough that you'll have time to eat breakfast, take a shower, and be fully alert by about 8:30, when you should start testing.

Your bedroom isn't the *worst* place to practice, but if possible, get yourself to a public place that you can expect to be fairly quiet, but that will have some ambient noise—a public library is perfect. Part of the SAT experience is the fact that someone next to you might be a nervous foot tapper, or have the hiccups, or have bad gas. A few minor distractions during your practice tests will help you to

---

* It's important to note that although practice tests are an important part of the prep experience, if you only take practice tests and do little else, your scores aren't likely to improve much. As a student of philosophy might say, practice tests are necessary but not sufficient.

** For links to all these things—and more as they become available—go to https://pwntestprep.com/resources/free-college-board-released-tests/

be better prepared when something noisy, smelly, or otherwise weird happens on test day.

Take the whole test in one sitting. And for Pete's sake, actually bubble your answers on the bubble sheet, rather than just circling them in your book. Bubbling takes time, and if you're doing an accurate simulation, you should account for that time. As you work, make sure to circle any question you're uncertain about on your answer sheet. That way, even if you get it right, you'll remember that it's something you should revisit during your review.

No finishing early and moving on to the next section. If the section's supposed to take 25 minutes, you work on it for 25 minutes. If it's supposed to take 55 minutes, *you work on it for 55 minutes*. You can give yourself a few short breaks between sections: 10 minutes after section 1, and five minutes after section 3.

For the math questions you missed, go to the Official Test Breakdown at the back of this book (page 470), and mark all your mistakes. This way, each time you take a practice test you'll be building a database of your weak areas, which you can then use to focus your prep. You should refer to this section every time you take a test to make sure you're recognizing all the opportunities to employ your new bag of tricks. If I suggest a technique that you didn't try the first time, try it! See if that would be a better way for you to go next time you see a similar problem.

We're only talking about math in this book, but this last point goes for all sections: *do not simply grumble about your score and then take another test*. Taking the test helps you build stamina, but reviewing the test is how you actually learn. A good rule of thumb is that you should take at least as long to review the test as it took you to take it in the first place. Go back and look at all your mistakes, and think them through until you'd be able to explain them to a total SAT neophyte. If there are any questions that, despite your best efforts at review, you still don't understand, ask someone for help.

As you work through this book, consider taking a practice test after you get through the Techniques, Problem Solving and Data Analysis, and Heart of Algebra major sections, and then again after you get through Passport to Advanced Math and Other Topics. I know I just said this above, but I'll say it again: don't forget to track your practice test progress in the Official Test Breakdown section!

At the end of each unit in this book, I provide a list of Official Test questions that can be solved with the techniques I've just discussed. These lists are meant to give you a rough idea of how often you can expect to use the techniques you're learning, and are a useful reference if you want to see all the different ways a concept might be tested. Just don't spoil official practice tests you haven't taken by peeking at half their questions first.

What about Khan Academy?

Use it—it's free! I imagine some folks might buy this book once they've exhausted the resources on Khan Academy, and other folks will be working through this book at the same time they're working through that site. Either way is fine. I categorize questions in the way I think is most helpful here in this book, but you should be able to figure out without much effort how my categorizations overlap with those on the Khan Academy site. Your mission, regardless of the resources you use and the order you use them in, is to identify your weaknesses and drill them into strengths.

What about the new digital SAT?

Well, it's not here yet. But it was announced just as I was getting ready to publish this edition. As it stands now, international students will start taking the digital test in spring 2023 and US students will start taking it in spring 2024. I'll update this book again as info is released—6th edition, here we come!—but for now all signs point to minimal changes to math content despite major changes to format. If you're looking ahead to a digital test, you can ignore the distinctions in this book between Calculator and No Calculator questions, and any format-specific advice (e.g., target scores), but the content and practice questions should still be useful. Keep your eye on pwntestprep.com for more info as I get it.

Alternative study plan

I know not everybody will buy this book with months to go before their SAT, and therefore not everybody will have time to read it cover-to-cover. *I still really think you should try—I think everything in here is important.* However, here's another path you might choose to take if you're in a hurry—but not like, a crazy hurry. This plan will still take a while. It's *barely* a shortcut.

1. **Take Official Test #1.** Correct it.

   a) Highlight every question you got wrong in the Official Test Breakdown of Test #1 (page 471), and write down the relevant techniques.

   b) Work through every chapter that you've written down more than once.

   c) Do the drills at the end of each chapter. Use the solutions section at the end of the book to understand any mistakes you make.

   d) *Important:* Go back to the Official Test you just took, and redo every question in the test you got wrong, making efforts to apply the concepts you read about in this book. New techniques won't be easy or feel natural the first time, but if you want to change your scores, you're going to have to change your approach.

2. **Take Official Test #3.** Correct it and repeat steps a) through d) above for Official Test #3. Make special note of problem types you've been missing over and over again. At this point, it's safe to call those weaknesses. Reread the chapters corresponding to your weaknesses again.

3. **Hit Khan Academy.** Drill your weaknesses until you run out of questions.

4. **Take Official Test #5.** Correct it and repeat review steps a) through d).

5. **Take Official Test #6.** Time it so that you're doing this a few days before (*not* the day before) your SAT. You want this to be an accurate prediction of your score on test day. Think of it like your dress rehearsal.

6. **Get in there and PWN the SAT for real.** Do it.

General Test Strategies

When baseball was invented, bunting was not part of the game. Every batter's intention was to hit the ball hard every time. Soon, however, it became apparent that it could sometimes be useful to put the ball in play by simply holding the bat over the plate and hitting the ball a few feet. And thus, the bunt was born. The rules didn't forbid it, and it created desirable outcomes, so it became a part of the game.

There are parallels here to the SAT. You need to play the game the way it's played today, not the way it was intended to be played when it was conceived in 1947. You must use the test's design to your advantage, whether its designers meant for you to do so or not. Read on for a few SAT-specific strategies that might help raise your score.

The hardest questions are the least important ones

Imagine you're given the task of picking as many apples as you can from a particular apple tree in a limited amount of time. You know that none of the apples on the tree are any more or less delicious than any of the others, but of course the higher up they are, the harder they are to get.

Are you going to climb right to the top to get the most difficult apples first? Not if you want to pick the most apples! I guess if it's important to you to brag to your friends that you got the highest apple, you might do that. But if that's what you want to brag about to your friends, maybe it's time to look at your life and look at your choices.

Rushing to get to the hard questions faster is like climbing to the top of the tree before you've picked all the easier-to-get apples towards the bottom—the ones you can reach from the ground without climbing at all. You're risking your entire day's work by doing so. You'll probably get fired from your apple picking job for being so inefficient. How will you afford your Xbox Live subscription without that job?

In the SAT math section, the questions go roughly in order from easiest to hardest, but each question carries the same point value. There's no bonus for getting the hardest ones right. So if you're rushing through the easy questions to get to the hard ones, *you're doing it wrong*. You're climbing to the top of the tree first. You're spending precious time on questions that are very difficult without giving enough thought to questions that are much easier. If you prioritized your time differently, you might very well see a higher score. Put another way: if you stop rushing to get to the hardest questions, laboring through them, and often still getting them wrong, you'll probably make fewer errors on the easier questions. You'll make your test experience *less stressful* as you *raise your score*.

Generally speaking, you can expect to find easier stuff *mostly* in the first few multiple choice questions of each section and in the first couple grid-ins, but you'll also find some hard questions mixed in at the beginning and some easy questions mixed in at the end. Bottom line: just make sure you're spending the bulk of your time working on questions that you feel you have a good chance of getting right. That's how you'll maximize your score.

Don't worry if you don't get to the hardest question or two in a section. If you run out of time, just guess on the ones you haven't answered. Generally speaking, sacrificing speed for accuracy is a good trade-off. Slow down, work carefully, and bask in the glow of your score report when it arrives and proves me right.

Know your target

On the next page is a summary of the math scoring tables from the official practice tests. For each raw score—AKA number of questions you get right—starting at 20, you can see the highest, lowest, and "probable" scaled score (the "probable" is the average over the 8 tests, rounded to the nearest 10).

If you have a specific goal score in mind, this can help you make some important prep decisions. For example, say you know you need to hit 650 to qualify for a scholarship. The table below shows that you'll be pretty darn safe if you get 45 out of 58 questions right (a raw score of 45 is 650 on even the most punishing scale), and you might still be OK even if you get a few less than that. Therefore, you can safely ignore a few less-common question types (like complex numbers, which appear less than once per test) and focus on perfecting the most commonly tested concepts.

Raw Score (# Correct)	Probable Scaled Score	Low Scaled Score	High Scaled Score
20	460	440	480
21	470	450	490
22	480	460	500
23	490	470	510
24	500	480	520
25	510	490	530
26	520	500	540
27	520	510	550
28	530	510	560
29	540	520	570
30	550	530	580
31	560	530	590
32	560	540	600
33	570	550	600
34	580	550	610
35	590	560	620
36	600	570	630
37	610	580	640
38	610	590	650
39	620	590	660
40	630	600	670
41	640	610	680
42	650	620	690
43	660	630	700
44	670	640	710
45	670	650	710
46	680	660	720
47	690	670	730
48	700	680	730
49	710	680	740
50	720	690	750
51	720	700	750
52	740	720	770
53	750	730	780
54	760	740	790
55	770	760	790
56	780	770	800
57	790	790	800
58	800	800	800

Guess when you're stumped

You may have noticed that a couple pages ago, I told you to guess if you run out of time. On the *old* SAT, that wouldn't have been good advice: there used to be a penalty for wrong answers that would negate the benefit of random guessing. *On the current SAT, there is no such penalty.* So let me just make this really easy for you: you should never, ever, EVER leave a multiple choice question blank. If you're stumped, guess. If you're running out of time and you have 3 questions left, use your last 5 seconds to bubble in answers for those 3 questions. You have nothing to lose. (You also have only a little to gain; guessing isn't going to improve your score much, but even marginal gains matter on the SAT.)

Of course, my hope is that you won't need to guess at all on test day. If you find yourself guessing often, you'd probably benefit from redoubling your prep efforts. The only way to improve your score more than a minuscule amount is to learn some techniques to help you actually get the questions right *without* uncertainty, and that's what we'll spend most of this book discussing. Still, you need a plan for how you're going to deal with uncertainty on test day; no matter how well you prepare, there's always the possibility of a head-scratcher or two.

Be suspicious of "easy" answers to "hard" questions

Since you've been paying such close attention, you know by now that the difficulty of math questions *generally* increases as a section progresses. The earlier questions are usually easier, and the later questions are usually harder (with the occasional hard question early and easy question late to keep you on your toes). Duh, right? I've already beaten you over the head with this, and also, if you've ever taken an SAT or PSAT/NMSQT, it's likely that you noticed it yourself. But have you thought about what it means for you, intrepid test taker?

This easy-to-hard section structure has two important implications:

→ Easy questions are more important than the hard ones for your score (which we just talked about).

→ You should be leery of "easy" answers to "hard" questions (which we're about to talk about).

When you're faced with a question that's supposed to be more difficult, you should resist the urge to jump on an answer choice that seems immediately obvious. It's probably best to illustrate this with an example. Say you're cruising through the Calculator section and at question #19, you see the following.

Stephen wins the lottery and decides to donate 30% of his winnings to charity. Then he decides to give 20% of what he has left to his mother. What percent of his winnings does Stephen have left for himself?

A) 67%

B) 56%

C) 54%

D) 50%

This question isn't too tough and you might not need my help to solve it, but before we get to the solution I want to ask you something: what choice should you *not even consider*? Well, if this question was just asking you to start with 100%, and subtract 30% and 20% and end up at 50%, it wouldn't be a #19. It'd be a #1. So there's *no flippin' way* it's D. Since we know where we are in the test, we know there must be something else going on here. And sure enough, we see that Stephen gives 20% of what he has left *after* he's already donated 30% to charity.

I want to be clear: although it's sometimes presented as such, being suspicious of answers that seem too easy is *not* a technique for answering a question correctly, and anyone who tells you otherwise hasn't spent enough time learning about the SAT. But it *is* helpful to remember that, once you're about halfway through a math section, the questions are supposed to require some thought, so you shouldn't fall for answers that seem to require no thought at all.

This is not a way to get questions right; this is a way to avoid getting questions wrong.

To get it right, as we'll often do with percent questions, we're going to **plug in** (We'll talk much more about this technique starting on page 24).

Say Stephen won $100. He gives 30% of that ($30) to charity. Now he's got $70 left, 20% of which he gives to his poor old mother. 20% of 70 is 14, so he gives his mom \$14. \$70 – \$14 = \$56, so he's got \$56 left for himself. Because he started with \$100, that's 56% of his original winnings. The answer is **B**.

Actually read the question

I'll be honest: I hate that I'm actually devoting space in this guide to reminding you to read each question very carefully, but I am because I've worked with enough kids to know that errors due to misreading (and *misbubbling*[*]) are amazingly, unspeakably common.

If there's a way a question could possibly be misinterpreted by a test taker, the SAT writers have usually anticipated that error and made it an incorrect answer choice. So if you don't read the question carefully the first time, you'll feel warm and fuzzy about your incorrect answer. You *might* catch your mistake if you finish early and have time to review your answers, but there's also a pretty good chance your warm-and-fuzzy will carry all the way through until you get your score report back and see that you missed #6 and you're all like WTFFFFFF.

The SAT has, historically, been known to do things like:

➜ Give all the question information in feet and ask for an answer in inches. Of course, make the same answer in feet an incorrect choice.

➜ Ask testers to solve for x^2, which is 49 (a perfect square—those *monsters*). Make 7 an incorrect answer choice to give the warm-and-fuzzy to everyone who automatically solved for x like they do every other day of the year.

➜ Write a question about John and Susie buying iguana treats or something. Ask how many Susie bought. Make the number John bought a choice too.

So yeah. Just like the aforementioned suspicion of "easy" answers to "hard" questions, this isn't really a strategy so much as it is me imploring you to actually put your eyes on the paper and read the question carefully because the SAT has a long history of humbling those who don't.

---

[*] Misbubbling just gets a footnote. If I gave it its own chapter, I'd probably rip my hair out before I finished writing it. *Triple check* your bubbling. I can't tell you how many *very smart* kids I've worked with who have lost points to bubbling errors on the SAT. It's unbelievable to me. And they always just laugh it off! "Oops, I misbubbled, LOL." "Oops, I threw my shoe at you, LOL. Oops I threw my other one too! LOLLERCOASTER!!!1one"

Example 2: No calculator

The perimeter of an equilateral triangle with sides of length s is p. What is the perimeter of a square with sides of length $3s$, in terms of p ?

A) p^2

B) $12p$

C) $4p$

D) $3p$

Recognize that on a question like this, there's almost always going to be a choice—and often more than one—meant to seem attractive to you when you're rushed and stressed on test day.

On this question, you could breeze through the question too quickly, miss the fact that you're asked about the perimeter of a *square* after you're given information about an *equilateral triangle*, and gravitate towards $3p$. D is a classic misread answer.

The other incorrect answers are also designed to look good to someone who's completely panicked (p^2 because you know, *squares*). It's actually a helpful mental exercise to try to figure out how the wrong answers are selected because it gives you insight into the way the test is written. Enough insight like that, and you'll be well on your way to earning your SAT black belt.

The solution, again, is found most easily by **plugging in**. (Are you recognizing a theme? I push plugging in hard.)

Say $s = 2$. An equilateral triangle with sides of length 2 has a perimeter of 6, so $p = 6$. Since $3s = 6$, the square with sides of length $3s$ (AKA 6) has a perimeter of 24; that's the number we're looking for in the answer choices. What's 24 in terms of p when $p = 6$? $4p$, of course! The correct answer is **C**.

Anyway, read the question carefully. *Always*. You may be laughing now. You won't be when you lose precious points because of careless errors.

Miscellaneous Things You Must Know

There are some things you need to know for the SAT that don't warrant entire
chapters being dedicated to them—things like definitions of terms and potent but
rarely applicable techniques. A responsible and thorough SAT prep book like the
one you hold in your hands must mention these things, though, so I'm putting
them here. Please review this chapter carefully, even if the first few things you
read are familiar. If you're shaky on any of these things, the SAT will exploit that
weakness. And we don't want that. No, we don't want that at all.

Make sure you know what's going on with

→ **Integers.** An integer is a whole number, not a fraction. Integers can be
positive, negative, or zero. The following are all integers: –5, 31, 100, 0. The
following are *not* integers: 0.5, $-\frac{2}{3}$, π.

→ **Even and odd.** This was featured much more heavily on the old SAT, but
you should still know it. Be able to predict what will happen when you
perform basic arithmetic operations on generic even or odd numbers.

⇨ Odd × Odd = Odd

⇨ Odd × Even = Even

⇨ Even × Even = Even

⇨ Even ± Odd = Odd

⇨ Odd ± Odd = Even

⇨ Even ± Even = Even

⇨ *Zero is even.*

→ **Positive and negative.** Know these cold.

⇨ Negative × Negative = Positive

⇨ Negative × Positive = Negative

⇨ *Zero is neither positive nor negative.*

→ **Multiples and factors of integers.** The positive *factors* of 8 are 1, 2, 4,
and 8. Positive *multiples* of 8 are 8, 16, 24, 32, 40, etc.

→ **Prime numbers.** A prime number is a positive integer greater than 1 that
has no positive divisors other than itself and 1. You should have the first

few memorized. Here are all the prime numbers less than 100 (you might want to memorize the bold ones): **2, 3, 5, 7, 11, 13, 17, 19, 23, 29**, 31, 37, 41, 43, 47, 53, 59, 61, 67, 71, 73, 79, 83, 89, 97.

⇨ 1 is *not* a prime number.

⇨ The only even prime number is 2.

→ **Fractions.** Personally, I convert them to decimals whenever possible, but sometimes you can't escape working with fractions on the SAT. The top number in a fraction is called the *numerator*. The bottom number is called the *denominator*. Given a positive numerator and denominator ($a > 0$ and $b > 0$), the following points are true.

⇨ The greater the numerator, the greater the fraction: $\dfrac{a+2}{b} > \dfrac{a}{b}$

⇨ The greater the denominator, the smaller the fraction: $\dfrac{a}{b+2} < \dfrac{a}{b}$

→ **Remainders.** On vanishingly rare occasion, you might be asked about remainders on the SAT. It's probably been a while since you dealt with remainders, so here are two shortcuts:

⇨ If asked for a remainder, remove the decimal from the result you get when you divide, and multiply it by your original divisor. That's your remainder. Doing this on your calculator will look something like this:

The remainder, when 13 is divided by 5, is 3. You could also, of course, just do long division.

⇨ If you're given a specific remainder and a specific divisor, and you need to find a number that, divided by the divisor, produces the remainder, simply add the remainder to the divisor (or a multiple of the divisor). Sorry, that was the most confusing sentence ever. Here's an example: if you need a number that gives you a remainder of 5 when divided by 8, $8 + 5 = 13$ will work just fine: $13 \div 8 = 1$ R 5. In fact, 5 greater than any multiple of 8 will work: $8k + 5$, where k is a positive integer and therefore $8k$ is a positive multiple of 8, will always have a remainder of 5 when divided by 8.

→ **Digit places.** In the number 5,764.312, 4 is the *units (ones) digit*, 6 is the *tens digit*, 7 is the *hundreds digit*, and 5 is the *thousands digit*. The decimal places have names, too: 3 is the *tenths digit*, 1 is the *hundredths digit*, and 2 is the *thousandths digit*.

→ **Inequalities.** We use the $<$ symbol for *less than* and the $\leq$ symbol for *less than or equal to*. Likewise, $>$ means *greater than* and $\geq$ means *greater than or equal to*. Remember, *least* just means *farthest to the left* on a number line, and *greatest* means *farthest to the right*. On a number line, we represent $>$ and $<$ with open circles (like this: ○), and $\geq$ and $\leq$ with closed circles (like this: ●).

⇨ **Special note because I always see kids screw this up:** -11 is *less than* -5 because it's farther to the left on a number line. If you ever have any doubt about an inequality, draw a number line.

→ **Sets.** A set is really just a group of numbers. You'll sometimes see it spelled out, like "Set A contains the integers 3, 4, and 5." Other times, you'll see a set denoted this way: "Set $B = \{5, 6, 7\}$." Occasionally, you may find it useful to visualize the intersection of sets by using a Venn diagram:

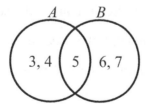

→ **Other assorted symbols.** There aren't many symbols you need to recognize, but you should know that

⇨ ⊥ means *perpendicular.* $\overline{AB} \perp \overline{CD}$ means the segment between points A and B forms a right angle with the segment between points C and D.

⇨ **||** means *parallel.* $\overline{EF} \parallel \overline{GH}$ means segments $\overline{EF}$ and $\overline{GH}$ will never touch, never ever ever, no matter how far they're extended. There is therefore no angle between them.

⇨ **≠** means *not equal to.* $2 \neq 3$.

→ **Variables and constants.** A *variable* is a placeholder that can have more than one value. In the line $y = 3x$, y and x are both variables and there are an infinite number of solutions to the equation. A *constant* must remain exactly that—constant. It can only ever be one thing. In questions that involve both constants and variables, the SAT will tell you exactly what's what. When the SAT says an equation is "true for all values of x," that means x is a variable.

⇨ It's important to know the difference between variables and constants in polynomials: in the equation $y = ax^2 + bx + c$, x and y are variables and a, b, and c are constants.

→ **Cartesian graphs.** I assume you already understand the basic layout of the Cartesian coordinate plane (also known as the *xy*-plane). Specifically, I expect that you already know how to find a point given an ordered pair like (3, 4). You should also know the following:

⇨ **Intercepts.** A graph's *y-intercept* is the point at which it crosses the *y*-axis. Since it's understood that the *x*-coordinate is always zero at the *y*-intercept, often the *y*-intercept is given as only the y-coordinate. For example, when a graph has a *y*-intercept of 5, that means the graph crosses the *y*-axis at (0, 5). Of course, the same is true for *x-intercepts*: a graph with an *x*-intercept of 3 crosses the *x*-axis at (3, 0).

⇨ **Domain.** The domain of a function is all the values of x for which the function is defined.

⇨ **Range.** The range of a function is the set of all *y*-values that a function hits at some point in its domain.

⇨ **Increasing and decreasing.**

When a graph is moving up as it goes left to right, we say it's *increasing*. When a graph is moving down as it goes left to right, we say it's *decreasing*. Because the same graph can be increasing and decreasing depending on what part you're looking at, we usually say that a

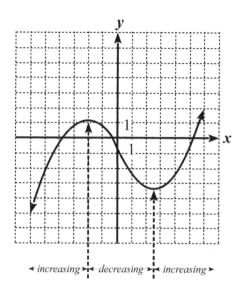

graph is increasing or decreasing over a certain interval. For example, the graph above is increasing until $x = -2$, then decreasing from $x = -2$ to $x = 2.5$, then increasing again from $x = 2.5$ on. Note the relationship between the concept of increasing and decreasing graphs and the concept of *slope*: a line with a positive slope is always increasing, and a line with a negative slope is always decreasing.

⇨ **Vertical Asymptotes.** A graph has a vertical asymptote when, in its most simplified form, a certain value of x will create a zero in the function's denominator. For example, $y = \dfrac{x^2 + 3x + 2}{x - 5}$ will have a vertical asymptote at $x = 5$ because when $x = 5$, the denominator is 0.

⇨ **Horizontal Asymptotes.** A graph has a horizontal asymptote when, in its most simplified form, it has a numerator and a denominator with the same degree (AKA the same highest power of the variable). For example, $y = \dfrac{3x^2 + x + 10}{x^2 + 6x + 4}$ will have a horizontal asymptote because the highest power of x is 2 on both the top and the bottom of the fraction. To calculate where the asymptote will be, divide the leading coefficient of the numerator by the leading coefficient of the denominator. In the example, the leading coefficient of the numerator is 3 and the leading coefficient of the denominator is 1. $\dfrac{3}{1} = 3$, so the horizontal asymptote of the function will be at $y = 3$.

⇨ **Even functions.** If a function is symmetrical about the y-axis, it is an *even function*. Another way to say the same thing: when a function f is even, $f(x) = f(-x)$ for all values of x in the domain of f. Examples of even functions include $f(x) = x^2$ and $f(x) = -x^4 + 5x^2$. Check out this sweet symmetry:

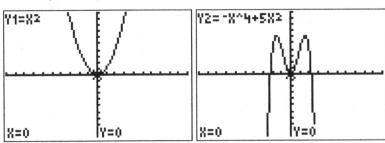

⇨ **Odd functions.** If a function is symmetrical about the origin, then it is an *odd function*. Another way to say the same thing: when a function f is odd, $f(-x) = -f(x)$ for all values of x in the domain of f. Examples of odd functions include $f(x) = x^3$ and $f(x) = -x^7 + 3x^5 - x^3$. Here's what those bad boys look like:

Techniques

Let me just say this right up front: *yes, every SAT problem can be solved with some combination of algebra, geometry, and reasoning—mostly algebra.* You'll never encounter a question that can't be solved without employing some arcane test prep trickery. Any flesh-hungry zombie can be killed with one's bare hands, too, but it's still probably best, when preparing for a zombie apocalypse, to learn a few more expedient tactics for zombie extermination. I hope you see where I'm going with this because I think I'm doing an awesome job crafting an argument for learning some math-avoidant techniques—even *if you're really good at and really enjoy math.*

The following techniques won't come easily right away if this is the first time you're seeing them, but make no mistake: if you practice plugging in and backsolving until they're second nature, then you'll be in a much better position to improve your math score than you'd be in if you just drilled yourself on purely mathematical content all day.

Plugging in

When I say that *the SAT is not like other math tests*, this is one of the primary reasons. On the SAT, it's often completely unnecessary to do the math that's been so carefully laid out before you. A lot of the time, and on a lot of otherwise onerous problems, all you need to do is make up numbers.

Sounds crazy, right? It's not. It would be crazy to just make up numbers on just about any other number-driven task—for instance, it would be a pretty bad idea just to make up numbers on your taxes—but you'll be dumbstruck by how often doing so works in your favor on the SAT. Of course, you'll have to practice **plugging in** a fair amount before it becomes second nature. That way, when an opportunity to do it on the real test pops up, you don't panic and blow it. This kind of thing is precisely why you and I have come together.

The best way to teach you how to plug in is just to show you how it works, so let's get right into an example that's *begging* to be solved by plugging in.

Example 1: No calculator

If a and b are not equal to zero, and $a + b = c$, which of the following is equal to $a^2 + b^2$?

A) $c + 2ab$

B) c^2

C) $c^2 - ab$

D) $c^2 - 2ab$

Now, maybe you see an algebraic solution here and maybe you don't. For our purposes right at this moment, it doesn't matter. We're going to solve this one by plugging in so that we can do arithmetic, not algebra. Start by assigning values to a and b. I like to keep my numbers small, and it's my book, so let's say $a = 2$ and $b = 3$. Of course, since the question tells us that c is the sum of a and b, we can't just make up anything I want for *c*. *When we have an equation, we can't plug in values for both sides; we have to choose one side on which to plug in, and then see what effects our choices have on the other side.* Once I've chosen $a = 2$ and $b = 3$, now I have to say that $c = 5$:

$$a + b = c$$
$$2 + 3 = 5$$

Next, we need to figure out what $a^2 + b^2$ is:

$$a^2 + b^2 = 2^2 + 3^2 = 13$$

From here, all we need to do is plug our values for *a*, *b*, and *c* into each answer choice to see which one gives us 13!

A) $c + 2ab = 5 + 2(2)(3) = 5 + 12 = 17$ ✗   (too big...)

B) $c^2 = 5^2 = 25$ ✗   (even bigger...)

C) $c^2 - ab = 5^2 - (2)(3) = 25 - 6 = 19$ ✗   (warmer...)

D) $c^2 - 2ab = 5^2 - 2(2)(3) = 25 - 12 = 13$ ✓   **(yes!)**

Sure enough, only one answer choice works, and we didn't need to do any algebra to figure out which one. Cool, right?

Note that if we'd used different numbers for *a* and *b*, we still would have gotten the same answer. That's the beautiful thing about plugging in! Try it yourself: what happens when $a = 11$ and $b = 19$?

Example 2: Calculator; Grid-in

If $\dfrac{m}{n} = \dfrac{2}{3}$, what is the value of $\dfrac{2n}{m} + 5$?

Same basic idea here, only this time it's a grid-in, so we know right off the bat that we're not going to have answer choices to check against. Does that make you nervous? It shouldn't! This question is *begging* for a plug in.

Let's make our lives as easy as possible and say $m = 2$ and $n = 3$. Obviously, in that case $\frac{m}{n} = \frac{2}{3}$. What's $\frac{2n}{m} + 5$?

$$\frac{2(3)}{2} + 5 = 8$$

Sure looks like the answer is 8. Awesome, right? Since we're new at this, though, let's try one more set of numbers just to be sure. Now say $m = 6$ and $n = 9$. That'll still simplify to $\frac{m}{n} = \frac{2}{3}$, and look at this:

$$\frac{2(9)}{6} + 5 = 8$$

Still works!

Let's do one more example together. This one's a little tougher; it might not be obvious right away that you can plug in.

Example 3: Calculator

If k is an integer constant greater than 1, which of the following values of x satisfies the inequality $\frac{x}{3} + 1 \geq k$?

A) $k - 3$

B) k

C) $3k - 4$

D) $3k - 2$

OK. Forget for a minute that this can be solved with algebra and think about how to solve it by plugging in. Remember, if you don't practice plugging in on problems you know how to do otherwise, you won't be able to plug in well when you come to a problem you don't know how to solve otherwise!

We know k is a positive integer greater than 1, so let's say it's 2. If $k = 2$, then we can do a little manipulation to see that x has to be greater than or equal to 3:

$$\frac{x}{3} + 1 \geq 2$$

$$\frac{x}{3} \geq 1$$

$$x \geq 3$$

Again, note that we don't just make up a number for x! Once we've chosen a value for k, we've constrained the universe of possible values of x.

So, which answer choice, given our plugged in value of $k = 2$, gives us a number greater than or equal to 3 for x?

    A) $k - 3 = 2 - 3 = -1$ ✗   (too low...)

    B) $k = 2$ ✗   (nope...)

    C) $3k - 4 = 6 - 4 = 2$ ✗   (dude, naw...)

    D) $3k - 2 = 6 - 2 = 4$ ✓   **(yes!)**

Rock. On. Note once again that if we had picked a different number for k, we still would have been OK. Try running through this with $k = 10$ to see for yourself.

When to plug in

→ When you see variables in the question *and* the answer choices, you might want to try plugging in.

→ On percent questions, you'll probably benefit from plugging in (and using 100 as your starting value).

→ In general, if you're plugging in on a geometry question, just make sure that all the angles in your triangles and straight lines add up to 180°. On triangle questions where no angles are given, you might want to try plugging in 60 for all angles.

→ Anytime you're stuck because you don't know something that you think it would be helpful to know, *try making it up!* The worst that can happen is you're no better off than before.

Plug in dos and don'ts

→ As a general rule, ***don't*** plug in 0. When you multiply things by 0, you always get 0, and when you add 0 to anything, it stays the same. I trust you see why this would be bad: too many answer choices will work.

→ Similarly, ***don't*** plug in 1, since when you multiply things by 1, they don't change. Again, this will often make more than one choice seem correct.

→ ***Don't*** plug in random numbers on both sides of an equal sign—equal signs must remain true! Remember back to Example 1: once we plugged in for *a* and *b*, we only had one choice for *c* to keep the equal sign true.

→ ***Do*** try to keep your numbers small. Don't plug in 245 when 2 will do.

→ ***Do*** think for a minute before picking your numbers. Will the numbers you're choosing result in messy fractions or negative numbers? We plug in to make our lives *easier*, so try to avoid these scenarios! With a little practice, picking good numbers will become second nature.

→ ***Do*** check every single answer choice when you plug in on a multiple choice question because there's always a small chance that more than one answer will work. If that happens, *don't panic*...just try new numbers. You can greatly mitigate this risk by adhering to the first two rules above—don't plug in 0 or 1.

Practice questions: Plugging in

Remember: Plugging in on the SAT is good. Doing so on your taxes is bad.

Note: All of these problems can be solved without plugging in, of course, but you'll have plenty of time to practice algebraic solutions later. You're here to practice plugging in. Don't be intractable in your methods. Flexibility and nimbleness beget success.

1 No calculator

If $r + 9$ is 4 more than s, then $r - 11$ is how much less than s ?

A) 9

B) 11

C) 16

D) 20

2 No calculator

If $x < y$ and $-3x > y$, which of the following must be true?

A) $x < 0$

B) $y > 0$

C) $|x| > y$

D) $x^2 > y$

3 No calculator

If Brunhilda went to the casino and lost 40% of her money playing Pai Gow poker before doubling her remaining money playing roulette, the amount of money she had after playing roulette is what percent of the amount of money she started with?

A) 20%

B) 80%

C) 100%

D) 120%

4 No calculator

If $2x + y = 8$ and $x < 7$, which of the following must be true?

A) $y > -6$

B) $y < -6$

C) $-6 < y < 7$

D) $y < 6$

5 No calculator

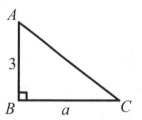

The figure above shows the right triangle *ABC* with legs of length 3 and a. What is the value of $\sin A$?

A) $\dfrac{a}{\sqrt{9 + a^2}}$

B) $\dfrac{a}{\sqrt{9 + 6a + a^2}}$

C) $\dfrac{a}{9 + a^2}$

D) $\dfrac{a}{3}$

Remember: Plugging in on the SAT is good. Doing so on your taxes is bad.

6 Calculator

If $x^3 = y$, and $y > x > 0$, then what is the difference between x^6 and x^3, in terms of y?

A) y^3

B) y^2

C) $y(y - 1)$

D) $2y - y$

7 Calculator

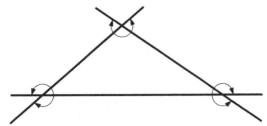

What is the sum of the measures of the marked angles in the figure above?

A) 1080°

B) 900°

C) 720°

D) 540°

8 Calculator

If $2x + 3y = 11$, what is the value of $4^x 8^y$?

A) 2^{15}

B) 2^{11}

C) 2^9

D) 2^8

9 Calculator

If $x > 4$, which of the following is equivalent to $\dfrac{x}{x-4} - \dfrac{2}{x+6}$?

A) $\dfrac{x^2 + 4x + 8}{x^2 + 2x - 24}$

B) $\dfrac{x^2 + 4x - 8}{x^2 - 2x - 24}$

C) $\dfrac{x + 8}{x - 6}$

D) $\dfrac{x - 4}{x + 3}$

10 Calculator

In a certain office, there are c chairs, d desks, and e employees. Five desks are not occupied, and all other desks are occupied by exactly one employee. All but two of the employees have two chairs at their desks, and all the other desks, whether they are occupied or not, have one chair. If $e > 2$, then which of the following expressions is equal to c?

A) $2(d - 5) + e$

B) $2(d - e)$

C) $2(d - 2)$

D) $2e + 3$

Answers:

1	C		6	C
2	A		7	B
3	D		8	B
4	A		9	A
5	A		10	D

Solutions on page 351.

You can plug in to solve the following questions on Official Tests. You might not need to plug in on all these, but this table should make clear it's a common option.

Test	Section	Questions
1	3: No calculator	8, 13, 14
	4: Calculator	20, 31
2	3: No calculator	4, 15
	4: Calculator	1, 23, 25
3	3: No calculator	11
	4: Calculator	13, 14
4	3: No calculator	5, 6, 12
	4: Calculator	26, 29
5	3: No calculator	13
	4: Calculator	21
6	3: No calculator	7, 12
	4: Calculator	28
7	3: No calculator	7, 13
	4: Calculator	2
8	3: No calculator	5, 6, 8
	4: Calculator	1, 13, 23, 25, 26
9	3: No calculator	12
	4: Calculator	14, 18, 21, 25
10	3: No calculator	5
	4: Calculator	1, 34
PSAT/NMSQT 1	3: No calculator	1, 11
	4: Calculator	18
PSAT/NMSQT 2	3: No calculator	1, 2
	4: Calculator	21, 24

Backsolving

It's important to be ever-cognizant of the fact that on this multiple choice test, one —and *only* one—of the four answers has to be right. It's sometimes possible to exploit this aspect of the SAT's design to answer a question correctly by starting with the answer choices and working backwards. Many in the prep world call this **backsolving**, and it's so powerful on the SAT because *the SAT generally puts numerical answer choices in order*, so it's easy to backsolve efficiently. On the SAT, as on many other multiple choice exams, this is an indispensable technique.

As we did in the plug in chapter, let's begin with a fairly simple example.

Example 1: Calculator

Shira keeps both dogs and cats as pets; she has 7 pets in total. A dog eats 4 pounds of food per day, and a cat eats 1 pound of food per day. If Shira uses 16 pounds of food per day to feed her pets, how many dogs does she have?

A) 2

B) 3

C) 4

D) 5

Alright. So this problem isn't that hard, and I'm sure you could solve it with algebra, but hold off on that for now. I want to talk about backsolving, and if you can't backsolve on an easy question, you're not going to be able to use this technique when it's really useful on a hard question. Instead of trying to write equations, then, let's use the fact that one of the four answers has to be right to our advantage. If we start with answer C, we'll have to try *at most* 2 answers, since C is one of the middle answers and if it's not right we'll know right away whether we need to go higher or lower. Either C is too low, which would mean D is right, or C is too high and we need to try A or B to see which is right.

Note that, since we know the total number of pets, we also know how many cats Shira would have in each answer choice. For example, if she has 4 dogs like it says in choice C, then she has 3 cats to make 7 total pets. We can represent this information in a handy table:

Answer choice	Dogs	Cats
C	4	3

But wait. We also know how much food each kind of pet eats. Let's throw that into the table, too! Each dog eats 4 pounds per day, and each cat eats 1.

Answer choice	Dogs	Dog food (lbs per day)	Cats	Cat food (lbs per day)	Total food (lbs per day)
C	4	16	3	3	19

Hopefully what you're seeing there is that we're using too much food. The question said we're supposed to use 16 pounds of food per day, but if choice C were right, we'd be using 19 pounds. So choice C is wrong, and we've got a pretty clear direction to move in: we need to use less food for Shira's 7 pets, so we need fewer dogs (who eat a lot of food) and more cats (who eat less food). So let's try choice B:

Answer choice	Dogs	Dog food (lbs per day)	Cats	Cat food (lbs per day)	Total food (lbs per day)
~~C~~	~~4~~	~~16~~	~~3~~	~~3~~	~~19~~
B	**3**	**12**	**4**	**4**	**16**

And there you have it. When there are 3 dogs and 4 cats, Shira uses 16 pounds of food per day, just like the question said. So B is the correct answer.

The beauty of this technique is that, while it might take a bit of practice to internalize, it'll eventually feel very intuitive. You start with one of the two middle choices, and if the one you chose doesn't work, the question pushes you in the right direction. Again, this was a fairly easy one, and you might not have had any trouble writing equations to solve it, but it's important that you start to look at the SAT differently if you want to change your score. Adding a technique like backsolve to your bag of tricks will make you a more formidable test taker, whether you use it all the time or not.

Let's do one more together, shall we? What's that? You want a *harder* one? I suppose I can make that happen.

Example 2: Calculator

Rex is a carnivorous dinosaur who lives on an island that is also inhabited by people. He eats one fourth of the people on his island on Monday, 13 of them on Tuesday, and half as many as he ate on Monday on Wednesday. If there are 22 people left on the island on Thursday, and nobody came to the island or left in a way other than being eaten in that time period, how many people were on the island before Rex's rampage?

A) 56

B) 64

C) 68

D) 74

As I did for the last question, I'm going to use a table to keep track of what's going on here. When you get comfortable backsolving you might decide you don't need to use a table, but doing so has always been useful to me.* Your call. You just need to pick an answer choice to start with—I usually go with C—and follow the instructions in the question to see whether everything is internally consistent.

---

* My handwriting isn't super neat. Tables help me keep things organized, so I can make sense of my work when I go back to check it.

PWN Test Prep

Answer choice	People on island before rampage	People eaten Monday ($\frac{1}{4}$ total)	People eaten Tuesday (13)	People eaten Wednesday ($\frac{1}{2}$ eaten Mon)	People left Thursday
C	68	−17	−13	−8.5	29.5

As the table above shows, if C is true and 68 people were on the island before the carnage, then 17 were eaten Monday. 13 people were eaten Tuesday. Finally, half the number of people who were eaten Monday were eaten Wednesday, which means on Wednesday Rex only ate 8.5 people. We know C isn't right if it's going to leave us with a fractional person, but more importantly, we know that $68 - 17 - 13 - 8.5 = 29.5$, which means the number of people left according to C is too big! Remember, we're trying to end up with 22 people left on the island, so fewer than 68 people must have started on the island.

Let's try B instead:

Answer choice	People on island before rampage	People eaten Monday ($\frac{1}{4}$ total)	People eaten Tuesday (13)	People eaten Wednesday ($\frac{1}{2}$ eaten Mon)	People left Thursday
~~C~~	~~68~~	~~−17~~	~~−13~~	~~−8.5~~	~~29.5~~
B	64	−16	−13	−8	27

As you can see, 64 doesn't work either, but it got us closer. At this point, we're pretty confident A is our answer, but it also shouldn't take us very much longer to confirm it:

Answer choice	People on island before rampage	People eaten Monday ($\frac{1}{4}$ total)	People eaten Tuesday (13)	People eaten Wednesday ($\frac{1}{2}$ eaten Mon)	People left Thursday
~~C~~	~~68~~	~~−17~~	~~−13~~	~~−8.5~~	~~29.5~~
~~B~~	~~64~~	~~−16~~	~~−13~~	~~−8~~	~~27~~
A	**56**	**−14**	**−13**	**−7**	**22**

Alright. Nice. We've successfully summarized a gruesome scene[*] with a neat and tidy table. High five!

When to try backsolving

→ If the answer choices are numbers (in numerical order—they always will be), there's a decent chance backsolving will work.

→ If the question is a word problem, your chances get even better.

→ Even if neither of these conditions is met, you still might be able to backsolve. Always be on the lookout for chances to work backwards from the answers!

Things to keep in mind while backsolving

→ You're almost always going to want to start with B or C, but if a question asks for a least possible value, start with A or D, whichever is least. Same goes, obviously, for questions that ask for greatest possible value.

→ Sometimes it won't be obvious to you which direction to move in if the first choice you try doesn't work. If this happens, don't freak out, just pick a direction and go. Remember, backsolving is supposed to *save* you time, so don't spend all day trying to figure out how to be efficient and not try any extra wrong choices by mistake. You'll spend less time on the question if you just go in the wrong direction first.

→ Practice, of course, will make all this easier, and reveal subtle nuances to the technique that might not be obvious right away. As with any new technique, you'll want to make sure backsolving is second nature for you before you sit down for the real test. So practice it on hard questions *now*, and reap the benefits on test day.

---

[*] This is probably obvious without me saying it, but you'll never see a question so macabre on the SAT. I'm just trying to keep you awake. :)

Practice questions: Backsolving

Note: As was true in the plug in drill, all of these problems have non-backsolve solutions, but you should resist the urge to fall back on your algebra skills. The same old methods you've already been using will just get you the same old score you've already been getting. Use this drill to practice backsolving.

1 No calculator

Rajesh sells only hats and scarves at his store, for which he charges \$13 and \$7, respectively. On Monday, he sold 15 items and made \$123. How many hats did Rajesh sell on Monday?

A) 3

B) 4

C) 5

D) 6

2 No calculator

From where he lives, it costs Jared \$4 more for a round-trip train ticket to Chaska than it does for one to Waconia. Last month, Jared took round-trips to Chaska 7 times and to Waconia 8 times. If he spent a total of \$103 on train tickets, how much does Jared spend on one round-trip ticket to Waconia?

A) \$12

B) \$10

C) \$7

D) \$5

3 No calculator

$$(9 + ai)(1 - i) = 12 - 6i$$

In the equation above, a is a real number constant and $i = \sqrt{-1}$. What is the value of a?

A) 6

B) 3

C) 2

D) −3

4 No calculator

$$3x + 2y = 15$$

$$5x - y = 12$$

Which of the following ordered pairs (x, y) satisfies the system of equations above?

A) (3, 3)

B) (2, 3)

C) (4, 8)

D) (5, 0)

5 | No calculator

$$12 - 13x > \frac{x+1}{x-9}$$

Which of the following values of x is a solution to the inequality above?

A) 5

B) 3

C) 1

D) 0

6 | Calculator

The audience of a reality TV show cast a total of 3.4 million votes, and each vote went to either Brian or Susan. If Susan received 34,000 more votes than Brian, what percent of the votes were cast for Brian?

A) 45%

B) 49%

C) 49.5%

D) 49.9%

7 | Calculator

Marisol has two different methods of commuting to and from work: she either takes the subway, which costs $2.75 per one-way trip, or she takes a car service, which costs $18.50 per one-way trip. Last week, she worked 5 days, commuting to and from work each day. If her total commuting cost for the week was $74.75, how many times did she take the car service?

A) 2

B) 3

C) 4

D) 6

8 Calculator

$$V(n) = 8100\left(\frac{7}{6}\right)^n$$

A number of years ago, Andy purchased $8,100 worth of stock in PGHH Corporation. The value, in dollars, of his stock n years after purchase is given by the function V, above. If the stock is worth $11,000 now, roughly how many years ago did Andy purchase his stock?

A) Five

B) Four

C) Three

D) Two

9 Calculator

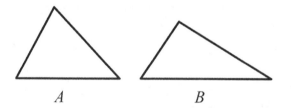

A   B

The two triangles in the figure above, labeled A and B, each have the same area. The base of triangle B is p percent longer than the base of triangle A, and the height of triangle B is r percent less than the height of triangle A. If $p - r = 5$, which of the following could be the value of p?

A) 15

B) 18

C) 23

D) 25

10 Calculator

In the xy-plane, a line containing the points (a, a^3) and $(10, 40)$ passes through the origin. Which of the following could be the value of a?

A) −3

B) −2

C) 3

D) 4

Answers:

1	A		6	C
2	D		7	B
3	B		8	D
4	A		9	D
5	D		10	B

Solutions on page 353.

You can backsolve the following Official Test questions. As with plugging in, this chart demonstrates the opportunities, even if you don't need to backsolve on all of them.

Test	Section	Questions
1	3: No calculator	9
	4: Calculator	8, 10, 11, 19, 25, 26
2	3: No calculator	2, 5, 6, 8
	4: Calculator	3, 8, 29
3	3: No calculator	13
	4: Calculator	16, 22, 24, 26, 27
4	3: No calculator	9, 13
	4: Calculator	1, 6
5	3: No calculator	3, 5
	4: Calculator	6, 24
6	3: No calculator	4, 13
	4: Calculator	4, 10
7	3: No calculator	3, 7, 8, 15
	4: Calculator	5, 6, 14, 25
8	3: No calculator	1, 7, 10, 13
	4: Calculator	8, 9, 14
9	3: No calculator	7, 11, 15
	4: Calculator	1, 13, 15, 19, 24
10	3: No calculator	1, 6, 14
	4: Calculator	15, 16, 23
PSAT/NMSQT 1	3: No calculator	5
	4: Calculator	
PSAT/NMSQT 2	3: No calculator	3, 4
	4: Calculator	

Interlude: Look for Trends

I'm constantly reminding students to look for trends on the SAT because the key to transcendent scores is a deep understanding of the way the test works. If you want to be a truly adroit test taker, you're going to have to devote yourself to taking every test you take *actively*. You should be looking for trends in the kinds of mistakes you're making, and you should also be making mental (or heck, *physical*) notes of every question you see that strikes you as something new or novel.

Do you play video games? How about poker? Do you ever go outside and play baseball? When I was your age....

True domination in any game comes only after you have internalized the systems in which the game is played. When you start playing a new first person shooter, *even if you're good at FPS games in general*, you have to spend time getting shot in the back right after you spawn until you've really learned the maps. You have to master the trajectories of projectiles that don't go in a straight line (grenades, etc). You must learn the timing of the sniper rifle. You have to learn the game's physics, inside and out, and then you need to start recognizing the common behaviors of other players. For example, you might notice that most guys run right for the rocket launcher when they spawn anywhere near it. Can you use that knowledge to your advantage?

Poker is similar. Decent poker players know how to bet given the hand they have because they know something about probability. *Good* poker players know what their opponents have based on how their opponents bet. When a good poker player sits down at a new table, she spends time learning about her opponents. Who likes to bluff? Who plays fast, and who plays slow? What are these players' tells?

For one more example, consider baseball. Professional baseball players don't face a pitcher they've never seen before without reading a scouting report to try to learn what pitches they're likely to see in which situations. Ever try to hit a curve ball before? It's really hard to do! But you know what makes it a little easier? *Knowing a curve ball is coming.* Pitchers do the same thing with batters. They know who not to pitch inside and low, for example, and who can't lay off the slider in the dirt.

I've compiled this book to help you identify the common trends on the SAT, but don't just sit back and allow me to do all the work. As you work through this book and the Official Tests, be on the lookout for familiar themes. When you take ownership of these observations, when you treat the entire SAT like a game of you vs. them, when you start to feel like you know what the SAT is going to throw your way before you even open the test booklet, *that's* when you're ready to PWN it.

Heart of Algebra

The SAT places a heavy emphasis on the "Heart of Algebra," which is a bizarre and tortured euphemism for, basically, working in various ways with linear equations. I know you took algebra in 8th grade and feel like a pro at this point—you're taking calculus for Pete's sake! Still, don't take this section lightly. The SAT has a long, long history of writing very tricky questions with very simple concepts. You ignore the basics at your peril.

There will be 19 Heart of Algebra questions on your test, and your performance on them will determine your Heart of Algebra subscore. I don't think subscores are going to be all that important once this test is out in the world, but of all the math subscores, you'll want your Heart of Algebra one to be solid.

Now is also a good time to remind you that even though algebra practice is paramount here, you should also keep your eyes peeled for opportunities to plug in and backsolve. Those techniques might really save your hide on test day, but only if you become adept at spotting opportunities to use them. Some of the questions in the units that follow will *require* algebra; others will be algebra-optional. How well you distinguish between the two will be a great predictor of your eventual score improvement.

Let's do this.

Translating between Words and Math

The SAT math section has always had a profusion of questions that, if we're being really honest, require you to do more careful reading than difficult math. This is unfortunate in that I have known a lot of students over the years whose raw math skills are not represented in their SAT math scores due to susceptibility to intentionally tricky language. If you aren't good at translating from words to math and —a little less often—from math to words, you'd better start working on it. This is a weakness that, if you have it, will *really* weigh down your score.

In this chapter, I'm going to touch on the way arithmetic expressions are commonly presented in wordy ways, and parse them as best I can. When I say arithmetic, I'm talking about addition, subtraction, multiplication, division, exponents—you know, PEMDAS* stuff. You're probably pretty good at doing basic translations here, but when things get complicated even the sharpest students have to be *very* careful.

In order to calculate his final score in a convoluted game that is destined not to be a popular hit, David must subtract two times his number of penalty cards, p, from his number of achievement cards, a. He multiplies that difference by the number of other players, n, he faced in the game, and then divides by the number of hours, t, the game took to play. Which of the following expressions equals David's final score in this infernal game?

A) $\dfrac{a-2pn}{t}$

B) $\dfrac{an-2pn}{t}$

C) $(a-2p)nt$

D) $\dfrac{(a-2)pn}{t}$

---

* You know PEMDAS, right? It's a word that's often taught to students when they're first learning the order of arithmetic operations: PEMDAS stands for Parentheses, Exponents, Multiplication, Division, Addition, and Subtraction. That's the order in which arithmetic proceeds.

First things first: a lot of people see a question like this and get straight to plugging in. That's a fine way to go, but it's a bit beside the point: plugging in will only work for you if you're reading the math right. So let's talk about reading the math for a minute.

The way you do this without making mistakes is that you make two passes. First, you read the whole thing to know all the steps that are coming. On your first pass here, you see that David will need to subtract, multiply, and divide to calculate his score. The second pass is the important one: it's where you break the question into little pieces.

Let's start with this one: "David must subtract two times his number of penalty cards, p, from his number of achievement cards, a." Order of operations comes into play here. We do multiplication before we do subtraction, so we know our expression should have $a - 2p$, and not $2(a - p)$.

The next sentence begins by saying, "He multiplies that difference by the number of other players, n, he faced in the game..." What is meant by "that difference"? Well, $a - 2p$, of course. So we know we're multiplying the whole difference expression $a - 2p$ by n. We want to see $(a - 2p)n$, not $a - 2pn$.

Now all that's left is the second half of that sentence: "...and then divides by the number of hours, t, the game took to play." Easy enough, right? We need to divide by t.

At this point, we've built the expression we want to see in an answer choice:

$$\frac{(a - 2p)n}{t}$$

Turns out that isn't an answer choice, which is a bummer. But wait—what if we distribute that n? Well, then we get choice **B**: $\frac{an - 2pn}{t}$. That's our answer.

You won't always be asked to recognize an expression or formula, though. Sometimes you'll be asked to go one step further and resolve a big block of text to a simple number.

We good on this? This book will get hair-pullingly hard soon enough—if you want to stand a chance there, you need to be able to do this kind of stuff in your sleep. For that reason, I want you to take a few minutes to translate the following sentence describing arithmetic into algebraic expressions. Answers are at the bottom of the page.

✎ The product of x and y is five times the sum of a, b, and c.

✎ The square of the sum of x squared and y is equal to the product of p squared and q.

✎ Three times the sum of a and b is four less than the product of a and b.

✎ Ten more than four times the sum of x and y is twice the product of w and z.

✎ Eight less than p is five more than twice q.

✎ The sum of x and y is greater than the product of x and y.

Example 2: Calculator; Grid-in

Tariq and Penelope baked cookies and brownies for a school bake sale. Tariq made 30 brownies per hour, and Penelope made 48 cookies per hour. If the students worked for the same amount of time and produced 312 treats altogether, for how many hours did they work?

Answers: • $xy = 5(a + b + c)$ • $(x^2 + y)^2 = p^2 q$
• $3(a + b) = ab - 4$ • $4(x + y) + 10 = 2wz$
• $p - 8 = 2q + 5$ • $x + y > xy$

This, you might be thinking, is an easy question. It is! Recognize that you only need to write and solve one equation, and not two, because Tariq and Penelope worked for the same amount of time, and in the end we don't really care about the difference between brownies and cookies. So let's say h is the number of hours the students worked.

Hang with me for a minute because I sometimes see mistakes here. We know Tariq made 30 brownies per hour, so if he worked for h hours he made $30h$ brownies. Units are a helpful way to confirm that multiplication was the way to go, if you had any doubt:

$$\left(30\,\frac{\text{brownies}}{\text{hours}}\right)(h\,\text{hours})=30\,h\ \text{brownies}$$

Likewise, we can say that Penelope worked h hours, and produced in that time $48h$ cookies.

Let's write the equation. We know the total treats produced should be the sum of $30h$ and $48h$, and we know from the question that the actual number of treats produced was 312. So we write the equation and solve:

$$30h + 48h = 312$$
$$78h = 312$$
$$h = 4$$

Not so bad, right? Let's do a drill.

Practice questions: Translating between Words and Math

Translating = good ×

The product of x and y is three halves of the product of a and b.

Which of the following equations is equivalent to the statement above?

A) $3ab = 2xy$

B) $3xy = 2ab$

C) $\dfrac{3}{2} = \dfrac{ab}{xy}$

D) $\dfrac{3}{2ab} = xy$

Francesca, Geraldine, and Hilda each have prepaid gift cards to spend at the mall. Geraldine has $20 more than Francesca has, and Hilda has one third of the money Geraldine has. If the dollar amounts Francesca, Geraldine, and Hilda have are represented by f, g, and h, respectively, which of the following equations is true?

A) $\dfrac{1}{3}h = g$

B) $\dfrac{1}{3}h = f + 20$

C) $3h = f + 20$

D) $g - 20 = 3h$

Nadine works in a call center. Last week, she took x calls on Monday. On Tuesday, she took 13 more calls than she took Monday. On Wednesday, she took 9 fewer calls than she took on Tuesday. On Thursday, she took 5 fewer calls than she took on Wednesday. On Friday, she took 118 calls. Which of the following expressions shows how many calls Nadine took during her Monday-to-Friday work week, in terms of x ?

A) $28x + 118$

B) $4x + 134$

C) $x + 117$

D) $4x + 117$

The product of a and b is 17 more than the sum of a and $2b$. If $a = 3$, what is the value of b ?

Kent has half as many marbles as Justine has. Justine has twice as many marbles as Eloise has. If Kent has 68 marbles, how many marbles does Eloise have?

6 Calculator

A biologist wants to understand how a certain hormone affects digestion in rats, so she designs an experiment during which some rats will be injected with the hormone. Seven technicians work in the biologist's lab, and each one can inject one rat with the hormone per minute. Which of the following equations could be used to model the number of rats, y, still waiting to be injected after x minutes if the biologist wants to inject a total of 119 rats in her study?

A) $y = 7x + 119$

B) $y = 7x - 119$

C) $7x + y = 119$

D) $7y + x = 119$

7 Calculator

A store manager calculates his store's monthly utility expenses using two expense rates, r_1 for the dollar cost per hour the store was open during the month and r_2 for the dollar cost per hour the store was not open during the month. During September, which has 30 days, the store was open 8 hours a day, except one day when it was open for 15 hours for a special sale. Which of the following expressions should the manager use to calculate the store's utility expenses, in dollars, for September?

A) $247r_1 + 473r_2$

B) $(247r_1)(473r_2)$

C) $473r_1 + 247r_2$

D) $\dfrac{473r_1}{247r_2}$

8 Calculator; Grid-in

Peter owns a number of apartments, which he rents to tenants on a monthly basis. At the end of every year, he projects his monthly rental income for the next year by calculating the product of his average monthly rent in the previous year and the number of apartments he owns, and then subtracting 10 percent for vacancies to keep his projection conservative. In 2015, Peter owned 6 apartments and his average rent was \$740 per month. What is Peter's projected monthly income, in dollars, for 2016 ? (Disregard the \$ sign when gridding your answer.)

Translating = good ×

9 Calculator; Grid-in

$$A(m) = 4{,}523 + km$$

On June 1, 2010, there were 4,523 accounts on a certain online forum site. On June 1, 2015, the same site had 41,783 accounts. The site's administrator recently lost his analytics data in a crash, so he wants to model his historical data with the equation above to approximate the number of accounts on the site during the time for which he does not have data. If $A(m)$ represents the approximate number of accounts on the site m months after June 1, 2010, what value should the administrator use for k ?

10 Calculator; Grid-in

Gus plans to sell a limited number of T-shirts printed with a design he made. It costs him $690 to purchase the unprinted T-shirts and the screen printing supplies he needs to produce his finished product. He prints 50 shirts, and is sure he will sell them all because his designs are in high demand. He wants his profit (the difference between his sales revenue and his expenses) to be at least 60% of his expenses. If he will only sell his shirts for a whole dollar amount (for example, $8.00), what is the lowest price Gus can set for the shirts? (Disregard the $ sign when gridding your answer.)

Answers:

1	A		6	C
2	C		7	A
3	B		8	3996
4	20		9	621
5	68		10	23

Solutions on page 355.

The following Official Test questions will test whether you're an effective translator. There are so many of them that I was afraid I'd run out of room! This is an *important* skill, often tested in combinations with other skills.

Test	Section	Questions
1	3: No calculator	3, 4, 6
	4: Calculator	4, 19, 20, 32
2	3: No calculator	3, 14, 16
	4: Calculator	1, 6, 8, 9, 12, 21, 23, 34, 35, 37, 38
3	3: No calculator	1, 4, 15, 19
	4: Calculator	8, 17, 22, 24, 31, 35, 37, 38
4	3: No calculator	7, 12, 20
	4: Calculator	1, 2, 3, 5, 6, 16, 17, 31, 32, 34, 35, 37, 38
5	3: No calculator	7, 8, 13, 15, 16
	4: Calculator	6, 7, 25, 35
6	3: No calculator	1, 2, 14, 19
	4: Calculator	2, 3, 4, 9, 10, 18, 19, 23, 29, 31, 33, 37, 38
7	3: No calculator	1, 6, 8, 9, 14
	4: Calculator	11, 17, 26, 33
8	3: No calculator	5, 10, 13, 19
	4: Calculator	1, 6, 7, 12, 15, 20, 21, 29, 37
9	3: No calculator	4, 5
	4: Calculator	10, 13, 14, 18, 19
10	3: No calculator	2, 3, 16
	4: Calculator	1, 2, 3, 21, 22, 29, 31
PSAT/NMSQT 1	3: No calculator	1, 5, 7, 8, 9
	4: Calculator	1, 2, 7, 11, 25, 29, 30, 31
PSAT/NMSQT 2	3: No calculator	6, 7, 9, 10, 15
	4: Calculator	2, 19, 23, 28, 30, 31

Algebraic Manipulation

I can't stress this enough: algebraic manipulation is where the rubber hits the road, folks. You need to be able to deftly add to, subtract from, multiply, and divide both sides of an equation to solve for a variable like x, or an expression like $\dfrac{5p}{w}$. If you want a high score on the SAT, you need to be able to do this in your sleep. Performing well on pretty much any question that falls under "Heart of Algebra" (or "Passport to Advanced Math," for that matter) will require your mastery of algebraic manipulation.[*]

When we talk about algebraic manipulation, we're really talking about the basic operations: addition, subtraction, multiplication, and division. You need to know how to deploy those operations to maximum effect when, for example, you need to solve for x, but it's in the denominator of a fraction. Hmm...that seems like something we should actually do in an example!

Example 1: Calculator

$$\frac{k+7}{x+1} = \frac{5}{2}$$

If $k = 3$ in the equation above, and $x > 0$, what is the value of x ?

A) 2

B) 3

C) 4

D) 5

First of all, yes. Total backsolve.[**] You might see this and choose to backsolve instantly on the real test, and you'd get the right answer. However, because we're talking about algebraic manipulation, let's manipulate.

---

[*]   Forgive me for hovering on every step in this chapter—I'll move more quickly later, but right now we really want to make sure this stuff is solid. I know for some people their first algebra class was a long time ago, and I cannot stress enough how much you're going to need to be automatic with this by test day.

[**] *Always* be on the lookout for opportunities to plug in or backsolve—that way you'll be ready by test day!

PWN Test Prep

First, substitute 3 in for k:

$$\frac{3+7}{x+1}=\frac{5}{2}$$

$$\frac{10}{x+1}=\frac{5}{2}$$

Now the important part. When you have x (or whatever you want to solve for) in a denominator, then you're going to have to multiply by that denominator to be able to manipulate it freely. In this case, we're going to multiply both sides of the equation by $x + 1$:

$$\frac{10}{x+1}(x+1)=\frac{5}{2}(x+1)$$

$$10=\frac{5}{2}(x+1)$$

The $x + 1$ cancels from the left, and now it's there on the right, in a much easier place to deal with. Let's do one more thing to rid ourselves of that last fraction—let's multiply both sides by 2 to cancel out the denominator in $\frac{5}{2}$, and then distribute that 5:

$$10(2)=(2)\frac{5}{2}(x+1)$$

$$20=5(x+1)$$

$$20 = 5x + 5$$

Now we're home free, right? Subtract 5 from each side, then divide by 5 and you've got x:

$$20 - 5 = 5x + 5 - 5$$

$$15 = 5x$$

$$\frac{15}{5}=\frac{5x}{5}$$

$$3 = x$$

No sweat—the answer is **B**.

Again, I know you might be thinking, *yeah Mike, I get it; I've been solving for x for years. Take me to the questions about dividing polynomials!* Well, you can jump to those yourself, I suppose (page 144), but let me caution you: I have worked with many bright students over the years, and I've learned never to be surprised when someone who has a 98 average in calculus gets turned around solving for x when it's in a denominator. The SAT tests you on stuff you haven't really had to practice in years; take a little time to shake the rust off.

Practice solving these five equations for x, then (finally) we'll move on. (Answers are at the bottom of the page.)

✎ $\dfrac{8}{x-2}=2$

✎ $\dfrac{16}{2x-1}=\dfrac{18}{x}$

✎ $\dfrac{90+x}{x}=31$

✎ $\dfrac{11}{x+6}=\dfrac{2}{x-3}$

✎ $\dfrac{16}{x+1}=\dfrac{19}{x-11}$

Now, let's move on to something a bit trickier, shall we?

Example 2: No calculator

$$P = x + rn - wn - c$$

Ms. Blackburn owns a construction business. She uses the equation above to calculate the profit, P, she makes on a project. Her revenues are a flat fee, x, plus the product of an hourly rate per worker, r, and the number of workers on the project, n. From that she subtracts the product of n and the average hourly wage her workers earn, w, and all other costs (raw materials, tools, insurance, fuel, etc.) she incurs to complete the project, which she lumps together as c. What is n in terms of P, x, r, w, and c?

A) $\dfrac{P-x+c}{rw}$

B) $\dfrac{P-x-c}{r+w}$

C) $\dfrac{P-x+c}{r-w}$

D) $\dfrac{P+x-c}{r-w}$

Total plug in question, right? Make up numbers for x, r, n, w, and c, and put them into the equation to get P. Then put all those into each answer choice to see which equals n! I hope you'll try that on your own, for the practice, but again, in the manipulation chapter, I'm going to do manipulation. First, let's get everything that doesn't have an n in it on one side of the equation:

$$P - x + c = rn - wn$$

Now we still have a problem: we have more than one n written there! We need to factor n out of each term on the right hand side:

$$P - x + c = n(r - w)$$

Once we've done that, we can divide by $r - w$ and be done with this!

$$\frac{P - x + c}{r - w} = n$$

So the answer is **C**.

Final thoughts

Here's a short list of things you should be very careful to do if you want to be unstoppable on basic algebraic manipulation questions.

→ Be careful with your signs. Perhaps the most common kind of mistake on these questions is the flipped negative.

→ Think before you leap. Before you go on autopilot, make sure you know what you're trying to accomplish.

  ⇨ Know what the question wants you to solve for.

  ⇨ Make sure that every step you take actually gets you closer to that goal.

→ Remember that anything you do to one side of an equation *must* also be done to the other side.

1 No calculator

If $\dfrac{x+3}{x-3} = 4$, what is the value of x ?

A) 1

B) 3

C) 5

D) 12

2 No calculator

$$(5x + 1) - (3x + 2) + 3(x + 5)$$

If the expression above is rewritten in the form $ax + b$, where a and b are constants, which of the following statements is true?

A) $a > b$

B) $a < b$

C) $a = b$

D) $a = -b$

3 No calculator

$$P = x + \dfrac{t - 70}{10}$$

The pressure of a gas in a container depends on its temperature. An auto mechanic uses the formula above to estimate actual tire pressure, P, in pounds per square inch (psi), given the temperature outside, t, in degrees Fahrenheit, and the pressure, x, in psi to which the tire was originally inflated in a factory environment that is air conditioned to 70° Fahrenheit. Which of the following expressions could be used to determine the approximate temperature outside given a tire's actual pressure and original inflated pressure?

A) $10P - 10x + 70$

B) $10P - 10x + 700$

C) $10P + 10x - 70$

D) $P + 10x - 70$

4 No calculator; Grid-in

If $\dfrac{m}{2n} = 15$, what is the value of $\dfrac{m}{3n}$?

5 No calculator; Grid-in

If $\dfrac{1}{3}x + \dfrac{4}{9}x = \dfrac{5}{9} - \dfrac{1}{6}$, what is the value of x ?

6 Calculator

$$9ax + b - 3c$$

$$-2ax + b + c$$

If a, b, and c are constants, which of the following is the sum of the two expressions above?

A) $7ax + b + 2c$

B) $-18ax + b - 3c$

C) $7ax + 2(b - c)$

D) $11ax - 4c$

7 Calculator

For what value of x is $19 = 6 + \dfrac{x}{31}$?

A) 403

B) 496

C) 589

D) 775

8 Calculator

$$\frac{pqr}{mn} + 34a = 374$$

If m and n are both greater than zero, then according to the equation above, which of the following is equal to a ?

A) $11 - \dfrac{pqr}{34mn}$

B) $374\left(\dfrac{mn}{pqr}\right) - 34$

C) $374\left(\dfrac{pqr}{mn}\right) - 34$

D) $11 + \dfrac{mn}{34pqr}$

9 Calculator; Grid-in

If $11y + 6 = 139$, what is the value of $22y - 6$?

10 Calculator; Grid-in

$$8x - 1 < 2x + 5$$

If $x > 0$, what is one value of x that satisfies the inequality above?

Answers:

1	C	6	C
2	B	7	A
3	A	8	A
4	10	9	260
5	.5 or 1/2	10	$0 < a < 1$

Solutions on page 357.

The following Official Test questions will require you to perform algebraic manipulation. There are a lot of them.

Test	Section	Questions
1	3: No calculator	1, 5, 7, 8, 13, 16, 20
	4: Calculator	9, 10, 11
2	3: No calculator	1, 5, 12, 17
	4: Calculator	3, 6, 22, 24, 34, 37, 38
3	3: No calculator	2, 5, 16, 17
	4: Calculator	6, 7, 13, 19, 30, 33
4	3: No calculator	5, 9, 10, 13, 14
	4: Calculator	16, 19
5	3: No calculator	5, 6, 15, 16, 17, 19
	4: Calculator	4, 8, 10, 21, 26, 33
6	3: No calculator	6, 7, 17
	4: Calculator	1, 5, 17, 29, 31, 32
7	3: No calculator	2, 16, 20
	4: Calculator	2, 6, 9, 19, 20, 26
8	3: No calculator	1, 3, 12
	4: Calculator	8, 9, 27, 32
9	3: No calculator	2, 7, 8, 11, 12, 17
	4: Calculator	1, 3, 16
10	3: No calculator	1, 8
	4: Calculator	4, 6, 17, 21, 27
PSAT/NMSQT 1	3: No calculator	2, 7, 11, 14, 15, 16
	4: Calculator	4
PSAT/NMSQT 2	3: No calculator	1, 2, 17
	4: Calculator	9, 10, 21

Solving Systems of Linear Equations

One of the kinds of questions you *know* you're going to see, probably more than once, on your SAT is solving systems of linear equations. For example:

$$17x + 3y = 40$$
$$19x - 6y = 26$$

Which ordered pair (x, y) satisfies the system of equations above?

A) $(2, -2)$

B) $(2, 2)$

C) $(-2, 2)$

D) $(-2, -2)$

There are a bunch of good ways to solve such a problem, and I think you should know all of them. So, I'm going to talk about all of them. That's what you bought this book for, after all.

Substitution

To solve by substitution, first you'll want to get one of the variables in one of the equations alone. It doesn't matter which variable, and it doesn't matter which equation, so pick the one that looks easiest to isolate. I'm gonna get the y from the first equation by itself. First, I'll subtract the x term from each side, then divide each side by 3 to get y alone:

$$17x + 3y = 40$$
$$3y = 40 - 17x$$
$$y = \frac{40}{3} - \frac{17x}{3}$$

Once I've got y alone, I'm going to substitute what I now know y equals into the *other* equation. This is important! You won't get anywhere if you substitute back into the equation you just manipulated—you'll eventually just end up at $0 = 0$. Yeah, it's a valid equation, but it's not getting you anywhere.

$$19x - 6y = 26$$
$$19x - 6\left(\frac{40}{3} - \frac{17x}{3}\right) = 26$$

Now I'm going to simplify and solve that equation for x:

$$19x - (80 - 34x) = 26$$
$$19x - 80 + 34x = 26$$
$$53x - 80 = 26$$
$$53x = 106$$
$$x = 2$$

Once I've got my x, I can put it into one of the previous equations (it doesn't matter which) to get y. I like to use the equation I already solved for y to save me a step or two:

$$y = \frac{40}{3} - \frac{17x}{3}$$
$$y = \frac{40}{3} - \frac{17(2)}{3}$$
$$y = \frac{40}{3} - \frac{34}{3}$$
$$y = \frac{6}{3}$$
$$y = 2$$

So there you have it. Choice B is the answer: $(2, 2)$ is a solution for that system.

Elimination

Substitution is the classic approach—the mainstay of algebra teachers everywhere. Most students I run into know how to do it and are comfortable with it, and even those who are a little rusty are at least familiar with the technique. Elimination, to my constant amazement, seems less universally known. I say to my amazement because elimination is awesome. Let me show you just *how* awesome by solving the same question with elimination that we just solved with substitution.

Example 1 (again): Still No calculator

$$17x + 3y = 40$$
$$19x - 6y = 26$$

Which ordered pair (x, y) satisfies the system of equations above?

A) $(2, -2)$

B) $(2, 2)$

C) $(-2, 2)$

D) $(-2, -2)$

To solve the same problem with elimination, what we'll want to do is instead of trying to isolate any variables, find a way to multiply one of the equations by something so that either the coefficients of x or the coefficients of y can cancel each other out. I see an easy way to do that:

$$2(17x + 3y) = 2(40)$$
$$34x + 6y = 80$$

That's what I'm talking about! I've got a $6y$ there, and a $-6y$ in the other equation: $19x - 6y = 26$. Now all I need to do is add one equation to the other, eliminating the $6y$ terms, making it *very* easy to solve for x:

$$34x + 6y = 80$$
$$\underline{+\ 19x - 6y = 26}$$
$$53x + 0y = 106$$

$$53x = 106$$
$$x = 2$$

Easy, right? Now to find y, we just substitute 2 in for x in either equation:

$$19x - 6y = 26$$
$$19(2) - 6y = 26$$
$$38 - 6y = 26$$
$$-6y = -12$$
$$y = 2$$

Cool, right? Unsurprisingly, because math works, we landed on the same answer with both methods. Let's try a tougher one with elimination.

$$\frac{1}{3}x + \frac{1}{6}y = 12$$

$$2x + 5y = 21$$

Which ordered pair (x, y) satisfies the system of equations above?

A) $\left(\dfrac{339}{8}, -\dfrac{51}{4}\right)$

B) $(18, 36)$

C) $\left(\dfrac{1}{2}, 4\right)$

D) $\left(-3, \dfrac{29}{5}\right)$

Again, to solve with elimination we're going to find a way to multiply one of the equations by something so that either the x-coefficients in each equation are equal, or the y-coefficients are equal. I see an easy way to do that:

$$\frac{1}{3}x + \frac{1}{6}y = 12$$

$$6\left(\frac{1}{3}x + \frac{1}{6}y\right) = 6(12)$$

$$2x + y = 72$$

There—now we have a $2x$ in both equations. All we need to do now is subtract one equation from the other, and we'll be left with nothing but y terms!

$$\begin{array}{r} 2x + 5y = 21 \\ -\,(2x + y = 72) \\ \hline 0x + 4y = -51 \end{array}$$

$$4y = -51$$

$$y = -\frac{51}{4}$$

Awesome, right? And because there's only one choice with $-\frac{51}{4}$ as a y-value, we're able to conclude that the answer is A and move on, assuming we trust ourselves not to have made any calculation errors. (But then again, I never like to assume I haven't made an error if I have time to *confirm* that I haven't made an error, so I'm going to finish the problem.)

$$2x + 5y = 21$$
$$2x + 5\left(-\frac{51}{4}\right) = 21$$
$$2x - \frac{255}{4} = 21$$
$$2x - \frac{255}{4} = \frac{84}{4}$$
$$2x = \frac{339}{4}$$
$$x = \frac{339}{8}$$

So there you go—substitution and elimination are two great ways to solve systems of equations. But we're not done yet, folks. We've barely even gotten started!

Backsolving

A multiple choice question like this can also be solved by backsolving. All you have to do is try answer choices by making sure they work *in both equations*. Only the correct answer choice will result in true outcomes when substituted into the given equations.

Example 2 (again): Calculator still OK

$$\frac{1}{3}x + \frac{1}{6}y = 12$$

$$2x + 5y = 21$$

Which ordered pair (x, y) satisfies the system of equations above?

A) $\left(\dfrac{339}{8}, -\dfrac{51}{4}\right)$

B) $(18, 36)$

C) $\left(\dfrac{1}{2}, 4\right)$

D) $\left(-3, \dfrac{29}{5}\right)$

Here's what happens when you backsolve with a wrong answer choice (I'll use choice B):

$$\frac{1}{3}x + \frac{1}{6}y = 12$$

$$\frac{1}{3}(18) + \frac{1}{6}(36) = 12$$

$$6 + 6 = 12$$

$$12 = 12$$

That worked for the first equation. But let's see what happens in the second equation:

$$2x + 5y = 21$$

$$2(18) + 5(36) = 21$$

$$36 + 180 = 21$$

$$216 = 21$$

Nope—that's not true at all! It's evil! Kill it with a heavy thing!

The right answer, though, will work beautifully:

$$\frac{1}{3}x + \frac{1}{6}y = 12$$

$$\frac{1}{3}\left(\frac{339}{8}\right) + \frac{1}{6}\left(-\frac{51}{4}\right) = 12$$

$$\frac{113}{8} - \frac{17}{8} = 12$$

$$\frac{96}{8} = 12$$

$$12 = 12$$

Yep!

$$2x + 5y = 21$$

$$2\left(\frac{339}{8}\right) + 5\left(-\frac{51}{4}\right) = 21$$

$$\frac{339}{4} - \frac{255}{4} = 21$$

$$\frac{84}{4} = 21$$

$$21 = 21$$

Yep again! That's a good answer.

Of course, I'm showing a lot of intermediate steps you might not need to do yourself if you're in the calculator section. You can backsolve this problem with two lines in your calculator. All you need to do is type the left-side of the equation, with the ordered pair you want to try out substituted in for x and y, into your calculator and see what you get.

Look at the calculator screen on the right. When you see that both equations worked out the way the question said they would, equaling 12 and 21, respectively, then you know that the ordered pair $\left(\frac{339}{8}, -\frac{51}{4}\right)$ satisfies that system!

Graphing

Always remember, as you're taking the SAT, that when two graphs intersect, they do so at a point (x, y) that is a solution for the two equations that make those graphs. If you're in the section where calculators are allowed (and with the numbers in this question we're playing with, you probably would be), then you have still more weapons for solving systems of equations at your disposal. Let's look at that question again.

$$\frac{1}{3}x + \frac{1}{6}y = 12$$

$$2x + 5y = 21$$

Which ordered pair (x, y) satisfies the system of equations above?

A) $\left(\frac{339}{8}, -\frac{51}{4} \right)$

B) $(18, 36)$

C) $\left(\frac{1}{2}, 4 \right)$

D) $\left(-3, \frac{29}{5} \right)$

To solve a system of equations by graphing, first get each equation into $y =$ form:

$$\frac{1}{3}x + \frac{1}{6}y = 12 \qquad\qquad 2x + 5y = 21$$

$$\frac{1}{6}y = 12 - \frac{1}{3}x \qquad\qquad 5y = 21 - 2x$$

$$y = 72 - 2x \qquad\qquad y = \frac{21}{5} - \frac{2}{5}x$$

Pop those into your calculator and graph! If your window is currently set to standard zoom, you'll probably only see one line, as shown below. You should expect this to happen from time to time—the writers of the SAT would love to see you doing the algebra, not taking graphing shortcuts.

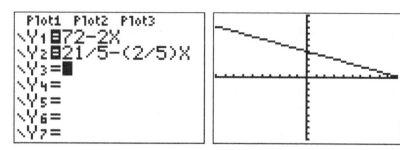

Try zooming out a bunch by setting your window to go from −100 to 100 in both axes, instead of the standard −10 to 10. Ahh, that's better.

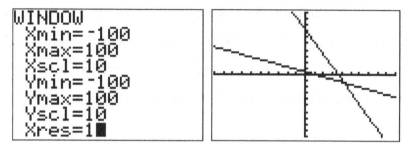

Now just use your calculator's intersect function! On a TI-83 or TI-84, you're going to hit [2nd] [TRACE] to open up the CALC menu, and then select intersect. Hit ENTER on the first line for First curve,* then hit ENTER on the second line for Second curve. The calculator asks for a Guess next— you don't need to do anything here but hit ENTER.** Look, here's what you should see at every step:

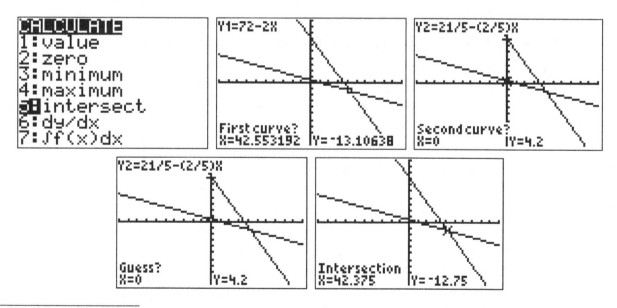

---

* The calculator asks for "curves," but that's only because this same calculator command will also find intersections of non-linear graphs—a line is a curve for our purposes.

** When you are finding intersections of curves that intersect more than once, which we'll do later, then the guess prompt becomes important. In that case, you'll need to put the cursor closest to the intersection you want.

Of course, those are the decimal values of the answers we already know are correct:

$$\left(\frac{339}{8}, -\frac{51}{4}\right) = (42.375, -12.75)$$

Solving for expressions

There's one last thing worth mentioning, which I'll introduce with a goofy metaphor. If I were to tell you that today is my birthday and then ask you for a cake, what would you do? (Let's assume, for the moment, that you like me and want me to be happy.) You've got two choices: buy a bunch of ingredients and start baking, or go to a different aisle in the same grocery store and just buy the friggin' cake.

Baking a cake yourself is not only more time consuming than just buying one; it also gives you more opportunities to screw up (for example, if you mistake salt for sugar, you'll bake the grossest cake of all time). Since you know I'm a shameless crybaby who will never let you forget it if you ruin my birthday, you should just buy the cake in the cake aisle, and then use your time to do something more fun than baking.

Example 3: No calculator

If $3x - y = 17$ and $2x - 2y = 6$, what is the value of $x + y$?

A) 8
B) 9
C) 11
D) 23

The SAT is asking you for a cake here. Baking it yourself will still result in a cake, but it will also give you multiple opportunities to screw up. Moreover, baking a cake takes longer than just buying one. In this question, nobody cares if you buy the ingredients (x and y), so don't waste time solving for them! All that matters is the finished cake, the value of the expression $x + y$, and we might be able to solve for that directly without ever finding x or y individually.

To do so, stack up the equations we're given and the expression we want:

$$3x - y = 17$$
$$2x - 2y = 6$$
$$x + y = ?$$

Do you see it yet? How about now:

$$3x - y = 17$$
$$\underline{-(2x - 2y = 6)}$$
$$x + y = ?$$

That's right. All we need to do is subtract one equation from the other, just like we were doing earlier in this chapter with the elimination technique. Distribute that negative and solve:

$$3x - y = 17$$
$$\underline{-2x + 2y = -6}$$
$$\mathbf{x + y = 11}$$

The answer is **C**.

Note that the old SAT had *tons* of questions like this. On the old SAT it was almost never necessary to solve systems of linear equations using substitution or graphing; it was pretty rare to even have to solve for an individual variable rather than an expression you could land on in one step. On the current SAT, well, you're going to be doing a lot more of the actual math, but the test writers haven't fully broken their old habits. You should still keep your eye out for the opportunity to solve directly for an expression if asked for one. If the SAT asks for a cake, in other words, try to buy the cake before you go shopping for the ingredients.

Practice questions: Solving Systems of Linear Equations
Some funny line about intersections

1 No calculator

$$x + 2y = 7$$
$$2x + 3y = 11$$

Which ordered pair (x, y) satisfies the system of equations above?

A) $(1, -3)$

B) $(1, 3)$

C) $(-1, 3)$

D) $(-1, -3)$

2 No calculator

$$-3x - 2y = 5$$
$$8x + 2y = 0$$

Which ordered pair (x, y) satisfies the system of equations above?

A) $(-1, -1)$

B) $(1, -4)$

C) $(-4, -1)$

D) $(-4, 4)$

3 No calculator

If $3x + 7y = 22$ and $2x + 6y = 12$, what is the value of $13x + 13y$?

A) 34

B) 58

C) 130

D) 156

4 No calculator; Grid-in

Bethany is a camp counselor. She has n lollipops to distribute to the campers in her group. She calculates that if she were to give each camper 7 lollipops, she would have 10 left over. She then realizes that if she eats one of the lollipops herself, she can give each camper 8 lollipops and have none left over. How many campers does Bethany have in her group?

5 No calculator; Grid-in

$$x + 2y - 3z = 92$$
$$2x - y + z = 36$$
$$4x - y + 2z = 12$$

Based on the system of equations above, what is the value of x ?

Practice questions: Solving Systems of Linear Equations
Some funny line about intersections

6 Calculator

$$3x - 2y = 16$$

$$\frac{2}{5}x - 2y = 4$$

Which ordered pair (x, y) satisfies the system of equations above?

A) $\left(3, \dfrac{7}{2}\right)$

B) $(10, 0)$

C) $\left(\dfrac{9}{2}, -\dfrac{9}{10}\right)$

D) $\left(\dfrac{60}{13}, -\dfrac{14}{13}\right)$

7 Calculator

$$x\sqrt{2} + 3y = 13$$

$$5x\sqrt{2} + 20y = 70$$

Which ordered pair (x, y) satisfies the system of equations above?

A) $\left(5\sqrt{2}, 1\right)$

B) $\left(\sqrt{2}, \dfrac{11}{3}\right)$

C) $\left(\sqrt{2}, 3\right)$

D) $\left(10\sqrt{2}, -\dfrac{7}{3}\right)$

8 Calculator; Grid-in

Seth and Dan decided to share the cost of a new television for their dorm room. The television cost $190.00, plus 8% sales tax. Dan spent $30.80 more than Seth did. Rounded to the nearest dollar, how much did Dan spend? (Disregard the $ sign when gridding your answer.)

9 Calculator; Grid-in

$$2x\sqrt{5} - 3y\sqrt{45} = 12\sqrt{5}$$

$$5x - 9y = 18$$

If the ordered pair (x, y) that satisfies the system of equations above is (a, b), what is the sum of a and b ?

10 Calculator; Grid-in

$$y \geq -4x - 3$$

$$y \geq \frac{1}{2}x + 3$$

A point with coordinates (m, n) lies in the solution set of the system of inequalities above, graphed in the xy-plane. What is the minimum possible value of n ?

Answers:

1	B		6	D
2	B		7	A
3	C		8	118
4	9		9	1.11 or 10/9
5	20		10	2.33 or 7/3

Solutions on page 358.

The following Official Test questions will require your ability to solve systems of linear equations.

Test	Section	Questions
1	3: No calculator	9, 11, 18
	4: Calculator	18, 28
2	3: No calculator	2, 9, 20
	4: Calculator	34
3	3: No calculator	6, 19
	4: Calculator	24, 29, 36
4	3: No calculator	3, 11, 19
	4: Calculator	6
5	3: No calculator	18
	4: Calculator	6, 12, 13
6	3: No calculator	
	4: Calculator	11
7	3: No calculator	3
	4: Calculator	16, 33
8	3: No calculator	6, 18
	4: Calculator	27
9	3: No calculator	1
	4: Calculator	13, 17, 19, 36
10	3: No calculator	19
	4: Calculator	25
PSAT/NMSQT 1	3: No calculator	3
	4: Calculator	5, 25, 29
PSAT/NMSQT 2	3: No calculator	5
	4: Calculator	27

Lines

We just finished talking about solving of systems of linear equations by graphing them and finding their intersections. That's important stuff—lines (and, more generally, graphs) are really useful tools for solving algebra problems without doing algebra. That said, there are enough things you should know about lines that *don't* have to do with solving systems of equations that they warrant their own chapter.

We'll get into the mathy math about lines in a minute, but before we do I want you to try to remember the first time a math teacher introduced the concept of slope to you. Chances are you were taught that the slope of a line is a ratio that tells you how steep the line is by telling you how much it "rises" for every unit it "runs." In those halcyon days, your mantra might very well have been: "rise over run." I don't want to belabor this point because if you're reading this you've likely been working with slope for quite some time. I simply bring it up because questions about lines and slopes are some of the easiest questions to overcomplicate. Make a conscious effort to keep line questions as simple as possible, and you might save yourself a good deal of aggravation.

Example 1: No calculator

Line j has a slope of $\frac{1}{3}$ and passes through the point (1, 1). Which of the following points is NOT on line j ?

A) (–2, 0)

B) (0, –3)

C) (4, 2)

D) (7, 3)

Don't even *think* of writing an equation here! Just apply the first thing you ever learned about slope: that it's the **rise** (up and down) over the **run** (left and right). You can easily list other points on the line simply by adding 1 to the *y*-value for every 3 you add to the *x*-value. In the following graph, I've drawn the line by starting at (1, 1) and figuring out one more point based on the slope. Specifically, I added 1 to the *y*-value and 3 to the *x*-value to get (4, 2). That means we can eliminate D right away, of course, but it should be enough to eliminate *every* incorrect choice.

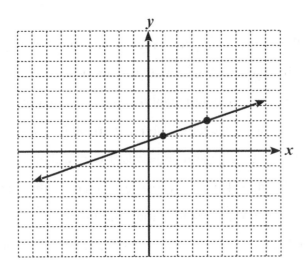

Which answer choice doesn't fall on the graph? Choice B is nowhere close: (0, –3) is very far from the line. So B has to be your answer! All of the other points clearly fall on the graph.

OK, on to the mathy math

If you're going to do algebra, you're going to want to use **slope-intercept form** whenever possible. If you're given the equation of a line and it's *not* in slope-intercept form already, your first step is to get it there. Many questions will consist of nothing more than comparing the slopes of numerous lines, so make sure you know this:

Slope-intercept form of a line
$y = mx + b$
m is your slope; *b* is your *y*-intercept.

Some times you won't be given a line equation at all, just two points. In that case, you can calculate the slope using this formula:

Slope formula

$$\text{slope} = m = \frac{y_2 - y_1}{x_2 - x_1}$$

(given (x_1, y_1) and (x_2, y_2) as two points on a line)

One interesting thing to point out about the slope formula: if one of the points you're dealing with is the origin, $(0, 0)$, then it's *really* easy to calculate the slope. Say you know a line goes through $(2, 9)$ and $(0, 0)$. The slope is $\frac{9-0}{2-0} = \frac{9}{2}$. The reason this is really helpful is that if you know a line goes through the origin, then you know that any two points (x, y) on that line will have the same $\frac{y}{x}$ ratio.* Take a look at this question:

Example 2: Calculator; Grid-in

Line m passes through the origin and has a positive slope. If $(2, a)$ and $(a, 8)$ are both on line m, what is the value of a ?

Because the question says the line passes through the origin, you know that the $\frac{y}{x}$ ratio of both given points must be the same. So we can say:

$$\frac{a}{2} = \frac{8}{a}$$

We can solve that for a by cross-multiplying:

$$a^2 = 16$$

$$a = \pm 4$$

---

* It's worth noting here (in a footnote, anyway) that when a line goes through the origin, its equation represents a direct proportion. When we talk about direct proportionality and we say the ratio of the two variables must always be the same, that's not really different from noting that when a line goes through the origin, its slope is $\frac{y}{x}$ for any point (x, y) on the line.

Since we know the line in question has a positive slope—and, really, since we know that grid-ins can only have positive answers—we know the answer is 4.

One other thing you should know about slopes: you should be able to identify whether one is positive, negative, zero, or undefined quickly by sight.

Other line facts to know cold

→ The x-intercept of a line is the x-value of the equation when $y = 0$.

→ The y-intercept of a line (b in the slope-intercept form) is the y-value of the equation when $x = 0$.

→ **Parallel lines** have the same slope. When lines are parallel, they never intersect. This means there is no ordered pair (x, y) that satisfies the equations of those lines—there are no solutions.

→ **Perpendicular lines** have negative reciprocal slopes (so if one line has a slope of 2, a perpendicular line has a slope of $-\frac{1}{2}$; if one has a slope of $-\frac{16}{5}$, the other has a slope of $\frac{5}{16}$). Another way of saying this is that the product of the slopes of perpendicular lines is always -1.

→ If a system of equation has **infinite solutions**, that means that the equations are equivalent. In other words, you only have infinite solutions when the two lines you're dealing with are actually the same line. When this is true, your lines will have the same slope *and* the same y-intercept.

→ When you reflect a line over *either axis*, the slope is negated. If you reflect a line over the x-axis, its y-intercept is also negated. If you reflect a line over the y-axis, its y-intercept stays the same. Consider the implications for the slope-intercept form of a line. The reflection of $y = 3x + 2$ over the x-axis is $y = -3x - 2$; the reflection of $y = 3x + 2$ over the y-axis is $y = -3x + 2$. (More on reflections and other graph manipulations on page 98.)

One other reminder that deserves its own heading

When you are told that a particular point is on a line, that's the same as being told that the equation of the line works out when that point is plugged into the equation for *x* and *y*. In other words, (4, 6) is on the line $y = x + 2$ because $6 = 4 + 2$. When a question gives you a point and an equation, *put the point into the equation*.

Variants of the following question are fairly common. Let's see if, given what we know about lines, we can figure it out.

Line *p* has a slope of $-\dfrac{2}{3}$ and a positive *y*-intercept. Line *q* passes through the origin, is perpendicular to line *p*, and intersects line *p* at the point $(c, c + 1)$. What is the value of *c* ?

A) 1

B) 2

C) 3

D) 4

With only a cursory glance, it might seem like we don't have much to work with here. Look closer. Note that the question states that line *q* passes through the origin. *This is very important*. It's common for the SAT writers to tell you that, and it's also common for students to completely breeze by it. When a line passes through the origin, that means we have the *y*-intercept (zero). It also, more generally, means we have a *point*, which ends up being the key to solving lots of questions.

So we know the y-intercept of line q is 0, and we can easily calculate the slope. Line q is perpendicular to line p, so its slope has to be the negative reciprocal of p's slope. Since the slope of p is $-\frac{2}{3}$, the slope of q is $\frac{3}{2}$.

$$y\text{-intercept} = b = 0$$

$$\text{slope} = m = \frac{3}{2}$$

We can write the equation of the line:

$$y = mx + b$$

$$y = \frac{3}{2}x + 0$$

$$y = \frac{3}{2}x$$

Then we can drop the point $(c, c + 1)$ into that equation, and solve:

$$c + 1 = \frac{3}{2}c$$

$$2(c + 1) = 3c$$

$$2c + 2 = 3c$$

$$2 = c$$

The answer is **B**.

The SAT writers are adept at writing difficult line questions, and as I said above, questions like this one are not uncommon. Make sure you understand what's going on here because it's a good bet that you'll see something like this again.

Practice questions: Lines

I can't think of anything funny to say about lines.

1 No calculator

What is the x-intercept of $y = 5x - 20$?

A) -20

B) -4

C) 4

D) 5

2 No calculator

If a line has a slope of -2 and it passes through the point $(-3, 2)$, what is its y-intercept?

A) 6

B) 0

C) -4

D) -6

3 No calculator

Which of the following sets of points forms a line that is parallel to $3y = 2x + 11$?

A) $(-1, 3)$ and $(3, -1)$

B) $(12, 4)$ and $(3, -2)$

C) $(6, 2)$ and $(8, 5)$

D) $(7, 4)$ and $(5, 7)$

4 No calculator

Line l has the equation $y = 3x + c$ and line m has the equation $4y - 3x = 11 - d$, for some constants c and d. If lines l and m intersect at $(-3, -2)$, what is the sum of c and d ?

A) -7

B) 7

C) 10

D) 17

5 No calculator; Grid-in

In the xy-plane, the line determined by the points $(8, 3)$ and (a, b) passes through the origin. If $a \neq 0$, what is the value of $\dfrac{b}{a}$?

6 Calculator

Which of the following is the equation of a line that is perpendicular to $y + 3 = 3x - 8$?

A) $3y + x = 26$

B) $9y - 6x = 18$

C) $y + 3x = 9$

D) $y - 3x = 10$

7 Calculator

$$7x + 12y = 31$$

$$ky = x + 19$$

For what value of k will the system of equations above have no solutions?

A) $\dfrac{7}{12}$

B) $\dfrac{12}{7}$

C) $-\dfrac{7}{12}$

D) $-\dfrac{12}{7}$

8 Calculator

$$p = 100 - 7\left(\dfrac{d}{2}\right)$$

Karen is a serious golfer; she keeps careful statistics in order to help herself improve. Based on a season's worth of data, she has written the equation above to model the percentage of putts, p, she made when she was d feet from the hole. Which of the following best summarizes the model?

A) For every 2 feet farther Karen's ball is from the hole, she loses 7% accuracy.

B) For every half foot farther Karen's ball is from the hole, she loses 7% accuracy.

C) For every 7 feet farther Karen's ball is from the hole, she loses 1% accuracy.

D) For every 7 feet farther Karen's ball is from the hole, she loses 2% accuracy.

9 Calculator

Line l in the xy-plane contains points from Quadrants I and IV, but no points from Quadrants II or III. Which of the following must be true?

A) The slope of line l is positive.

B) The slope of line l is negative.

C) The slope of line l is zero.

D) The slope of line l is undefined.

10 Calculator; Grid-in

$$f(x) = 3x + 8$$

$$g(x) = ax + b$$

In the system of equations above, a and b are constants. If the lines defined by f and g are perpendicular and intersect at (2, 14), what is the value of $a + b$?

Answers:

1	C		6	A
2	C		7	D
3	B		8	A
4	D		9	D
5	3/8 or .375		10	43/3 or 14.3

Solutions on page 361.

The following Official Test questions will require your ability to work with lines.

Test	Section	Questions
1	3: No calculator	12
	4: Calculator	15, 16
2	3: No calculator	6, 9, 20
	4: Calculator	25, 28
3	3: No calculator	8, 9
	4: Calculator	4, 26, 36
4	3: No calculator	8
	4: Calculator	8, 17
5	3: No calculator	1
	4: Calculator	11, 13, 28
6	3: No calculator	5
	4: Calculator	2, 14, 25, 35
7	3: No calculator	6, 19
	4: Calculator	5, 17, 21, 28, 32
8	3: No calculator	2, 10, 13, 19
	4: Calculator	7, 21, 25, 29, 33, 35
9	3: No calculator	3, 8, 14, 20
	4: Calculator	8, 14, 15, 20, 29, 30, 32, 36
10	3: No calculator	4, 9, 15
	4: Calculator	1, 23
PSAT/NMSQT 1	3: No calculator	
	4: Calculator	8, 28
PSAT/NMSQT 2	3: No calculator	6, 8
	4: Calculator	4

Absolute Value

I trust you already know the very basics of absolute value: that $|5| = 5$ and $|-5| = 5$, etc. Taking the absolute value of a positive number has no effect on the number. Taking the absolute value of a negative number makes it positive. This applies, of course, to variables and expressions as well. The absolute value of x is just plain old x when x is positive, and it's $-x$ when x is negative.

When $x < 0$	When $x \geq 0$
$|x| = -x$	$|x| = x$

You might also find it helpful to think about absolute value as it relates to a number line.

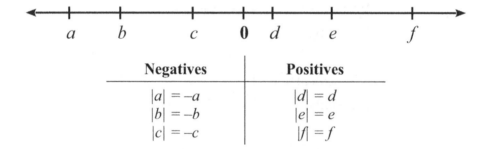

Negatives	Positives
$|a| = -a$	$|d| = d$
$|b| = -b$	$|e| = e$
$|c| = -c$	$|f| = f$

If you don't know whether something is positive or negative, *you must account for both possibilities*. When $|x| = 5$, then either $x = 5$, or $x = -5$.

$$|x| = 5 \begin{array}{l} \nearrow\ x = 5 \\ \searrow\ x = -5 \end{array}$$

Is this bending your brain a bit? Or is it like *duh*? Stick around, please, either way, because now it's time to talk about the ways this stuff will appear on the SAT.

If a is the value of x at which $|x - 3| + 5$ will equal its minimum value, and b is that minimum value, then what is the value of $a + b$?

The key to dealing with a question like this is to recognize that the smallest possible value you're going to get from the $|x - 3|$ part of the expression is 0. Because that whole bit is inside absolute value brackets, it can't ever be less than 0. Therefore, when that expression equals 0 (that is to say, when $x = 3$), the whole $|x - 3| + 5$ expression will equal its minimum value. So you know $a = 3$.

From there, it's pretty easy to find b:

$$b = |a - 3| + 5$$
$$b = |3 - 3| + 5$$
$$b = |0| + 5$$
$$b = 5$$

So there you go—$a = 3$, $b = 5$, and $a + b = 3 + 5 = \textbf{8}$. Easy enough, right?

Absolute value and inequalities

Interesting things start happening when absolute values are combined with inequalities, so one of the SAT writers' occasional tricks is to kill two birds with one stone and test absolute value and inequalities concomitantly. Remember that $|x| = 5$ means that $x = 5$ or $x = -5$. You can draw similarly simple conclusions with inequalities.

If I told you that $|y| < 3$, and y is an integer, then what are the possible values for y? There aren't many: y could equal 2, 1, 0, –1, or –2. In other words, y has to be less than 3, *and* greater than –3. You can get rid of the absolute value brackets in $|y| < 3$ by translating the expression into a range: $-3 < y < 3$.

Let's try another example, shall we? And what the heck, let's get weird.

Example 2: Calculator

In order to be considered "good for eating" by the La'Urthg Orcs of Kranranul, a human must weigh between 143 and 181 pounds. Which of the following inequalities gives all the possible weights, *w*, that a human in Kranranul with normal self-preservation instincts should NOT want to be?

A) $|w - 143| < 38$

B) $|w - 162| < 19$

C) $|w + 38| < 181$

D) $|w - 181| < 22$

First of all, it's possible to plug in here, although it matters greatly what numbers you choose. Picking a number right in the middle of the range (like 165) probably won't help you out much. To plug in successfully, choose weights that should *just barely* be within the range (like 144 or 180) and then, if you still haven't eliminated all the answers, choose weights that should *just barely* be outside the range (like 142 or 182). Be careful with this second part! You're looking to eliminate any choices that *work* when you know you picked a number that *shouldn't work*.

Let's start with *w* = 144 and see what happens. A person who weighs 144 pounds should try to lose weight, pronto, lest he become a meal for the orcs. Right now, he's in the "good for eating" range! Since 144 is in the range, we're looking for choices that will

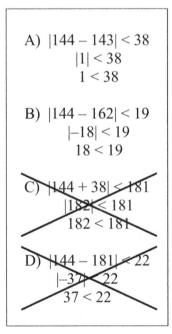

A) $|144 - 143| < 38$
    $|1| < 38$
    $1 < 38$

B) $|144 - 162| < 19$
    $|-18| < 19$
    $18 < 19$

C) $|144 + 38| < 181$
    $|182| < 181$
    $182 < 181$

D) $|144 - 181| < 22$
    $|-37| < 22$
    $37 < 22$

give us *true* inequalities when we plug it in. Have a look at the column on the right for how this all works out.

So, bummer. Our first plug-in only eliminated 2 out of 4 choices. What happens when we plug in a number that shouldn't work, like 141? Remember, now we're looking to eliminate anything that gives us a *true* inequality: a 141 pound person is NOT considered on the menu by the orcs. Note that I'm not bothering with **C** and **D** since we've already eliminated them.

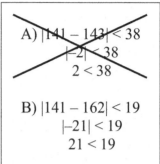

Only **B** was true when we needed it to be true and false when we needed it to be false, so that's our answer. But if plugging in here seems cumbersome to you, you're not alone. I actually prefer to do questions like this another way.

Let's have a look at B, our correct answer, and convert it like we did at the beginning of the chapter:

$$|w - 162| < 19 \longrightarrow -19 < w - 162 < 19$$

Now things are about to get crazy. Add 162 to each side to get w by itself:

$$-19 + 162 < w - 162 + 162 < 19 + 162$$
$$\mathbf{143 < w < 181}$$

Wow, that's exactly what we were looking for. I mean, I knew that was coming, and I'm *still* amazed. I can't even imagine how you must feel.

So on a question like this, you can just convert every answer choice in this way to see which one gives you what you want, or you can even take it one step further. If and when you get a question like this, the correct answer will look like this:

To say that a variable falls into a particular range:

|variable – middle of range| < distance from middle to ends of range

---

This formula tells you how far from a central value you can get before being outside of the desired range. Let's look at how it applies to the question we just answered:

Variable:	w
Desired range:	$143 < w < 181$
Middle value:	162
Distance from middle to ends:	19

$$|w - 162| < 19$$

Not bad, right? What $|w - 162| < 19$ is really saying is that the ideal eating weight of a human, w, is less than 19 pounds away from 162.

Absolute value and functions

As you hopefully know, order of operations dictates that you don't apply absolute value brackets until you've completed all the operations inside the brackets:

GOOD: $|-8 + 5| = |-3| = 3$
BAD: $|-8 + 5| = 8 + 5 = 13$

Seriously, don't do that second one. *Don't*.

The same is true if you have absolute value brackets around a function, like $|f(x)|$. The order of operations is such that the absolute value brackets don't take effect until the function has done its thing inside. If the function comes out positive on its own, the brackets have no effect. If the function comes out negative, it becomes positive:

x	$f(x)$	$|f(x)|$
1	−8	8
2	−3	3
3	−1	1
4	4	4
5	6	6

See? Now here's the important part: what happens to the *graph* of a function when you take the absolute value of the function? Well, when the function is positive, as we see in the table above *nothing at all happens to it*. When the function is negative, it reflects off the x-axis. In other words, it bounces. BOING!

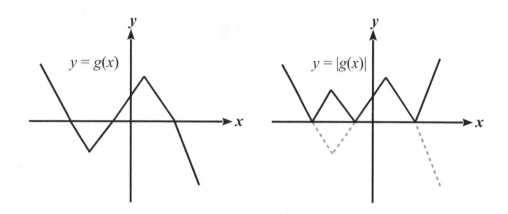

Don't forget: the graph of $|g(x)|$ is identical to the graph of $g(x)$ whenever $g(x)$ is positive. The only changes occur when $g(x)$ is negative.

Wanna see something rad? Have a look at the graph of $y = |\sin x|$. What do you think it'll look like?

Cool, right?

Practice questions: Absolute Value

1 No calculator

Which of the following expressions is never equal to 0 for any value of x ?

A) $|x + 3| - 1$

B) $|x - 3| - 1$

C) $|x - 1| + 3$

D) $|x + 1| - 3$

2 No calculator

For what value of y is $|y - 3| + 3$ equal to 2 ?

A) 0

B) 2

C) 3

D) There is no such value of y.

3 No calculator

$$y \geq |3x| - 7$$

According to the inequality above, if $x \leq 0$, what is the minimum value of y ?

A) −7

B) 0

C) 21

D) There is no minimum value of y.

4 No calculator; Grid-in

Whether a taxpayer is eligible for a certain government subsidy is determined by that taxpayer's annual gross income. In order to estimate the cost of the subsidy, a data engineer writes a program to search a tax return database and show only single taxpayers whose gross annual incomes are x dollars, such that $|x - 24{,}800| \leq 13{,}500$. What is the maximum gross annual income, <u>in thousands of dollars</u>, that a single taxpayer can make and still qualify for this subsidy? (Round your answer to the nearest tenth; disregard the $ sign when gridding your answer.)

5 No calculator; Grid-in

If $|x - 9| + 1 = 7.5$, what is the minimum value of x ?

6 Calculator

If $|a| + |b| = 7$ and a and b are integers, which of the following could NOT equal $a + b$?

A) 5

B) 0

C) −3

D) −7

Practice questions: Absolute Value

Strengthen your core! (Get it? Because "absolute" has "abs" in it? High five!)

7 Calculator

If $h(x) = 2x - 10$, which of the following is NOT true?

A) $h(3) < |h(3)|$

B) $h(1) = |h(1)|$

C) $h(10) = |h(10)|$

D) $h(10) = |h(0)|$

8 Calculator

All the bowlers on Robbie's bowling team, Strike Force, have average scores between 215 and 251. Which of the following inequalities can be used to determine whether a bowler with an average score of s could be on the team?

A) $|s - 233| < 36$

B) $|s - 251| < 215$

C) $|s - 18| < 233$

D) $|s - 233| < 18$

9 Calculator

x	$g(x)$
3	−3
5	8
9	12
13	−11
17	15

The table above shows a few values for the function g. According to the table, which of the following statements is NOT true?

A) $|g(3)| = 3$

B) $|g(5)| > g(5)$

C) $g(17) - g(9) = |g(3)|$

D) $|g(13)| < g(9)$

10 Calculator; Grid-in

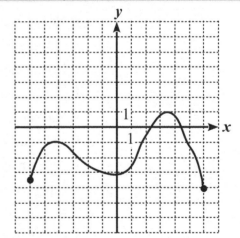

The function $g(x)$ is graphed above. What is an integer value of a for which $g(a) = |g(a)|$?

Answers:

1	C		6	B
2	D		7	B
3	A		8	D
4	38.3		9	B
5	2.5		10	3 or 4

Solutions on page 364.

The following Official Test questions will test your ability to work with absolute values. As you can see, there aren't many, and the ones that are there aren't particularly hard. Take that into consideration as you prioritize concepts to prep.

Test	Section	Questions
1	3: No calculator	
	4: Calculator	8
2	3: No calculator	
	4: Calculator	
3	3: No calculator	
	4: Calculator	
4	3: No calculator	1
	4: Calculator	
5	3: No calculator	
	4: Calculator	
6	3: No calculator	
	4: Calculator	28
7	3: No calculator	
	4: Calculator	
8	3: No calculator	
	4: Calculator	
9	3: No calculator	
	4: Calculator	
10	3: No calculator	17
	4: Calculator	
PSAT/NMSQT 1	3: No calculator	
	4: Calculator	
PSAT/NMSQT 2	3: No calculator	
	4: Calculator	

Passport to Advanced Math

Let me be really honest for a minute. Way back in the Spring of 2014, when College Board first announced revisions to the SAT, and gave a big, self-congratulatory press conference, I first chuckled, then scoffed at the name "Passport to Advanced Math." Not quite as much as I did at "Heart of Algebra," of course, but still. A *hearty* chuckle. The content in this unit is no laughing matter, though.

There will be 16 Passport to Advanced Math questions on your test. The subscore for these questions will theoretically represent your ability to solve "complex" algebraic equations (like ones where the variable is in the denominator, or ones that involve exponents or radicals). Basically, this is everything that can be called algebra that *isn't* linear equations, which are captured in the Heart of Algebra subscore.

As the math gets more and more complex, it actually becomes harder for question writers to create questions that aren't susceptible to plugging in or backsolving. Opportunities to use those techniques abound in Passport to Advanced Math. Stay frosty.

Functions

Think of a function question like you think of a car wash. Not like a fundraiser car wash you do to raise money for your next band trip, but an automatic car wash. Have you ever been to one of those? They're super cool. Anyway, if I drive my bird-poop-covered silver Toyota Yaris up to the car wash, what's going to happen? First it'll get sprayed with water, then with soap, then it'll get to the spinning brushes, then those dangly-slappy things that don't seem to serve much of a purpose, then the rinse, then the biggest hairdryer of all time will blow it dry. What comes out on the other end? A clean silver Yaris. *Not* a clean blue Honda; that'd be crazy. However, if a dirty blue Honda went in after my Yaris, then all the same stuff would happen to it as happened to my car, and then a clean blue Honda *would* come out.

The point is that you can always predict what's going to come out of a car wash based on what goes into it. Functions are the same way.

You've probably been working with the $f(x)$ notation in school for some time now, but let's review some of the things you'll see over and over again on the SAT.

Interpreting function notation

One thing you're definitely going to need to be able to do is interpret function notation. For some questions, it's enough to remember that saying $f(x) = x^3$, for example, is basically the same as saying $y = x^3$.

For other questions, you're going to need to take that a bit further and identify points on a graph using function notation. Here's a quick cheat for you: **when you have $f(x) = y$, that's the same as having the ordered pair (x, y).** For example, if you know that $f(4) = 5$, then you know that the graph of the function f contains the point $(4, 5)$. Likewise, if you know that $h(c) = p$, you know that the graph of function h contains the point (c, p). And so on.

$$
\begin{array}{cc}
f(x) & = y \\
\downarrow & \downarrow \\
(x, & y)
\end{array}
$$

Basically, whatever is inside the parentheses is your x-value, and whatever's across the equal sign is your y-value. This is important. If you don't understand yet, read it over and over until you do. Might help to write it down. Just sayin'.

To make sure you've got this, think about what the following things mean (answers at the bottom of the page).

✎ $f(0) = 3$

✎ $p(12) = 0$

✎ $s(3) = r(3)$

Nested functions (functions in functions)

Have you ever seen those dolls where you open them up and there are smaller ones inside? They're called Russian nesting dolls. Google them sometime.

Anyway, sometimes the SAT might put a function inside another function to try to bamboozle you. Don't let yourself get stymied here. All you need to do is follow the instructions, same as you do with all other function questions.

Example 1: No calculator

If $f(x) = x^2 - 10$ and $g(x) = 2f(x) + 3$, what is the value of $g(\sqrt{2})$?

A) 7

B) −5

C) −7

D) −13

Answers: ● The graph of $y = f(x)$ contains $(0, 3)$, so it has a y-intercept of 3

● The graph of $y = p(x)$ contains $(12, 0)$, so it has an x-intercept of 12

● The graphs of $y = s(x)$ and $y = r(x)$ are equal when $x = 3$, so they intersect when $x = 3$

Let's just take this one step at a time. First, let's take the $\sqrt{2}$ we're given and put it in for every x we see in $g(x)$.

$$g(\sqrt{2}) = 2f(\sqrt{2}) + 3$$

Not too bad, right? Now let's replace the $f(\sqrt{2})$ with an expression we can actually work with. Remember that $f(x) = x^2 - 10$, so we write:

$$g(\sqrt{2}) = 2((\sqrt{2})^2 - 10) + 3$$

See how this is working? Now just simplify to arrive at **choice D**:

$$g(\sqrt{2}) = 2(-8) + 3$$
$$g(\sqrt{2}) = -13$$

Tables and function notation

Now that you're good with function notation by itself, it's time to talk about how functions can be represented in table form. It's pretty common for the SAT to present a function to you this way:

x	2	3	4	5	6
$f(x)$	13	18	25	34	45

We can use this table to find points. For example, $f(5) = 34$. See if you can do the following questions(answers at the bottom, natch):

✎ If $f(p) = 18$, what is one possible value for p?[*]

✎ What is $f(6 - 4)$?

✎ What is $f(6) - f(4)$?

✎ Holy crap those are different?

---

[*] The function f here turns out to be quadratic, and there are 2 values that could produce 18, one of which is 3. In a function, each input can only have one output, but multiple inputs can have the same output. To go back to the car wash example, a blue Honda (input) that goes through can *only* result in a clean blue Honda (output). However, there are many blue Hondas in the world, so multiple inputs can produce the same output.

Answers: ● p could equal 3 ● $f(2) = 13$ ● $45 - 25 = 20$ ● ...yup.

Graphs and function notation

Now that you're good with tables, let's talk about function notation as it pertains to graphs. Using function notation to interpret graphs is one of the most common bugaboos of SAT math students. If you're willing to put in a few minutes of focused practice here, however, you'll laugh in the face of these dangerous questions.

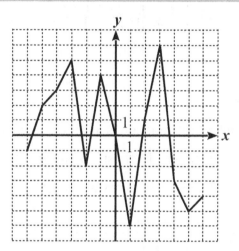

The figure above shows the graph of $f(x)$ from $x = -6$ to $x = 6$. If $f(3) = p$, what is the value of $f(p)$?

A) −4

B) −2

C) 3

D) 6

The first thing I want to point out, since I've found it to be a sticking point for a lot of students, is that you don't need to know the equation for $f(x)$. All the information you need to know is in the figure! To solve a question like this, you must remember a simple but important fact that we've already discussed: that "$f(a) = b$" is just shorthand for saying "the function f contains the point (a, b)." So when this question tells you that $f(3) = p$, it's telling you that the function f contains the point $(3, p)$. All you need to do is go to the graph and see where it is when $x = 3$.

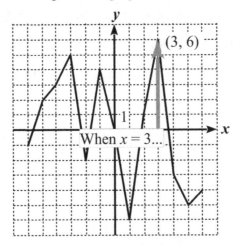

When $x = 3$, the graph of the function is at $(3, 6)$. So $f(3) = 6$, and therefore $p = 6$. And now you're almost done! To finish up, just go to the graph one more time to find $f(p)$, which you now know is really just $f(6)$.

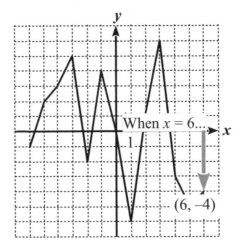

And there you have it. When $x = 6$, the graph of the function is at $(6, -4)$. This means that $f(6) = -4$, so **A** is your answer.

Becoming deft with questions like this simply requires practice. So...you should do some practice. Let's use the same graph, and I'll ask you some more questions, increasing the complexity as I go.

The answers to these questions are at the bottom of the page.

✐ What is the *y*-intercept of *f*(*x*)?

✐ When, in the given interval, is *f*(*x*) greatest?

✐ If *f*(4) = *a*, what is *f*(*a*)?

✐ If *f*(–2) = *b*, what is *f*(*b*)?

✐ If *f*(–1) = *e*, what is *f*(*e*) – 6?

✐ If *f*(1) = *g*, what is *f*(–*g*)?

✐ If *f*(5) = *c*, what is *f*(*c* + 1)?

✐ If *f*(*s*) = 0, how many possible values are there for *s* in the given interval?

✐ If *f*(2) = *d*, what is 2*f*(2*d*)?

✐ If *f*(6) = *m* and *f*(2) = *n*, what is 3*f*(*m* – *n*)?

✐ If *f*(–3) = *r*, what is *f*(*f*(*r*))?

These are super fun, right?

_____

Answers: ● 0 ● *f*(3) = 6 ● 5 ● –2 ● –9 ● –4
● *f*(5) = –5, so *f*(–5 + 1) = *f*(–4) = 3
● 6 (*f*(*x*) = 0 means an *x*-intercept, and there are 6 of those)
● *f*(2) = 1, so *d* = 1 and 2*d* = 2. 2*f*(2) = 2 × 1 = 2
● *f*(6) = –4 and *f*(2) = 1, so *f*(*m* – *n*) = *f*(–5). 3*f*(–5) = 3 × 2 = 6
● *f*(–3) = 5, so *f*(*f*(*r*)) = *f*(*f*(5)) = *f*(–5) = 2

Graph translation, reflection, and amplification

Sometimes the SAT likes to test you on whether you can figure out how a graph will react to some manipulation of its equation. Usually, though, they won't give you the equation. They'll draw some crappy squiggly line, call it $g(x)$, and then ask what will happen to $g(x + 1)$.

I'm including the rules for common manipulations, but I *strongly* recommend that you remind yourself of them with your calculator if you should need them on your SAT. It's very easy to set a simple function (like $f(x) = x^2$, which you've seen a million times) as your starting point and experiment with your graphing calculator to see how the graph reacts when the function is modified:

Graph translation rules:

$f(x + 1) \Rightarrow$ graph moves **LEFT** one
$f(x - 1) \Rightarrow$ graph moves **RIGHT** one
$f(x) + 1 \Rightarrow$ graph moves **UP** one
$f(x) - 1 \Rightarrow$ graph moves **DOWN** one

$$y = f(x)$$

When $f(x) = x^2$:

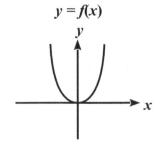

$y = f(x + 1)$	$y = f(x - 1)$	$y = f(x) + 1$	$y = f(x) - 1$
			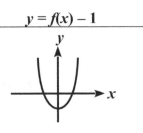

Note that the graph does just what you expect it to when the operation is outside the function (+ means up, – means down) but behaves differently when it's inside the function (+ means *left*, – means *right*).

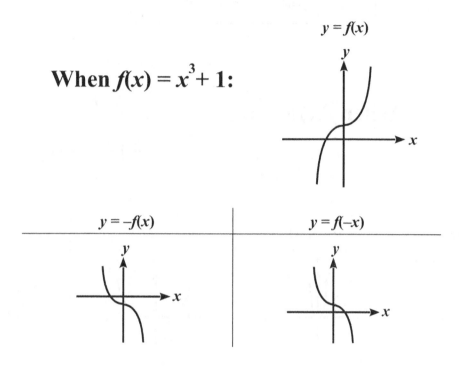

When $f(x) = x^3 + 1$:

$y = f(x)$

$y = -f(x)$ | $y = f(-x)$

Notice that when you have a reflection about the x-axis (as you do on the left), the x-intercept remains the same. When you have a reflection about the y-axis, the y-intercept likewise remains the same. The intercepts that don't remain the same are negated. Makes sense, right? Math is awesome.

This was mentioned in the Lines chapter already, but when you reflect a line over *either* axis, the slope is negated. If you reflect it over the y-axis, the y-intercept stays the same. If you reflect it across the x-axis, the y-intercept and slope are both negated. For example, consider the line $y = 3x + 2$, with a slope of 3 and a y-intercept of 2. Its reflection across the y-axis will be $y = -3x + 2$ (slope negated), and its reflection across the x-axis will be $y = -3x - 2$ (slope and y-intercept negated).

> **Graph amplification rules:**
>
> **x-intercepts remain the same, but for other points on the graph**
>
> $2f(x) \Rightarrow$ graph moves **FARTHER** from x-axis
>
> $\frac{1}{2}f(x) \Rightarrow$ graph moves **CLOSER** to x-axis

When $f(x) = x^2$:

$y = f(x)$

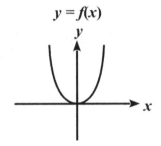

$y = 2f(x)$	$y = 3f(x)$	$y = \frac{1}{2}f(x)$	$y = \frac{1}{3}f(x)$

 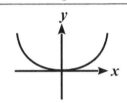

As you can see above, when a parabola is amplified by a coefficient greater than 1, it gets skinnier. When it's amplified by a coefficient between 0 and 1, it gets fatter.

It's not a bad idea for you to see this effect on a function that has more than one x-intercept. Use your graphing calculator right now to see the difference between the graphs of $y = \sin x$, $y = 2\sin x$, and $y = \frac{1}{2}\sin x$. Go ahead...I'll wait.

1 No calculator

The figure above shows the graph of $y = f(x)$. If $f(-1) = k$, which of the following is equal to $2f(k)$?

A) -3

B) 2

C) 4

D) 6

2 No calculator

If $f(x - 1) = x + 1$ for all values of x, which of the following is equal to $f(x + 1)$?

A) $x + 3$

B) $x + 2$

C) $x - 1$

D) $x - 3$

3 No calculator

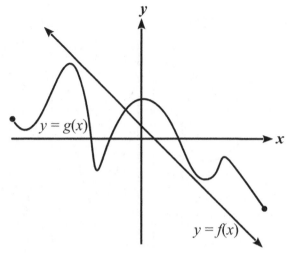

The figure above shows the graphs of $f(x)$ and $g(x)$. If $f(b) = g(b)$, which of the following could be the value of b ?

A) -3

B) 0

C) 1

D) 7

4 No calculator; Grid-in

If $f(x) = 2x - 1$, what is the value of $f(10) - f(5)$?

5 No calculator; Grid-in

If $f(x + 3) = 10x + 4$ for all values of x, what is the value of $f(8)$?

6 Calculator

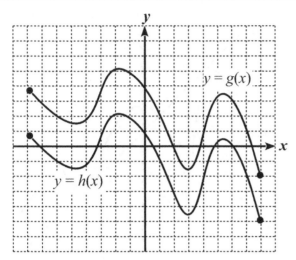

The figure above shows the complete graphs of $y = g(x)$ and $y = h(x)$. Which of the following could be an expression of $h(x)$ in terms of $g(x)$?

A) $h(x) = g(x + 3)$

B) $h(x) = g(x - 3)$

C) $h(x) = g(x) + 3$

D) $h(x) = g(x) - 3$

7 Calculator

If $f(x) = 3x^2 + 8$, what is $f(-2x)$ equal to?

A) $-6x^2 + 8$

B) $-6x^2 - 16$

C) $12x^2 + 8$

D) $12x^2 - 16x$

8 Calculator

x	1	3	5	7	9
$g(x)$	–2	15	6	–3	–10

The table above gives values of the function g for selected values of x. If $f(x) = |g(x)|$, and $f(7) = t$, what is the value of $f(t)$?

A) –3

B) –2

C) 6

D) 15

9 Calculator; Grid-in

$$f(x) = 2x^2 - 14x + k$$

In the function above, k is a constant. If $f(11) = 50$, what is the value of $f(13)$?

10 Calculator; Grid-in

x	$f(x)$	$g(x)$
1	11	m
2	18	–20
3	k	43
4	–29	88
5	–33	107

In the table above, k and m are unknown values of the functions f and g, respectively. If $f(4) = m + 9$ and $g(4) = 2k - 4$, what is the value of $f(3) + g(1)$?

Answers:

1	B		6	D
2	A		7	C
3	A		8	D
4	10		9	118
5	54		10	8

Solutions on page 365.

The following selected Official Test questions are all about that sweet function action.

Test	Section	Questions
1	3: No calculator	10
	4: Calculator	17
2	3: No calculator	10
	4: Calculator	10, 26, 33
3	3: No calculator	7
	4: Calculator	4, 16
4	3: No calculator	2, 4
	4: Calculator	12
5	3: No calculator	14
	4: Calculator	2, 23, 28
6	3: No calculator	8
	4: Calculator	15, 25
7	3: No calculator	5
	4: Calculator	
8	3: No calculator	15
	4: Calculator	30, 35, 38
9	3: No calculator	18, 20
	4: Calculator	24
10	3: No calculator	3, 4, 7
	4: Calculator	5, 9
PSAT/NMSQT 1	3: No calculator	10
	4: Calculator	
PSAT/NMSQT 2	3: No calculator	
	4: Calculator	26

Exponents and Exponential Functions

You can be sure that you're going to encounter exponents on the SAT. Sometimes it'll be in the context of standard exponent and radical operations. Other times, it'll be working with exponential growth or decay equations. Once you've been through this chapter, you'll look forward to the opportunity to spank both types of questions.

Basic exponent rules

Rule	Example
Don't forget what a regular integer exponent means!*	$x^4 = xxxx$
Anything raised to the first power equals itself.	$y^1 = y$
Anything raised to the zero power equals 1.**	$m^0 = 1$
When you multiply like bases, you *add* their exponents.	$p^3 p^5 = p^{3+5} = p^8$
When you divide like bases, you *subtract* their exponents.	$\dfrac{r^9}{r^4} = r^{9-4} = r^5$
When you apply one exponent to another, you *multiply* the exponents.	$\left(z^3\right)^7 = z^{3 \times 7} = z^{21}$
When you apply an exponent to a single term in parentheses, you can *distribute* the exponent. Be careful, though! You *cannot distribute* an exponent to multiple terms (i.e., terms separated by + or − sign) in parentheses.	$(xy)^7 = x^7 y^7$ $(x+y)^7 \neq x^7 + y^7$
When you're adding or subtracting like bases with different exponents, you can factor if that would be helpful but otherwise *you can't do JACK.*	$y^4 + y^3 = y^3(y+1)$ $y^4 + y^3 \neq y^7$

That last one is important: there's no simplifying when exponents are separated by a + or − sign. If you make the mistake of adding or subtracting exponents when you shouldn't, people will laugh at you. It'll be like that nightmare where

---

* Don't be ashamed to do this when you're stuck. You'll be amazed how often doing so will unstick you. All the rules that follow are derived directly from this basic principle.

** Except zero. There's some debate about what 0^0 equals. Some people say it equals 1, others say it's undefined. You needn't worry about this for the SAT. I've never seen 0^0 appear there.

you somehow went to school in only your underwear, only it'll be worse and it'll be real. Don't do it.

Before we go further, let's make sure you've got the above. Try simplifying the following. (Answers at the bottom of the page.)

✎ $t^9 t^2 =$

✎ $\dfrac{3^n}{3^2} =$

✎ $\left(xy^3\right)\left(x^5 y\right) =$

✎ $\left(8^m\right)^2 =$

✎ $\left(3x\right)^3 =$

✎ $r^{16} - r^{12} =$

Fractional and negative exponents

These are less common, but you still need to know them.

Here's what you need to know about **fractional exponents**:

➔ The numerator of the exponent is the *power*

➔ The denominator of the exponent is the *root*

➔ In radical notation, the power can go inside or outside the radical symbol, like so:

$$y^{\frac{3}{5}} = \sqrt[5]{y^3} = \left(\sqrt[5]{y}\right)^3 \qquad r^{\frac{5}{11}} = \sqrt[11]{r^5} = \left(\sqrt[11]{r}\right)^5$$

Answers: • t^{11} • 3^{n-2} • $x^6 y^4$ • $8^{2m} = 64^m$ • $27x^3$
• $r^{16} - r^{12}$, unless you choose to factor for some reason. If you do, you can get all the way down to this: $r^{12}(r^2 + 1)(r + 1)(r - 1)$.

And here's what you need to know about **negative exponents**:

→ An expression with a negative exponent is the reciprocal of the corresponding expression with a positive exponent, like so:

$$p^{-5} = \frac{1}{p^5} \qquad y^{-\frac{3}{5}} = \frac{1}{y^{\frac{3}{5}}} = \frac{1}{\sqrt[5]{y^3}}$$

What's nice is that even though these rules might be a bit more confusing, fractional and negative exponents follow the same rules as integer exponents. Stare at these for a minute to see what I mean:

$$\frac{m^4}{m^{\frac{1}{2}}} = m^{\frac{7}{2}} \qquad \frac{2^x}{2^{-y}} = 2^{x-(-y)} = 2^{x+y} \qquad \frac{1}{p^5} = \frac{p^0}{p^5} = p^{-5}$$

Example 1: Calculator

If $x^{\frac{3}{5}} = m$ and $y^{-\frac{3}{5}} = n^{-1}$, which of the following is equal to xy?

A) $(mn)^{\frac{3}{5}}$

B) $m^{\frac{5}{3}} n^{-\frac{5}{3}}$

C) $(mn)^{\frac{5}{3}}$

D) $\dfrac{n}{m}$

You have two options here. You could plug in, or you could work through this using the exponent rules. Since this is the exponent chapter, I'm going to use the exponent rules, but you should solve this by plugging in, too, just for the extra practice.

The first thing to do is get rid of those pesky negatives in the second equation. Remember that as long as you do the same thing to both sides of an equation, it's cool, man. Nobody gets hurt. So raise both sides of that equation to the -1 power. Remember what the rule says about raising exponents to other exponents? You *multiply* them.

$$\left(y^{-\frac{3}{5}}\right)^{-1}=\left(n^{-1}\right)^{-1}$$

$$y^{\frac{3}{5}}=n$$

That's better, right? Now let's do the real work. This is, at its core, a solve-for-the-expression question. Look at what you've got, and ask yourself how on earth you're going to transform that into what you want.

$$x^{\frac{3}{5}}=m$$

$$xy = \underline{\quad}$$

$$y^{\frac{3}{5}}=n$$

Looks to me like our first step has to be multiplication. Let's combine the two equations by multiplying the left and right sides of each together.

$$x^{\frac{3}{5}}\, y^{\frac{3}{5}}=mn$$

$$(xy)^{\frac{3}{5}}=mn$$

Almost there now, right? We'll get rid of that pesky $\frac{3}{5}$ the same way we got rid of the -1: we'll raise both sides to a clever exponent that will leave us with what we want. What do I multiply $\frac{3}{5}$ by to make it go away? Yep, $\frac{5}{3}$. I *knew* you had it in you.

$$\left((xy)^{\frac{3}{5}}\right)^{\frac{5}{3}}=(mn)^{\frac{5}{3}}$$

$$xy=(mn)^{\frac{5}{3}}$$

So the answer is **C**. Whew! That was beautiful. I got chills.

How different bases react to being raised to powers

It's pretty important that you understand how different kinds of numbers will react when raised to powers. You should know, for example, that numbers between 0 and 1 will shrink when raised to a positive power: $0.5^2 = 0.25$. You should also know that negative numbers will turn positive when raised to even powers, but stay negative when raised to odd powers: $(-2)^2 = 4$, $(-2)^3 = -8$.

Example 2: Calculator

Each of the following inequalities is true for some value of a EXCEPT

A) $a^3 < a < a^2$

B) $a < a^3 < a^2$

C) $a^3 < a^2 < a$

D) $a^2 < a^3 < a$

The best way to avoid careless errors on questions like this is to plug in. Pro tip: use values for a that are greater than 1, between 0 and 1, between -1 and 0, and less than -1. Here's a little table I whipped up. We're looking for a choice that can't be true, so when a plugged-in value results in an order that matches an answer choice, we eliminate that choice.

a	a^2	a^3	Order	Eliminate
2	4	8	$a < a^2 < a^3$	Not a choice
0.5	0.25	0.125	$a^3 < a^2 < a$	C
-0.5	0.25	-0.125	$a < a^3 < a^2$	B
-2	4	-8	$a^3 < a < a^2$	A

That eliminates everything except for D, so **choice D** is the answer. No sweat.

Exponential functions: Growth and decay

The SAT will throw one other kind of exponent question your way. You've almost certainly learned at some point how to calculate simple compound interest, so you've worked with exponential growth and decay before. An **exponential function** is one where the variable is found in an exponent. For example, $f(x) = 3^x$ is an exponential function. The first thing you need to remember—and the reason I put Example 2 before this section—is this: **exponential functions grow when the base is greater than 1, and get smaller (we call it decay) when the base is between 0 and 1.**

The second thing you need to remember is the basic structure of a compound interest equation, which you might encounter on test day.

Compound Interest Equation

$$A = P\left(1 + \frac{r}{n}\right)^{nt}$$

A = amount
P = principal (AKA initial investment)
r = interest rate (as a decimal!)
n = number of times interest compounds in a period
t = number of periods

Don't freak out about this, even though it looks complicated and even though you've probably had to deal with tricky versions of it in school. On the SAT, they'll *mostly* go easy on you with this by making $n = 1$, which is to say they'll make the interest compound only once per period. That makes the whole equation much easier to swallow. Still, if you're shooting for tiptop scores, you should know how to deal with n. I'll hit you with such a question in the drill.

One other note: this works with positive or negative interest rates. If r is negative, you've got decay instead of growth, but the math is the same.

Randy opened a savings account by making a deposit of $750. The savings account earns 5 percent interest, compounded annually. Which of the following expressions should Randy type into his calculator if he wants to know how much money he will have in 10 years, assuming he makes no other deposits?

A) $750(1.5)^{10}$

B) $750(1.05)^{10}$

C) $750(10)^{1.05}$

D) $10(1.05)^{750}$

Questions like this are really just translation questions. 5 percent is 0.05, so the r you want is 0.05. The interest in this account compounds annually, and you're talking about 10 years, so $n = 1$ and $t = 10$. The initial investment is $750. Put all those into the equation and simplify.

$$A = 750\left(1 + \frac{0.05}{1}\right)^{(1)(10)}$$

$$A = 750(1.05)^{10}$$

That's **choice B**! Note that for this question you're not even required to calculate what the account will be worth in 10 years—you just have to be able to recognize the right formula. That's fairly common.

Practice questions: Exponents and Exponential Functions

More like exPWNents, amirite?!

1 No calculator

If $x^6 = 60$ and $w^{10} = 20$, what is the value of $x^{12}w^{-10}$?

A) 36

B) 60

C) 180

D) 360

2 No calculator

If z, p, and q are each positive constants, which of the following is equivalent to z^q ?

A) $z^{pq} - z^p$

B) $\dfrac{z^{pq}}{z^p}$

C) $\dfrac{z^p}{z^{p-q}}$

D) $2z^{\frac{q}{2}}$

3 No calculator

Year	Value
1	$3,000
2	$3,300
3	$3,630
4	$3,993

Anson deposited $3,000 in a savings account in year 1, and took note of the value of his account in each of the next three years, as shown in the table above. Assuming Anson does not deposit any more money and his interest rate does not change, which of the following expressions can be used to calculate the value of Anson's account at the end of year 7?

A) $3000(1.1)^6$

B) $3000(1.1)^7$

C) $3000(1.01)^7$

D) $3000(0.1)^7$

4 No calculator; Grid-in

$$\sqrt[10]{x^2 x^3} = x^a$$

According to the equation above, what is the value of a ?

5 No calculator; Grid-in

$$A = 800(1.0025)^x$$

Chihiro has a savings account that earns 3% interest, compounded monthly. She wants to use the equation above to determine how much money she will have at the end of 8 years if she deposits $800 now. What value should she use for x ?

6 Calculator

$$P(n) = 5,000,000(0.92)^n$$

A wildlife biologist uses the function above to model the population, P, of species X from 1990 to 2010, where n represents the number of years since 1990. Which of the following statements would the biologist disagree with?

A) The population of species X has been decreasing at a rate of 8 percent per year.

B) The population of species X has been increasing by 92 percent each year.

C) The population of species X was 5 million in 1990.

D) The population of species X decreased by more than 80 percent from 1990 to 2010.

7 Calculator

A microbiologist observes that a certain species of thermophilic bacteria reproduces at its maximum rate at a temperature of 59° Celsius, and that for every degree cooler than 59° Celsius, the bacteria's reproduction rate is reduced by 20 percent. By what percent will the bacteria's reproduction rate be reduced from its maximum at a temperature of 56° Celsius?

A) 60.0 percent

B) 51.2 percent

C) 48.8 percent

D) 0.8 percent

8 Calculator; Grid-in

When the frequency at which a guitar string is vibrating doubles, the note the string is producing goes up one octave. If a string vibrating with a frequency of 82.41 Hz produces a certain note, what will be the frequency, in Hz, of a string producing a note two octaves higher, rounded to the nearest integer?

9 Calculator; Grid-in

If $(m + n)^2 = m^2 + n^2$, what is the value of $(3^m)^n$?

10 Calculator; Grid-in

$$\left(x^5\right)^6 x^{\frac{2}{3}} = x^a$$

According to the equation above, what is the value of a ?

Answers:

1	C		6	B
2	C		7	C
3	A		8	330
4	.5 or 1/2		9	1
5	96		10	30.6, 30.7, or 92/3

Solutions on page 367.

The following selected Official Test questions are examples of this stuff in the wild.

Test	Section	Questions
1	3: No calculator	14, 20
	4: Calculator	37, 38
2	3: No calculator	7, 14
	4: Calculator	
3	3: No calculator	3
	4: Calculator	21, 28
4	3: No calculator	
	4: Calculator	13, 14, 15, 20
5	3: No calculator	12, 14
	4: Calculator	
6	3: No calculator	9, 16
	4: Calculator	37
7	3: No calculator	11
	4: Calculator	27
8	3: No calculator	
	4: Calculator	13, 23, 38
9	3: No calculator	
	4: Calculator	4, 21
10	3: No calculator	5
	4: Calculator	9, 22, 26
PSAT/NMSQT 1	3: No calculator	
	4: Calculator	
PSAT/NMSQT 2	3: No calculator	12
	4: Calculator	25

Quadratics

You're going to have to solve yourself some quadratics on the SAT—for real. This is important stuff, score-wise. I want to focus on three ways to pwn quadratics questions. You might already know them all, but make sure you've got them locked and loaded on test day.

Example 1: No calculator; Grid-in

$$f(x) = x^2 + 6x - 7$$

The function $f(x)$ is defined above. If $f(k) = 0$ and $k > 0$, what is the value of k?

Like I was saying—three ways to go here. First, we could always use the quadratic formula. This is one of those things that's not given to you on the reference sheet in the beginning of the test but that you *absolutely must* have memorized.[*]

Quadratic Formula
IF: $ax^2 + bx + c = 0,$
THEN: $x = \dfrac{-b \pm \sqrt{b^2 - 4ac}}{2a}$

In this case, we know $a = 1$, $b = 6$, and $c = -7$, so we can grind out the zeros thusly:

$$x = \frac{-6 \pm \sqrt{6^2 - (4)(1)(-7)}}{2(1)}$$

$$x = \frac{-6 \pm \sqrt{36 - (-28)}}{2}$$

$$x = \frac{-6 \pm \sqrt{64}}{2}$$

$$x = \frac{-6 \pm 8}{2}$$

$$x = -7 \text{ or } x = 1$$

---

[*] You might also want to make a quadratic formula program in your calculator (if your calculator doesn't already have one) to speed you up in the calculator section. Search pwntestprep.com for a video that will help you do that.

Since the question told us that $k > 0$, we now know that $\pmb{k = 1}$. GRID IT IN!

The quadratic formula might totally end up being your go-to first stop on a question like this, but let's make sure we talk about the other two ways to solve this problem anyway. Here it is again:

$$f(x) = x^2 + 6x - 7$$

The function $f(x)$ is defined above. If $f(a) = 0$ and $a > 0$, what is a ?

If you're fond of factoring, it's probably a faster way to go here. Let's set that quadratic equal to zero again and try to factor it:

$$x^2 + 6x - 7 = 0$$

You've probably already done this in your head, but I'm going to go very much step-by-step here. First, note that the first term has a coefficient of 1. Pretty much the only time you're going to want to factor to solve something like this rather than just use the quadratic formula is if the leading coefficient is 1, or if you can neatly divide the whole quadratic by something to make the leading coefficient 1. Anyway, when the leading coefficient is 1, you know that both factors will begin with x.

$$(x \quad)(x \quad) = 0$$

You also have a negative constant at the end, there. That tells you that one of your factors will be $x +$ something, and other will be $x -$ something.

$$(x + \ )(x - \ ) = 0$$

Finally, you know that the blanks you've got left must multiply to -7, and sum to 6. The only way that happens is if they're 7 and -1.

$$(x + 7)(x - 1) = 0$$

There—that's nice.* Since we're multiplying two things together and getting zero, we know one of those things must be zero. Either $x = -7$ or $x = 1$, same as before.

Example 2: Calculator

What are the solutions to $x^2 - 3x - 7 = 0$?

A) $x = 6 \pm \sqrt{19}$

B) $x = \dfrac{3 \pm \sqrt{28}}{2}$

C) $x = \dfrac{3 \pm \sqrt{37}}{2}$

D) $x = 3 \pm \sqrt{41}$

You're not going to be able to factor that one. You can use the quadratic formula, of course, but since the calculator is allowed on this problem, why don't we try something wild and crazy? Let's graph it!

 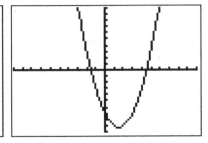

The calculator will calculate zeros for you. Mine only does them one at a time, which is a bit annoying, but look at those answer choices! They're different enough that one is all we need. So let's choose the zero function, set our bounds, humor our calculator with a guess, and then see what we find.

---

* This is almost too obvious to mention, but it's really easy to check your work when you factor like this—just FOIL the factors back out to make sure you end up back where you started!

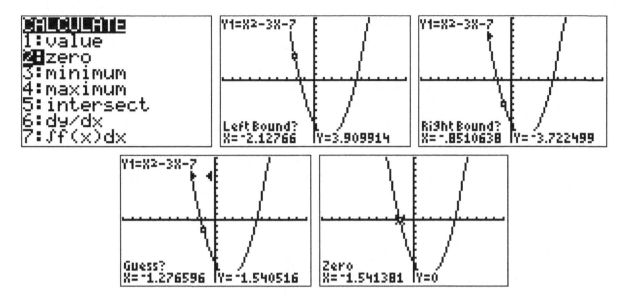

Now, look again at those answer choices. We know we found the lesser of the two zeros, so let's just change all those ± signs to – signs, start with choice A, and try each one until a choice gives us –1.541381...

```
6-√(19)
         1.641101056
(3-√(28))/2
        -1.145751311
(3-√(37))/2
        -1.541381265
```

Yep! That last one did it. The answer is **C**.

As I was saying before, it's likely that for most quadratics where you need to find zeros, you'll turn right to the equation. That's good! Just don't let it be the only tool in your belt. This test is about being nimble; there will be plenty of questions that will be much easier to solve by factoring.

Extraneous solutions

Another fun trick the SAT will play on you is to throw an extraneous solution at you once in a while. Like so:

$$x+1=\sqrt{x+3}$$

What is the solution set of the equation above?

A) $\{1, -2\}$

B) $\{1, 2\}$

C) $\{-2\}$

D) $\{1\}$

To solve this without a calculator, you're going to have to square both sides:

$$(x+1)^2=\left(\sqrt{x+3}\right)^2$$
$$x^2+2x+1=x+3$$

Now combine like terms to get this into true quadratic form:

$$x^2+x-2=0$$

You can throw that in the quadratic formula if you wish, but I'm just gonna factor (like a boss):

$$(x+2)(x-1)=0$$

So, great! We have two solutions: $x=-2$ and $x=1$. NOT SO FAST!

Whenever you square both sides of an equation like this to allow you to solve, you introduce the possibility of an extraneous solution—one that doesn't actually work in the original equation. Try both of these solutions out in the original equation and see what happens.

$$x=-2 \qquad\qquad x=1$$
$$(-2)+1=\sqrt{(-2)+3} \qquad (1)+1=\sqrt{(1)+3}$$
$$-1=\sqrt{1} \qquad\qquad 2=\sqrt{4}$$
$$-1\neq 1 \qquad\qquad 2=2$$

Plugging -2 back into the original equation made trouble for us! That's not an actual solution—it's extraneous. So the only actual solution we have is $x=1$. The correct answer is **D**.

I know this was a no-calculator problem, but now that we've done it I think the calculator might provide a useful visual. Why isn't $x = -2$ an actual solution?

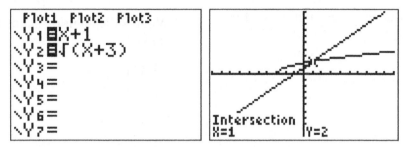

Well, there you go. That's why. When $x = -2$, the $y = x + 1$ line is below the x-axis; the $y = \sqrt{x + 3}$ graph never gets below the x-axis!

One more note about extraneous solutions. It's easy to avoid getting screwed up here if you backsolve. If you look back at the answer choices, there are only three possible solutions between the four of them: –2, 1, and 2. Because of that, we *could have* skipped all the squaring, combining, and factoring work above and just jumped to checking possible solutions. The only work we would have needed:

$$x = -2 \qquad\qquad x = 1 \qquad\qquad x = 2$$
$$(-2) + 1 = \sqrt{(-2) + 3} \qquad (1) + 1 = \sqrt{(1) + 3} \qquad (2) + 1 = \sqrt{(2) + 3}$$
$$-1 = \sqrt{1} \qquad\qquad 2 = \sqrt{4} \qquad\qquad 3 \neq \sqrt{5}$$
$$-1 \neq 1 \qquad\qquad 2 = 2$$

Pretty cool, no?

Practice questions: Quadratics

Don't let these question FOIL you.

$$(x + 3)(x - 4) = 8$$

Which of the following is the solution set for the equation above?

A) $\{-3, 4\}$

B) $\{-4, 3\}$

C) $\{-5, 4\}$

D) $\{-4, 5\}$

$$3x^2 - 5x - \frac{11}{12} = 0$$

If $x > 0$ in the equation above, which of the following is true about the value of x ?

A) $0 < x < 1$

B) $1 < x < 2$

C) $2 < x < 3$

D) $3 < x < 4$

$$\sqrt{2x-1} = x - 2$$

What is the solution set of the equation above?

A) $\{1\}$

B) $\{5\}$

C) $\{-1, -5\}$

D) $\{1, 5\}$

4 No calculator; Grid-in

If $x + 3$ is a factor of $x^2 + bx - 6$, what is the value of b ?

5 No calculator; Grid-in

If $x + 2$ is a factor of $x^2 + px + p$, what is the value of p ?

120

PWN Test Prep

Practice questions: Quadratics

Don't let these question FOIL you.

What are the solutions to $4x^2 - 10x + 2 = 0$?

A) $\dfrac{5 \pm \sqrt{17}}{4}$

B) $\dfrac{-5 \pm \sqrt{11}}{2}$

C) $3 \pm \sqrt{15}$

D) $2 \pm \dfrac{\sqrt{2}}{2}$

$$f(x) = \dfrac{x^2 + 3x + 6}{(x-3)^2 - 6(x-3) + 9}$$

For what value of x is the function above undefined?

A) -9

B) -3

C) 3

D) 6

$$\sqrt{x+3} = x - 2$$

What is the solution set of the equation above?

A) $\left\{ \dfrac{5 + \sqrt{29}}{2}, \dfrac{5 - \sqrt{29}}{2} \right\}$

B) $\left\{ \dfrac{5 + \sqrt{29}}{2} \right\}$

C) $\left\{ \dfrac{5 + \sqrt{21}}{2} \right\}$

D) $\left\{ \dfrac{3 + \sqrt{5}}{2}, \dfrac{3 - \sqrt{5}}{2} \right\}$

$$h = -4.9t^2 + t + 1.5$$

The equation above expresses the approximate height, h, in meters, of a coin t seconds after it is flipped vertically upward from a height of 1.5 meters with an initial velocity of 1 meter per second. After how many seconds will the coin land on the ground?

What is the sum of all values of x that satisfy $3x^2 - 5x = 30$?

Answers:

1	D	6	A
2	B	7	D
3	B	8	C
4	1	9	.664 or .665
5	4	10	1.66 or 1.67 or 5/3

Solutions on page 369.

The following Official Test questions will test your quadratic skills.

Test	Section	Questions
1	3: No calculator	
	4: Calculator	25, 36
2	3: No calculator	13
	4: Calculator	
3	3: No calculator	14
	4: Calculator	
4	3: No calculator	9, 13, 15
	4: Calculator	
5	3: No calculator	3
	4: Calculator	35
6	3: No calculator	13
	4: Calculator	20
7	3: No calculator	
	4: Calculator	35
8	3: No calculator	7, 8, 14, 16
	4: Calculator	8, 14, 19
9	3: No calculator	11, 15
	4: Calculator	
10	3: No calculator	13, 14
	4: Calculator	
PSAT/NMSQT 1	3: No calculator	6, 17
	4: Calculator	
PSAT/NMSQT 2	3: No calculator	4, 16
	4: Calculator	20

Binomial Squares and Difference of Two Squares

The SAT might occasionally test your ability to factor special expressions into their binomial components. This won't be a very long chapter because there's not much to say other than to show you the forms you need to know and walk you through a few questions. Once you know the forms cold, you'll probably find that you get a little bit excited when you spot one of these questions.

So, let's get right into it. You should commit to memory the forms of the two binomial squares and the difference of two squares. These should be close enough to the front of your mind that you can deploy them without much thought should you encounter a question that requires them on the SAT.

Binomial squares:

$$(x + y)^2 = x^2 + 2xy + y^2$$
$$(x - y)^2 = x^2 - 2xy + y^2$$

Difference of two squares:

$$(x + y)(x - y) = x^2 - y^2$$

Example 1: No calculator; Grid-in

If $(x - y)^2 = 25$ and $xy = 10$, then what is the value of $x^2 + y^2$?

What do you see going on here? Do you see that you've been provided with pieces of a particular puzzle?

To solve, let's start by expanding what we were given. FOIL works here, of course; however, making the effort to memorize the contents of the table above—the binomial squares and difference of two squares—will save you precious time on the test.

$$(x - y)^2 = 25$$
$$x^2 - 2xy + y^2 = 25$$

And would you look at that! We're pretty much already done. Just substitute the value you were given for xy, and do a little manipulating:

$$x^2 - 2(10) + y^2 = 25$$
$$x^2 - 20 + y^2 = 25$$
$$\mathbf{x^2 + y^2 = 45}$$

Note that we didn't need to solve for x or y individually to find this solution; all we needed to do was move some puzzle pieces around. Note also that actually solving for the individual variables would have been a pain.

Your mantra for questions like this needs to be: *"How do I quickly go from what they gave me to what they want?"*

Example 2: No calculator

$$a^4 - b^8$$

Which of the following expressions is equivalent to the expression above?

A) $(a^2 + b^4)(a + b^2)(a - b^2)$

B) $(a^2 - b^4)(a + b^2)(a - b^2)$

C) $(a^2 + b^4)^2$

D) $(a^2 - b^4)^2$

As I'm fond of saying, this one looks way gnarlier than it is. All you need to do to get it is recognize the difference of two squares form: a^4 is a perfect square and so is b^8. So we can factor:

$$a^4 - b^8$$
$$= (a^2 + b^4)(a^2 - b^4)$$

And look $a^2 - b^4$ is *still* a difference of two squares! We can factor further.

$$= (a^2 + b^4)(a + b^2)(a - b^2)$$

So the answer is **choice A**.

Practice questions: Binomial Squares and Difference of Two Squares
How will you get from where you are to where you want to be?

1 No calculator

$$\frac{x^2 - y^2}{x - y}$$

Which of the following is equivalent to the expression above for all values of x and y such that $x \neq y$?

A) $x - y$

B) $x + y$

C) 1

D) 0

2 No calculator

$$25a^6 - 40a^3b + 16b^2$$

Which of the following is equivalent to the expression above?

A) $(5a^3 - 4b)^2$

B) $(5a^2 - 2b)^3$

C) $(5a^3 + 4b)(5a^3 - 4b)$

D) $(5a^3 - 2b)^2$

3 No calculator

If $a + b = -8$ and $a^2 + b^2 = 50$, what is the value of ab ?

A) 14

B) 10

C) 9

D) 7

4 No calculator; Grid-in

If $p^2 - r^2 = 18$ and $p - r = 2$, what is the value of $p + r$?

5 No calculator; Grid-in

$$a^2 - b^2 = -24$$

In the equation above, a and b are constants. If $a - b = -8$, what is the value of b ?

Practice questions: Binomial Squares and Difference of Two Squares

How will you get from where you are to where you want to be?

6 Calculator

If $(x - y)^2 = 71$ and $x^2 + y^2 = 59$, what is the value of xy ?

A) 6

B) 3

C) –6

D) –12

7 Calculator

If $x + y = m$ and $x - y = n$, then what is $x^2 + y^2$, in terms of m and n ?

A) mn

B) $\dfrac{m^2 + n^2}{2}$

C) $(m - n)^2$

D) $\dfrac{m^2 - n^2}{2}$

8 Calculator; Grid-in

If $a^2 + b^2 = 258$, what is the value of $(a + b)^2 + (a - b)^2$?

9 Calculator; Grid-in

$$16x^4 - 81 = (ax^2 + b)(cx + d)(cx - d)$$

In the equation above, a, b, c, and d are constants. If the equation is true for all values of x, what is the sum of a, b, c, and d ?

10 Calculator; Grid-in

$$(x + a)^2 + b = x^2 + 10x + 36$$

In the equation above, a and b are constants. If the equation is true for all values of x, what is the value of b ?

Answers:

1	B		6	C
2	A		7	B
3	D		8	516
4	9		9	18
5	5.5 or 11/2		10	11

Solutions on page 372.

The following Official Test questions involve binomial squares and/or difference of two squares.

Test	Section	Questions
1	3: No calculator	
	4: Calculator	
2	3: No calculator	4
	4: Calculator	
3	3: No calculator	
	4: Calculator	
4	3: No calculator	
	4: Calculator	
5	3: No calculator	10
	4: Calculator	30
6	3: No calculator	4, 15
	4: Calculator	
7	3: No calculator	15
	4: Calculator	
8	3: No calculator	8
	4: Calculator	
9	3: No calculator	
	4: Calculator	
10	3: No calculator	6, 20
	4: Calculator	
PSAT/NMSQT 1	3: No calculator	
	4: Calculator	
PSAT/NMSQT 2	3: No calculator	17
	4: Calculator	

Parabolas

Parabolas are the graphical representations of quadratic functions—if the greatest power in a function is 2, then that function makes a parabola. It was tempting, therefore, for me to lump all of the following information in with the quadratics chapter. I decided not to because questions about parabolas have a different feel than other questions about quadratics. And besides, two chapters instead of one means twice as many practice problems—that can only be a good thing if you want to be prepped to the max.

In this chapter, we're going to talk about the parabola equation forms you should know, what those forms tell you, and how to convert between them. We'll also talk about parabola symmetry because even though it's tested less commonly, it is still fair game and with a little practice it's easy to master.

Standard form of a parabola

The standard form of a parabola is the most common parabola form—the one that most math teachers would consider "simplified."

> **Standard form of a parabola**
> $$y = ax^2 + bx + c$$

The coefficients in the standard form tell you a few important things at a glance:

→ The constant a tells you whether the parabola opens up or down. If a is positive, the parabola's a smiley face. If a is negative, it's a frowny face. Easy to remember, no?

→ The constant c is the parabola's y-intercept. If there is no c, that means your parabola has a y-intercept of 0. In other words, it goes through the origin.

→ The x-coordinate of the parabola's vertex is at $-\dfrac{b}{2a}$.

Sometimes questions about this form might be as simple as being given an equation, and having to match it to the correct parabola graph. In that case, if your equation has a positive a, eliminate the parabolas that open down. Then focus on y-intercepts. If your equation has a positive c, only one remaining choice will have a positive *y*-intercept. It'll be that simple. Other times, you'll have to do a *little* more critical thinking about the information provided by the standard form.

Which of the following quadratic equations, when graphed in the *xy*-plane, will not intersect the line with equation $y = 3$?

A) $y = 3x^2 + 3x + 3$

B) $y = -3x^2 + 3x - 3$

C) $y = 3x^2 + 3x - 3$

D) $y = 3x^2 - 3x - 3$

At first glance, it might not seem like you have enough information here to answer the question without a lot of work, especially when you can't use your calculator. But wait! Just a quick look at the answer choices tells us this:

    A)   Opens up; *y*-intercept at 3

    B)   Opens down; *y*-intercept at –3

    C)   Opens up; *y*-intercept at –3

    D)   Opens up; *y*-intercept at –3

Obviously, choice A goes right away—if its *y*-intercept is 3, then it clearly intersects the $y = 3$ line. Maybe not *quite* as obviously, but still *pretty obviously*, choices C and D can also be eliminated! If they open up, and have a *y*-intercept lower than 3, then obviously they're going to have to cross the $y = 3$ line at some point! So, without much work at all, we're left with only the correct answer: **B**.

Vertex form of a parabola

The vertex form of a parabola tells you—as you'd expect from the name—where the parabola's vertex is.

> ### Vertex form of a parabola
> $$y = a(x - h)^2 + k$$

➜ The constants h and k tell you the vertex of the parabola—the vertex is at (h, k).

⇨ Note that this is just an application of the graph translation rules we discussed in the Functions chapter on page 98. If $f(x) = ax^2$, which would have a vertex at $(0, 0)$, then $f(x – h) + k = a(x – h)^2 + k$ would move the vertex to (h, k).

⇨ Also note the negative inside the parentheses, which is the trickiest thing about the vertex form of a parabola. The parabola with equation $y = 3(x + 4)^2 + 1$ will have its vertex at $(–4, 1)$, not $(4, 1)$!

➜ The constant a still tells you whether the parabola opens up or down, just like it does in the standard form.

Example 2: Calculator; Grid-in

$$y = 2(x + 1)^2 + 3$$

What is the slope of the line that contains the vertex and the y-intercept of the parabola with the equation above?

To solve this, first we must note that the parabola is given in vertex form. So we know the vertex is $(–1, 3)$.

Now we need to find the y-intercept. The fastest way to do this is to plug in zero for x, since the y-intercept will always be where $x = 0$.

$$y = 2(0 + 1)^2 + 3$$
$$y = 2(1) + 3$$
$$y = 5$$

Of course, the standard form of the parabola also tells us the y-intercept. We can FOIL to get there—we'll still find that the y-intercept is 5:

$$y = 2(x + 1)^2 + 3$$

$$y = 2(x^2 + 2x + 1) + 3$$

$$y = 2x^2 + 4x + 5$$

So the y-intercept of the parabola is 5, meaning the other point on the line for which we're finding the slope is $(0, 5)$.

All we need to do now is calculate the slope!

$$\text{slope} = \frac{5 - 3}{0 - (-1)}$$

$$\text{slope} = \frac{2}{1}$$

$$\text{slope} = 2$$

And there you have it. Not so bad, right?

Example 3: No calculator

$$y = x^2 - 2x - 3$$

Which of the following is an equivalent form of the equation above in which the minimum value of y appears as a constant or coefficient?

A) $y = x(x - 2) - 3$

B) $y = (x - 1)^2 - 4$

C) $y = (x - 3)(x + 1)$

D) $y = x^2 - 2\left(x - \frac{3}{2}\right)$

If you're on your game, you recognize that only choice **B** is even in vertex form, so that's almost certainly the answer. To prove it, I'd like to take a few minutes to review a concept for getting equations into certain forms that you've probably seen but might not have used for a while: completing the square. When we complete the square, we recognize that the first part of the given polynomial, $x^2 - 2x$, is the beginning of a binomial square: $(x-1)^2 = x^2 - 2x + 1$.

This is useful because it will allow us to convert from standard form to vertex form. If we add 1 to each side of the equation it stays balanced, and we can use that to our great advantage:

$$y = x^2 - 2x - 3$$
$$y + \boxed{1} = x^2 - 2x + \boxed{1} - 3$$

See those circles? That's the 1 I'm adding to each side.* Now I can group the binomial square and factor it:

$$y + 1 = (x^2 - 2x + 1) - 3$$
$$y + 1 = (x - 1)^2 - 3$$

Now just subtract 1 from each side to get y alone again, and you've got your parabola in vertex form:

$$y = (x - 1)^2 - 4$$

There it is: choice **B**. Just like we thought.

At this point I should mention that most students I know do not use completing the square here. Instead, they prefer to use the fact that the x-coordinate of the vertex in the originally provided standard form is $-\dfrac{b}{2a} = -\dfrac{-2}{2(1)} = 1$. Once they've got that figured out, they can plug 1 in for x to find the minimum y-value:

$$y = (1)^2 - 2(1) - 3$$
$$y = -4$$

From there, you can scan the answer choices for –4s. Only choice **B** has one.

Oh man—this is so much fun I want to mention one more thing! I know I said this was a no calculator question, but if it weren't then one other option available to us is to do some graphing. First, graph the original equation:

---

* The reason we call this "completing the square" is that when $x^2 - 2x$ becomes $x^2 - 2x + 1$, the square, $(x-1)^2$, is complete.

Now use the calculator's minimum function to find the vertex:

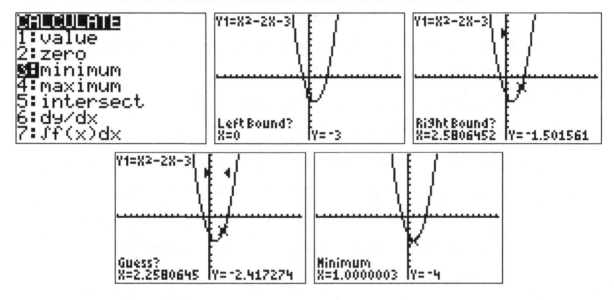

Ugh—ignore the fact that sometimes these stinking calculators are off by 3 ten millionths. The minimum here is clearly (1, –4), and you know from the original equation that the leading coefficient is 1, so if you know your vertex form, you can write it:

$$y = (x - 1)^2 - 4$$

Then, if you're at all concerned that you might have made a mistake or forgotten something, you can graph *that* and make sure it matches your previous graph:

Yep, that looks right!

Factored form of a parabola

Once in a while, a quadratic in a parabola question will be given to you in a factored form.

> **Factored form of a parabola**
> $$y = a(x - m)(x - n)$$

→ The constants m and n tell you the parabola's x-intercepts.

⇨ Not every parabola has x-intercepts. If a parabola doesn't have x-intercepts, though, it won't be given in this form.

→ The constant a still tells you whether the parabola opens up or down, just like it does in the standard and vertex forms.

⇨ If a parabola opens up, then the part of the parabola between the x-intercepts is negative (that is, below the x-axis) and the parts outside the x-intercepts are positive. If it opens down, then the part between the x-intercepts is positive and the parts outside the x-intercepts are negative.

Of course, if you're given a parabola in factored form and you need it in standard or vertex form, your first step is to FOIL. Before you do that, though, think about whether you can solve the problem without converting.

Example 4: No calculator

$$f(x) = -5(x - 2)(x + 3)$$

When the function above is graphed in the xy-plane, the result is a parabola. Which of the following is positive?

A) $f(1)$

B) $f(2)$

C) $f(3)$

D) $f(4)$

You can't use your calculator to graph this, but don't panic! You know from the -5 that the parabola opens down, and you know it has x-intercepts at $x = 2$ and $x = -3$. Therefore, you know that values between $f(-3)$ and $f(2)$ will be positive. Only $f(1)$ fits in that range, so choice **A** is the answer. (Of course, it also wouldn't be so bad just to backsolve this one. Just put 1, 2, 3, and 4 in for x and see which one gives you a positive result!)

Parabola width

In the all three forms we've discussed, the leading coefficient, a, that tells you whether a parabola opens up or down, also tells you how fat or skinny the parabola is. The bigger a is (or smaller, in the case of negative values of a), the skinnier the parabola. A good point of reference: when $a = 1$, the points 1 to the left and 1 to the right of the parabola's vertex will each be 1 higher than the vertex. When $a > 1$, those points will be higher. When $0 < a < 1$, those points will be lower.

Look at the following graphs of $y = x^2$, $y = 2x^2$, and $y = 0.5x^2$. Note that while the first contains the points $(-1, 1)$, $(0, 0)$, and $(1, 1)$, the latter two graphs do not.

Parabola Symmetry

Test writers like parabola symmetry with good reason: even though symmetry is an easy enough concept to understand, there are still some great ways to ask tricky questions about it. Most parabola questions on the SAT are equation-based, but you should still spend a few minutes on this. If you're presented with a parabola question and you're not given an equation—or enough information to quickly derive an equation—think symmetry.

Every parabola has a vertical line of symmetry that goes through its vertex. Each point on the parabola to the left of that line will have a point exactly mirroring it on the right.*

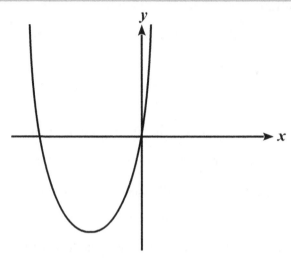

The graph above represents the quadratic function $f(x)$. If the function's minimum is at $f(-3)$, and $f(0) = 0$, which of the following is equal to 0?

A) $f(3)$

B) $f(-1)$

C) $f(-5)$

D) $f(-6)$

Right. So let's translate this into English first. What they're saying here is that the line of symmetry for this parabola is at $x = -3$, and that the function goes right through the origin: $f(0) = 0$ means that this graph contains the point $(0, 0)$. They're basically asking us to find the other x-intercept.

---

*   I'm talking about vertical parabolas only, here. Horizontal parabolas are pretty unlikely to appear on the SAT—because they're not functions, I guess—so I'm not mentioning them. Obviously, if you had a horizontal parabola, its line of symmetry would be horizontal.

Here's where the whole symmetry thing really comes in. If we know the line of symmetry, and we know one of the *x*-intercepts, it's a piece of cake to find the other. Both *x*-intercepts have to be the exact same distance from the line of symmetry. Since (0, 0) is a distance of 3 from the line of symmetry at

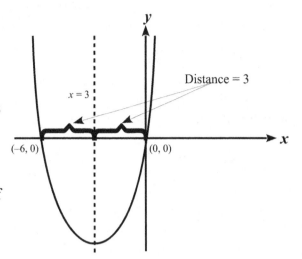

$x = -3$, our other *x*-intercept has to be a distance of 3 away from the line of symmetry too!

So we're looking for the point $(-6, 0)$. Choice **D** is the one that does that for us: $f(-6) = 0$.

Can they find ways to make symmetry questions difficult? You bet. Will you be ready for them? I'd say so.

Summary

The table below summarizes the different parabola forms and what they tell you.

	Standard	Vertex	Factored
Equation	$y = ax^2 + bx + c$	$y = a(x - h)^2 + k$	$y = a(x - m)(x - n)$
What the constants or coefficients tells you	c is the *y*-intercept; $-\dfrac{b}{2a}$ is the *x*-value of the vertex.	(h, k) is the vertex.	*m* and *n* are the *x*-intercepts.
What the coefficient *a* always tells you	If $a > 0$, the parabola opens upwards; if $a < 0$, the parabola opens downwards. The greater the value of $|a|$, the thinner the parabola.		

Practice questions: Parabolas

Parabola schmarabola.

$$g(x) = x^2 + 8x - 9$$

Which of the following is an equivalent form of the function g above in which the minimum value of g appears as a constant or coefficient?

A) $g(x) = x(x + 8) - 9$

B) $g(x) = -(x^2 - 8x + 9)$

C) $g(x) = (x + 9)(x - 1)$

D) $g(x) = (x + 4)^2 - 25$

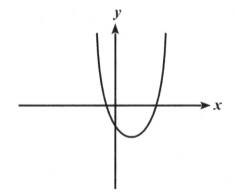

The parabola in the figure above has its minimum at $x = 2$. Which of the following could be the equation of the parabola?

A) $y = (x - 3)(x - 1)$

B) $y = (x + 3)(x + 1)$

C) $y = (x - 5)(x + 1)$

D) $y = (x + 5)(x - 1)$

Which of the following equations represents the reflection of the parabola $y = (x + 3)(x - 5)$ across the y-axis in the xy-plane?

A) $y = x^2 - 2x - 15$

B) $y = x^2 + 2x + 15$

C) $y = x^2 + 2x - 15$

D) $y = -x^2 + 2x + 15$

In the xy-plane, a parabola passes through the points $(0, 3)$ and $(8, 3)$, and has its minimum at $(p, -2)$. What is the value of p ?

In the xy-plane, the line $y = k$, where k is a constant, intersects the parabola

$y = 2(x + 5)^2 + 19$ at exactly one point. What

is the value of k ?

Parabola schmarabola.

6 Calculator

If a and b are constants, and the graph of $g(x) = (x - a)^2 + b$ has its minimum at $g(6)$, which of the following pairs of points could also be on the graph of $g(x)$ in the xy-plane?

A) $(5, -9)$ and $(8, -9)$

B) $(0, 6)$ and $(10, 10)$

C) $(5, 6)$ and $(7, 8)$

D) $(2, -5)$ and $(10, -5)$

7 Calculator

$$g(x) = -6x^2 + 3x$$

Which of the following is true about the graph of the function g defined above?

    I   It passes through the origin.

    II   It is increasing from $x = 1$ to $x = 6$.

    III $g(-6)$ is negative.

A) I only

B) II only

C) I and III only

D) I, II, and III

8 Calculator

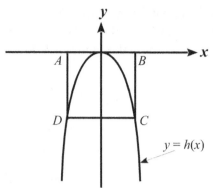

Note: Figure not drawn to scale.

In the figure above, $ABCD$ is a square that intersects the graph of $h(x)$ at points C and D. A and B lie on the x-axis. If the area of $ABCD$ is 36 and $h(x) = kx^2$, what is the value of k ?

A) $\dfrac{1}{3}$

B) $-\dfrac{1}{6}$

C) $-\dfrac{1}{3}$

D) $-\dfrac{2}{3}$

Practice questions: Parabolas

Parabola schmarabola.

When the parabola $y = (-x + 3)(x + 11)$ is graphed in the xy-plane, its maximum value is at (a, b). What is the value of b ?

The function $f(x) = (x - 11)^2 + 9$ is graphed in the xy-plane. The point (a, a) lies on the graph. What is one possible value of a ?

Answers:

1	D		6	D
2	C		7	C
3	C		8	D
4	4		9	49
5	19		10	10 or 13

Solutions on page 373.

The following selected Official Test questions are examples of parabolas in their natural habitat.

Test	Section	Questions
1	3: No calculator	10
	4: Calculator	30
2	3: No calculator	
	4: Calculator	7, 29
3	3: No calculator	10, 12
	4: Calculator	
4	3: No calculator	11, 13
	4: Calculator	28
5	3: No calculator	4
	4: Calculator	
6	3: No calculator	11
	4: Calculator	30
7	3: No calculator	7, 12
	4: Calculator	24
8	3: No calculator	
	4: Calculator	
9	3: No calculator	13
	4: Calculator	26, 27, 28
10	3: No calculator	10, 13
	4: Calculator	19, 28, 36
PSAT/NMSQT 1	3: No calculator	13
	4: Calculator	28, 30, 31
PSAT/NMSQT 2	3: No calculator	13
	4: Calculator	22

Polynomials

The SAT will test you on your understanding of, and your ability to perform basic operations on, polynomials. Here's the stuff you need to know.

Zeros

When we use the word "zeros" in the context of talking about polynomials, we're talking about instances where some value of x makes the polynomial equal zero. I often find it useful to think about zeros graphically: whenever the graph of a polynomial function crosses the x-axis, that x-value is one of the polynomial's zeros.

Example 1: Calculator

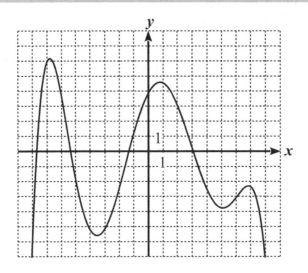

A section of the graph of $y = f(x)$ is shown above. How many zeros does $f(x)$ have for $-8 < x < 8$?

A) 3

B) 4

C) 5

D) 6

This is too easy, right? Especially after I *just* told you that every time a graph crosses the x-axis, that's a zero. Just count the x-intercepts! There are 4 of them, so the answer is **B**! (Don't count the y-intercept, unless it's at the origin and therefore also an x-intercept. We only care about where $y = 0$.)

Unless you get a question that looks almost exactly like the one above, though, you're going to want to know how to actually calculate zeros. In almost all cases, this will be for quadratics, which we just spent a whole section on.

The only other thing you'll need to know is that if a polynomial has a zero at, say, $x = 3$, then $x - 3$ will be a factor of that polynomial.

Example 2: No calculator

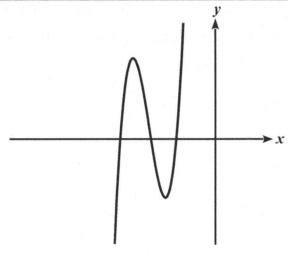

The figure above shows the graph of the function $f(x)$ in the xy-plane. If $f(x) = (x + a)(x + b)(x + c)$, where a, b, and c are integer constants, then which of the following statements must be true about a, b, and c?

A) All three are positive.

B) All three are negative.

C) One of the three is equal to 0.

D) Two are positive and one is negative.

Not much pencil work to do here—you just have to see that all those zeros on the graph are negative, and then draw the right conclusion. Let's plug in to make things a bit more intuitive. Say one of those zeros is $x = -7$. If that's true, then we know that $x + 7$ is a factor of $f(x)$. That's x plus a positive number. Since all the zeros are negative, all the factors will be x plus a positive number! So the answer is **A**, which says a, b, and c are all positive.

Long division of polynomials

When I first saw that they were adding long division of polynomials to the SAT, I could barely believe it, but sure enough it's in there—there's a question that requires this skill in all but one of the practice tests released by College Board at the time of this writing. So, my slack-jawed disbelief aside, you should expect to see this on test day. The good news is that the basic process is actually not that hard to do, even if you've never done it in school. So I'm going to walk you through the algorithm a few times, and then throw a few practice problems your way, and we'll call it a day, mmmkay?

$$f(x) = 3x^2 + 17x + 25$$

What is the remainder when $f(x)$, above, is divided by $x + 2$?

Right, so how do we do this? Well, we start by setting up the long division, just like we used to do in 3rd grade when we were only dividing integers, only now we have to put on our big boy and big girl pants and deal with variables. Yay!

$$x+2 \overline{\smash{\big)}\,3x^2+17x+25}$$

Just like we'd do if we were doing long division of integers, our first step is to figure out how many times $x + 2$ can go into the first part of the polynomial: $3x^2 + 17x$. And it turns out that it can go into that $3x$ times. All that ends up meaning, practically, is that we multiply by whatever we need to multiply to match the leading term. In this case, if we multiply $x + 2$ by $3x$, then we'll get $3x^2 + 6x$, which has $3x^2$ as a leading term. That's what we want.

$$
\begin{array}{r}
3x \\
x+2{\overline{\smash{\big)}\,3x^2+17x+25}} \\
\underline{-\left(3x^2+6x\right)} \\
11x+25
\end{array}
$$

See what's going on there? $3x$ becomes part of the quotient. The product of $3x$ and $x + 2$ is $3x^2 + 6$, which gets subtracted from the original polynomial, and leaves us with $11x + 25$. Our next step is basically a repeat of the process again, only now instead of matching our leading term to $3x^2$, we're going to match it to $11x$.

$$
\begin{array}{r}
3x \\
x+2{\overline{\smash{\big)}\,3x^2+17x+25}} \\
\underline{-\left(3x^2+6x\right)} \\
11x+25 \\
\underline{-\left(11x+22\right)} \\
3
\end{array}
$$

So again, we multiplied $x + 2$ by 11, which gave us $11x + 22$. We did that so that we'd have a leading term of $11x$, which would cancel out and leave us only with a constant term when we subtracted. That constant we're left with, 3, is our remainder. That's what we'd bubble in on this grid-in question.

We also now know, although we didn't need it for this question, the full quotient: $3x + 11$. In math speak: when $3x^2 + 17x + 25$ is divided by $x + 2$, the quotient is $3x + 11$ and the remainder is 3.

Another way we can write the same information:

$$
\frac{3x^2+17x+25}{x+2} = (3x+11) + \frac{3}{x+2} \quad \text{--- remainder}
$$

quotient

Got all that? Good. Now I want to show you something.

Example 3 (again): Calculator; Grid-in

$$f(x) = 3x^2 + 17x + 25$$

What is the remainder when $f(x)$, above, is divided by $x + 2$?

What if, instead of going through that whole long division process, we just wanted to test whether $x + 2$ was a factor of $f(x)$? A great way to do that would be to just plug $x = -2$ into $3x^2 + 17x + 25$ to see whether we got 0. (In other words, we'd test whether $f(-2) = 0$ is true.)

Of course, because we already did the problem, we know that $f(-2) \neq 0$. What does it equal, though?

$$f(x) = 3x^2 + 17x + 25$$
$$f(-2) = 3(-2)^2 + 17(-2) + 25$$
$$f(-2) = 12 - 34 + 25$$
$$f(-2) = 3$$

And just like that, a shortcut is born. **For any constant a, if all you need to know is the remainder when a polynomial is divided by $x - a$, just plug a into the polynomial for x and see what gets spit out. If you get 0, then $x - a$ is a factor of the polynomial. If you get anything other than 0, that's your remainder.**

Now, let's have you try a few. For each of the following polynomial division problems, find the quotient and the remainder using long division. Then confirm that you're right about the remainder by using the shortcut above.

✎ $(x^2 + 11x + 5) \div (x + 9)$

✎ $(x^2 - 3x + 8) \div (x - 1)$

✎ $(x^2 - 5x - 7) \div (x - 5)$

✎ $(x^3 + 5x^2 - 18) \div (x - 3)$

Answers: ● Quotient: $x + 2$; Remainder: -13 ● Quotient: $x - 2$; Remainder: 6 ● Quotient: x; Remainder: -7 ● Quotient: $x^2 + 8x + 24$; Remainder: 54

Corresponding coefficients in equivalent polynomials

I've had more students tell me they don't remember learning this in school than just about any other concept I've covered with them as a tutor:

When two polynomials equal each other for all values of *x*, the polynomials are equivalent and their corresponding coefficients are equal.

For nonzero constants *a*, *b*, *c*, *p*, *q*, and *r*,

IF: $ax^2 + bx + c = px^2 + qx + r$, for all values of *x*,

THEN: $a = p$, $b = q$, and $c = r$

$$ax^2 + bx + c = px^2 + qx + r$$

To me, the easiest way to understand why this is true is to think about two parabolas. (Quadratics are the polynomials you'll probably see tested if you see this concept tested at all.) If two parabolas intersect once, then their polynomials are equal for *one* value of *x*. The polynomials are only equal for *all* values of *x* if the parabolas are right on top of each other—they're the same parabola!

You might find it useful, when you're presented with equivalent polynomials, to stack them on top of each other just like I did in the box above and put circles around the corresponding coefficients. *I* find it useful to do that, anyway.

Example 4: Calculator; Grid-in

$$(x + 9)(x + k) = x^2 + 4kx + p$$

In the equation above, *k* and *p* are constants. If the equation is true for all values of *x*, what is the value of *p* ?

To solve this, first FOIL the left hand side:

$$(x + 9)(x + k)$$
$$= x^2 + 9x + kx + 9k$$

Let's factor x out of those middle terms:

$$= x^2 + (9 + k)x + 9k$$

Pay close attention to what just happened there. If we're going to compare coefficients of x in two equivalent polynomials, then we need *one* coefficient of x on each side of the equation. Factoring $9 + k$ out accomplishes this for us. Now stack up the two sides, and see what equals what:

$$x^2 + (\mathbf{9 + k})x + \mathbf{9k}$$
$$= x^2 + (\mathbf{4k})x + \mathbf{p}$$

So we know two things:

$$9 + k = 4k$$

$$9k = p$$

From here, this is cake, no?

$$9 + k = 4k$$

$$9 = 3k$$

$$3 = k$$

$$9(3) = p$$

$$27 = p$$

There—that wasn't so bad. This kind of problem can really throw you for a loop the first time you see one, but you can get very good very quickly once you understand the process. And that, my friend, is what good SAT prep is all about!

Poly-YES-mials

1 No calculator

If $(a + b)x^3 = cx^3$ for all values of x, which of the following must be true about constants a, b, and c ?

A) $a - b = c$

B) $b - c = a$

C) $a - c = b$

D) $c - a = b$

2 No calculator

$$ax^2 - bx + c = rx^2 + sx + t$$

If the equation above is true for all values of x, and a, b, c, r, s, and t are nonzero constants, which of the following is FALSE?

A) $b = s$

B) $c = t$

C) $b^2 = s^2$

D) $a + c = r + t$

3 No calculator

$$r(x) = 2(x^2 - 11x + 3) + 7(x + m)$$

In the polynomial defined above, m is a constant. If $r(x)$ is divisible by x, what is the value of m ?

A) 6

B) $\dfrac{5}{2}$

C) $-\dfrac{6}{7}$

D) -7

4 No calculator; Grid-in

$$\frac{18x^2 - 16x + 3}{ax + 1} = 2x - 2 + \frac{5}{ax + 1}$$

The equation above is true for all values of $x \neq -\dfrac{1}{a}$, where a is a constant. What is the value of a ?

5 No Calculator; Grid-in

$$(x - 3)(x - d) = x^2 - 2dx + m$$

In the equation above, d and m are constants. If the equation is true for all values of x, what is the value of dm ?

6 Calculator

$$(x-5)(x-7) = x^2 + mx + n$$

The equation above is true for all values of x; m and n are constants. Which of the following equals $n - m$?

A) 2

B) 12

C) 30

D) 47

7 Calculator

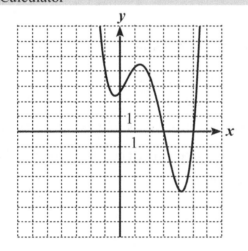

Part of the graph of the polynomial function $f(x)$ is shown above. Which of the following could be a factor of $f(x)$?

A) $x + 1$

B) $x + 3$

C) $x - 2$

D) $x - 5$

8 Calculator

$$f(x) = 3x^3 + 9x^2 - 30x$$
$$g(x) = x^2 + 3x - 10$$

The polynomials $f(x)$ and $g(x)$ are defined above. Which of the following statements is FALSE?

A) $g(x)$ is a factor of $f(x)$

B) $f(x)$ is divisible by $(x - 5)$

C) $g(x)$ has two real zeros

D) If $h(x)$ is defined as $h(x) = f(x) + 2g(x)$, then $h(x)$ is divisible by $3x + 2$

9 Calculator; Grid-in

$$g(x) = x^2 + 8x - 20$$

The equation for the function g is given above. If $g(a) = 0$ and $g(b) = 0$ and $a \neq b$, what is the value of $|a + b|$?

10 Calculator; Grid-in

$$\frac{3x^2 - 4x + 2}{x+3} = 3x - 13 + \frac{a}{x+3}$$

The equation above is true for all $x \neq -3$. What is the value of a?

Answers:

1	D		6	D
2	A		7	D
3	C		8	B
4	9		9	8
5	27		10	41

Solutions on page 375.

The following selected Official Test questions show the ways you can expect to see polynomials tested.

Test	Section	Questions
1	3: No calculator	15
	4: Calculator	29
2	3: No calculator	4, 15, 17
	4: Calculator	
3	3: No calculator	7, 13
	4: Calculator	12, 33
4	3: No calculator	18
	4: Calculator	25
5	3: No calculator	
	4: Calculator	
6	3: No calculator	12
	4: Calculator	
7	3: No calculator	10, 13
	4: Calculator	
8	3: No calculator	11, 17
	4: Calculator	19
9	3: No calculator	10
	4: Calculator	27
10	3: No calculator	
	4: Calculator	35
PSAT/NMSQT 1	3: No calculator	12
	4: Calculator	
PSAT/NMSQT 2	3: No calculator	14, 16, 17
	4: Calculator	20

Working with Advanced Systems of Equations

On relatively rare occasion, the SAT will ask you to solve a system of equations where one (or maybe even both) of the equations are polynomials with degrees greater than one. We've already basically covered the techniques you'll need to employ to achieve this, but that doesn't mean we shouldn't still do a few more examples together. As I did in the chapter about solving systems of linear equations, I'm going to use our discussion in this chapter to solve the same couple questions in multiple ways.

Example 1: No calculator

$$y = x^2 + 4$$
$$4x - y = -1$$

Which of the following sets of ordered pairs (x, y) contains ALL ordered pairs that satisfy the system of equations above?

A) $\{(1, 5), (3, 13)\}$

B) $\{(1, 5)\}$

C) $\{(3, 13)\}$

D) $\{(-1, 3), (5, 13)\}$

Substitution

Let's do this algebraically first, using substitution. If we substitute the value for y we're given in the first equation into the second equation, we get a quadratic, and it happens to be easily factorable:

$$4x - (x^2 + 4) = -1$$
$$4x - x^2 - 4 = -1$$
$$-x^2 + 4x - 3 = 0$$
$$x^2 - 4x + 3 = 0$$
$$(x - 3)(x - 1) = 0$$

So we know that the values of x that will satisfy the equation are 3 and 1. Plugging those back into either equation will give us our y-values. I'll use the first equation for ease since it's already in $y =$ form.

$$y = 1^2 + 4 = 5$$
$$y = 3^2 + 4 = 13$$

So there we have it: our solution set is $\{(1, 5), (3, 13)\}$, which is **choice A**.

But is pure algebra the fastest way to go? As is often the case, no. First of all, once we solved the quadratic and found the x-values that worked, we should have checked back with the answer choices. Only choice A has both 1 and 3 as x-values! More importantly, we could have been backsolving from the very beginning!

Backsolve

Let's look at that same question with new eyes.

Example 1 (again): No calculator

$$y = x^2 + 4$$
$$4x - y = -1$$

Which of the following sets of ordered pairs (x, y) contains ALL ordered pairs that satisfy the system of equations above?

A) $\{(1, 5), (3, 13)\}$

B) $\{(1, 5)\}$

C) $\{(3, 13)\}$

D) $\{(-1, 3), (5, 13)\}$

I'd argue that the *fastest* way to get through this question is just to note that the answer choices actually only contain four unique ordered pairs. Trying them all in one of the equations should be a very fast way to see which ones work. Start with choice B since it contains 1, which is easy to work with. Does (1, 5) satisfy both equations?

$$5 = 1^2 + 4 \leftarrow \text{Yes, that's true.}$$
$$4(1) - 5 = -1 \leftarrow \text{Yes, that's also true.}$$

So (1, 5) works. Choices C and D don't have (1, 5), so we can cross them right off. Now all we need to do is try (3, 13) to see whether the right answer is choice A or choice B.

$$13 = 3^2 + 4 \leftarrow \text{Yes, that's true.}$$
$$4(3) - 13 = -1 \leftarrow \text{Yes, that's also true.}$$

Turns out (3, 13) also works, so the answer must be **choice A**.

Graphing

When we're allowed to use our calculator to solve a system of equations, we can graph. The basic idea here is the same as it was when we talked about solving linear equations by graphing. The only difference is that now we will sometimes need to account for multiple points of intersection, so the Guess? prompt will be important.

Example 2: Calculator; Grid-in

$$y = (x - 3)^2 - 4$$
$$y - 2x = -7$$

When the system of equations above is graphed in the *xy*-plane, the graphs intersect at a point (a, b) such that $a > b > 0$. What is the value of a ?

So, I think you should graph these equations right away. All you need to do first is put the linear equation into $y = mx + b$ form: $y = 2x - 7$. Here we go:

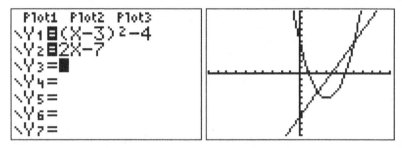

From the graphs, it's quite obvious that there are two points of intersection. Since one of them is in Quadrant IV, though, where x is positive and y is negative, we know that's not the intersection we're looking for. Remember—the question told us that both a and b are greater than zero, so the y-coordinate can't be negative! So let's use our trusty calculators to find the intersection in Quadrant I.

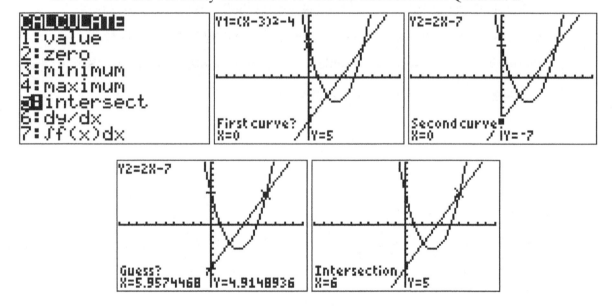

Note how I placed the cursor near the intersection I cared about before I submitted my Guess. The cursor's starting position is at $x = 0$, so if I hadn't done that, the calculator would have given me the intersection closer to $x = 0$, which is not the one I wanted. Anyway, the calculator has served up the answer on a silver platter: The intersection in question is at $(6, 5)$, so $a = 6$.

Of course, we could have also solved this algebraically by substituting:

$$(x - 3)^2 - 4 = 2x - 7$$
$$(x^2 - 6x + 9) - 4 = 2x - 7$$
$$x^2 - 6x + 5 = 2x - 7$$
$$x^2 - 8x + 12 = 0$$
$$(x - 6)(x - 2) = 0$$

That tells us that there are intersections at $x = 2$ and $x = 6$. We still need to put those values back into one of the equations to figure out which one fits the $a > b > 0$ constraint.

$$2(2) - 7 = -3 \leftarrow \text{That's a negative } y\text{-value. :(}$$
$$2(6) - 7 = 5 \leftarrow \text{That's a positive } y\text{-value. :)}$$

Of course, as always, we get the same answer both ways: $a = 6$. As you're hopefully agreeing with me at this point, though, graphing is a much more straightforward way to solve this problem. This will *very often* be the case. Know how to play your calculator like a Stradivarius.

Practice questions: Working with Advanced Systems of Equations

All systems are go.

$$f(x) = (x - 1)^3$$

$$g(x) = (x + 1)^3$$

For how many values of x do the functions above have the same value?

A) 0

B) 1

C) 2

D) 3

$$f(x) = x^2 - 2x + 8$$

$$g(x) = -x^2 + 18x + 4$$

The two functions defined above are equal to each other when $x = 5 \pm a$, where a is a constant. What is the value of a ?

A) $\sqrt{23}$

B) $\sqrt{19}$

C) $\sqrt{17}$

D) $\sqrt{13}$

For two functions f and g, $f(0) = g(0)$ and $f(5) = g(5)$. If $g(x) = x^2 + 3x - 10$ and $f(x)$ is a linear function, which of the following could be the definition of $f(x)$?

A) $f(x) = 10x - 10$

B) $f(x) = 8x - 10$

C) $f(x) = 2x + 40$

D) $f(x) = 5x + 50$

$$y \geq (x - 2)^2 + 4$$

$$y \leq -(x - 2)^2 + 6$$

The ordered pair $(a, 5)$, where a is a constant, satisfies the system of inequalities above. What is the least possible value of a ?

What is the slope of the line that contains both of the points of intersection when the equations $y = 2(x - 4)^2 - 2$ and $y = (x - 3)^2$ are plotted in the xy-plane?

6 Calculator

$$y = x^2 + 7x + 10$$

Which of the following lines, when plotted in the xy-plane, does not have any points of intersection with the parabola formed by the equation above?

A) $y = -2x + 1$

B) $y = -\dfrac{1}{2}x + 1$

C) $y = \dfrac{1}{2}x + 1$

D) $y = 2x + 1$

7 Calculator

$$y = 2x^2 + 12x + 16$$

$$y = x^2 + 4x + 1$$

How many ordered pairs (x, y) satisfy the system of equations above?

A) 0

B) 1

C) 2

D) More than 2

8 Calculator

In the xy-plane, where a and b are positive constants, the graphs of $y = a(x - 5)^2 + 6$ and $y = b(x - 5)^2 + 5$ never intersect. Which of the following could be true?

    I $a > b$

    II $a = b$

    III $a < b$

A) I only

B) III only

C) I and II only

D) II and III only

9 Calculator; Grid-in

When the equations $y = -(x - 4)^2 + 8$ and $y = 2(x - 4)^2 + 5$ are graphed in the xy-plane, the intersections between the parabolas formed lie on the line $y = k$. What is the value of k?

10 Calculator; Grid-in

$$y = x^2 - 12x + 41$$

$$y = -x^2 + bx - 57$$

In the two equations above, b is a constant. When the equations are graphed in the xy-plane, the parabolas they form intersect at $(a, 6)$ where a is a constant. What is one possible value of b?

Answers:

1	A		6	D
2	A		7	C
3	B		8	C
4	1		9	7
5	4		10	16, 17.6, 88/5

Solutions on page 377.

The following selected Official Test questions make you wrangle more than one equation at a time, at least one of which is "advanced." As I said in the chapter, these are pretty rare in the practice tests released so far.

Test	Section	Questions
1	3: No calculator	
	4: Calculator	
2	3: No calculator	
	4: Calculator	
3	3: No calculator	
	4: Calculator	
4	3: No calculator	11, 13
	4: Calculator	
5	3: No calculator	9
	4: Calculator	
6	3: No calculator	
	4: Calculator	34
7	3: No calculator	
	4: Calculator	35
8	3: No calculator	
	4: Calculator	35
9	3: No calculator	9
	4: Calculator	
10	3: No calculator	
	4: Calculator	
PSAT/NMSQT 1	3: No calculator	
	4: Calculator	28
PSAT/NMSQT 2	3: No calculator	3
	4: Calculator	29

Problem Solving and Data Analysis

Your SAT will have 17 Problem Solving and Data Analysis questions, and they will *all* occur in the section where calculators are allowed. The calculator section has 38 questions; this type of question constitutes almost half of them, even though many of them will not require any calculations at all. This category is the main reason the calculator and no calculator sections feel so different.

In this unit you'll practice a bunch of different kinds of things—some stuff like percents and ratios will probably be pretty familiar, and other things like interpreting scatterplots might be a bit more novel. Don't be lulled into complacency even by the familiar stuff, though, even if you were introduced to many of these concepts when you were in elementary school. The writers of the SAT have always been quite adept at finding ways to test simple concepts with difficult questions.

Percents and Percent Change

Let's begin our discussion of Problem Solving and Data Analysis questions by making sure you're flawless on simple percent calculations. Different people use different methods to work through such things, and if you're comfortable with percents then you might choose to ignore this tip, but here's how I translate sentences describing percents into mathematical notation:

→ The word "what" is a variable to be solved for, like x (or any other variable if x is already in use)

→ The word "is" translates to an equal sign.

→ The word "of" means multiplication.[*]

→ The word "percent" (or the % symbol) means "divided by 100."

So, for example, the sentence "What is 14 percent of 83?" translates to "x equals 14 divided by 100 times 83," or:

$$x = \frac{14}{100} \times 83$$

Solve that for x, and you'd know 14 percent of 83. Here's one more: "12 is 89 percent of what number?" translates to "12 equals 89 divided by 100 times x," or:

$$12 = \frac{89}{100} \times x$$

Cool? How about you try a few, just as a warm up before we get into the fun stuff? (Answers are at the very bottom of the page.)

✎ What is 11 percent of 110?

✎ 93 is what percent of 31?

✎ 62 is 16 percent of what?

---

[*] Sometimes "of" doesn't mean multiplication, like in the phrases "the square root of x," or "f of x." When you're dealing with percents or fractions, though, "of" always means multiplication.

Answers: ● 12.1 ● 300 ● 387.5

OK, so that was fun, right? Of course it was. Believe it or not, many of the percent questions on the SAT will be basically this straightforward. They'll often make you read a graph or table to figure out what numbers you need to use, but really, they'll basically come down to simple percent calculations.

Example 1: Calculator

A market researcher surveyed 193 high school students about whether or not they had read a young adult fiction novel about a dystopian future where children murder each other. The data are shown in the table below.

	Have read the book	Have not read the book	Total
9th graders	37	11	48
10th graders	44	9	53
11th graders	41	15	56
12th graders	29	7	36
Total	151	42	193

Which of the following is closest to the percent of those surveyed who were in 11th grade?

A) 21%

B) 25%

C) 29%

D) 73%

Doesn't this drive you nuts? Look at all that data! But all you have to do is find the two numbers the question cares about, and then solve. How many students constitute "those surveyed?" 193. How many of them were in 11th grade? 56? 56 is what percent of 193?

$$56 = \frac{x}{100} \times 193$$

$$29.02... = x$$

Of course, you can also just take the shortcut most of you have been taking for years: $\frac{56}{193} = 0.2902...$. That's a fine way to go and I endorse it. In fact, let's take a minute or two and talk about some other percent shortcuts.

Because the same thing always happens when you divide by 100, it's natural to eventually get away from writing out the "over 100" fractions like I've been doing so far in this chapter and just instantly translating "27 percent of 49" to "0.27×49." Pretty much every student I've ever worked with does that. Totally cool.

One thing I'm often surprised students *don't* know, though, is that you can use similar shortcuts for percent increases and decreases. Say, for example, that you wanted to calculate the total bill if you know the TV you're buying costs $382 plus 8.5% sales tax. You could calculate 8.5% of $382 separately and add it to $382. That's two steps, but they're easy steps. You could also simply take 108.5% of $382 and be done in one step. Why? Start with the first way—the two-step way:

$$382 + (0.085)382 = 414.47$$

Now factor the 382 out of the left side of the equation above:

$$(1 + 0.085)382 = 414.47$$
$$(1.085)382 = 414.47$$

The same thing works with percent decreases. To calculate the price of a $220 coat that's 30% off:

$$220 - (0.30)220 = 154$$
$$(1 - 0.30)220 = 154$$
$$(0.70)220 = 154$$

Not exactly revolutionary, I admit, but this stuff is important to know.[*]

---

[*] It's also context for why interest or exponential decay formulas look like they do. If you're skipping around, those are covered in the Passport to Advanced Math section.

Example 2: Calculator

Stepping Out Footwear is having a clearance sale for the end of the season, so a 15 percent discount is applied to every product in the store. Denise, the store manager, has had her eye on a certain pair of shoes all season and decides to take advantage of the store-wide sale, which can be combined with her 19 percent employee discount. She will still need to pay 6 percent sales tax. If the original price of the shoes was x dollars, which of the following represents the total amount, in dollars, that Denise will pay including sales tax?

A) $(0.85)(0.81)(1.06)x$

B) $(0.85)(0.81)(0.94)x$

C) $(0.15)(0.19)(0.06)x$

D) $(1 - 0.15 - 0.19 + 0.06)x$

Let's do this using the shortcuts we just discussed, one discount at a time. First, let's tackle the 15% store-wide discount. That's going to make the shoes, which originally cost x dollars, cost:

$$(1 - 0.15)x = 0.85x$$

From there, let's apply the 19% employee discount. $1 - 0.19 = 0.81$, so applying a 19% discount is the same as taking 81% of a price. Since the discounts can be combined, we take 81% of the store-wide discount price of $0.85x$. So now we're at:

$$(0.81)0.85x$$

That's the price she'll pay, before sales tax. Note that I'm staying aware of my surroundings—the answer choices aren't simplified, so I'm not bothering to go to my calculator and multiply 0.81 and 0.85. Get on my level.

The last step is to apply the 6% sales tax. Sales tax is an increase, so we add the 6% to 1, rather than subtracting it as we've done in the last two steps. $1 + 0.06 = 1.06$, so we're going to multiply everything by 1.06:

$$(1.06)(0.81)0.85x$$

Do a little rearranging, and you'll see that the answer is **choice A**.

Note that this question might also be made easier with some simple plugging in, which will allow you to avoid writing everything in one expression if that stresses you out. Say the shoes start off at $100. The store discount brings them to $85. The employee discount on top of that brings them down to $68.85. Add sales tax on there, and you're at $72.981. Which answer choice gives you that when you put 100 in for x? Only choice A.

Percent change

When I was in high school, I weighed 120 pounds fully clothed and soaking wet. I couldn't do anything to change it, either. That was the worst part. I yearned to play varsity baseball, but at my weight, I just wasn't big enough.

College was mostly the same, although I filled out a little. I'd say my average weight in college reflected the "freshman fifteen," but for me it was a welcome change.

Then I graduated and got a job. I spent a few years living a largely sedentary existence and eating too much fast food. Before I knew it, I weighed 150 pounds.

So over the years, I put on 30 pounds. What was the percent increase in my weight?

Here's the general formula for this kind of question:

$$\text{Percent Change (Increase or Decrease)} = \frac{\text{Amount of Change}}{\text{Original Value}} \times 100\%$$

Drop my values in:

$$\text{Percent Change}_{\text{Mike's march towards decrepitude}} = \frac{30 \text{ lbs}}{120 \text{ lbs}} \times 100\% = 25\%$$

And would you look at that? My weight increased by 25%! Holy moly. So say then I went on a diet and *lost* 30 pounds, so I'm right back where I started at 120. What will be my percent change then? (If the answer was just going to be 25% again, I probably wouldn't be wasting your time with this.)

$$\text{Percent Change}_{\text{Mike's crazy diet}} = \frac{30 \text{ lbs}}{150 \text{ lbs}} \times 100\% = 20\%$$

Whoa. So it was a 25% increase, but now it's only about a 20% decrease? That doesn't seem fair!

An important thing to remember about percents is that the bigger the numbers are, the less difference a difference makes:

→ If you owe your friend $20, you can reduce your debt by 50% by paying him $10. If you end up taking out student loans when you go to college, it will be much harder to reduce your debt by 50%.

→ The more you weigh, the more pounds you have to gain to increase your weight by 10%.

→ If you're 16 years old and your little brother is 13, you're about 123% his age. But when you were 4 and he was 1, you were 400% his age. The older you both get, the smaller the percent difference will be, but you'll always be 3 years older than him.

Practice questions: Percents and Percent Change

What difference does a difference make?

When Lucy complained to her boss that she was only making $75 per hour while her coworker Stephanie was making $100 per hour for the same work, her boss gave her a 25% raise. Lucy's hourly wages are now what percent of Stephanie's?

A) 110%

B) 100%

C) 93.75%

D) 75%

March	$2,000
April	$2,400
May	$3,000
June	$3,500
July	$4,300

The table above represents the money Debbie earned, by month, for the last five months. When was the percent change in her income the greatest?

A) From March to April

B) From April to May

C) From May to June

D) From June to July

What is 500% of 45% of 22% of n ?

A) $0.0495n$

B) $0.495n$

C) $4.95n$

D) $49.5n$

If p is q percent of r, what is r in terms of p and q?

A) $\dfrac{100p}{q}$

B) $\dfrac{100q}{p}$

C) $\dfrac{pq}{100}$

D) $\dfrac{100}{pq}$

Questions 5-7 refer to the following information.

The graph below show the number of births that took place at County Hospital during the week that began Monday November 2nd.

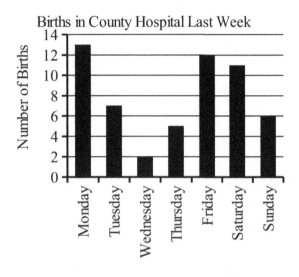

Births in County Hospital Last Week

5 Calculator

Between which two days was the greatest percent decrease in the number of births at the hospital?

A) Between Monday and Tuesday

B) Between Tuesday and Wednesday

C) Between Friday and Saturday

D) Between Saturday and Sunday

6 Calculator

Which of the following is closest to the percent of the babies born last week that were born on Thursday?

A) 23 percent

B) 20 percent

C) 11 percent

D) 9 percent

7 Calculator

If n percent fewer babies are born during the following week (beginning Monday November 9th) there will be 49 births. What is the value of n ?

A) 12.5

B) 2.5

C) 8.5

D) 7.0

8 Calculator

There are 30 more boys than girls in Monroe Township's intramural soccer league. If there are g girls in the league, then, in terms of g, what percent of participants in the league are girls?

A) $\dfrac{g}{g+30}\%$

B) $\dfrac{g}{200(g+30)}\%$

C) $\dfrac{100g}{2g+30}\%$

D) $\dfrac{100g}{g+30}\%$

9 Calculator; Grid-in

Week	Customers
1	673
2	813
3	780
4	x
5	1365
6	1436

The table above shows the number of customers a new business served each week during its first 6 weeks. There was a 40% increase in customers served from week 3 to week 4, and an n percent increase in customers served from week 4 to week 5. What is the value of n ?

10 Calculator; Grid-in

After appearing in 16 games this season, a certain baseball pitcher had thrown 1550 pitches, exactly 70% of which were strikes. In his 17th appearance, he threw 99 pitches, and increased his season-long strike percentage to greater than 71%. What is the least number of strikes he could have thrown in the 17th game?

Answers:

1	C		6	D
2	B		7	A
3	B		8	C
4	A		9	25
5	B		10	86

Solutions on page 380.

The following selected Official Test questions are examples of percent stuff in the wild.

Test	Section	Questions
1	3: No calculator	
	4: Calculator	13, 20, 26, 32
2	3: No calculator	
	4: Calculator	5, 17
3	3: No calculator	
	4: Calculator	5, 27
4	3: No calculator	
	4: Calculator	22
5	3: No calculator	
	4: Calculator	22, 24, 25, 38
6	3: No calculator	19
	4: Calculator	24, 38
7	3: No calculator	
	4: Calculator	12, 30
8	3: No calculator	
	4: Calculator	22, 29
9	3: No calculator	
	4: Calculator	35, 38
10	3: No calculator	18
	4: Calculator	12, 16, 18
PSAT/NMSQT 1	3: No calculator	
	4: Calculator	10, 14, 19
PSAT/NMSQT 2	3: No calculator	7
	4: Calculator	12, 15, 16

Ratios and Proportionality

In many contexts, the words **ratio** and **proportion** can be used to achieve the same purpose: there's no meaningful difference between asking, "what is the ratio of boys to total students?" and asking, "boys make up what proportion of total students?"[*] You'll see both on the SAT, although ratio is used a bit more commonly on the stuff that's been released as of this writing. But that's more language than math—mathematically, ratios and proportions are both just fractions. The fraction $\dfrac{\text{number of boys}}{\text{number of total students}}$ is both the ratio of boys to total students and the proportion of total students that are boys.

It's worth talking notation for a second here. When you read "the ratio of x to y," that means "$\dfrac{x}{y}$". The first thing listed in a ratio statement is the numerator of the fraction, and the second thing listed is the denominator. You might also, once in a great while, see the ratio of x to y written as $x{:}y$. I don't know why anyone does that, but if you ever come across two numbers separated by a colon, now you know. Just convert them to a fraction. 3:4 is $\dfrac{3}{4}$.

Many questions on the SAT involving ratios and proportions are really just asking you to read a graph or table and then divide two of the numbers in there. We'll touch on those in the chapters on reading graphs and tables that'll come a little later in this book. In *this* chapter, I want to talk about questions that actually require you to write an equation and solve.

Such questions usually turn out to be pretty easy, provided you're fastidious in keeping track of units. That means, when you set up a proportion, you actually *write the units* next to each number. Make sure you've got the same units corresponding to each other before you solve the proportion, and you're home free. Pass Go, collect your $200, and spend it all on Lik-M-Aid Fun Dip.

---

[*] A rule of thumb used by some is that if you're talking about a part-to-part relationship (e.g., boys to girls), use ratio, and if you're talking about a part-to-whole relationship (e.g., boys to total students), use proportions. The more you know...

A certain farm has only cows and chickens as livestock. The ratio of cows to chickens is 2 to 7. If there are 63 livestock animals on the farm, how many cows are there?

A) 13

B) 14

C) 16

D) 18

The SAT writers would love for you to set up a simple proportion here and solve:

$$\frac{2}{7} = \frac{x}{63}$$

Hooray! $x = 18$! That's answer choice D! *Not so fast, Dr. Moreau.*

You just conjured a terrifying hybrid beast, the *COWNIMALKEN*. Let's look at that fraction more carefully, with the units included:

$$\frac{2 \text{ cows}}{7 \text{ chickens}} = \frac{x \text{ cows}}{63 \text{ animals}}$$

So when you casually multiplied by 63 and solved, you solved for a unit that won't do you any good: the $\frac{\text{cow} \times \text{animal}}{\text{chicken}}$ —the *COWNIMALKEN*. That's terrifying. Nature never intended it to be so. Also, you're getting an easy question wrong. You decide which is worse.

Before we can solve this question, we need to make sure our units line up on both sides of the equal sign. So let's change the denominator on the left to match the one on the right. Get rid of "7 chickens" and replace it with "9 animals." Get it? Because cows count as animals, if there are 2 cows for every 7 chickens, that means there are 2 cows for every 9 animals.

$$\frac{2 \text{ cows}}{\textbf{9 animals}} = \frac{x \text{ cows}}{63 \text{ animals}}$$

What we're doing here is important and common to ratio problems: we're converting from a part:part ratio (cows and chickens are both parts of the total livestock population) to a part:whole ratio (total animals being the whole). Anyway, *Now*, we can solve: $x = 14$. There are 14 cows. That's choice **B**.

See how the units cancel out nicely when you've properly set up a ratio question? That should make the hairs on your neck stand on end.

You know what? Let's just drive home the part:part to part:whole conversion process with some extra practice. Do the three quick exercises below. Answers at the bottom of the page.

✎ If the ratio of dogs to cats in a pet store that sells only dogs and cats is 3 to 7, what is the ratio of cats to all animals in the store?

✎ If the ratio of boys to total students on a school bus is 8 to 13, what is the ratio of girls to boys?

✎ At a certain middle school, students choose whether to study chemistry or earth science in 8th grade. They cannot study both. If the ratio of chemistry students to earth science students is 9 to 19, and in total 168 students take one of those sciences, how many take chemistry?

Working with multiple ratios

Here's another thing you might want to watch out for. You might one day be given units that aren't so easily converted. Like so:

Example 2: Calculator

The ratio of students to teachers at a certain school is 28 to 3. The ratio of teachers to cafeteria workers is 9 to 2. What is the ratio of cafeteria workers to students?

A) 1 to 42

B) 3 to 37

C) 9 to 56

D) 3 to 14

Answers: ● 7/10 ● 5/8 ● 54

Here, we have a few options. First, it's not too hard to find a number of teachers that will work with both ratios. There are 9 teachers in one ratio and 3 in the other. If we just unsimplify the students to teachers ratio, we can get to 9 teachers in both ratios, at which point the teachers become irrelevant.

$$\frac{28 \text{ students}}{3 \text{ teachers}} \times \frac{3}{3} = \frac{84 \text{ students}}{9 \text{ teachers}}$$

If there are 84 students for every 9 teachers, and 2 cafeteria workers for every 9 teachers, then there are 2 cafeteria workers for every 84 students. Simplify that ratio, and you've got your answer: 2 to 84 simplifies to 1 to 42. That's choice **A**.

Let me also point out that there's a pretty elegant solution here that comes from simply multiplying the two ratios together, essentially solving for the expression we're looking for without the (admittedly minor) manipulation we had to do above. Peep the skillz:

$$\frac{28 \text{ students}}{3 \text{ teachers}} \times \frac{9 \text{ teachers}}{2 \text{ cafeteria workers}}$$

What happens to the teachers? *They cancel!* So multiply, and simplify:

$$\frac{28 \text{ students}}{3 \text{ teachers}} \times \frac{9 \text{ teachers}}{2 \text{ cafeteria workers}} = \frac{252 \text{ students}}{6 \text{ cafeteria workers}} = \frac{42 \text{ students}}{1 \text{ cafeteria worker}}$$

Since the question asked for the ratio of cafeteria workers to students, just flip it and you're done! 1 cafeteria worker to 42 students. That's still choice **A**! Ahh-mazing.

Proportionality

The old SAT required you to know the difference between direct proportionality and inverse proportionality.[*] Inverse proportionality occurred incredibly rarely, though, and it looks like on the current SAT, it's been retired completely. (Good riddance, I say.) So all we need to talk about here is **direct proportionality**, which is basically just ratios, which is why this chapter exists.

---

[*]   You might be more familiar with terms like *direct variation* and *inverse variation*. Po-tay-to, Po-tah-to.

There are two ways worth knowing to represent direct proportionality mathematically. Math teachers the world over like to say that when x and y are directly proportional, $y = kx$ for some nonzero constant k. This definition is correct of course—and it's often useful—but since it introduces an extra value into the mix, it doesn't lend itself as easily to the kinds of questions you'll usually be asked on the SAT. I much prefer to say that *direct proportionality means the ratio of the two proportional variables will always be the same.*

When x and y are directly proportional:

$$y = kx \quad \text{and} \quad \frac{y_1}{x_1} = \frac{y_2}{x_2}$$

Note that the proportionality constant k remains in the second equation—both fractions equal k—we just don't have to deal with it directly anymore. I like to streamline.

In a direct proportion, as one value gets farther from zero, the other one also gets farther from zero by the same factor. As one gets closer to zero, the other also gets closer to zero by the same factor. If you're dealing with a positive proportionality constant (most of the time), you can say it even more simply: as one gets bigger, the other gets bigger by the same factor. As one gets smaller, the other gets smaller by the same factor.

If p and q are directly proportional:

p	q	What happens?
4	10	Start here.
8	20	p goes UP, so q goes UP.
40	100	p goes UP, so q goes UP.
2	5	p goes DOWN, so q goes DOWN.
1	2.5	p goes DOWN, so q goes DOWN.

One last way you might like to think about direct proportionality if you like graphs: when two variables are in direct proportion with proportionality constant k, they form a line with slope k that passes through the origin. That's right—$y = kx$ and $y = mx + b$ are closely related. Isn't that cool? Don't you roll your eyes at me!

For easy direct proportion questions, all you'll need to do is plug values into the general proportion form, $\dfrac{y_1}{x_1} = \dfrac{y_2}{x_2}$, and solve. And the "hard" direct proportion questions won't actually be much harder.

Example 3: Calculator

The amount of money a tutor earns in a week is directly proportional to the number of students he sees that week. If a particular tutor earns p dollars in a week during which he sees 8 students, how much money does he make in a week during which he sees 11 students?

A) $\dfrac{11p}{8}$ dollars

B) $\dfrac{8p}{11}$ dollars

C) $\dfrac{11}{8p}$ dollars

D) $\dfrac{8}{11p}$ dollars

What makes this question tricky is that you're given p instead of an actual dollar value, but that's no big deal—we can still use the same setup we would use if we'd actually been told what the tutor made. Just say that x is the amount of money the tutor made in the 11-student week, and set up the proportion:

$$\frac{p \text{ dollars}}{8 \text{ students}} = \frac{x \text{ dollars}}{11 \text{ students}}$$

Our units line up, so all we have to do to solve that for x is multiply both sides by 11.

$$\frac{11 \ \cancel{\text{students}} \times p \text{ dollars}}{8 \ \cancel{\text{students}}} = x \text{ dollars}$$

$$\frac{11p}{8} \text{ dollars} = x \text{ dollars}$$

No big deal, right? The answer is **A**.

At this point, you might be asking yourself: *OK...so what's the difference between solving a direct proportion problem and solving a ratio problem?* That's a good question, and the answer is: as long as you know what the words mean, there isn't really one. In both cases, all we're doing is setting fractions equal to each other, making sure units coordinate, and solving carefully.

Practice questions: Ratios and Proportionality

Mad props, yo.

In Ms. Picker's 3rd grade class, the ratio of boys to girls is 7 to 5. If there are 14 boys in the class, then how many students are in the class?

A) 10

B) 20

C) 24

D) 36

The ratio of pens to pencils in Dore's drawer is 3 to 1. The ratio of sharpened pencils to unsharpened pencils in the drawer is 2 to 1. If there are 18 pens in the drawer, how many pencils in the drawer are sharpened?

A) 2

B) 4

C) 6

D) 10

If k is a nonzero constant, which of the following does NOT represent a proportional relationship between x and y ?

A) $y = x + k$

B) $\dfrac{y}{x} = k$

C) $y = k^2 x$

D) $y = \dfrac{x}{k}$

4 Calculator

A certain Witch's Brew recipe calls for $1\frac{1}{2}$ cups werewolf hair and 1 eye of newt, and makes enough brew to curse 2 princesses. If Cheryl, who is a witch, wants to make enough Witch's Brew to curse 7 princesses, how many cups of werewolf hair will she need?

A) $5\frac{3}{4}$

B) $5\frac{1}{4}$

C) $4\frac{3}{4}$

D) $3\frac{3}{4}$

5 Calculator

The ratio of pennies to quarters in Garrett's pocket is 4 to 1. If there are only pennies and quarters in Garrett's pocket, which of the following could be the amount of money in his pocket?

A) $0.54

B) $1.12

C) $1.45

D) $1.66

6 Calculator

Which of the following could represent a directly proportional relationship between x and $f(x)$?

A) $f(3) = 5, f(5) = 7, f(15) = 17$

B) $f(3) = 6, f(5) = 10, f(15) = 30$

C) $f(3) = 9, f(5) = 25, f(15) = 225$

D) $f(3) = 5, f(5) = 3, f(15) = 1$

Mad props, yo.

7 Calculator

Alistair runs a 5000 meter race in 22 minutes. If he runs at a constant pace, which of the following is closest to the distance he runs in 45 seconds?

A) 103 meters

B) 170 meters

C) 227 meters

D) 303 meters

8 Calculator; Grid-in

If r and s are directly proportional and $r = 18$ when $s = 15$, what is the value of r when $s = 20$?

9 Calculator; Grid-in

Andy and Sean are in a fantasy baseball league. Last month, the players on Andy's team struck out 7 times for every 2 home runs they hit. In the same month, Sean's players hit 9 home runs for every 5 home runs Andy's players hit. If Andy's players struck out 105 times last month, how many home runs did Sean's players hit over the same span of time?

10 Calculator; Grid-in

A certain political district has an area of 34 square miles and a population density of 88 people per square mile. If the lines of the district are redrawn such that 2 square miles and 432 people are no longer in the district, what will be the district's new population density in people per square mile?

Answers:

1	C		6	B
2	B		7	B
3	A		8	24
4	B		9	54
5	C		10	80

Solutions on page 383.

The following Official Test questions will test you on ratios and proportions.

Test	Section	Questions
1	3: No calculator	
	4: Calculator	2, 6, 23, 34
2	3: No calculator	
	4: Calculator	2, 4, 15, 20, 31, 32
3	3: No calculator	
	4: Calculator	9, 14, 19, 38
4	3: No calculator	
	4: Calculator	3, 4, 7, 9, 33
5	3: No calculator	
	4: Calculator	3, 5, 9, 16, 17, 18, 31, 32, 37, 38
6	3: No calculator	
	4: Calculator	26
7	3: No calculator	
	4: Calculator	3, 10, 15, 25, 31
8	3: No calculator	
	4: Calculator	3, 11, 31, 34
9	3: No calculator	
	4: Calculator	2, 11, 12
10	3: No calculator	
	4: Calculator	14, 34, 37, 38
PSAT/NMSQT 1	3: No calculator	
	4: Calculator	6, 7, 15, 16
PSAT/NMSQT 2	3: No calculator	
	4: Calculator	3, 7, 13, 17

Measures of Central Tendency and Variability

Yeah, so that's a fancy title for a chapter, right? Are you intimidated? You probably shouldn't be: we're going to talk about a few different concepts here, but you've probably dealt with all of them before, and you probably already mostly know how they work. We're going to talk here about **average** (AKA arithmetic mean[*]), **median**, **mode**, **standard deviation**, and **range**. With the SAT's heavy emphasis on data, these concepts are usually tested in the context of data sets rather than in tricky word problems.

Average (arithmetic mean)

The concept of average or mean is the most versatile of the kinds of questions we'll discuss here: the SAT can and will ask you about averages in a number of different ways. Some questions will be super straightforward and require nothing of you other than basic table reading and calculator work. Others will be a little more conceptual and require some algebra to solve. Let's get right into a few.

Example 1: Calculator; Grid-in

Fishing Boat	Fish Caught (lbs)
Peleg	167
Bits'n Pieces	182
Lila Mae	
M.T. Monkey	213

The incomplete table above shows the pounds of fish caught in a single day by four fishing boats that operate in the same waters. If the average (arithmetic mean) weight of the day's catch for the four boats was 173 pounds, how many pounds of fish came in on the Lila Mae?

---

[*] The word average is not exclusive to the concept we typically think of when we hear the word. For example, an average speed is not actually an arithmetic mean. For this reason, whenever the SAT wants you to think about the kind of average we'll be discussing in this chapter, it'll make sure you're clear by putting "(arithmetic mean)" after the word "average."

So, if you remember nothing else from this chapter, remember this: the key to most average questions is to work with sums. Let's look for a minute at the classic average formula:

$$\text{Average of Values} = \frac{\text{Sum of Values}}{\text{Number of Values}}$$

Now watch what happens when we multiply both sides of that equation by the Number of Values:

$$\boxed{\text{Number of Values} \times \text{Average of Values} = \text{Sum of Values}}$$

Obvious, right? Obvious and important. Write that down.

All we need to do to solve this fishing boat question is multiply the average we know we're supposed to have by the number of boats to get the total sum of pounds of fish.

$$173 \text{ lbs per boat} \times 4 \text{ boats} = 692 \text{ lbs}$$

Since we know how much the weight that came in on each other boat, all we need to do to get Lila Mae's total is subtract!

$$692 - 167 - 182 - 213 = \mathbf{130}$$

See? Easy.

Example 2: Calculator

After four tests, Lauren's average (arithmetic mean) score in her statistics class is 86. There are two more tests in the semester, and Lauren wants to bring her average up to 90. What is the average score she will need to achieve on her last two tests to reach her goal?

A) 92

B) 94

C) 96

D) 98

OK, so if Lauren's first four test scores have an average of 86, then they have a sum of $4 \times 86 = 344$. To have a 90 average over six tests, she'll need to get up to a sum of $90 \times 6 = 540$.

That means that she needs to score a total of $540 - 344 = 196$ points over her next two tests. That's 98 points per test. The answer is **D**.

Median

The median is the middle value in an ordered list of numbers. If the list of numbers you're given isn't in numerical order, it still has a median, but to find it you're going to have to put it in numerical order first. If the set contains an even number of values, the median is the average of the two middle values. That's it. That's all you need to know about the median. Find the median of each of the following sets. (Answers below.)

✎ {4, 6, 7, 9, 12, 16, 30}

✎ {9, 30, 16, 4, 7, 6, 12}

✎ {2, 200, 300, 700}

✎ {17, 22, 6, 99, 68, 52, 29, 86}

If you've got all those, I guess it's time we tried an SAT-inspired question.

Answers: ● 9 ● 9 (changing the order does not change the median)
● 250 (the avg of 200 and 300) ● 40.5 (the avg of 29 and 52)

Player	Height (inches)	Player	Height (inches)
Aisha	76	Marla	72
Taryn	70	Kristine	74
Luisa	69	Madison	67
Juliana	70	Sara	68
Carolyn	65	Salma	72

The table above shows the heights of 10 players on the Southeast High School women's basketball team. If the coach takes Aisha out of the game and substitutes Kristine in her place, and makes no other substitutions, which of the following must be true? (Note: In basketball, five players from a team are allowed on the court at a time.)

A) The median height of players on the court from Southeast will not change.

B) The median height of players on the court from both teams will not change.

C) The median height of players on the court from Southeast will decrease.

D) The median height of players on the court from both teams will decrease.

They key to this one is recognizing that Aisha and Kristine are the tallest players on the team, so when one replaces the other, all that's happening is that the height of the tallest girl on the court from Southeast is changing. Since the median is the middle value in a set, changing the greatest value has no impact on the median. The answer is **A**.

But wait, how can I just ignore choice B? Well, we're not given any information at all about the other team, *and* I've already convinced myself that choice A must be true—those are pretty good reasons. But if you want the actual reason that B doesn't *have* to be true, here it is. Since we're not told anything about that team, it's theoretically possible that every single person on the court from the other team is taller than Aisha. In that case, the median height of all the players on the court would be the average of Aisha's height and that of the shortest player from the other team of *very* tall women. If that were true, then replacing Aisha with Kristine would change the median height of all players on the court.

Mode

The mode of a list of numbers is the number that appears most in that list.
We don't need to discuss it much because the likelihood of it appearing on your test is pretty low (it doesn't appear in *any* of the existing Official Tests), but you should know what it is on a very basic level. Be aware that it's possible for a list to have multiple modes, but all modes will appear the same number of times, and no other number will appear more often. For example check out this set:

$$\{4, 4, 5, 5, 5, 6, 6, 6, 7, 8\}$$

In the set above, 5 and 6 are both modes. 4 is not a mode, even though it appears more often than 7 and 8, because it doesn't appear as often as 5 and 6. Easy, right?

Find the mode(s) for each of the following sets. (Answers below.)

✎ $\{2, 4, 2, 7, 9, 3, 2\}$

✎ $\{2, 4, 2, 7, 9, 7, 3, 2, 7\}$

✎ $\{1, 1, 200, 300, 400\}$

✎ $\{p, q, r, s, t, t, s, t\}$

If you're good on those, let's try some SAT-type stuff (which you will probably *not* encounter on test day—mode questions are rare).

Answers: • 2 • 2 *and* 7 (both appear 3 times) • 1 • *t*

PWN Test Prep

$$\{2, 3, 9, 4, 11, 4m - 8, 3n - 4\}$$

The modes of the set above are 2 and 11. If m and n are constants, what is one possible value of $m + n$?

OK. In order for 2 and 11 to be the modes of the set above, each need to appear an equal number of times, and more often than any other value in the list. Which means one of two things must be true:

$$4m - 8 = 2 \text{ and } 3n - 4 = 11$$

—or—

$$4m - 8 = 11 \text{ and } 3n - 4 = 2$$

Let's deal with the first possibility:

$$4m - 8 = 2$$
$$4m = 10$$
$$m = 2.5$$

$$3n - 4 = 11$$
$$3n = 15$$
$$n = 5$$

So one possibility is that $m = 2.5$ and $n = 5$.

$$m + n = 2.5 + 5 = \textbf{7.5}.$$

I'll spare you the algebra for the second possibility; I'm sure you can handle it on your own. The other acceptable solution is **6.75**.

Standard deviation

Let's get this out of the way up front: you *do not* need to be able to calculate the standard deviation of a set on the SAT. Really, you don't even need to know how it's calculated. You just need to know that the **standard deviation is a measure of variability**: the higher a data set's standard deviation is, the greater its variability.

But wait—what's variability? Glad you asked. Variability refers to how far the values in a set are from the mean. Super simple example:

$$A = \{1, 2, 3, 4, 5\} \qquad B = \{1, 1, 3, 5, 5\}$$

Both sets above have a mean of 3, but the values in B are slightly farther from the mean than the values in A. So set B has higher variability and a higher standard deviation.

Chances are good that if you get asked about standard deviation at all on your SAT, it will be a very visual question. Like so:

Example 5: Calculator

The histogram above represents the number of apartments with one, two, three, four, or five bedrooms in two neighboring apartment buildings in Ravenholm. Which of the following is true about the data shown for these two buildings?

A) The standard deviation of bedrooms per apartment in Building 1 is larger.

B) The standard deviation of bedrooms per apartment in Building 2 is larger.

C) The standard deviation of bedrooms per apartment in Building 1 and the standard deviation of bedrooms per apartment in Building 2 are the same.

D) No conclusions about the standard deviations of bedrooms per apartment in these buildings can be drawn from the data shown.

OK, so this isn't as gnarly as it looks. All you need to see (or calculate, if it'll make you feel better) is that the means for both buildings are between two and three bedrooms per apartment. However, in Building 1, most of the apartments have two bedrooms, and *no* apartments have five bedrooms. In Building 2, there's much more variability: more apartments have one bedroom than have two, and a bunch of apartments are very far from the mean with five bedrooms. Therefore, the standard deviation of Building 2 is greater. **Choice B is correct.**

Range

Remember how I was just saying that you don't need to know much about standard deviation other than what it is, and how there's a great chance you won't even see it on test day? Same goes for the other basic measure of variability, the range. It's a crazy simple concept: you just need to know what it is. **The range of a set of data is just the difference between the largest and the smallest value in a set.**

$$\{49, 18, 24, 59, 71, 30\}$$

In the set above, the range is $71 - 18 = 53$. What could be easier than that?

All other things being equal, comparing the ranges of two sets can help you get a sense of their relative variability. If two equally sized sets have the same mean but different ranges, the one with the bigger range will *usually* have a greater standard deviation. Given the fact that you won't need to calculate standard deviation on the SAT even on standard deviation questions, it's very unlikely that you'll encounter an exception to this rule of thumb.

Practice questions: Measures of Central Tendency and Variability

Prove that you are above average.

1 Calculator

The average (arithmetic mean) test score in a class of 12 students was 74. If 4 students who averaged 96 were removed from the class, what would be the new average score of the class?

A) 70

B) 63

C) 58

D) 44

2 Calculator

The average (arithmetic mean) of 5 numbers is f. The sum of 3 of those numbers is g. What is the average of the remaining numbers?

A) $\dfrac{5f-g}{3}$

B) $\dfrac{5f-3g}{2}$

C) $\dfrac{f-3}{g}$

D) $\dfrac{5f-g}{2}$

3 Calculator

For the first m days of the month of July, the average (arithmetic mean) of the daily peak temperatures in Culver City was 87° Fahrenheit. If the peak temperature the next day was 93° and the average daily peak temperature for July rose to 89°, what is the value of m ?

A) 7

B) 6

C) 4

D) 2

4 Calculator

Sam's job is to deliver pizza, and he keeps careful track of the tips he earns. After work on Wednesday this week, he notes that his average (arithmetic mean) nightly tip total for Monday, Tuesday, and Wednesday is $75. How much would Sam have to earn in tips on Thursday and Friday, in total, to bring his 5-day average nightly tip total to $100?

A) $275

B) $280

C) $300

D) $325

Practice questions: Measures of Central Tendency and Variability
Prove that you are above average.

Questions 5 and 6 refer to the following information.

The histogram below compares the average wind speeds recorded every day on the summit of Mount Washington in June 2014 and June 2015.[*]

Daily Average Wind Speed on Mount Washington
■ June 2014 ■ June 2015

5 Calculator

Given the data shown for June 2014, which of the following is true?

A) The mean wind speed for the month is greater than the median daily average wind speed for the month.

B) The median daily average wind speed for the month is greater than the mean wind speed for the month.

C) The median daily average wind speed is between 25 and 30 miles per hour.

D) It was windier at the beginning of the month than it was at the end of the month.

6 Calculator

Given the data shown, which of the following is greater for June 2014 than it is for June 2015?

   I   The mean wind speed.

   II The median daily average wind speed.

   III The range of average daily wind speeds.

A) I only

B) III only

C) I and II only

D) I, II, and III

---

*   Data source: Mount Washington Observatory. Accessed 2015-11-24 at https://www.mountwashington.org/experience-the-weather/mount-washington-weather-archives/monthly-f6.aspx

7 Calculator

Score	Frequency	Score	Frequency
12	3	17	5
13	4	18	5
14	0	19	6
15	8	20	2
16	4	21	3

Olaf calculated the standard deviation for the data presented in the frequency distribution above. However, he then realized that he forgot some data points and had to add the following data points to his set: 16, 17, 17, 17, and 18. When he recalculates the standard deviation with the complete data set, which of the following will be true?

A) The new standard deviation will be higher.

B) The new standard deviation will be lower.

C) The standard deviation will not change.

D) No conclusion can be made about the standard deviation from the data given.

8 Calculator

Runner	Time	Runner	Time
John	6:21	Kevin	6:15
Chris	5:32	Millicent	6:01
Erik	6:20	Dario	5:50
Devon	5:56	Maryanne	6:31
Clive	5:45	Lakshmi	6:08

The table above shows the automatically recorded mile times for individual members of the City Runners Track Team at a recent meet. The team coach believes that a system malfunction caused Maryanne's time to be recorded incorrectly. If Maryanne's time is changed to 6:20, which of the following statistics for the club's mile times will NOT change?

    I   Range

    II   Mean

    III   Median

A) I only

B) II only

C) III only

D) I and II only

Practice questions: Measures of Central Tendency and Variability

Prove that you are above average.

The table below shows the scores that Octavia's 10 classmates have achieved in a beanbag tossing game.

3	15	11	3	9
6	10	11	10	12

Octavia is the last person to play. Her score increases the class average score by 1 but does not change the median. What is Octavia's score?

11 is both the median and the mode of a set of five positive integers. What is the least possible value of the average (arithmetic mean) of the set?

Answers:

1	B		6	B
2	D		7	B
3	D		8	C
4	A		9	20
5	A		10	7

Solutions on page 384.

The following Official Test are all about measures of central tendency (mostly) and variability (a bit).

Test	Section	Questions
1	3: No calculator	
	4: Calculator	12, 14
2	3: No calculator	
	4: Calculator	19
3	3: No calculator	
	4: Calculator	32, 35
4	3: No calculator	
	4: Calculator	23, 29
5	3: No calculator	
	4: Calculator	27
6	3: No calculator	10
	4: Calculator	22, 26
7	3: No calculator	
	4: Calculator	22, 37
8	3: No calculator	
	4: Calculator	17, 28
9	3: No calculator	
	4: Calculator	22, 34, 37
10	3: No calculator	
	4: Calculator	11, 20, 33
PSAT/NMSQT 1	3: No calculator	
	4: Calculator	13, 20
PSAT/NMSQT 2	3: No calculator	
	4: Calculator	11, 14

Data Analysis 1: Graphs and Tables

Let's just tell it like it is: the SAT is basically *obsessed* with data analysis. This is not bad news. Once you get the hang of reading the different kinds of graphical and tabular summaries the test writers are so fond of, you'll probably look forward to these questions. They usually won't require many calculations. (They sometimes won't require *any* calculations.) They *will* require some careful reading and critical thinking, though. So...we're going to practice that. A lot.

That's why I'm breaking our discussion of data analysis into two chapters. The chapter you're currently in will be a potpourri of different data summaries in graphical and tabular form, just to acclimate you to the way data questions might be asked on your test. Then the next chapter will delve more deeply into two widely used methods of summarizing and modeling data that you may not be all that familiar with if you haven't taken stats.

Let's get right into it, shall we?

Example 1: Calculator

Steps Recorded in Javier's Fitness Tracker	
Monday	11,281
Tuesday	15,048
Wednesday	9,843
Thursday	10,020
Friday	13,068
Saturday	11,547
Sunday	12,788

Javier wears a fitness tracker on his wrist that records the number of steps he takes every day. The table above shows the number of steps he took each day last week. Javier's goals are to walk at least 10,000 steps every day and to walk an average of 12,000 steps per day in every three-day period. During which three-day period last week did Javier achieve both of his goals?

A) Monday, Tuesday, Wednesday

B) Tuesday, Wednesday, Thursday

C) Thursday, Friday, Saturday

D) Friday, Saturday, Sunday

Do you see what's being asked of you here? The right answer will be a three-day period during which Javier hits his daily goal of 10,000 steps every day, *and* during which his three-day average exceeds 12,000 steps.

You see right away that he didn't hit his daily goal on Wednesday, so cross off choices A and B. It doesn't matter that his average for Monday through Wednesday was greater than 12,000—the question asks about the period during which he achieved *both* of his goals.

Javier achieved his single-day 10,000 step goal on all the days in choices C and D, so we have to consider his three-day goal. You may calculate the average for each of those three day periods if you like, but I want to point out that you don't have to. You know the right answer must be C or D, and both C and D contain Friday and Saturday. Therefore, in choosing between choices C and D, you're really just choosing between Thursday and Sunday. Javier walked more steps on Sunday, so the answer is going to be **choice D**. His average steps will not exceed 12,000 on Thursday through Saturday, but they will on Friday through Sunday.

The question we just worked through required careful reading of the table and the question, but not much else. You'll also need to be able to perform simple calculations on the data in those graphs and tables. Percents, ratios, and measures of central tendency are all fair game, as are arithmetic operations: addition, subtraction, etc.

Example 2: Calculator; Grid-in

	Felt confident	Did not feel confident
Ate breakfast	12	3
Did not eat breakfast	8	4

Before giving her first period class a calculus test, Ms. Suarez surveyed her students, asking everyone whether they felt confident about the test and whether they had eaten breakfast that morning. The results are summarized in the table above. If one of the students who felt confident about the test is chosen at random, what is the probability that he or she ate breakfast that morning?

The Official Tests that have been released so far have barely mentioned probability at all, but it does appear, and it is fair game. However, you shouldn't worry about having to do complicated, confusing probability calculations—when probability appears on the SAT, it'll simply be a special kind of part-to-whole ratio. And that's all we need to do here.

First, note that all we care about are the students who felt confident since we know the student chosen at random here felt confident. So cross off the part of the table you don't care about. All we need to look at is this:

	Felt confident
Ate breakfast	12
Did not eat breakfast	8

Of those confident students, how many ate breakfast? 12 did. How many students were confident in total? 12 + 8 = 20 were confident. So what is the probability that our randomly selected confident student ate breakfast?

$$\frac{12}{20} = \frac{3}{5} = 0.6$$

You don't have space to grid in 12/20, but you do have space for either **3/5 or .6**, which are the acceptable answers.

Analyze this.

Questions 1 and 2 refer to the following information.

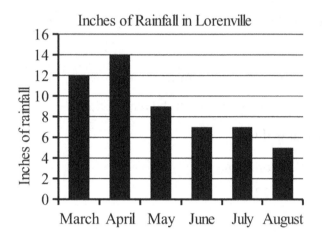

Inches of Rainfall in Lorenville

The table above shows the total inches of rainfall, rounded to the nearest inch, in Lorenville for six consecutive months.

1 Calculator

Which of the following is closest to the percent decrease in rainfall from April to May?

A) 35.7%

B) 40.8%

C) 55.6%

D) 64.3%

2 Calculator

What was the median monthly rainfall in Lorenville for the six months measured?

A) 6 inches

B) 7 inches

C) 8 inches

D) 9 inches

3 Calculator

	Golf	Skiing	Movies
2011	$527.78	$450.55	$325.85
2012	$464.46	$327.56	$313.23
2013	$456.07	$233.84	$342.59
2014	$359.11	$575.06	$252.24

The table above shows Carey's spending over a four-year period on three of his favorite recreational activities. During which year was the ratio of spending on golf to spending on movies the greatest?

A) 2011

B) 2012

C) 2013

D) 2014

Analyze this.

Questions 4 and 5 refer to the following information.

Teacher Productivity

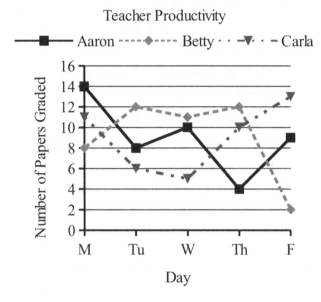

The graph above shows how many papers three teachers, Aaron, Betty, and Carla, graded each day last week.

4 Calculator

On Monday, Aaron graded the most papers and Betty graded the least. On which day was the opposite true?

A) Tuesday

B) Wednesday

C) Thursday

D) Friday

5 Calculator

On which day did Betty and Carla grade fewer papers, combined, than they did on all other days?

A) Tuesday

B) Wednesday

C) Thursday

D) Friday

6 Calculator

Country	Population Density $\left(\dfrac{\text{people}}{\text{km}^2}\right)$
X	7,698.19
Y	65.25
Z	421.68

The table above shows the population density, measured in people per square kilometer, for three countries. Country Y has an area of 70,273 km^2. Which of the following is the best approximation of the population of Country Y?

A) 4.59×10^4

B) 4.59×10^5

C) 4.59×10^6

D) 4.59×10^7

Analyze this.

Questions 7 and 8 refer to the following information.

The partially filled-in table below summarizes the number of pets in Capeside, and whether they have spots on their coats or not. The number of dogs that don't have spots is one third of the number of dogs that do have spots. The number of cats that don't have spots is one fourth of the number of cats that do have spots.

Species	Coat Pattern	
	Spots	No Spots
Dogs		
Cats		
Total	164	47

7 Calculator

Which of the following is closest to the probability that an animal with spots chosen at random is a dog?

A) 0.235

B) 0.439

C) 0.561

D) 0.750

8 Calculator

Which of the following statements about dogs and cats in Capeside is NOT true according to the information provided?

A) There are more dogs with spots than cats with spots.

B) There are more dogs without spots than cats without spots.

C) There are more cats than dogs.

D) Cats without spots comprise the smallest group in the table above.

Analyze this.

9 Calculator; Grid-in

10 Calculator; Grid-in

Number of Books Sold in 2014

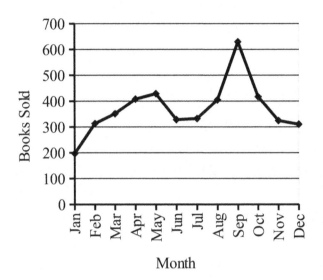

The table above shows the number of books an author sold each month in 2014. The total number of books she sold in 2014 was 4,443. During how many months did the author's sales exceed her monthly average number of books sold?

User	Apps	User	Apps
Anjali	259	Grace	102
Ben	58	Han	44
Colin	81	Ida	x
Dana	27	Jaco	47
Ephrem	74	Kate	61
Fatima	168	Leif	211

The table above lists the number of applications (apps) each of 12 smartphone users have on their phones. If the median number of apps for the group is 77, what is the value of x ?

Answers:

1	A		6	C
2	C		7	B
3	A		8	A
4	C		9	5
5	D		10	80

Solutions on page 386.

The following Official Test are all about analysis of tables and graphs.

Test	Section	Questions
1	3: No calculator	
	4: Calculator	1, 7, 13, 14, 21, 22, 23, 27, 33
2	3: No calculator	
	4: Calculator	11, 16, 19, 20
3	3: No calculator	
	4: Calculator	1, 2, 3, 10, 11, 29, 32
4	3: No calculator	
	4: Calculator	7, 9, 16, 17, 22, 23
5	3: No calculator	
	4: Calculator	1, 14
6	3: No calculator	
	4: Calculator	6, 8, 12, 13, 22, 23, 36
7	3: No calculator	
	4: Calculator	1, 13, 22, 25, 26, 37, 38
8	3: No calculator	
	4: Calculator	2, 10, 16, 37, 38
9	3: No calculator	
	4: Calculator	5, 6, 8, 9, 20, 33, 37, 38
10	3: No calculator	
	4: Calculator	2, 3, 8, 13, 14, 18
PSAT/NMSQT 1	3: No calculator	
	4: Calculator	3, 14, 15, 16, 17
PSAT/NMSQT 2	3: No calculator	
	4: Calculator	1, 8, 12, 16, 17, 18

Data Analysis 2: Histograms, Box Plots, and Scatterplots

As I was saying in the introduction to the last chapter, There are lots of different ways data can be summarized, and the SAT puts a really high value on data analysis, so it's going to throw lots of different kinds of questions about this your way. The two kinds of data summaries found in this chapter are a little more advanced, and offer the SAT the opportunity to ask a wide range of interesting questions, so I thought they warranted their own chapter.

Histograms

Sometimes, it's useful to look at data in terms of how often a data point occurs. Here's a super-relevant example in our current context: part of the process of constructing the scoring table for the SAT is determining the frequencies of each raw score over the population of test takers.

Anyway, in a histogram (AKA a bar graph), the horizontal axis displays the data we're concerned with, and the vertical axis displays how often each number occurs in the set of data. This kind of graph is usually used to help people visualize single-variable data sets (like raw scores for SAT math for a population of test takers).

Given a standard bar graph, you should be able to figure out:[*]

→ Total number of data points

→ Median

→ Average (arithmetic mean):

→ Mode

→ Standard deviation (you don't have to calculate this, but you should understand that standard deviation is a measure of variance and that the more volatile-looking the data set is, the higher its standard deviation will be.)

---

[*] Note that sometimes data are not numeric, and when that's the case you can't calculate median unless you have some other way of ranking the data, and you can't calculate average or standard deviation, period. If you're given a bar graph that shows the frequency of different colors of candy in a bowl, you can't calculate the median color, the average color, or the standard deviation of color. Those are meaningless phrases!

Anyway, let's have a look at a sample histogram and talk about each of those. The figure on the right shows the number of babies at a certain daycare facility with one, two, three, four, or five teeth.

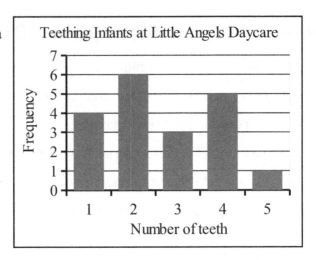

The first thing we'll want to know is how many data points we're dealing with. To figure that out, all we need to do is count! The graph tells us that there are 4 babies with 1 tooth each, 6 babies with 2 teeth each, 3 babies with 3 teeth each, 5 babies with 4 teeth each, and 1 baby with 5 teeth.

$4 + 6 + 3 + 5 + 1 = 19$, so there are 19 data points here. Easy, right?

Now let's calculate the **median**. If there are 19 data points, then there will be 9 points of data below or equal to the median, and 9 points of data above or equal to the median—the median will be both the 10th from the front and the 10th from the back of the line. So we just need to start at either side of the graph and count to 9. There are 4 babies with one tooth, and 6 babies with 2 teeth each, and that's 10 babies. That means the 10th baby, the median baby, has 2 teeth. Note that if we had counted from the right, of course, we'd get the same result: 1 baby with 5 teeth, 5 babies with 4 teeth each, and 3 babies with 3 teeth add up to 9 babies. The next baby, the 10th baby, will have 2 teeth. Cool? This is something you'll almost definitely be asked to do, so make sure you understand this paragraph.

OK, now let's calculate the **average (arithmetic mean)**. Of course, we already know the total number of babies is 19, so we just need to figure out the total number of teeth. To do that, multiply each number of teeth by its frequency: $4(1) + 6(2) + 3(3) + 5(4) + 1(5) = 50$. So the average number of teeth for babies at this daycare is $\frac{50}{19} \approx 2.63$.

Lastly, let's calculate the **mode**. The mode is the easiest thing to calculate, especially when you're doing so from a frequency graph, because the mode is just the most commonly occurring data point in the set! Look for the highest bar and you're done—more babies have 2 teeth than any other number of teeth, so the mode is 2.

As for **standard deviation**, well, as I said above (and back in the Measures of Central Tendency and Variability chapter), there's not much you need to be able to do with it other than to remember that it's a measure of variance, or how far each data point is from the mean. The data we're looking at are not just a bunch of babies in teething lockstep, each with 2 teeth, so the standard deviation of the number of teeth at Little Angels Daycare would be higher than the standard deviation of the number of teeth at Little Clones Daycare where every single child has 2 teeth.

It's worthwhile to know how a histogram like this is built since you could conceivable be presented with data in any stage of the following process and asked the same kinds of questions.

Number of teeth per infant at Little Angels Daycare		
1	2	1
2	4	3
4	4	2
5	2	2
3	1	3
4	2	4
1		

SORTING →

Number of teeth per infant at Little Angels Daycare		
1	2	4
1	2	4
1	2	4
1	3	4
2	3	4
2	3	5
2		

The first table above is what the same Little Angels Daycare data look like in raw form. Once someone goes to the trouble to sort them, the data look like the second table. For a small data set like the one we've got, honestly, that sorted table is pretty easy to deal with. A reasonable person might just leave it at that.

We, however, are not reasonable people. So we make a frequency table. From that frequency table on the right, hopefully you can see exactly where the bar graph comes from.

Number of teeth	Frequency
1	4
2	6
3	3
4	5
5	1

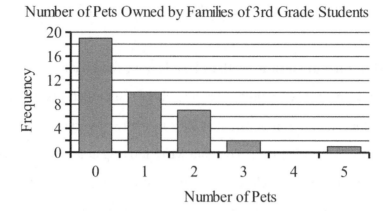

The bar graph above summarizes the number of pets owned by the families of the 39 children in the 3rd grade at Seymour Elementary School. Which of the following events could change the value of the median number of pets owned by the families of these students?

A) Alice, whose family had no pets, gets a dog.

B) Brianne's cat, which had been her only pet, has four kittens, and her family decides to keep them all.

C) Clyde's three hamsters—his only pets—escape, and he is too bereft to replace them.

D) Five of the students go to a carnival, and each wins one pet goldfish in a carnival game.

OK, to solve this, first figure out what the median is. If there are 39 families, then the median number of pets will be the 20th biggest and 20th smallest—19 families will have fewer or as many, and 19 will have as many or more. The graph tells you that 19 families have no pets, so the 20th family, the median family, has one pet.

Knowing that, and seeing what the graph looks like, you should be thinking that the best way to change the median is to raise the zero pets bar since one more student with no pets will cause the median number of pets to be zero. Choice **C** is the only choice that increases the number of families with zero pets, so that's the answer.

Finally, you should know that a histogram won't always have individual data points along the horizontal axis. Sometimes, it'll have ranges of data instead.* This is usually done to summarize data that would be too messy to represent visually if each value got its own bar. For example, if you wanted to graphically represent how much money each of 20 random strangers had in their pockets, and you used actual dollars and cents instead of ranges, you'd *probably* just have a bar graph with 20 different frequencies of 1: one guy has $2.28, one other guy has $2.47, one other lady has $8.00, etc. If you instead plotted how many people have $0–10 , $10–20, $20–30, etc., the graph would make more sense.

Using a histogram with ranges changes a little bit about what you can calculate just from looking at the graph. You won't be able to calculate a mode anymore, nor will you be able to calculate a precise mean or median. You *will* still be able to figure out ranges for the mean and median, though. Let's look at one.

The histogram above summarizes the final checks for all 29 tables served at Giovanni's Restaurant on a recent Saturday night. If the median and the mean value check both equal the same number *m* that night, what is one possible value of *m* ? (Disregard the $ sign when gridding your answer.)

---

* On the SAT, histogram bars will always include the data from the left endpoint of the range but not the right endpoint. So, someone who has exactly $10 in this example would be represented in the $10-20 bar, not the $0-10 bar.

To solve this question, we're going to need to find the theoretical ranges of both the mean and the median, and then pick a number that falls into both ranges. Let's do the mean first.

From the histogram, we can determine the minimum and maximum values contributed to the overall total by each bar. For example, We know 2 checks fell between $20 and $40, so we know the minimum that bar could have contributed to the overall total is 2($20) = $40. Similarly, we can calculate the minimum each other bar could contribute to the total. In order, the minimums each bar might have contributed to the total are: 4($0) = $0, 2($20) = $40, 8($40) = $320, 5($60) = $300, 7($80) = $560, and 3($100) = $300.

Add all those up, and you find that the absolute minimum Giovanni's could have made that night is $0 + 40 + 320 + 300 + 560 + 300 = $1,520. Divide that by the total number of checks (29) and you get roughly $52.41. So you know the mean must be greater than that.

Now let's find the maximum[*] Giovanni's could have made: 4($20) = $80, 2($40) = $80, 8($60) = $480, 5($80) = $400, 7($100) = $700, and 3($120) = $360. Add those up and you get $2,100. Divide by 29 to get the average and you get roughly $72.41. That's exactly $20 more than the minimum, which makes sense: if we know the $20 range into which each final check fell, we can figure out a $20 range into which the average check falls. The mean must be between $52.41 and $72.41.

Now we just need to find the range for the median. This is a little easier than finding the range of possible means—all we need to do is figure out which bar the median falls into, the same way we would with a histogram that wasn't giving us ranges. There are 29 checks, so there will be 14 checks less than the median check, and 14 checks greater than the median check. The first 3 columns represent 4 + 2 + 8 = 14 checks, so the median must fall in the $60–80 range.

You can grid in **anything greater than or equal to 60 and less than 72.4.**

---

[*] Note that, as I said in the footnote on the last page, for any histogram you encounter on the SAT, the upper bound will not actually be included in each bar. (This is called a "border condition," btw.) For simplicity's sake, I'm still using the upper bound for this calculation because it's a pain to use $19.99 instead of $20, $39.99 instead of $40, etc.

Box plots

A box plot is a way of summarizing a data set by showing five important numbers in one graph: the minimum, the maximum, the median, the first quartile, and the third quartile. (The first and third quartiles are like the medians of the top and bottom half of the data—more on these in a bit.) This is sometimes called the "five number summary."

Box plots look like this:

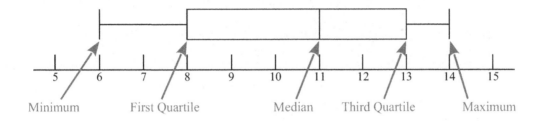

In a box plot, the skinny lines (also known as "whiskers") reach out to the minimum and maximum value in the data set. The box itself stretches from the first quartile to the third quartile, and the line in the middle of the box represents the median. The quartiles and median* split the data into quarters (this is why they're called quartiles). The box itself represents the half of the values that are closest to the median, sometimes called the "middle 50%" of the values, with 25% to the right of the box, and the other 25% to the left of the box.

So the box plot above represents a data set where the lowest value is 6, the highest value is 14, the median is 11, and half of the data falls between 8 and 13 (the first and third quartiles, respectively). Easy enough, right?

SAT questions about box plots may be as simple as showing you a box plot and asking you what the median of the data set is, but it could also get more complicated, like showing you data summarized in one way (like a histogram) and asking you what a box plot of the same data should look like. Let's try one of those.

---

* Fun (or not so fun) fact: the median is the second quartile.

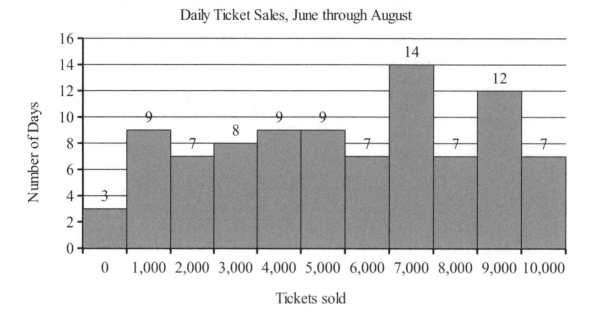

Daily Ticket Sales, June through August

A manager at an amusement park has summarized ticket sales over June, July, and August—a 92-day period—by rounding the number of tickets sold each day to the nearest thousand and compiling the histogram above. Which of the following box plots could represent this same ticket sale data?

A) Daily Ticket Sales, July through August

B) Daily Ticket Sales, July through August

C) Daily Ticket Sales, July through August

D) Daily Ticket Sales, July through August

OK, so get rid of choice D right away—we know from the histogram without doing any calculations that the minimum and maximum should reach all the way from 0 to 10,000.

After that, though, we're going to need to do a little figuring. First, let's figure out the median. We know there are 92 values, which means there will be 46 numbers equal to or below the median and 46 equal to or above it. The median will be the average of the 46th and 47th greatest numbers. So, let's count from either side of the histogram until we get to 46.

Counting from the left, $3 + 9 + 7 + 8 + 9 + 9 = 45$, and that gets us all the way through the 5,000 ticket bar. That means the 46th and 47th values will be in the 6,000 ticket bar, so the median will be 6,000—cross off choice A!

Choices B and C have different values for both the first and third quartile, so we really only need to pick one of those to check, but since this is practice we'll find both. Remember, the first quartile is the median of the numbers below the median, and the third quartile is the median of the numbers above the median. We established above that there are 46 numbers equal to or under the median, which means the median of those 46 will be the average of the 23rd and 24th values. Counting from the left again, we have $3 + 9 + 7 = 19$ getting us through the 2,000 bar, which means the 23rd and 24th values will be in the 3,000 bar. So the first quartile is 3,000. At this point we know that the answer is **B**, but for the sake of practice let's confirm by finding the third quartile.

Just like we counted from the left to find the first quartile, we can count from the right to find the third quartile: $7 + 12 = 19$ gets us through the 9,000 bar, so the 23rd and 24th highest values will be in the 8,000 bar—the third quartile is 8,000.

To be clear, box plot questions are rare on the SAT, but they do occur and each time they do, they seem to cause undue consternation for students. Fret not! As long as you remember what the box plots are meant to represent, you should have no problem working with them.

Scatterplots

A scatterplot is a way to show, graphically, whether and how two variables relate to each other. Scatterplots are neat because they can help folks model messy, real world data. Let's get right into an example.

Example 4: Calculator

The scatterplot above shows how far 28 employees at a vinyl record pressing plant live from the plant and their average commuting times. A line of best fit for the data is also provided. Lyla, a new employee not represented on the chart, lives 16 miles away from the plant and finds that her average commuting time is 23 minutes. Which of the following is the most accurate statement about Lyla's commute?

A) Lyla's commute is the shortest of all her coworkers' commutes.

B) Lyla has a shorter commute than the line of best fit would suggest.

C) Lyla's commute is longer than those of some coworkers who live farther from the plant than she does.

D) Lyla's commute will eventually get longer.

As this question illustrates, scatterplots can be useful to take a set of real-world data (almost always messy) and model it neatly. It stands to reason that the farther someone lives from work, the longer it would take him to commute. The real-world data show that, but of course not perfectly—some people drive faster than others, some have a route with fewer traffic lights, etc. At around 21 miles distance from the plant, you see three different workers with drastically different commuting times when they live almost the exact same distance from work! Still, the data clearly suggest a linear relationship between distance from the plant and length of commute, and we can draw a line of best fit that helps us model that relationship. If we want a rough estimate of how long a new worker's commute might be based on the data we have, that line of best fit is the way to go.

So, let's answer this question! To evaluate the statements about Lyla's commute, let's first plot her on the graph. She lives 16 miles away and has a commute of 23 minutes, so she'll be at (16, 23):

Once you've placed Lyla on the graph, it should be obvious that her commute is in fact shorter than what the trend line would suggest. The trend line looks like it would suggest a commuting time of more like 28 minutes for someone who lives 16 miles from the plant. The answer is **B**.

So this is one important skill you'll be tested on with scatterplots and lines of best fit—you'll need to know how to interpret the data presented and possibly go from there to making conclusions about new data.

Another thing scatterplot questions will test you on is whether you know what different kinds of growth look like and what relatively strong relationships look like versus relatively weak ones. The graph we just looked at, with distances from work and commuting times, was a pretty strong linear relationship. The table below will show you a few more examples of the kinds of relationships you should be able to recognize just by looking at them.

Linear relationships do not suggest any curvy shape. Positive linear relationships are higher on the right than they are on the left. Negative linear relationships are higher on the left than they are on the right.

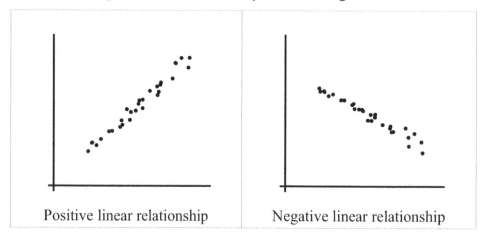

Positive linear relationship   Negative linear relationship

When data suggest a linear relationship, a **line of best fit** is often drawn to model that relationship (just like it was in Example 1). Like any other line, a line of best fit can be represented in $y = mx + b$ form.[*] If the relationship is positive, then the line of best fit will have a positive slope, and if the relationship is negative, then the line of best fit will have a negative slope. Duh, right?

Exponential relationships have a lot more shape to them than linear relationships do. **Exponential growth** looks exactly like you hope a graph of your personal income will look after you invent the next Instagram. **Exponential decay** drops off steeply, then flattens out at the bottom.

---

* You won't need to calculate a line of best fit with precision on the SAT, but you should understand its purpose: to take messy data set and summarize them with a neat (if imperfect) mathematical model. You should also be ready to choose from a list of possible equations for the line of best fit based a scatterplot. In this case, make your determination based on eyeball estimates for slope and intercept.

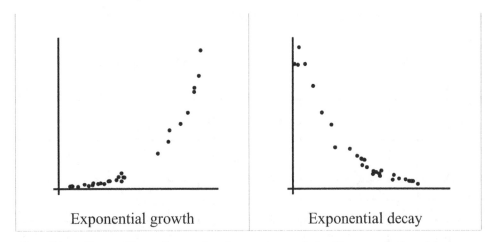

Exponential growth	Exponential decay

Just like a line of best fit can be drawn to model a linear relationship, an exponential function can be plotted that models an exponential relationship. It will have the form $y = ab^x$, where the constant a is a starting value—it's what y will equal when $x = 0$—and the constant b is a growth or decay factor. When $b > 1$, you'll have exponential growth. When $0 < b < 1$, you'll have exponential decay.[*] This formula should look familiar if you've already read the Passport to Advanced Math chapters in this book—exponential functions are how interest is calculated.

This stuff will mostly be tested in one of the following two ways: 1) you'll be shown a scatterplot and be asked to choose which written description of the data is most appropriate, or 2) a situation will be described in English, and you'll be asked to choose the scatterplot that best models the situation described. Of course, it's also possible that you might also be asked a question like the one on the next page.

---

[*] You probably won't need to come up with your own exponential function to model data on the SAT, but it's still good to know this stuff.

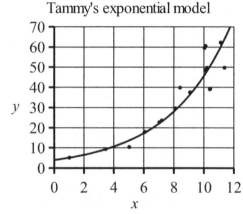

Kevin and Tammy are in the same statistical modeling class. Their teacher has given the class a partial set of data points from an experiment in the form of a scatterplot, but has not told them what the experiment was or what the axes on the scatterplot represent. Kevin thinks the data look like they represent a linear relationship, and draws a line of best fit to model that relationship. Tammy thinks the data look like they represent exponential growth, and draws her own exponential growth model. Both students' models, drawn on the same scatterplot, are above. The teacher offers to provide some additional data points to the class. Which of the following would best help Kevin and Tammy come to an agreement on the best model for the data?

A) Three more data points with x-values between 0 and 2

B) Three more data points with x-values between 3 and 5

C) Three more data points with x-values between 5 and 7

D) Three more data points with x-values between 8 and 10

This is a pretty theoretical question, huh? The way to think about it is to look for a couple things. First, where are the two models the most different? They're not very far off at $x = 4$, and they're pretty darn close at $x = 10$. They're pretty far from each other at $x = 0$, though, and as x continues to grow past 12, they'll be very different as well—the exponential model will start to shoot up very quickly, while the linear model will increase at a constant rate.

The other thing to look at is where the fewest data points exist. While there's pretty even coverage of data points on most of the graph, There's really only one point with an x-coordinate less than 3.

Since we have the least data where x is between 0 and 2, and since that's a place where the two models differ substantially, that'd be the best place to get a few more data points to help Kevin and Tammy decide on the best model. If they got three points like $(1, -10)$, $(0.5, -12)$ and $(1.5, -7.6)$, that would suggest that a linear model is best, and that the one point already shown is an outlier. If, on the other hand, they got three points near the point they already have, then they could feel more confident in choosing an exponential model. The answer is **A**.

Practice questions: Data Analysis 2: Histograms, Box Plots, and Scatterplots

It's OK to be a bit scatterbrained.

1 Calculator

Tomato Plant Height in Centimeters

The box plot above summarizes the heights, rounded to the nearest centimeter, of 20 tomato plants six weeks after they were planted. Which of the following MUST be true?

I   There is a tomato plant that is 14 centimeters tall.

II   There is a tomato plant that is 17 centimeters tall.

III   There is a tomato plant that is 19 centimeters tall.

A) I only

B) I and II only

C) I and III only

D) I, II, and III

2 Calculator

Andy, an aspiring musician, decided to play his guitar and sing in a subway station near his home for at least a few minutes every day for a month. (This practice is called busking.) He kept track of how long he played each day and how much he made in tips. He has plotted that data, and the line of best fit, in the scatterplot above. Which of the following is true?

A) When Andy spent more than 30 minutes busking, he usually made less in tips than the line of best fit would predict.

B) The line of best fit suggests that Andy made more than $1 per minute when he went busking.

C) Andy made the most money on the day he spent the longest time busking.

D) Most days, Andy spent more than 20 minutes busking.

Questions 3 and 4 refer to the following information.

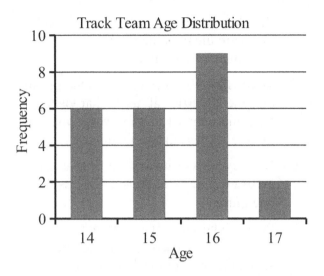

Track Team Age Distribution

The histogram above summarizes the distribution of ages on the Pleasantville High School track team.

3 Calculator

According to the histogram, what is the median age on the Pleasantville High School track team?

A) 14

B) 15

C) $15\frac{1}{2}$

D) 16

4 Calculator

This age distribution graph was made on March 15th, at the beginning of the spring track season. In April, three of the 16-year-olds had birthdays and turned 17. None of the other team members had birthdays in March or April. Which of the following are true?

I   The range of the ages of the track team members increased from March 15th to April 30th.

II   The median age on the track team increased from March 15th to April 30th.

III   The mean age on the track team increased from March 15th to April 30th.

A) I only

B) II only

C) III only

D) I and III only

It's OK to be a bit scatterbrained.

Questions 5 and 6 refer to the following information.

Hair Salon Website Visitors
Saturday, June 20, 2015

The owner of a hair salon is able to use his website's analytics feature to track roughly how far visitors are from his hair salon and how long those visitors stay on the website. Above is a scatterplot the salon owner made of the first 40 visitors to his website on a particular Saturday, and the line of best fit for that data.

5 Calculator

According to the data in the scatterplot, which of the following is closest to the amount of time the salon owner should expect a visitor who lives 4 miles from his salon to stay on the website?

A) 40

B) 75

C) 95

D) 105

6 Calculator

Which of the following statements is best supported by the data in the scatterplot?

A) People who visit the site from within 5 miles are the most likely to become customers of the salon.

B) Of the first 40 people who visited the site on June 20, 2015, all those that visited from more than 15 miles away stayed on the site for less than one minute.

C) Nobody who visits the site from within 5 miles ever stays on the site for less than one minute.

D) People who visit the site from more than 15 miles away leave quickly to keep searching for a closer hair salon.

It's OK to be a bit scatterbrained.

7 Calculator

Population of Children

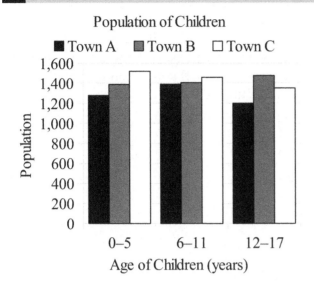

The populations of children, broken into three different age groups, in three neighboring towns of similar size are shown in graph above. Which of the following conclusions can be drawn from this graph?

A) There are more 7-year-old children in Town C than there are in Town B.

B) There are more children under the age of 12 in Town B than there are in Town A.

C) The median age of children in Town C is less than the median age of children in Town B.

D) Of the three towns, Town A has the smallest overall population.

8 Calculator

Weight of Black Bears Before and After Hibernation

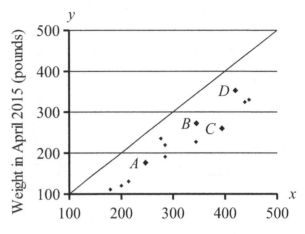

Weight in September 2014 (pounds)

A biologist weighed a number of black bears in September 2014, before they went into hibernation, and then again the following April, as they were coming out of hibernation. The biologist plotted this data in the scatterplot above with each bear's September weight on the x-axis and April weight on the y-axis. She also drew the $y = x$ line for reference. Which of the labeled points represents the bear that lost the most weight during hibernation?

A) A

B) B

C) C

D) D

It's OK to be a bit scatterbrained.

Questions 9 and 10 refer to the following information.

Number of Mumps Cases in the United States by Year

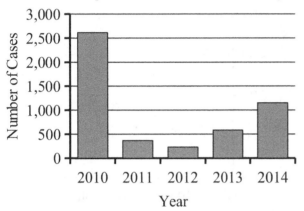

A student in a public health class created the histogram above to show the number of cases of mumps recorded in the United States in each year from 2010 to 2014.[*]

9 Calculator

Of the following, which best approximates the percent increase in mumps cases from 2012 to 2013 ?

A) 37%

B) 58%

C) 97%

D) 155%

10 Calculator

In 2010, the population of the United States was roughly 309.3 million. Which of the following is the best approximation of the fraction of the US population that developed a case of the mumps in 2010 ?

A) 8×10^{-3} %

B) 8×10^{-4} %

C) 8×10^{-5} %

D) 8×10^{-6} %

---

[*] Data source: US CDC. Accessed 2015-08-24 at
    http://www.cdc.gov/mumps/outbreaks.html

Answers:

1	A		6	B
2	D		7	B
3	B		8	C
4	C		9	D
5	C		10	B

Solutions on page 389.

The following Official Test are all about histograms and scatterplots.

Test	Section	Questions
1	3: No calculator	
	4: Calculator	5, 12
2	3: No calculator	
	4: Calculator	14, 27
3	3: No calculator	
	4: Calculator	20
4	3: No calculator	
	4: Calculator	10, 11, 15, 20, 21, 22, 27
5	3: No calculator	
	4: Calculator	17
6	3: No calculator	
	4: Calculator	30
7	3: No calculator	
	4: Calculator	7, 8, 18, 21
8	3: No calculator	
	4: Calculator	4, 17, 18
9	3: No calculator	
	4: Calculator	29, 30, 34
10	3: No calculator	
	4: Calculator	24
PSAT/NMSQT 1	3: No calculator	
	4: Calculator	9, 12, 13, 20, 22, 23, 24
PSAT/NMSQT 2	3: No calculator	
	4: Calculator	5, 6

Designing and Interpreting Experiments and Studies

The SAT will occasionally ask you to interpret the results of experiments or studies. For example, you may need to determine whether the results of a survey conducted by some students can be generalized to an entire population, or whether some experimental intervention has a causal impact. These questions will not be rocket science and will usually not require any math at all, even though they're in the math section. They will require some critical thinking and careful reading, though.

Randomization

Part of interpreting the results of an experiment, survey, or observational study is evaluating its design, and the key thing you need to be looking out for on the SAT when you have to do this is **randomization**. Generally speaking, the more randomized an experiment is, the stronger the conclusions that can be drawn.

If you're doing research, and you want to be able to generalize your findings over an entire population, then you have to randomly select the subjects for your study from that entire population. Say you want to know, on average, how likely a new driver in the United States is to have an accident within one year of getting his driver license. If you want to be able to generalize your findings to the entire population of new drivers in the United States, then you need to survey a random selection from that whole population. That's not going to be easy to do, of course, but good research is hard![*]

If you tried to take the easy way out and just went to your local shopping mall and asked the first hundred 17-year-olds you saw whether they'd been in an accident within a year of getting their licenses, then you could really only generalize your findings about the population of new drivers who visit that mall. Maybe going to that mall requires driving on a four-lane highway. Because some new drivers may avoid such a highway, the sample would likely not be representative of all new drivers. Maybe that mall is in a city, where fender benders are more

---

[*] If you want to generalize about all new drivers in the US, you're going to have to find someone who has the data you need. Maybe start calling the Department of Motor Vehicles in every state, or reach out to car insurance companies. If this sounds exciting to you, great! You might want to consider becoming a researcher.

likely to occur than they are in rural areas. Maybe people who shop in malls are more likely to get into car accidents than people who do most of their shopping online. You see?

If you want to be able to draw conclusions about an entire population from survey results, you need to randomly select a sample from that entire population.

Things get a bit more complicated when you're dealing with experiments, in which an intervention of some kind occurs, but the same basic idea holds. In an experiment, you can only generalize results to an entire population if you selected the experimental sample randomly from that population. Further, you can only argue that some intervention is causally responsible for some difference between experimental groups if the intervention is assigned to subjects within the sample randomly.

Say a cognitive scientist is trying to determine whether a certain intervention can be used to cause infants to exhibit object permanence earlier than they usually do. Say, further, that this researcher managed to obtain a truly random sample of infants.[*] If the data show that babies who received the intervention did, on average, exhibit object permanence earlier than those who did not receive the intervention, the cognitive scientist could only claim that the intervention caused the accelerated object permanence if the babies given the intervention were selected at random.

However—and this is a big important thing—it's also possible to assign an intervention randomly in a nonrandom sample. In that case, one might be able to make a convincing argument about causality in the sample, but one could not convincingly generalize that result to any broader population.

---

[*] This is very difficult because parents would need to sign off on such a thing, and maybe there's some difference between children of parents who would sign off and children of parents who wouldn't.

Julissa puts an ad in a local newspaper to find paid participants who are interested in improving their muscle tone for a study about a new personal training regimen she has designed. She finds 200 participants. She randomly assigns 100 of the participants to group A and the other 100 participants to group B. Group A is assigned Julissa's new training regimen, and group B is not assigned a training regimen. All 200 participants respond to questionnaires about their muscle tone at the beginning and end of the study. The final questionnaire data indicate that the overall muscle tone of the participants in group A improved significantly compared to that of group B. Which of the following is a reasonable conclusion?

A) It is likely that the personal training regimen improved the muscle tone of the participants in group A.

B) The personal training regimen will improve the muscle tone of anyone who follows it.

C) The personal training regimen will improve the muscle tone of anyone who lives in Julissa's town.

D) No conclusion about cause and effect can be made regarding the personal training regimen and participants in Julissa's study.

Because the only part of the study that was randomized was the assignment of the training intervention, Julissa can conclude that the training regimen probably caused improved muscle tone but only for the sample of 200 people in the study! Because respondents to a newspaper ad about a paid health training program are not a randomized sample, no broader conclusions can be made. The answer is **A**.

So, yeah. My longwindedness about randomization notwithstanding, experimental design questions really aren't hard—I promise. Just remember: if the question you get asks you to find a weakness in the design of an experiment, chances are very good that the answer will be something that's obviously not random.

Sample size and confidence

Remember that we use statistics to make generalizations about large populations based on observations we make of small groups from those populations. The small groups we use (randomly, if we're doing it right) are called samples. The number of members of the sample is called the **sample size**. Generally speaking, the bigger the sample size, the more likely it is that the sample is representative of the whole population.

Design and interpretation questions on the SAT will usually provide a sample size. In the released tests, there's no question where a too-small sample size is an experimental design problem, but I suppose it's possible that something like that could appear in the future. Rule of thumb: if your sample size is bigger than 100, it's probably fine. Only consider sample size a problem if it's *comically* small.

This kind of question will also sometimes make mention of a study's **margin of error** or **confidence interval**. If you've taken a statistics course, then you've probably had to calculate these things. You'll *never* have to do that on the SAT. You'll just have to know, in the most basic sense, what they are and why they're important.

When we generalize what we've observed in a sample to draw a conclusion about an entire population, we have to remember that there's a small possibility that we're wrong. For example, after measuring the heights of 300 randomly selected 33-year-old American males, we might say that we are 95% sure that the true average height height of 33-year-old American males is within 3 inches of the 70 inch average we found. 3 inches is our margin of error, and 67 to 73 is our confidence interval. As our sample size increases and we become more confident that the sample is representative of the population, our margin of error and confidence interval will shrink: we'll be able to say, with the same level of certainty, that the average we're finding is closer and closer to the true population average.

One more thing: the 95% in this example is called the confidence level—you'll probably only ever see confidence levels of 95% (maybe 99% once in a while). We include a confidence level to acknowledge that, even if we've designed our study carefully—randomized properly, made sure our sample size was sufficient, etc.—it's mathematically possible that our sample just won't repre-sent the overall population well.

Keep calm and randomize on.

1 Calculator

Tess wants to conduct a survey to test whether the proportion of left-handed people at her school is any different than the proportion of left-handed people in general. She has read that, in general, 10 percent of the population is left handed. One morning, before school has begun, Tess asks the first 10 people she sees whether they are left handed, and all 10 say no. Tess concludes that her school's population has a lower proportion of left handed people than does the general population. Is she justified in drawing this conclusion?

A) Yes, because if 10 percent of the population is left-handed then one of the people Tess asked should have said yes.

B) Yes, because in asking the first 10 people she saw, Tess randomized her sample.

C) No, because Tess cannot be sure that the people she asked told the truth.

D) No, because Tess's sample size was too small.

2 Calculator

Ms. Carlisle, a math teacher, offers extra help every Tuesday after school. She keeps careful attendance at these sessions. At the end of the school year, she compares the average score of the students who attended extra help regularly to the average score of the students who didn't and finds that students who attended extra help regularly did better in the class. Which of the following is an appropriate conclusion?

A) Attending extra help regularly will cause an improvement in performance for any student in any subject.

B) Attending extra help regularly will cause an improvement in performance for any student taking a math course.

C) Attending extra help regularly with Ms. Carlisle was the cause of the improvement for the students in Ms. Carlisle's class who did so.

D) No conclusion about cause and effect can be made regarding students in Ms. Carlisle's class who attended extra help regularly and their performance in the course.

3 Calculator

Bradley conducted a survey of a randomly selected group 18–24-year-old American males to determine how many movies young men of that age watch in a month. He then decided that his margin of error was too high and that he would conduct the survey again. Which of the following changes could Bradley make to decrease his margin of error?

A) Increase his sample size.

B) Decrease his sample size.

C) Increase the age range in his sample.

D) Include 18–24-year-old American females in his sample.

4 Calculator

A researcher is trying to estimate the average weight of the population of wild salmon in a certain river. She catches 100 salmon in a net, weighing each before releasing it back into the river. The researcher's conclusion is a 95% confidence interval of 3.3 to 3.8 pounds. Which of the following conclusions is most appropriate given that confidence interval?

A) 95% of the wild salmon in the river weigh between 3.3 and 3.8 pounds.

B) 95% of all wild salmon weigh between 3.3 and 3.8 pounds.

C) The true average weight of all wild salmon is likely to be between 3.3 and 3.8 pounds.

D) The true average weight of the wild salmon in the river is likely to be between 3.3 and 3.8 pounds.

5 Calculator

A college student is doing research to determine the proportion of students who leave campus for the weekend. He asked 120 students in a dining hall one Wednesday night during dinner service whether they would be staying on campus that weekend. 11 students refused to respond. Which of the following factors makes it least likely that the student can reach a reliable conclusion about the proportion of all students at the college who leave campus each weekend?

A) Where the survey was conducted

B) Sample size

C) Population size

D) The number of people who refused to respond

6 Calculator

Dean has taken an interest in politics and decides that he is going to try to predict the winner of a local election by conducting a poll in his home town. He begins dialing local phone numbers randomly on Monday evening at dinner time. He connects with 20 voters before stopping because he grew tired of being hung up on or cursed at. In total, 11 people told him the candidate they planned to vote for, and 9 people refused to respond. Which of the following factors makes it least likely that Dean can make a reliable prediction about the outcome of the election?

A) Population size

B) Sample size

C) The way the sample was selected

D) The number of people who refused to respond

7 Calculator

In order to determine if 30 minutes of intense cardiovascular exercise before bed can help people with insomnia sleep better, a research study was conducted. From a large population of people with insomnia, 500 participants were selected at random. Half of those participants were randomly assigned an intense cardiovascular exercise regimen to complete each night before bed. The other half were not assigned an exercise regimen. The resulting data showed that throughout the study, participants who were assigned an exercise regimen slept better than participants who were not assigned an exercise regimen. Based on the design and results of the study, which of the following is an appropriate conclusion?

A) Intense cardiovascular exercise is likely to help anyone who tries it sleep better.

B) Intense cardiovascular exercise is likely to help people with insomnia sleep better.

C) Any kind of exercise is likely to help people with insomnia sleep better.

D) No conclusion about cause and effect can be made regarding intense cardiovascular exercise and people with insomnia sleeping better.

8 Calculator

Courtney designed an experiment for his school's science fair. He planted 20 tomato plants in 20 identical pots and gave each plant the same amount of water each day at the same time. However, he kept 10 of the plants in a room without windows and with very low light, and the other 10 plants in a room that received four hours of direct sunlight. After four weeks, he measured the height of each plant and noted that the average height of the plants in the dark room was 40 percent less than the average height of the plants in the sunny room. Which of the following is the most appropriate conclusion?

A) Tomato plants grow more quickly when exposed to four hours of sunlight per day than they do in dark rooms.

B) Tomato plants grow 10 percent more per week when exposed to bright light than they do in dark rooms.

C) Tomato plants that grow in dark rooms are unlikely to bear fruit.

D) Tomato plants in dark rooms require more water to grow.

Keep calm and randomize on.

9 Calculator

A group of researchers conducted a phone survey of 300 people in Oakville in an attempt to calculate the mean amount spent by people in the town every month on groceries. They calculate that the mean is $197 with a margin of error of 6% at a 95% confidence level. Rounded to whole dollars, which of the following represents the confidence interval the researchers should report?

A) $102 to $192

B) $185 to $209

C) $187 to $207

D) $191 to $203

10 Calculator; Grid-in

An Internet research firm conducted a study with a sample of 1,134 American smartphone owners and reported a 95% confidence interval of 1.782 to 1.818 gigabytes for the mean cellular data per month consumed by American smartphone users. What was the study's margin of error?

Answers:

1	D	6	B	
2	D	7	B	
3	A	8	A	
4	D	9	B	
5	A	10	.018	

Solutions on page 391.

The following Official Test questions test you on experimental design and interpretation. You might not see this on your test. But if you do, you'll be prepared!

Test	Section	Questions
1	3: No calculator	
	4: Calculator	
2	3: No calculator	
	4: Calculator	13
3	3: No calculator	
	4: Calculator	15
4	3: No calculator	
	4: Calculator	
5	3: No calculator	
	4: Calculator	15, 22
6	3: No calculator	
	4: Calculator	7, 21
7	3: No calculator	
	4: Calculator	4
8	3: No calculator	
	4: Calculator	24, 26
9	3: No calculator	
	4: Calculator	23
10	3: No calculator	
	4: Calculator	7, 10
PSAT/NMSQT 1	3: No calculator	
	4: Calculator	
PSAT/NMSQT 2	3: No calculator	
	4: Calculator	

Interlude: Be Nimble

There's a question I love to throw at students early on in the tutoring process:

If $\dfrac{4^{999} + 4^{998}}{5} = 4^x$, what is x?

It's a beautiful question because no matter what, it's going to show me something about the kid with whom I'm working. Almost everyone goes to the calculator first. Once it becomes clear that the calculator won't help I see a few divergent paths, all illuminating:

1. If my student says it can't be done, I know one kind of question on which I'm going to have to drill her repeatedly.

2. If my student says $x = 1997$, then I know he just added the exponents in the numerator and completely ignored the denominator, so we're going to need to review the exponent rules and get his vision checked.

3. If my student factors 4^{998} out of the numerator to see that everything else cancels out and $x = 998$, then I know I'm going to have to really challenge her to get her score higher than it already is (full solution explained below).

4. If my student starts wrestling with other, more manageable numbers to try to get a foothold on the problem, I know I'm dealing with a kid who knows how to struggle and who doesn't back down from tough questions.

This fourth student might, for example, write the following:

$$\frac{4^3 + 4^2}{5} = 16 = 4^2 \text{, and } \frac{4^4 + 4^3}{5} = 64 = 4^3 \text{, so } \frac{4^{999} + 4^{998}}{5} = 4^{998}$$

Let's be clear here: it's fantastic to know how to do this question the right way, like the third student. She has a strong base of mathematical knowledge and has seen enough similar problems not to succumb to the pitfall of misusing exponent rules, and is creative enough to try pulling out the greatest common factor to see if anything good happens (and it does). As her tutor, this fills me with confidence and pride, but I'm also aware that I still don't know how she's going to react when she gets to a problem that's unlike any she's seen before (and on the SAT, that will indubitably happen, probably when it counts). So I'm going to keep watching her closely until I get to see what she does when a question makes her squirm.

The fourth student, though, is one who finds a way to claw out the correct answer even when faced with an intimidating problem that his tools seem at first not to be able to solve. He might not be as well-versed in math as the third student, but in the eyes of the SAT, she and he are exactly the same on that question. Because he's scrappy. He's nimble. And that will take him far.

In sports, you'll often hear a commentator say, "That's why you play the game," after an underdog team wins a game it wasn't expected to. It doesn't matter who looks better on paper. It matters who performs on game day. I've got faith in student #4 on game day.

If you want to take your place in the pantheon of great test takers, you're going to have to be nimble. You're going to have to grapple with tough problems sometimes. You're going to have to make mistakes, learn from them, and try not to repeat them. You're going to have to be flexible, and willing to try more than one approach.

This is, in a nutshell, why I want you to know how to plug in and backsolve, but I also want you to be able to do the math. Once in a while, no matter how good you are, the first thing you try isn't going to work. The best test takers, the most nimble, don't get frustrated when this happens. They always have one or two more approaches in reserve.

This, above all else, is the skill I'm trying to help you develop with this book

Solution

$$\frac{4^{999} + 4^{998}}{5} = 4^x$$

$$\frac{4^{998}(4+1)}{5} = 4^x$$

$$\frac{4^{998}(5)}{5} = 4^x$$

$$4^{998} = 4^x$$

$$998 = x$$

Additional Topics in Math

One of the many funny things about the SAT is the Additional Topics in Math question category. This is where geometry, which was such a large part of the previous version of the pre-2016 test, is now hidden away. Although geometry has been de-emphasized in terms of its prominence on the test, its scope has also been expanded: you need to know more geometry for fewer questions. Additional Topics in Math is also where basic trigonometry and complex numbers—which honestly feel out of place and aren't even guaranteed to appear *at all* on your test—have found a home.

You won't get a subscore for Additional Topics in Math (not that anyone's losing sleep over subscores anyway) and questions in this category only appear 6 times on the test—that's only about 10% of the questions! Funny, right? Hilarious.

So here's the deal: because folks who want to achieve the highest scores need to know more geometry than they used to have to know, the following section is pretty long and involved, but because Additional Topics in Math is such a small part of the new test, folks who are looking for a quick score boost might be fine to just ignore this section of the book altogether. People who love geometry* will curse the fact that their love won't pay off as hugely on the current SAT as it would have on the old one. People who hate geometry might rejoice that it's been relegated to this section, but lament that they'll have to learn more of it than before if they're shooting for top scores. Everybody loses!

Nah, I'm just kidding. This stuff still isn't that bad. You'll see. Come along on an adventure of the mind! We're gonna see shapes and stuff.

---

* If you love geometry, that's awesome! Me too. Let's start a club.

Angles, Triangles, and Polygons

Before we get into triangles, we need to take a very quick look at the ingredients of a triangle: line segments and angles. You probably already know this stuff:

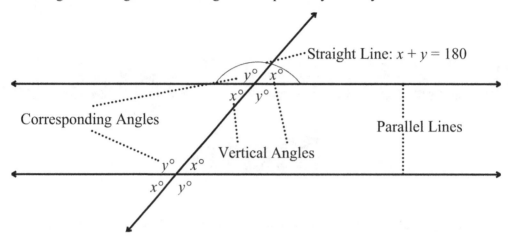

➔ The degree measure of a straight line is 180°.

➔ Angles directly across an intersection of two lines from each other are called *vertical angles* and they're congruent.

➔ When two lines are parallel, and a third line (called a *transversal*) intersects both of them, the angles created at one intersection correspond to the angles at the other, like in the figure above.

➔ If you have a transversal between two parallel lines and you know one angle, you can figure out all the rest using corresponding angles, vertical angles, and the fact that a straight line measures 180°.

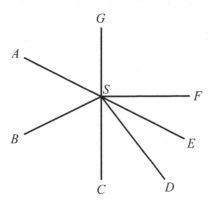

In the figure above, $\overline{AE}$, $\overline{BS}$, $\overline{CG}$, $\overline{DS}$, and $\overline{FS}$ intersect at point S. Which of the following pairs of angles must be congruent?

A) $\angle ASF$ and $\angle BSF$

B) $\angle ASG$ and $\angle CSE$

C) $\angle ASG$ and $\angle FSG$

D) $\angle ASB$ and $\angle ASG$

Which angles are vertical angles? We know that all these segments meet at point S, but which ones actually go through it? $\overline{AE}$ and $\overline{CG}$ both go all the way through, so they'll create a set of vertical angles: $\angle ASG$ and $\angle CSE$. We know vertical angles are always congruent, so **choice B** is the answer. You're really going to want to make sure you're solid on this kind of question.

Now let's talk triangles

There are only a few things you need to know about angles and triangles for the SAT, many of which are given to you at the beginning of each math section. This chapter is going to be long because there are a lot of different kinds of questions you might be asked and I want you to see all of them, but don't be daunted; I'm willing to bet you already know pretty much everything you need to know.

Now, as always, you just need to study the scouting report: know what the SAT will throw at you, and you'll have a better chance of knocking it out of the park. Note also that for now, I'm only going to cover non-right triangles. I'll devote the next chapter to the special case of right triangles (and the double-special cases therein).

➔ The sum of the measures of the angles in a triangle is 180°.

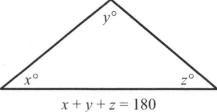

$$x + y + z = 180$$

➔ The area of a triangle can be found with $A = \dfrac{1}{2}bh$.

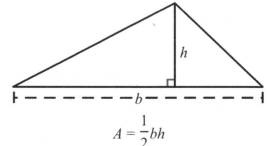

$$A = \dfrac{1}{2}bh$$

➔ In an isosceles triangle, the angles across from the equal sides are also equal.

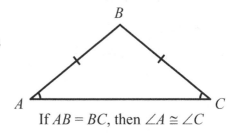

If $AB = BC$, then $\angle A \cong \angle C$

➔ In an isosceles triangle, a segment from the non-equal side to the opposite vertex is perpendicular to that side. This is called a perpendicular bisector.

If $\overline{AB} = \overline{BC}$ and D is the midpoint of $\overline{AC}$, then $\overline{BD} \perp \overline{AC}$

➔ In an equilateral triangle, all the angles are 60°, and all the sides are of equal length.

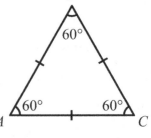

➔ The bigger the angle, the bigger its opposite side.

If $x < y < z$, then $AB < BC < AC$

➔ No side of a triangle can be as long as or longer than the sum of the lengths of the other two sides.

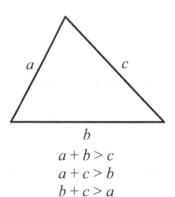

$$a + b > c$$
$$a + c > b$$
$$b + c > a$$

This last one is called the *Triangle Inequality Theorem*. The basic thrust: if the length of one side were equal to the sum of the lengths of the other two, would you have a triangle? No, you'd just have a straight line segment. And if one side were *longer* than the other two put together, then how would those two shorter ones connect to form the triangle? As hard as they might try, those poor little guys couldn't reach each other. They'd create a sadness gap. You don't want to make them make a sadness gap, do you?

To drive this home: imagine your forearms (apologies to my armless friends) are two sides of a triangle, and the imaginary line that connects your elbows is the third side. If you touch your fingertips together and pull your elbows apart, eventually

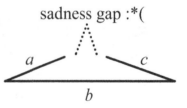

your fingertips have to disconnect...that's when the length between your elbows is longer than the sum of the lengths of your forearms. Neat, huh?

Similarity and congruence

When triangles are *similar*, they have all the same angles, and their corresponding sides are proportional to each other.[*] On the right, triangles

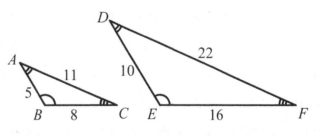

ABC and *DEF* are similar—their angles are all the same and the corresponding sides of *DEF* are twice the length of the corresponding sides of *ABC*.

---

* Fun fact: because every equilateral triangle has three 60° angles, all equilateral triangles are similar to each other.

You probably remember the similarity rules from your geometry class, but let's quickly review them here.

➜ **AA (Angle-Angle).** If two triangles have two pairs of congruent angles, then the triangles are similar. (You might know this one as AAA—same thing.)

➜ **SAS (Side-Angle-Side).** If two triangles have corresponding sides that are proportional in length, and the angles between those sides are congruent, then the triangles are similar.

➜ **SSS (Side-Side-Side).** If all the sides of one triangle are each proportional in length to the sides of another triangle, then the triangles are similar.

It's a good idea for you to be able to recognize common similar triangle configurations quickly. Have a look at the two figures below.

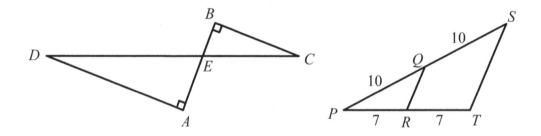

Look at the figure on the left first. $\angle A$ and $\angle B$ are right angles, so obviously those are congruent. Because $\angle BEC$ and $\angle AED$ are vertical angles, they are also congruent. Therefore, AA says you can bet your bottom dollar that $\triangle BEC$ is similar to $\triangle AED$!

On the right, note that $PQ = 10$, and $PS = 20$. Likewise, $PR = 7$, and $PT = 14$. So two sides of $\triangle PQR$ are proportional in length to two sides of $\triangle PST$. Because the angle between those sides is $\angle P$ for both triangles, and $\angle P$ is congruent to itself, $\triangle PQR$ is similar to $\triangle PST$ by SAS. Because in this case you know the ratio of the sides of $\triangle PQR$ to the sides of $\triangle PST$, you know that $\overline{ST}$ will be twice the length of $\overline{QR}$. Easy, right?

When the sides of similar triangles are in a 1:1 ratio—in other words, their sides are exactly the same—we say the triangles are *congruent*. That's right:

triangle congruence is really just a special case of triangle similarity. You'll probably remember that there are a bunch of special geometry theorems that can be used to prove triangle congruency,* but for SAT purposes, you don't really need to memorize them. If you know the conditions of triangle similarity well, and you know that congruence is when triangles are similar and their sides are in a 1:1 ratio, then you need not over-clutter your brain with a bunch of special case congruency rules.

Example 2: Calculator

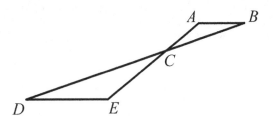

Note: Figure not drawn to scale.

In the figure above, the perimeter of $\triangle ABC$ is 15, and $\overline{AB} \parallel \overline{DE}$. If the ratio of AC to AE is 1:3, what is the perimeter of $\triangle EDC$?

A) 60

B) 45

C) 30

D) 5

OK, so the first thing you need to recognize is that you've got similar triangles here. Because $\overline{AB}$ and $\overline{DE}$ are parallel, angles A and E are congruent, and angles B and D are congruent. Of course, the angles in each triangle at point C are congruent because they're vertical.

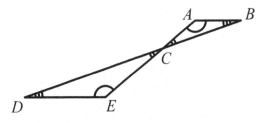

---

* Angle-Side-Angle (ASA), Angle-Angle-Side (AAS), Side-Angle-Side (SAS), Side-Side-Side (SSS)

Once you've got that bit down, you need to deal with the ratio. If $\frac{AC}{AE}=\frac{1}{3}$, then $\frac{AC}{CE}=\frac{1}{2}$. WHAAAT!? I'm throwing tricky ratio conversions at you in a triangle question!? What am I, some kind of sadist? No, silly. I'm just trying to prepare you for a test that is famous for testing multiple concepts at once.

If the ratio of AC to CE is 1:2, then the ratios of all the sides of $\triangle ABC$ to their corresponding sides in $\triangle EDC$ will be 1:2. Therefore, if the perimeter of $\triangle ABC$ is 15, the perimeter of $\triangle EDC$ will be 30. That's **choice C.**

So, that's basically it for triangles. Cool, right? It might feel like a lot, but just think back on everything you had to know when you were in the real thick of it with geometry. There's an *awful* lot to know about triangles if you're doing regular school math. You will never need to know the really arcane stuff like circumcenters or orthocenters of triangles. (Google them if you want a reminder, you lunatic.)

There are some who think you need to know things like the external angle rule, or rules about alternate interior angles and opposite exterior angles in transversals. I say that if you know a straight line measures 180° and you know a triangle's angles add up to 180°, you already know them! Why over-complicate your life with overlapping rules?

Polygons

The last thing we should touch on here is polygons. Polygons land in this chapter because they don't appear often enough to warrant their own chapter, and because, really, the best way to think about polygons is that they're just a bunch of triangles stuck together. Look:

That's a pentagon (5 sides) and an octagon (8 sides), broken into 5 and 8 triangles, respectively. Any convex* polygon with n sides can be broken into n triangles.

Some polygon facts worth knowing:

→ A polygon with n vertices has n sides.

→ A *regular* polygon is one in which all sides are the same length and all angles have the same measure. Although we typically use their simpler names, we can say that a square is a regular quadrilateral and an equilateral triangle is a regular triangle. The pentagon and octagon we were just looking at happen to be regular.

→ The sum of the degree measures of the interior angles in a convex polygon with n sides (sometimes called an "n-gon") can be found thusly:

$$180(n-2)$$

For example, a 5-sided polygon will have interior angles adding up to:

$$180(5-2)=180(3)=540 \text{ degrees}$$

→ In a regular n-gon, the degree measure of any interior angle is:

$$\frac{180(n-2)}{n}$$

For example, each interior angle in a 5-sided regular polygon will be:

$$\frac{180(5-2)}{5}=\frac{540}{5}=108 \text{ degrees}$$

→ The sum of the measures of the exterior angles of *any* polygon is 360°.

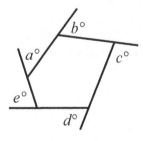

$$a+b+c+d+e=360$$

---

* A convex polygon is any polygon where every interior angle has a measure that is less than 180°. The SAT isn't going to subject you to concave polygons or other weird stuff like that.

➔ A regular polygon with *n* sides has *n* axes of symmetry. That is to say, you can fold a 7-sided regular polygon (called a heptagon) exactly in half along 7 different lines through the polygon. For example, each segment cutting through the regular heptagon below is an axis of symmetry. There are 7 of them.

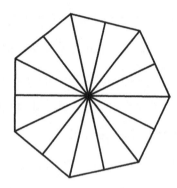

➔ When you break a regular hexagon into triangles as we were doing before, you form 6 equilateral triangles. (This might seem weirdly specific for me to be listing here, but it appeared a few times on the old SAT and it appears once in the current Official Tests, too. Someone over there likes to test this fact.)

Example 3: Calculator

The figure above shows a regular hexagon with two labeled vertices, *A* and *B*. If *AB* = 12, what is the perimeter of the hexagon?

A) 36

B) $36\sqrt{3}$

C) 72

D) $54\sqrt{3}$

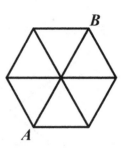

To solve this, just remember that neat fact I was *just* mentioning: that regular hexagons break out into equilateral triangles! If all those triangles are equilateral, and *AB* = 12, then each side of each triangle must have a length of 6. So the perimeter of the hexagon is 6 × 6 = 36. That's **choice A**.

Try angles.

1 No calculator

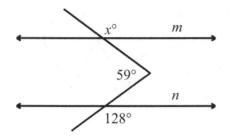

Note: Figure not drawn to scale.

In the figure above, $m \parallel n$. What is the value of x ?

A) 128

B) 167

C) 171

D) 173

2 No calculator

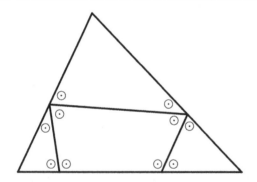

What is the sum of the measures of the marked (⊙) angles in the figure above?

A) 360°

B) 720°

C) 900°

D) 1080°

3 No calculator

If $\triangle RST$ is isosceles, $RS = 9$, and RT and ST are integers, then which of the following is NOT a possible perimeter of $\triangle RST$?

A) 15

B) 19

C) 22

D) 69

4 No calculator; Grid-in

What is the sum of the measures, in degrees, of the marked angles in the figure above?

5 No calculator; Grid-in

The area of a regular hexagon is $24\sqrt{3}$. What is its perimeter?

Try angles.

6 Calculator

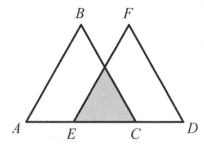

Note: Figure not drawn to scale.

In the figure above, $\triangle ABC$ and $\triangle DEF$ are congruent equilateral triangles. If E is the midpoint of $\overline{AC}$, and $AB = 14$, what is the perimeter of the shaded region?

A) 7

B) 14

C) 21

D) 28

7 Calculator

In $\triangle PQR$, $PQ > PR$. Which of the following MUST be true?

I $\quad PQ - QR < PR$

II $\quad$ The measure of $\angle PRQ$ is greater than the measure of $\angle PQR$

III $\quad 2PR > PQ$

A) I only

B) II only

C) I and II only

D) I, II, and III

8 Calculator

Note: Figure not drawn to scale.

If $y = 180 - x$ and all the triangle's side lengths are integers, which of the following could be the perimeter of the triangle in the figure above?

A) 19

B) 22

C) 23

D) 24

9 Calculator; Grid-in

The average interior angle measure in an irregular polygon with n sides is 156. What is the value of n ?

10 Calculator; Grid-in

The average of the measures of the exterior angles on a certain polygon is 22.5°. How many vertices does the polygon have?

Answers:

1	D		6	C
2	B		7	C
3	A		8	D
4	360		9	15
5	24		10	16

Solutions on page 392.

The following selected Official Test questions will show you how this content might appear on the test.

Test	Section	Questions
1	3: No calculator	17
	4: Calculator	3
2	3: No calculator	6, 8, 18
	4: Calculator	30, 36
3	3: No calculator	11, 18
	4: Calculator	
4	3: No calculator	16
	4: Calculator	
5	3: No calculator	20
	4: Calculator	36
6	3: No calculator	18
	4: Calculator	16
7	3: No calculator	17
	4: Calculator	14
8	3: No calculator	4
	4: Calculator	5
9	3: No calculator	
	4: Calculator	7
10	3: No calculator	8, 12
	4: Calculator	32
PSAT/NMSQT 1	3: No calculator	4
	4: Calculator	
PSAT/NMSQT 2	3: No calculator	11
	4: Calculator	

Right Triangles and Basic Trigonometry

So now that we've covered angles, and triangles in general, let's have a look at a special case. Right triangles get a chapter to themselves because they're special, and have rules of their very own. Like that one friend of yours whose parents let him get away with everything.

Ancient Greece was awesome

First, let's *briefly* discuss the **Pythagorean theorem**. You know this, yes? It is, after all, pretty much the most important thing to have come out of Ancient Greece.[*] Basically it says that the sum of the squares of the legs (short sides) of a right triangle are equal to the square of the hypotenuse (longest side, across from the right angle). Oh, you know it? OK, good.

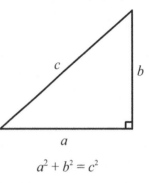

$$a^2 + b^2 = c^2$$

Example 1: Calculator

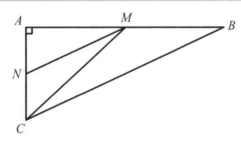

Note: Figure not drawn to scale.

In the figure above, $AC = 6$, $BC = 10$, and $CM = 2\sqrt{13}$. If N is the midpoint of $\overline{AC}$, what is $BM + MN$?

A) $3 + \sqrt{13}$

B) 9

C) $4 + 5\sqrt{3}$

D) 13

---

[*]   There was also, like, democracy and stuff.

Let's start by filling in what we know, which is how you should start basically every geometry problem you ever do. This diagram just contains what we're given. The slightly thicker lines, of course, are what we're trying to find.

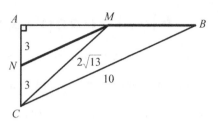

Note that we have two out of three sides of two different right triangles: $\triangle ABC$ and $\triangle ACM$. Let's Pythagorize (not a word) them both:

$$\triangle ABC: 6^2 + AB^2 = 10^2$$
$$36 + AB^2 = 100$$
$$AB^2 = 64$$
$$\boldsymbol{AB = 8}$$

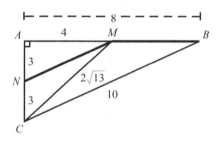

$$\triangle ACM: 6^2 + AM^2 = (2\sqrt{13})^2$$
$$36 + AM^2 = 52$$
$$AM^2 = 16$$
$$\boldsymbol{AM = 4}$$

OK, we've got BM now…it's $8 - 4 = 4$. Easy. How do we find MN? Help us Pythagoras, you're our only hope!

$$3^2 + 4^2 = MN^2$$
$$9 + 16 = MN^2$$
$$25 = MN^2$$
$$\boldsymbol{5 = MN}$$

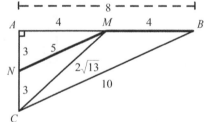

So our answer is $5 + 4 = 9$. That's choice **B**. Ain't no thang.

Special right triangles

Now, are you ready for some amazing news? Even though you should absolutely know the Pythagorean theorem inside out, you actually don't have to use it very often on the SAT provided you know the five special right triangles. *Five!? But they only give me two at the beginning of each section!* I know. I'mma give you some extra ones. You're welcome.

Above are the two special rights you're given at the beginning of every math section: the 45°-45°-90° (his friends call him "isosceles right") and the 30°-60°-90° triangles. Know the ratios of their sides cold…you'll need them often.

You should also know how to deal with a common SAT special right triangle trick: providing a whole number for the side that's usually associated with a radical. For example, the SAT might try to throw you by giving you a 45°-45°-90° with a hypotenuse of 20. Don't panic if this happens. Just divide the hypotenuse by $\sqrt{2}$ to find the legs. $\frac{20}{\sqrt{2}} = 10\sqrt{2}$, so the legs of a 45°-45°-90° triangle with a hypotenuse of 20 are each $10\sqrt{2}$.

Pythagorean triples

Below are three common right triangles that you *aren't* given in the beginning of each section, but nonetheless appear on the SAT—the first one quite often.

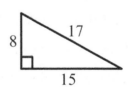

There's nothing worth saying about the angles; what's important are the sides. There aren't that many sets of integers that work nicely with each other in the Pythagorean theorem, but these three (and all their multiples) do.[*] These are called **Pythagorean Triples**, and you'll be seeing a bunch of them as you prep for

---

[*] There are actually a whole bunch of Pythagorean triples, including (7-24-25), (9-40-41), (11-60-61), (12-35-37), (13-84-85), etc. You get the point. For the purposes of the SAT, you probably needn't worry about all of these. I've noted the ones that appear on the test commonly above.

the SAT. Note that we saw the 3-4-5 (and its big brother the 6-8-10) in the example problem a few pages ago.

It's not *necessary* to know these, but quick recognition of them will save you 30 seconds of old-Greek-guy work. This is the kind of trend recognition that will pay off in small increments for you as you continue on your quest for SAT hegemony. Here are the few Pythagorean Triples I recommend you memorize (in convenient table form!):

3-4-5	**5-12-13**	**8-15-17**
6-8-10	10-24-26	16-30-34
9-12-15		
12-16-20		
15-20-25		

One more important note on right triangles

Remember that every part of an SAT problem (even the answer choices) might contain clues about the solution. If you see $\sqrt{2}$, $\sqrt{3}$, or any other radical in the answer choices for a hard question, that's a clue! There's a pretty good chance that a right triangle is involved—even if you don't see one in the figure provided. More on this when we get to working in 3-D on page 279.

Trigonometry

Look, when I first found out that the SAT was going to be including trigonometry, I got kinda nervous. Lots of people (myself included) find trig fun, but lots of other people find it really intimidating. And then you know what happened? College Board released some tests, and it turns out the only thing they care about you knowing is SOH-CAH-TOA. That's right—the only trig you need for the SAT is the most basic of basic trigonometry.[*] Trig haters rejoice! You're probably never even going to need to use the SIN, COS, or TAN keys on your calculator.

So, let's just cover our bases and talk for a minute about what SOH-CAH-TOA means, in case any of you were taught trigonometry by a math teacher who

---

[*] As you're certainly aware if you've studied trigonometry for any length of time, trig can be useful in many non-right-triangle situations, but those apparently won't be showing up on the SAT.

somehow resisted using the easiest, most ubiquitous math mnemonic ever. The letters in SOH-CAH-TOA stand for: $\text{Sine} = \dfrac{\text{Opposite}}{\text{Hypotenuse}}$, $\text{Cosine} = \dfrac{\text{Adjacent}}{\text{Hypotenuse}}$, and $\text{Tangent} = \dfrac{\text{Opposite}}{\text{Adjacent}}$. A bit of notation applies here: when we want to know what the sine of an angle is, say, the sine of angle A, we write "$\sin A$." The cosine and tangent of angle A would be written "$\cos A$" and "$\tan A$," respectively. I know, I know—you know this and I'm boring you. Just humor me for one more minute, and let's look at what that means in the context of a simple right triangle:

$$\sin A = \frac{a}{c} \qquad \cos A = \frac{b}{c} \qquad \tan A = \frac{a}{b}$$

$$\sin B = \frac{b}{c} \qquad \cos B = \frac{a}{c} \qquad \tan B = \frac{b}{a}$$

See how $\sin B = \cos A$, and $\sin A = \cos B$? That's important—it's always going to be true with complementary angles (AKA angles whose measures add up to 90°). *If two angles add up to 90°, the sine of one equals the cosine of the other.*

One last note before we do an example: *SOH-CAH-TOA only works in right triangles.* It's easy to remember this if you remember that only a right triangle has a hypotenuse: if you don't have a hypotenuse, then the H's in SOH-CAH-TOA are meaningless!

Example 2: No calculator; Grid-in

In triangle *DEF*, the measure of angle E is 90°, and the tangent of angle D equals $\dfrac{3}{4}$. What is the value of $\cos F$?

At first, it might not look like you've got much to go on here. But of course, you have plenty. First, draw the thing:

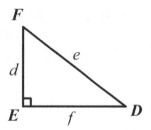

I've put placeholders in for the side lengths at the moment. We're told that $\tan D = \dfrac{3}{4}$. We know from our drawing that $\tan D = \dfrac{d}{f}$. Let's see what happens if we just plug in 3 for d and 4 for f. (You should be slowly nodding at this point, mouth slightly open, as this beautiful solution unfolds.) We just talked about Pythagorean triples, so I *know* you know that the hypotenuse of this triangle is 5 if the legs are 3 and 4.

What's the cosine of $\angle F$? Easy: The adjacent leg to $\angle F$ has a length of 3, and the hypotenuse of the triangle has a length of 5. So $\cos F = \dfrac{3}{5}$, and you grid in either **3/5** or **.6**.

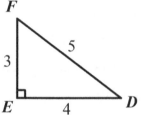

But wait! Why were we allowed to just plug in back there? Great question. Remember our discussion of similar triangles on page 239? When we learn the tangent of $\angle D$, we learn that we have Angle-Angle similarity with *every* right triangle where an angle has that tangent value. We could have plugged in any two numbers in a ratio of 3 to 4 and landed on the same final answer, so I went with the easiest ones to work with. Isn't math the coolest?

Practice questions: Right Triangles and Basic Trigonometry

You love triangles, right?

1 No calculator

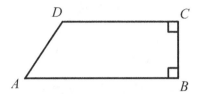

Note: Figure not drawn to scale.

In the figure above, $AB = 11$, $AD = 5$, and $DC = 8$. What is the perimeter of quadrilateral $ABCD$?

A) 24

B) 28

C) 29

D) 30

2 No calculator

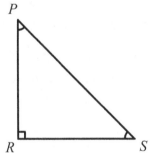

In the figure above, $\angle RPS$ and $\angle RSP$ each measure $45°$. If $PS = 10$, what is RS ?

A) $5\sqrt{2}$

B) $5\sqrt{3}$

C) 10

D) $10\sqrt{2}$

3 No calculator

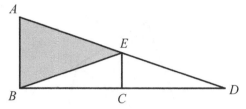

Note: Figure not drawn to scale.

In the figure above, $\overline{AB} \perp \overline{BD}$, $\overline{EC} \perp \overline{BD}$ and $\overline{EC}$ bisects both $\overline{BD}$ and $\overline{AD}$. If $ED = 13$ and $EC = 5$, what is the area of the shaded region?

A) 120

B) 90

C) 60

D) 40

4 No calculator; Grid-in

In the figure above, the sine of $n°$ is 0.4. What is the cosine of $m°$?

5 No calculator; Grid-in

If $\angle A$ and $\angle B$ are acute angles and $\cos A = \sin B$, then what is the sum of the measures of $\angle A$ and $\angle B$ in degrees? (Disregard the degree symbol when gridding your answer.)

Practice questions: Right Triangles and Basic Trigonometry

You love triangles, right?

6 Calculator

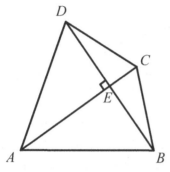

Note: Figure not drawn to scale.

In the figure above, point E lies on $\overline{AC}$ and is the midpoint of $\overline{BD}$. If $CD = 13$, $BD = 24$, and $AC = 21$, which of the following equals AB ?

A) $13\sqrt{2}$

B) $10\sqrt{5}$

C) 20

D) 22

7 Calculator

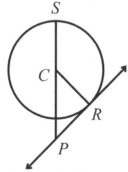

In the figure above, the line containing points P and R is tangent to the circle at R, and $\overline{CR}$ is a radius of length 3. If the measure of $\angle RCS$ is $135°$, what is the length of $\overline{SP}$?

A) $4\sqrt{2}$ (approximately 5.66)

B) 6

C) $3 + 3\sqrt{2}$ (approximately 7.24)

D) $6\sqrt{2}$ (approximately 8.49)

8 Calculator

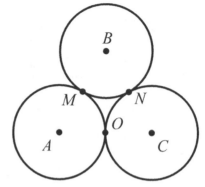

In the figure above, three congruent circles with centers A, B, and C are tangent to each other at M, N, and O. If $BO = 18$, what is the area of one of the circles?

A) $18\pi\sqrt{3}$

B) 72π

C) 81π

D) 108π

9 Calculator; Grid-in

In a right triangle, the hypotenuse has a length of 15 and the sine of one angle is $\dfrac{4}{5}$. What is the length of the triangle's shortest side?

10 Calculator; Grid-in

In triangle ABC, the measure of $\angle B$ is $90°$ and the value of $\sin A$ is $\dfrac{12}{13}$. What is the value of $\tan C$?

Answers:

1	B		6	C
2	A		7	C
3	C		8	D
4	.4 or 2/5		9	9
5	90		10	.416, .417, or 5/12

Solutions on page 394.

The following selected Official Test questions all about right triangles or trigonometry, and often both.

Test	Section	Questions
1	3: No calculator	19
	4: Calculator	
2	3: No calculator	19
	4: Calculator	36
3	3: No calculator	20
	4: Calculator	23
4	3: No calculator	17
	4: Calculator	
5	3: No calculator	
	4: Calculator	19
6	3: No calculator	18
	4: Calculator	
7	3: No calculator	
	4: Calculator	36
8	3: No calculator	
	4: Calculator	36
9	3: No calculator	19
	4: Calculator	25, 31
10	3: No calculator	12
	4: Calculator	30
PSAT/NMSQT 1	3: No calculator	
	4: Calculator	26
PSAT/NMSQT 2	3: No calculator	
	4: Calculator	

Circles, Radians, and a Little More Trigonometry

If you're like most students I know, then circles aren't exactly your favorite thing. You've got decent reasons for that: there are lots of ways to ask tough questions involving circles and lots of ways to incorporate circles into tough questions that are also about other geometrical or algebraic concepts. But don't despair! I'll tell you what you need to know, and it's not *that* much.

Here are the basics, which you're told in the beginning of every section. For circles with radius r and diameter d:

➔ The area of a circle can be calculated using $A = \pi r^2$.

➔ The circumference of a circle can be calculated using $C = 2\pi r$ (or $C = \pi d$).

➔ The number of degrees of arc in a circle is 360.

➔ The number of radians of arc in a circle is 2π.

I trust you have little problem with the facts above, but please remember that you don't need to be a memory hero—they're given to you in the beginning of each math section, and there's no shame in checking your formulas.

Tangents, secants, chords, and angles

Of course, if all the SAT asked about was *that* stuff, then I wouldn't even need to include a circles chapter in this book. Here are some other pieces of terminology you should know:

➔ A line is a *secant* line if it goes through a circle, intersecting the circle twice. The segment of the secant
that's actually inside the circle is called a *chord*. I don't
actually think you'll see the words secant or chord on
the SAT, but you still might see the concepts appear in
circle questions.

➔ A line is *tangent* to a circle when it intersects the circle at
exactly one point. A tangent line is always perpendicular
to the radius it intersects.

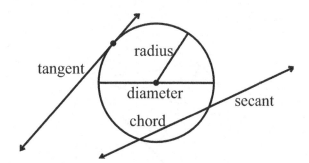

➔ The degree measure of an arc is equal to the degree measure of its central angle. In the figure on the right, The measure of arc *DF* is the same as the measure of ∠*DOF*.

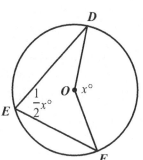

➔ When two chords intersect on a circle, they create what's called an *inscribed angle*. The measure of an inscribed angle is half the measure of the central angle that goes to the same intercepted arc. In the figure on the right, ∠*DEF* is inscribed, and the measure of ∠*DEF* is half the measure of ∠*DOF*.

➔ If you draw radii from the center of a circle to two ends of a chord, you're always creating an isosceles triangle because radii are always congruent. In the figure on the right, $\overline{PR}$ is a chord, and △*POR* is isosceles.

    ⇨ This means you can always draw a perpendicular bisector from the center of a circle to the midpoint of a chord. In the figure on the right, *M* is the midpoint of $\overline{AB}$, and therefore $\overline{OM} \perp \overline{AB}$.

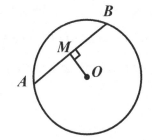

➔ There are a lot of theorems about chords, secants, and the angles they create that you don't need to know. If you're presented with a question that contains a chord that's not covered by the basics above, it's almost certainly a triangle question. In that case, of course, your job is to find the triangle.

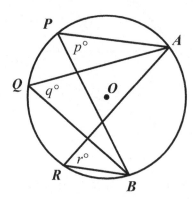

In the figure above, $\angle APB$, $\angle AQB$, and $\angle ARB$, measuring $p°$, $q°$, and $r°$, respectively, are inscribed in the circle with center O. Which of the following equations or inequalities must be true?

A) $p < q < r$

B) $p = q = r$

C) $\dfrac{p+r}{2} < q$

D) $p + q + r = 180$

The only thing you need to recognize to get this question right is that all three angles intercept the same arc *AB*. They're all, therefore, going to have the same angle measure. Choice D *might* be true in one special case where all three angles measure 60°, but **choice B** *must* be true, always.

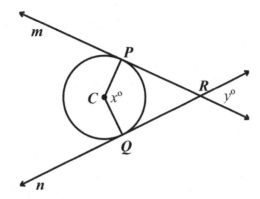

In the figure above, lines *m* and *n* are tangent to the circle at points *P* and *Q*, respectively, and *C* is the center of the circle. If *x* = 130, what is *y*?

This one isn't so bad at all if you know the rule about tangents being perpendicular to radii. Those tangent lines make 90° angles with $\overline{CP}$ and $\overline{CQ}$, and we know the measure of ∠*PCQ* is 130°. So we know 3 of the 4 angles in a quadrilateral. Since the angles in a quadrilateral add up to 360°*, we can easily calculate the fourth:

$$360° - 130° - 90° - 90° = 50°$$

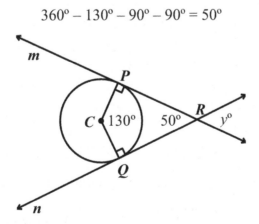

Since the angle marked *y*° is vertical to ∠*PRQ*, which measures 50°, ***y* = 50**.

---

* This is an extension of a rule you know: that the angles in a triangle add up to 180°. A quadrilateral is just two triangles mashed together! To see this, draw segment $\overline{CR}$.

Rolling wheels

I'm not really sure this little fact warrants its own header, but it's important to mention, and it doesn't fit nicely anywhere else. So here you go: When a wheel is rolling, it makes one revolution for every one circumference traveled, and vice versa.

Example 3: Calculator; Grid-in

A certain wheel has a radius of $\dfrac{1}{4\pi}$ meters. If the wheel rolls in a straight line without slipping for 10 meters, how many revolutions does it make?

Remember that a wheel makes one complete revolution when it travels a distance of one circumference. So if we can figure out how many circumferences go into 10 meters, we're good to go.

The circumference of a wheel with a radius of $\dfrac{1}{4\pi}$ meters is:

$$C = 2\pi r$$
$$C = 2\pi \left(\frac{1}{4\pi} \right)$$
$$C = \frac{1}{2} \text{ or } 0.5$$

Now that we know the wheel has a circumference of 0.5 meters, we can calculate how many revolutions it makes when it travels 10 meters by dividing.

$$\frac{10 \text{ meters}}{0.5 \text{ meters per revolution}} = 20 \text{ revolutions}$$

Not too shabby, right? Now let's get into my favorite kind of circle questions.

Sector areas and arc lengths

All of the above is well and good (and important), but if you want to be invincible on SAT circle questions, then we're only just getting started. Here's something else you have to know: some circle problems are actually ratio problems in disguise!

Let me 'splain. Picture a circle with radius 4. It'll have an area of $\pi(4)^2 = 16\pi$. Now, if I asked you for half of its area, that's easy, right? 8π. What about a 25% of its area? Still easy: 4π. What about the area of a 45° sector* of that circle? Hmm...

Wait a minute. Isn't this still easy? 45° is $\frac{1}{8}$ of 360°, is it not? So wouldn't the area of that sector simply be $\frac{1}{8}$ of 16π, or 2π? Yes, indeed it would. And in fact, finding the area of a sector (or the length of an arc) will *always* be this easy, as long as you know its central angle and its radius.

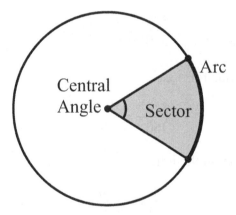

We can solve for the various parts of this circle with the following ratio:

$$\frac{\text{part}}{\text{whole}} = \frac{\text{part}}{\text{whole}}$$

Which can be expanded out into a more battle-ready form:

$$\frac{\text{Degree Measure of Central Angle}}{360°} = \frac{\text{Arc Length}}{\text{Circumference}} = \frac{\text{Area of Sector}\left(A_{sector}\right)}{\text{Area of Whole}\left(A_{whole}\right)}$$

If you can complete just one of these fractions (for example, if you know the ratio of arc length to circumference), you can figure out everything else. Often, all

---

* A sector is a part of a circle enclosed by two radii and their intercepted arc. But that's awfully technical. Most people I know just call it a pizza slice—see the diagram on this page.

you'll get will be the radius and a central angle, but as you're about to see, that's *plenty.*

Let's use these ratios to find the area and perimeter of PacMan. First, calculate the area and circumference of the whole circle (PacMan with his mouth closed):

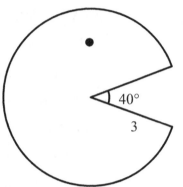

$$A_{whole} = \pi(3)^2 \qquad\qquad C = 2\pi(3)$$
$$A_{whole} = 9\pi \qquad\qquad\qquad C = 6\pi$$

Now we can use the angle of PacMan's gaping maw to find what we're looking for. Note that since PacMan's mouth is open at a 40° angle (which is empty space), we're actually looking for the part of the circle that is 320°. Let's tackle his area first:

$$\frac{320°}{360°} = \frac{A_{PacMan}}{A_{whole}}$$

Substitute in our value for A_{whole}:

$$\frac{320°}{360°} = \frac{A_{PacMan}}{9\pi}$$

Simplify the fraction on the left:

$$\frac{8}{9} = \frac{A_{PacMan}}{9\pi}$$

So we've solved for PacMan's area:

$$8\pi = A_{PacMan}$$

The process for his perimeter is very similar. Now, instead of looking for a part of the whole area of the circle, though, we're looking for a part of its circumference:

$$\frac{320°}{360°} = \frac{\text{Arc Length}_{PacMan}}{C}$$

Substitute, simplify, and solve:

$$\frac{8}{9} = \frac{\text{Arc Length}_{PacMan}}{6\pi}$$

$$\frac{16}{3}\pi = \text{Arc Length}_{PacMan}$$

But wait! We're not *quite* done yet. That's just the arc length around PacMan. To find his perimeter, we have to add the top and bottom of his mouth, too.

$$\frac{16}{3}\pi + 6 = P_{PacMan}$$

There we go. Arc length and sector area questions: not so bad, right? Don't panic, just work with the ratios.

I want to spend a *little* more time on arc length.

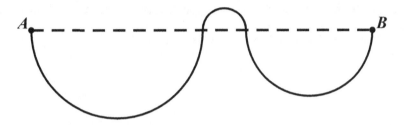

In the figure above, three semicircles with centers on $\overline{AB}$ form a continuous path from point A to point B. If the straight line distance between A and B is 26, what is the length of the path?

A) 13π

B) 18π

C) 26π

D) 51π

I know it might feel weird and like you don't have enough information, but consider plugging in. Say the diameters of the semicircles, from left to right, are 14, 2, and 10. That way, they add up to 26, just like they're supposed to.

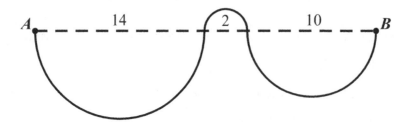

So your radii, then, are 7, 1, and 5, respectively. If you had full circles, you'd have circumferences of 14π, 2π, and 10π, respectively.

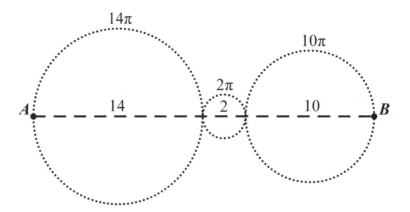

But you *don't* have full circles—you've got half circles. So your arc lengths are all half of their respective full circumferences, or 7π, π, and 5π, respectively. Sum those up and you get 13π, your total arc length. The answer is **A**.

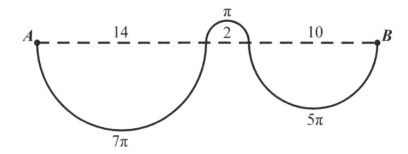

But wait a minute—we just plugged in random numbers! No way we're allowed to do that! Au contraire, mi amigo. We are *totally* allowed to do that. Try it again with different numbers. Say now our original diameters are 20, 2, and 4.

You'll get the same answer: $10\pi + \pi + 2\pi = 13\pi$. Diameters of 17, 1, and 8, will give you $8.5\pi + 0.5\pi + 4\pi = 13\pi$. As long as your diameters add up to 26, you'll get 13π as your answer.

In fact—and this is *really* cool—when semicircles* connect to form a continuous path between two points that lie on the same line as the semicircles' centers, like they do in this question, the arc lengths of the semicircles add up to the length of a single semicircular arc connecting the same two points.

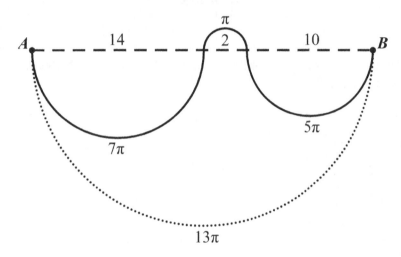

So there. Now you have something to impress your friends with at the next party you go to.

Circle equation

Yep, that's right. You have to know the equation of a circle in the *xy*-plane, even though you probably won't be asked about it. :/

Standard Equation of a Circle

$$(x - h)^2 + (y - k)^2 = r^2$$

(h, k) is the circle's center in the *xy*-plane; r is the circle's radius.

There are a couple things you'll need to be able to do with that. The first is easy: given an equation in that form, you'll need to remember it well enough to know which piece is which.

---
* Remember: A semicircle is exactly half a circle, not just part of a circle.

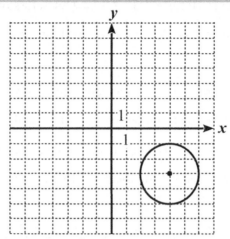

The figure above shows a circle in the *xy*-plane. Which of the following is the equation for that circle?

A) $(x - 4)^2 + (y + 3)^2 = 4$

B) $(x + 4)^2 + (y - 3)^2 = 2$

C) $(x + 4)^2 + (y + 3)^2 = 2$

D) $(x - 4)^2 + (y - 3)^2 = 4$

The center of that circle, you can see, is (4, –3). The radius of that circle is 2. You can plug those values into the standard circle equation to see that the correct answer is **A**:

$$(x - h)^2 + (y - k)^2 = r^2$$
$$(x - 4)^2 + (y - (-3))^2 = 2^2$$
$$(x - 4)^2 + (y + 3)^2 = 4$$

Lest you start thinking all circle equation questions will be cakewalks, though, I should tell you about the other thing you'll need to be ready to do on test day: complete the square. Yep, that's right. You might get a circle question where you have to complete the square to get a circle equation into the standard form. I know—I can't really believe it either. And yet, here we are.

$$x^2 + y^2 - 4x + 6y = 12$$

The equation above is that of a circle in the xy-plane. What is the circle's diameter?

It's best to start by doing a little rearranging, knowing that we're going to want to eventually have two binomial squares to wrestle this thing into the standard equation. To do that, we're going to complete the square, just as we did in the parabolas chapter (p 131).

$$x^2 - 4x + y^2 + 6y = 12$$

The key to completing the square is really knowing your binomial squares well—refer back to page 123 if you could use a refresher. Specifically, you need to be able to look at $x^2 - 4x$ and $y^2 + 6y$ and see the beginnings of perfect binomial squares, which you'll then complete.

I recognize $x^2 - 4x$ as the beginning of $(x - 2)^2 = x^2 - 4x + ④$ and I recognize $y^2 + 6y$ as the beginning of $(y + 3)^2 = y^2 + 6y + ⑨$ That tells me I'm going to need to add that circled 4 and that circled 9 to complete my squares. Remember—if you're going to add something to one side of an equation, you have to add it to the other side, too!

$$x^2 - 4x + ④ + y^2 + 6y + ⑨ = 12 + ④ + ⑨$$

$$x^2 - 4x + 4 + y^2 + 6y + 9 = 25$$

$$(x - 2)^2 + (y + 3)^2 = 5^2$$

So now we know the radius of the circle is 5. (We also know the center is at (2, –3), but we don't need that to answer this question.) Don't fall for the trap! The question asks for diameter, not radius, so the answer is **10**.

Radians

Holy cow, can you believe we're still doing circles!? I don't know who to feel sorrier for—me for having to write all this or you for having to study it all. Maybe we each deserve some sympathy. Sigh.

Anyway, the last thing we need to talk about here is radians, and honestly they're not so bad. You've probably dealt with them in school at least a little bit, and the level at which the SAT deals with them is pretty basic.[*] So! Here's what you need to know.

Radians are an angle measure that's used in circles: 1 radian is the central angle that inscribes an arc that's the same length as the radius. There are 2π radians of arc in a circle because the full circumference of a circle is $2\pi r$. Cool, right?

You can always convert from radians to degrees or vice versa using this relationship: 2π radians = 360°. So if you want to convert $\dfrac{5\pi}{6}$ radians to degrees, use a ratio:

$$\frac{\left(\dfrac{5\pi}{6}\right)}{2\pi}=\frac{x°}{360°}$$

$$\frac{5}{12}=\frac{x°}{360°}$$

$$150°=x°$$

Likewise, you can convert degrees to radians. Here's converting 80° to radians:

$$\frac{x}{2\pi}=\frac{80°}{360°}$$

---

[*] This is one of the many places in this book where I need to remind you that relative lack of actual test questions to go with makes me a bit nervous. There are only two questions involving radians in all the tests that have been released at the time of this writing. Given what we've seen, radians appear to be an afterthought, but let's not totally ignore the possibility that a tough radians question will appear once in a great while.

$$\frac{x}{2\pi} = \frac{2}{9}$$

$$x = \frac{4\pi}{9}$$

You should totally try these! (Answers are at the bottom of the page.)

✎ Convert 120° to radians

✎ Convert 200° to radians

✎ Convert $\frac{\pi}{9}$ radians to degrees

✎ Convert $\frac{7\pi}{6}$ radians to degrees

There are a few radian measures that you'll want to memorize. They corre-spond to the angles you already have memorized because they're super special. Look, I've summarized them in a table for you!

Radians	Degrees
$\frac{\pi}{6}$	30°
$\frac{\pi}{4}$	45°
$\frac{\pi}{3}$	60°
$\frac{\pi}{2}$	90°
π	180°
2π	360°

If you know those, and you're nimble in working with them (e.g., you can figure that $\frac{5\pi}{4}$ radians is 225° because it's $\pi + \frac{\pi}{4}$ and that's the same as 180° + 45°), then you pretty much know what you need to know.

Answers: ● 2π/3 ● 10π/9 ● 20° ● 210°

Example 7: Calculator; Grid-in

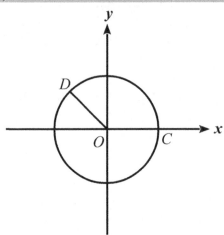

Note: Figure not drawn to scale.

In the *xy*-plane above, *O* is the center of the circle, and the measure of ∠*COD* is $\frac{3\pi}{4}$ radians. The coordinates of point *D* are (−5, *a*). What is *a*?

You get this question right by recognizing that $\frac{3\pi}{4}$ radians is a multiple of $\frac{\pi}{4}$ radians—it's a multiple of 45°! 135°, to be exact. This is going to be cake. First, draw a triangle, like I've done on the right. Label the angle and the lengths you know based on the fact that the coordinates of *D* are (−5, *a*): *D* will be 5 left of the *y*-axis, and *a* higher than the *x*-axis.

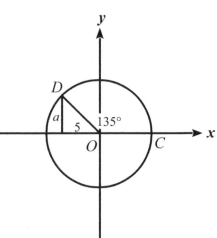

If ∠*COD* has a measure of 135°, then the triangle we drew is a special right triangle of the 45°-45°-90° variety! That's an isosceles right triangle. That means that *a* must be **5**.

Radians and trigonometry

No questions in any of the released tests deal with radians and trigonometry together, but it's probably a good idea for you to be prepared for such an eventuality. The College Board indicates as much in the "Additional Topics in Math" example problems in its Official Guide. Some history: there are things College Board said people would have to know before the last time they changed the test in 2005 that nobody ever ended up needing to know, so it's not outrageous to think that the same could happen again.

If I were you, though, I would know a *few* things. One thing that seems likely to come up: remember back in the last chapter where we said that if $x + y = 90$, then $\sin(x°) = \cos(y°)$? Well, of course that can be done with radians, too. For radian angle measures x and y such that $x + y = \dfrac{\pi}{2}$, $\sin x = \cos y$.

You should also either memorize (or be prepared to calculate quickly based on your crackerjack right triangle knowledge) the trigonometric ratios for the basic radian measures.

Radians	Degrees	Sine	Cosine	Tangent
$\dfrac{\pi}{6}$	30°	$\dfrac{1}{2}$	$\dfrac{\sqrt{3}}{2}$	$\dfrac{\sqrt{3}}{3}$
$\dfrac{\pi}{4}$	45°	$\dfrac{\sqrt{2}}{2}$	$\dfrac{\sqrt{2}}{2}$	1
$\dfrac{\pi}{3}$	60°	$\dfrac{\sqrt{3}}{2}$	$\dfrac{1}{2}$	$\sqrt{3}$
$\dfrac{\pi}{2}$	90°	1	0	D.N.E.

Example 8: No calculator

If $\sin\left(\dfrac{\pi}{4}\right) = \cos\left(\dfrac{\pi}{6} + A\right)$, and $0 < A < \dfrac{\pi}{2}$, which of the following equals $\sin A$?

A) $\cos\left(\dfrac{3\pi}{4}\right)$

B) $\cos\left(\dfrac{5\pi}{12}\right)$

C) $\cos\left(\dfrac{\pi}{3}\right)$

D) $\cos\left(\dfrac{\pi}{6}\right)$

To get this one, we need to recognize that if $\sin\left(\dfrac{\pi}{4}\right) = \cos\left(\dfrac{\pi}{6} + A\right)$, then $\dfrac{\pi}{4} + \dfrac{\pi}{6} + A = \dfrac{\pi}{2}$. Do a little subtracting there and you see that $A = \dfrac{\pi}{12}$.

From there, we can conclude that $\cos\left(\dfrac{5\pi}{12}\right)$ equals $\sin A$ because $\dfrac{5\pi}{12} + \dfrac{\pi}{12} = \dfrac{6\pi}{12} = \dfrac{\pi}{2}$. Piece of cake, right? This, by the way, is the kind of question you should only worry about if you're really shooting for 800.

Practice questions: Circles, Radians, and a Little More Trigonometry
Here, circular reasoning is a good thing.

1 No calculator

If a circle is divided evenly into 12 arcs, each measuring 3 cm long, what is the measure, in degrees, of an arc on the same circle that is 8 cm long?

A) 64°

B) 72°

C) 80°

D) 112°

2 No calculator

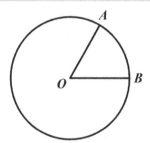

In the figure above, $OA = 1$ and the length of minor arc AB is $\frac{\pi}{3}$. What is the value of $\cos(\angle AOB)$?

A) $\frac{1}{2}$

B) $\frac{\sqrt{2}}{2}$

C) $\frac{\sqrt{3}}{2}$

D) 1

3 No calculator

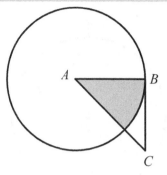

In the figure above, A is the center of the circle, $\overline{BC}$ is tangent to the circle at B, and $AB = BC$. If $AC = 8$, what is the area of the shaded region?

A) 4π

B) 8π

C) 16π

D) 24π

4 No calculator

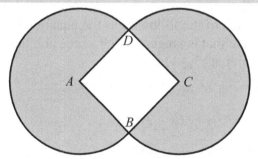

In the figure above, $ABCD$ is a square, and A and C are the centers of the circles. If $AB = 2$, what is the total area of the shaded regions?

A) 3π

B) 6π

C) $8\pi - 4$

D) $9\pi - 4$

Practice questions: Circles, Radians, and a Little More Trigonometry

Here, circular reasoning is a good thing.

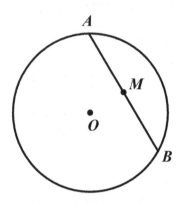

In the figure above, O is the center of the circle and M is the midpoint of $\overline{AB}$. If the radius of the circle is 5 and $AB = 5\sqrt{3}$. What is the length of $\overline{OM}$ (not shown)?

6 Calculator

Which of the following is the equation of a circle that is tangent to the y-axis and has its center at $(3, -1)$?

A) $x^2 + y^2 - 6x + 2y = -1$

B) $x^2 + y^2 + 6x - 2y = 1$

C) $x^2 + y^2 - 6x + 2y = -7$

D) $x^2 + y^2 + 6x - 2y = 7$

7 Calculator

Note: Figure not drawn to scale.

In the figure above, P is the center of a circle, and Q and R lie on the circle. If the length of arc QR is π and $PQ = 6$, what is the measure of $\angle RPQ$ in radians?

A) $\dfrac{\pi}{2}$

B) $\dfrac{\pi}{3}$

C) $\dfrac{\pi}{4}$

D) $\dfrac{\pi}{6}$

8 Calculator

Which of the following is true about a circle whose equation is $x^2 + y^2 + 8x = 36$?

   I   Its center is on the x-axis.
   II   Its radius is 6 units long.
   III It passes through the point $(2, 4)$.

A) I only

B) I and III only

C) II and III only

D) I, II, and III

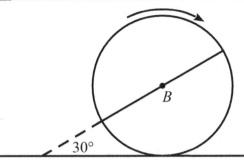

In the figure above, a wheel with center B and a radius of 12 cm is resting on a flat surface. A diameter is painted on the wheel as shown. Jasmine calculates that when the wheel begins to rotate in a clockwise direction and rolls along the surface without slipping, B will travel $b\pi$ cm before the painted diameter is perpendicular to the surface for the first time. What is the value of b ?

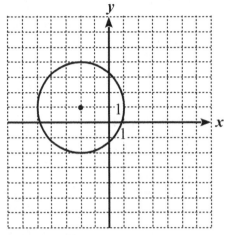

The figure above shows a circle in the xy-plane with equation $x^2 + y^2 + 4x - 2y = a$, where a is a constant. What is the value of a ?

Answers:

1	C		6	A
2	A		7	D
3	A		8	B
4	B		9	8
5	2.5 or 5/2		10	4

Solutions on page 397.

The following selected Official Test questions will require all of your circle knowledge.

Test	Section	Questions
1	3: No calculator	
	4: Calculator	24
2	3: No calculator	19
	4: Calculator	24, 36
3	3: No calculator	
	4: Calculator	34
4	3: No calculator	
	4: Calculator	24, 36
5	3: No calculator	2
	4: Calculator	20, 29, 36
6	3: No calculator	20
	4: Calculator	27
7	3: No calculator	18
	4: Calculator	29, 34
8	3: No calculator	9, 20
	4: Calculator	
9	3: No calculator	6
	4: Calculator	31
10	3: No calculator	11
	4: Calculator	
PSAT/NMSQT 1	3: No calculator	
	4: Calculator	
PSAT/NMSQT 2	3: No calculator	
	4: Calculator	15

Working in Three Dimensions

Although the College Board has signaled a willingness to test you on your ability to work in 3-D,[*] such questions have appeared sparingly and without much variety in the original Official Tests. *Therefore, you should consider this section of the book pretty speculative, and not worry about mastering these concepts until you've nailed down basically everything else.*

Volume

Generally speaking, the SAT will give you every volume formula that you need, either in the beginning of the section (where you're given formulas for the volume of a rectangular solid, a right cylinder, a sphere, a right cone, and a pyramid, as shown below) or in the question itself in a case where you'll have to deal with the volume of a different kind of solid. Volume questions will often be more about your ability to interpret and manipulate the formulas than your ability to visualize things in 3-D space.

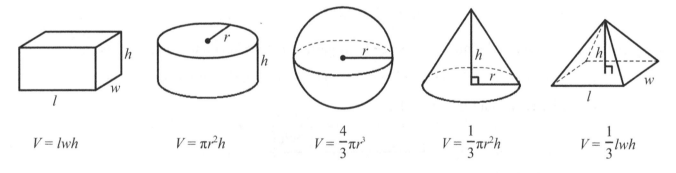

$$V = lwh \qquad V = \pi r^2 h \qquad V = \frac{4}{3}\pi r^3 \qquad V = \frac{1}{3}\pi r^2 h \qquad V = \frac{1}{3}lwh$$

It's worth mentioning that, while you're only given the formulas for the volume of two special-case right prisms,[**] the volume of *any* right prism can be calculated by finding the area of its base and multiplying that by its height. For example, if you needed to calculate the volume of a prism with an equilateral triangle base, you'd start by finding the area of an equilateral triangle:

---

[*] Tough 3-D questions appear in the College Board's initial—and now somewhat outdated—test specifications and also in the Official SAT Study Guide's review section. Volume formulas are also provided at the beginning of every math section.

[**] Right circular cylinders and rectangular solids are both special cases of right prisms: a right prism is any prism whose top lines up directly above its bottom.

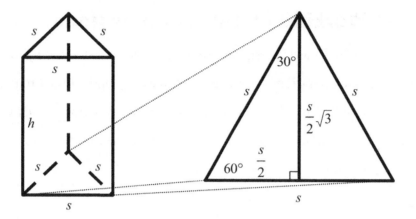

$$A_{\text{Triangle}} = \frac{1}{2}bh$$

$$A_{\text{Equilateral Triangle}} = \frac{1}{2}(s)\left(\frac{s}{2}\sqrt{3}\right)$$

$$A_{\text{Equilateral Triangle}} = \frac{s^2\sqrt{3}}{4}$$

And multiply that by the height of the prism:

$$V_{\text{Equilateral Triangular Right Prism}} = \frac{s^2\sqrt{3}}{4}h$$

You almost definitely won't need this particular formula on the SAT, but it's nice to know how to find the volume of a right prism in general: just find the area of the base, and multiply it by the height.

$$\boxed{V_{\text{Right Prism}} = A_{\text{base}} \times \text{height}}$$

The SAT will often require you to maneuver between the volume of a solid and its dimensions. Let's try one.

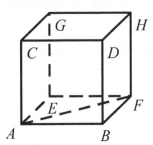

If the volume of the cube in the figure above is 27, what is the length of $\overline{AF}$?

A) 3

B) $3\sqrt{2}$

C) $3\sqrt{3}$

D) $3\sqrt{5}$

Remember that a cube is a special case of a rectangular solid where all the edges are equal, so the volume of a cube is the length of one edge CUBED:

$$V = 27 = s^3$$
$$s = 3$$

So far, so good, right? Now it's time to do the thing that you're going to find yourself doing for almost every single 3-D question you come across: work with one piece of the 3-D figure in 2-D.

The segment we're interested in is the diagonal of the square base of the cube. If we look at it in 2 dimensions, it looks like this:

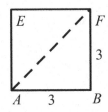

The diagonal of a square is the hypotenuse of an isosceles right triangle, so we can actually skip the Pythagorean Theorem here since we're so attuned to special right triangles. $\overline{AF} = 3\sqrt{2}$. That's choice **B**.

Note that after the fairly trivial step of figuring out the dimensions of the solid from its volume, this was basically a right triangle question. Most difficult 3-D questions, it turns out, end up being right triangle questions. More on this in a bit.

Surface area

The surface area of a solid is simply the sum of the areas of each of its faces. Easy surface area problems are really easy. Trickier surface area problems will often also involve volume. Have a go at this one:

The volume of a certain cube is v cubic inches, and its surface area is a square inches. If $v = 8p^3$, which of the following is NOT a value of p for which $a > v$?

A) 0.5

B) 1

C) 2

D) 4

Yuuuuck. What to do? Well, to find the surface area of a cube, you need to know the areas of its faces. To find those areas, you need to know the lengths of the cube's edges. Luckily for us, it's pretty easy to find the lengths of the edges of this cube because we know that the volume is $8p^3$. Let's call the length of one edge of the cube s. We know that $v = s^3$, so we can find s in terms of p:

$$v = s^3 = 8p^3$$
$$s = \sqrt[3]{8p^3}$$
$$s = 2p$$

If an edge of the cube is $2p$, then the area of one face of the cube is $(2p)^2$, or $4p^2$. There are 6 faces on a cube, so the surface area of the cube is found thusly:

$$a = 6 \times 4p^2$$
$$a = 24p^2$$

From here, it's trivial to either backsolve—try that on your own for practice—or solve the inequality spelled out in the question:

$$a > v$$
$$24p^2 > 8p^3$$
$$3p^2 > p^3$$
$$3 > p$$

The answer must be **D**, the one choice for which the inequality is *not* true.

A little more about right triangles

Since almost every solid you're going to be dealing with on the SAT is a right prism, *almost every solid you're going to be dealing with is going to contain right angles, and thus, right triangles.* The most difficult 3-D questions might require you to use the Pythagorean Theorem twice: once in the plane of one of the sides of the solid (usually the base), and once cutting through the solid. This will feel atrociously complicated the first few times you do it, but if you practice this enough for it to become second nature to you, you'll be unstoppable on tough 3-D problems.

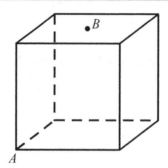

Point B is the center of the top face of a cube, and A is at one of the cube's vertices, as shown in the figure above. If each edge of the cube has a length of 3, what is the distance between A and B?

A) $\dfrac{3\sqrt{3}}{2}$

B) $\dfrac{3\sqrt{6}}{2}$

C) $3\sqrt{3}$

D) $3\sqrt{2}$

Yikes. In order to find the distance between A and B, we're going to have to work with the right triangle formed by the dotted lines and the edge of the cube in the drawing on the right. And in order to do *that*, we're going to have to deal first with just one face of the cube. Let's look at the top face by itself.

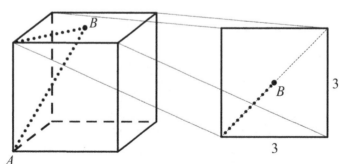

Of course, any face of a cube is a square. Note that B lies at the midpoint of the square's diagonal. If the sides of the square have a length of 3, then the diagonal must be $3\sqrt{2}$. So the distance from the corner to B must be half that: $\dfrac{3\sqrt{2}}{2}$.

Now let's have a look at our triangle, drawn in its own plane for clarity's sake. We can find the distance between A and B using the Pythagorean Theorem:

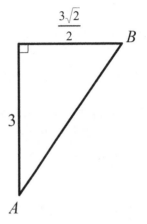

$$3^2 + \left(\frac{3\sqrt{2}}{2}\right)^2 = AB^2$$

$$9 + \frac{18}{4} = AB^2$$

$$\frac{27}{2} = AB^2$$

$$\sqrt{\frac{27}{2}} = AB$$

$$\frac{3\sqrt{3}}{\sqrt{2}} = AB$$

Since that's not an answer choice, rationalize by multiplying top and bottom by $\sqrt{2}$:

$$\frac{3\sqrt{3}}{\sqrt{2}} \times \frac{\sqrt{2}}{\sqrt{2}} = AB$$

$$\frac{3\sqrt{6}}{2} = AB$$

Bam! We've arrived at choice **B**.

Once you get accustomed to their patterns, you'll be able to rip through these double-Pythagorean 3-D questions with ninja-efficiency. Your friends are going to flip out so hard!

Let's try one more together before I set you loose on a drill.

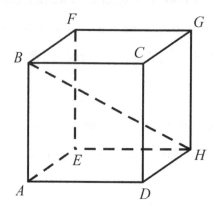

In the figure above, $\overline{BH}$ connects vertices of a cube with edges of length 8. What is the length of $\overline{BH}$?

A) $8\sqrt{2}$

B) $8\sqrt{3}$

C) $8\sqrt{5}$

D) $8\sqrt{7}$

Before we get into the solution, a bit of terminology that I might as well mention: $\overline{BH}$ is what's called the *long diagonal* of the cube. Other long diagonals in this cube (not shown) are $\overline{DF}$, $\overline{CE}$, and $\overline{AG}$. The reason we have the term long diagonal is to contrast it with the *short diagonal*, or side diagonal, like $\overline{AH}$, which runs along a face of the cube, instead of cutting through it.

Anyway, just like we did before, we're going to solve this with right triangles. $\overline{BH}$ is the hypotenuse of right triangle ABH. We know $AB = 8$, so we just need to find AH, and then Pythagorize.

If you've been paying attention to this chapter so far, finding AH should be no problem. If you haven't been paying attention, turn down the Skrillex or whatever and note that short diagonal $\overline{AH}$ is the diagonal of square $AEHD$. The diagonal of a square always cuts the square into

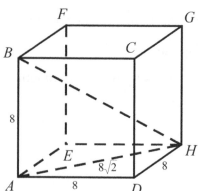

two 45°-45°-90° triangles, so it will always be the length of the square's sides times $\sqrt{2}$. The sides of *AEHD* have a length of 8, so $AH = 8\sqrt{2}$.

Now drop your values into the Pythagorean theorem to solve for *BH*:

$$AB^2 + AH^2 = BH^2$$
$$8^2 + (8\sqrt{2})^2 = BH^2$$
$$64 + 128 = BH^2$$
$$192 = BH^2$$
$$\sqrt{192} = BH$$
$$8\sqrt{3} = BH$$

So there you go—the answer is **B**.

Major shortcut

It turns out that the long diagonal of a cube with edges of length *s* will always have a length of $s\sqrt{3}$. *This only applies to long diagonals of cubes!* If you're not dealing with that very special case, you can either solve the "long way," with right triangles, like we did above, or apply the following general case shortcut:

For a rectangular solid with sides of length *l*, *w*, and *h*, the length of the long diagonal can be found thusly:

length of long diagonal $= \sqrt{l^2 + w^2 + h^2}$

Break it down.

1 No calculator

What is the surface area of a cube with a volume of 27 ?

A) 54

B) 36

C) 27

D) 9

2 No calculator

$$V = \frac{2}{3}\pi\left(a^3 - b^3\right)$$

Larry is using a 3-D printer to construct semi-spherical bowls. He uses the equation above to find the volume, V, of material needed to construct the bowl with an outer radius of a and an inner radius of b. Which of the following expressions represents the maximum amount of liquid such a bowl could contain once it is constructed?

A) $\frac{4}{3}\pi b^3$

B) $\frac{2}{3}\pi b^3$

C) $\frac{4}{3}\pi a^3$

D) $\frac{2}{3}\pi a^3$

3 No calculator

In the figure above, each empty box (□) is to be filled by the value of the length of one edge of the right triangular prism. If four unique constants, a, b, c, and d, are needed to fill the squares, and if the surface area of the prism equals $ab + ad + bd + cd$, then which constant represents the length of the longest edge of the prism's base?

A) a

B) b

C) c

D) d

4 No calculator; Grid-in

Cube A has edges that are 4 units long, and cube B has edges that are 5 units long. The volume of cube B is how much greater than the volume of cube A, in cubic units?

5 No calculator; Grid-in

Marc is calculating the volume of a right cone with a radius of 6 inches and a height of h inches. If he correctly calculates that the cone's volume is 24π cubic inches, what is the value of h, in inches?

7 Calculator

Xorgar H'ghargh is building a pyramid to honor himself on the planet Geometrox. If the pyramid has a square base with edges 50 meters long, and its other four sides are equilateral triangles, how tall will the pyramid be, in meters?

A) $50\sqrt{3}$

B) $50\sqrt{2}$

C) $25\sqrt{3}$

D) $25\sqrt{2}$

6 Calculator

John is holding a cylindrical cardboard tube in his hand, and two ants are crawling around on it. If the cylinder is 12 inches long and has a radius of 2.5 inches, what is the farthest the two ants could possibly be from each other and still both be on the tube?

A) 12 inches

B) 12.25 inches

C) 13 inches

D) $12\sqrt{2}$ inches

8 Calculator

The radius of a certain baseball is 73.2 millimeters, and the radius of a certain soccer ball 226.0 millimeters. Which of the following is true?

A) The volume of the soccer ball is roughly 29 times that of the baseball.

B) The volume of the soccer ball is roughly 18 times that of the baseball.

C) The volume of the soccer ball is roughly 14 times that of the baseball.

D) The volume of the soccer ball is roughly 10 times that of the baseball.

Break it down.

9 Calculator

Note: Figure not drawn to scale.

Mackenzie is in her school's wood shop and is about to drill a cylindrical hole from the center of one face of a wooden cube to the center of the the opposite face, as shown in the figure above. The cube's edges are 3 inches long and the diameter of the hole will be 2 inches. Of the following, which is closest to the volume of the resulting piece of wood?

A) 24.5 in^3

B) 17.6 in^3

C) 16.3 in^3

D) 8.2 in^3

10 Calculator; Grid-in

Priya pours water into a fish tank with interior dimensions of 3 feet wide, 4 feet long, and 2 feet high until the water is 1 foot deep. She then places a solid stone cube with edges 6 inches long into the tank. The cube sinks to the bottom of the tank. How much does the water level rise, in inches, when Priya places the stone into the tank? (1 foot = 12 inches)

Answers:

1	A		6	C
2	B		7	D
3	C		8	A
4	61		9	B
5	2		10	1/8 or .125

Solutions on page 399.

The following selected Official Test questions are examples of these rare beasts in the wild.

Test	Section	Questions
1	3: No calculator	
	4: Calculator	35
2	3: No calculator	
	4: Calculator	
3	3: No calculator	
	4: Calculator	25
4	3: No calculator	
	4: Calculator	18
5	3: No calculator	11
	4: Calculator	26
6	3: No calculator	
	4: Calculator	33
7	3: No calculator	
	4: Calculator	23
8	3: No calculator	
	4: Calculator	15
9	3: No calculator	16
	4: Calculator	
10	3: No calculator	
	4: Calculator	15
PSAT/NMSQT 1	3: No calculator	
	4: Calculator	
PSAT/NMSQT 2	3: No calculator	
	4: Calculator	24

Complex Numbers

Look, you're not going to need to be a total wizard with imaginary and complex numbers for the SAT—you're just going to have to know what they are and how they work on a basic level. So let's start with the basics and make sure you're solid on those, then work through some SAT-type questions that might get thrown your way. You know, like we have done in every other chapter in this book. I'm not going to change it up on you at this point.

What is an imaginary number?

As you're probably aware, the imaginary unit, i, is defined as the result of taking the square root of -1.

$$\sqrt{-1} = i$$

We call i imaginary because, well, it's not real (as in, it's not a Real Number, unlike 3, -9, π, or $\sqrt{13}$). Any time you take the square root of a negative number, you end up with an i in your solution:

$$\sqrt{-64}$$
$$= \sqrt{(64)(-1)}$$
$$= \sqrt{64}\sqrt{-1}$$
$$= 8i$$

So far, so good, right? You've seen all this before? Cool.

Powers of imaginary numbers

One thing you'll need to know is what happens when i is raised to a power. This is easy stuff—you might have even *enjoyed* it when you learned it, but in my experience this is something many students can use a quick refresher on by the time they're prepping to take the SAT. Remember that $i = \sqrt{-1}$. When you square the square root of something, you neutralize the radical, so you know what's going to happen when you square i:

$$i^2$$
$$= \left(\sqrt{-1}\right)^2$$
$$= \left(\sqrt{-1}\right)\left(\sqrt{-1}\right)$$
$$= -1$$

What happens when you raise i to the 3rd power?

$$i^3$$
$$=\left(\sqrt{-1}\right)^3$$
$$=\left(\sqrt{-1}\right)\left(\sqrt{-1}\right)\left(\sqrt{-1}\right)$$
$$=(-1)\left(\sqrt{-1}\right)$$
$$=-i$$

And what happens when you raise i to the 4th power?

$$i^4$$
$$=\left(\sqrt{-1}\right)^4$$
$$=\left(\sqrt{-1}\right)\left(\sqrt{-1}\right)\left(\sqrt{-1}\right)\left(\sqrt{-1}\right)$$
$$=(-1)(-1)$$
$$=1$$

That pattern, you might recall from math class, is going to repeat, and it's going to repeat *forever*. Any time i is raised to a power that's a multiple of 4, the result is 1. The result of i^8, i^{12}, i^{80}, and i^{400} is 1. Since the pattern repeats, if you know $i^{400} = 1$, then you know $i^{401} = i$, $i^{402} = -1$, $i^{403} = -i$, and $i^{404} = 1$ again.[*]

Working with complex numbers

You need to know the basics of imaginary numbers the SAT will sometimes test your ability to work with **complex numbers**. A complex number is a number with a real component and an imaginary component. Generally speaking, it'll take the form $a + bi$, where a and b are real numbers, and i is, well, you know what i is. We call the a term the real component and the bi term the imaginary component.

---

[*] You can, therefore, very easily tell what i^{341} is, as long as you're able to find the closest multiple of 4 to 341. 340 is a multiple of 4, so $i^{340} = 1$, and therefore $i^{341} = i$. Note that another way to think about this is in terms of remainders. 341 divided by 4 gives a remainder of 1, so i^{341} will equal the first term in the i, -1, $-i$, 1, ... pattern. Weirdly, the SAT doesn't seem interested in testing this concept.

Complex Numbers

$$a+bi$$

Real component   Imaginary component

Above, a and b are real constants, and i is the imaginary unit.

Just like real numbers, you can add, subtract, multiply, and divide complex numbers. It just gets a little more...complex. (Ba-dum-bum!)

Adding and **subtracting** are super easy; you can proceed just like you would adding or subtracting non-complex polynomials. For example:

$(2 + i) + (8 - 4i) = 10 - 3i$ because $2 + 8 = 10$ and $i - 4i = -3i$.

Multiplication is basically FOILing. Look:

$$(1+2i)(3+5i)$$
$$=3+5i+6i+10i^2$$
$$=3+11i+10i^2$$

You just have to remember at the end that $i^2 = -1$:

$$=3+11i+10(-1)$$
$$=3+11i-10$$
$$=-7+11i$$

Why don't you make sure you've got this down by multiplying a few complex numbers? Answers are at the bottom of the page, of course.

✎ $(3 + 2i)(5 - 3i) =$

✎ $(9 + 4i)^2 =$

✎ $(7 + 3i)(7 - 3i) =$

Did you notice, with that last one, that it looked like a difference of two squares? More importantly, did you notice that, when simplified, the i term went away? $(7 + 3i)$ and $(7 - 3i)$ are called complex conjugates. When you multiply complex conjugates, you end up with a real number. It's probably not important that you remember what they're called, but you should definitely know what they are and why they work.

Complex conjugates end up being pretty useful for **division** of complex numbers—the trickiest operation of the bunch. When you divide complex numbers, you set up a fraction, then use the complex conjugate of the denominator to get the imaginary part out of the denominator. Here, let's do $\frac{8+4i}{2+2i}$.

To simplify, we're going to create a clever form of 1 out of the complex conjugate of $2 + 2i$, and then multiply. In other words, we're going to multiply $\frac{8+4i}{2+2i}$ by $\frac{2-2i}{2-2i}$. We can get away with that because $\frac{2-2i}{2-2i}$ is equal to 1. THAT'S THE MULTIPLICATIVE IDENTITY, BABY!

$$\frac{8+4i}{2+2i} \times \frac{2-2i}{2-2i}$$
$$= \frac{(8+4i)(2-2i)}{(2+2i)(2-2i)}$$
$$= \frac{24-8i}{8}$$
$$= 3-i$$

To summarize all that, when you're performing arithmetic operations on complex numbers, you're generally going to want to treat i like it's a variable or unknown constant until you've done everything else you can do. Then, once you've done everything else, you'll clean up by doing one or both of the following:

➔ Simplify any exponents on i, as we practiced above, or

➔ Multiply by clever forms of 1 to remove any imaginary components from the denominators of any fractions you have.

That second bullet is what the SAT is most interested in. Let's try one.

$$\frac{3-4i}{3-i}$$

If the expression above is rewritten in the form $a + bi$, where a and b are real numbers, what is the sum of a and b? (Note: $i = \sqrt{-1}$)

A) -1

B) $\frac{2}{5}$

C) $\frac{5}{8}$

D) 4

Just like we did before, let's get that unsightly fraction into $a + bi$ form by multiplying by a clever form of 1 made up of the complex conjugate of the denominator.

We want to lose the $3 - i$ in the denominator. To do that, we're going to multiply the fraction by $\frac{3+i}{3+i}$.

$$\frac{3-4i}{3-i} \times \frac{3+i}{3+i}$$

Now we're going to FOIL.

$$= \frac{9 + 3i - 12i - 4i^2}{9 - i^2}$$

$$= \frac{9 - 9i - 4i^2}{9 - i^2}$$

So far, so good, right? Now let's simplify those i^2 terms.

$$= \frac{9 - 9i - 4(-1)}{9 - (-1)}$$

$$= \frac{13 - 9i}{10}$$

$$= \frac{13}{10} - \frac{9}{10}i$$

So, there you go! You've got $a = \frac{13}{10}$ and $b = -\frac{9}{10}$. The sum of a and b, then, is $\frac{4}{10}$, which simplifies to $\frac{2}{5}$. Bubble in choice B.

As I said above, even if you haven't really worked with complex numbers before, this should have felt a bit familiar. Getting complex numbers out of a denominator is exactly the same as getting radicals out of a denominator—we multiply by a clever form of 1. And multiplying complex numbers is basically FOILING. Oh, and of course, that complex conjugate we used to get the i term out of the denominator? That's easy to remember, too, because all we're doing there is creating a difference of two squares! Because of the unique property of i that causes it to disappear when squared, creating a difference of two squares turns out to be a very handy trick indeed for complex numbers.

Your calculator can handle complex numbers (maybe)

A lot of people don't know this, but there's a pretty good chance that your calculator knows how to deal with imaginary numbers. If you have a TI-83 or TI-84, then you can enter i by hitting 2nd and then the decimal point key.[*] (If you want your calculator to give you i solutions when you take the square root of negative numbers, instead of giving you errors, then you have to change modes. Go to the MODE menu and change Real to $a+bi$.) That's the good news. The bad news is that from what we've seen so far it looks like College Board is putting all the complex numbers in the section where calculators are prohibited.

The reason I even bring this up is that you can write yourself complex number algebra problems to solve all day long for practice and check your work with your calculator. That's nice. Also, of course, in the event that a complex number problem *does* appear in the section where calculators are allowed, you'll be glad you know how to work with them on your machine.

---

[*] If you don't have one of those calculators, do a Google search with your calculator model number to see if your calculator works with complex numbers.

Practice questions: Complex Numbers

Why'd you have to go and make things so complexated?

If $(3 + 6i)(3 + bi) = 45$, where b is a real number, what is the value of b?
(Note: $i = \sqrt{-1}$)

A) -6

B) -3

C) 3

D) 6

For $i = \sqrt{-1}$, which of the following complex numbers is equal to $(5+8i)-(6i^2+3i^3)$?

A) $-1 + 5i$

B) $11 + 11i$

C) $2 - 2i$

D) $8 + 14i$

Which of the following complex numbers is equivalent to $\dfrac{5-i}{1-i}$? (Note: $i = \sqrt{-1}$)

A) $3 + 2i$

B) $2 + 3i$

C) $3 - 2i$

D) $2 - 3i$

Which of the following complex numbers is equivalent to $\left(\sqrt{5}+2i\right)^2$, for $i = \sqrt{-1}$?

A) $9 + 4i\sqrt{5}$

B) $3 + 2i\sqrt{5}$

C) $1 + 4i\sqrt{5}$

D) 1

Which of the following complex numbers is equivalent to $(3 + 2i)(2 + 3i)(3 - 2i)$?
(Note: $i = \sqrt{-1}$)

A) $39 - 26i$

B) $26 + 39i$

C) $15 - 10i$

D) $10 + 15i$

6 No calculator; Grid-in

For $i = \sqrt{-1}$, what is the value of

$$(4+4i)\left(\frac{1}{2}-\frac{1}{2}i\right)?$$

7 No calculator; Grid-in

If $(4-2i)(6+bi) = 30$, where b is a positive real number, what is the value of b?
(Note: $i = \sqrt{-1}$)

8 No calculator; Grid-in

If the product of the complex numbers $3 + 8i$ and $5 + 9i$ equals $m + ni$, where m and n are real numbers and $i = \sqrt{-1}$, what is the sum of the values of m and n?

9 No calculator; Grid-in

If $\dfrac{9-bi}{1-2i} = 5+2i$ and b is a real number greater than 0, what is the value of b?
(Note: $i = \sqrt{-1}$)

10 No calculator; Grid-in

$$\frac{3+8i}{6+16i}$$

If the expression above is rewritten in the form $a + bi$, where a and b are real numbers, what is the value of ab? (Note: $i = \sqrt{-1}$)

Answers:

1	A		6	4
2	B		7	3
3	A		8	10
4	C		9	8
5	B		10	0

Solutions on page 401.

The following table refers you to examples of complex number questions on the Official Tests.

Test	Section	Questions
1	3: No calculator	2
	4: Calculator	
2	3: No calculator	11
	4: Calculator	
3	3: No calculator	
	4: Calculator	
4	3: No calculator	14
	4: Calculator	
5	3: No calculator	
	4: Calculator	
6	3: No calculator	3
	4: Calculator	
7	3: No calculator	4
	4: Calculator	
8	3: No calculator	
	4: Calculator	
9	3: No calculator	
	4: Calculator	
10	3: No calculator	
	4: Calculator	
PSAT/NMSQT 1	3: No calculator	
	4: Calculator	
PSAT/NMSQT 2	3: No calculator	
	4: Calculator	

Extra Practice

The questions that follow have all been part of my Daily PWN question of the day service. (Sign up for that here, but expect some repeats: http://bit.ly/DailyPWN) The topics covered here aren't exhaustive, nor are they proportionally representative of the question types that appear on the SAT. They are, unscientifically, the kinds of questions I've seen students struggle with most.

When people answer these questions on my site, the site tracks the number of correct and incorrect responses. That's the data I used to arrange the questions in this book by difficulty. The later a question appears in this section, the smaller a percentage of respondents got it right. The first few questions about 90% of respondents got correct—the last few, more like 40%.

Take the above percentages with a grain of salt. People who sign up for the Daily PWN are not exactly a random sample of test takers. Other limitations to these percents and ranking including but are not limited to:

- Users can answer questions as many times as they want. This is not common practice, but it's also not controlled for.
- Multiple choice questions are far more likely than "grid-ins" to be guessed correctly, but I couldn't think of a good way to account for that in my ranking, so I just didn't.

Still, seeing all these questions laid out in order of difficulty, it does feel mostly right.

The answers to all these questions can be found on page 349, and detailed solutions begin on page 403. In the detailed solutions section, you'll find question categorizations that will refer you back to the relevant chapters in this book.

Good luck and happy prepping!

1 Calculator; Grid-in

Marble Run Results

14%   18%

26%   20%

22%

☐ Bucket 1
☐ Bucket 2
▨ Bucket 3
☐ Bucket 4
■ Bucket 5

Franklin created a marble run with multiple paths the marbles can take due to a number of random intersections. There are five possible buckets that the marbles can land in at the end of the run. Franklin ran 50 marbles through the run and created the pie chart above based on the number of marbles each bucket collected. How many more marbles landed in Bucket 3 than landed in Bucket 5?

2 Calculator

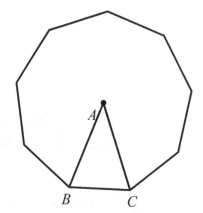

In the figure above, A is the center of a regular polygon with nine sides. Points B and C are adjacent vertices of the polygon. What is the measure of angle BAC ?

A) 40°

B) 36°

C) 35°

D) 32°

3 Calculator

$$f(x)=x^3$$
$$g(x)=\sqrt{x}$$

Functions f and g, above, are defined for all $x \geq 0$. If a and b are greater than zero, and $a = b^6$, then what does $f(g(a))$ equal, in terms of b ?

A) b^{18}

B) b^9

C) $\sqrt{b^9}$

D) b^3

4 Calculator

$$y = 3x + a$$
$$y = -2x + b$$

In the system of equations above, a and b are constants. If $b = a + 15$, what value of x satisfies the system of equations?

A) -2

B) 1

C) 2

D) 3

5 Calculator; Grid-in

$$y = a(x - 6)^2 + 5$$

In the equation above, a is a constant. When the equation is graphed in the xy-plane, it passes through the point $(8, 8)$. What is the value of a ?

6 Calculator

What is the value of x that satisfies the equation $\dfrac{1}{x} + \dfrac{4}{2x} = \dfrac{27}{3x^2}$?

A) -3

B) -2

C) 2

D) 3

7 Calculator

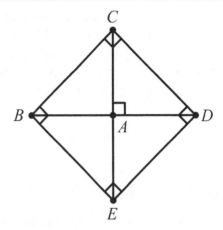

In the figure above, $BCDE$ is a square, and the area of triangle ABC is 2 cm^2. What is the perimeter of $BCDE$?

A) $2\sqrt{2}$ cm

B) 4 cm

C) $8\sqrt{2}$ cm

D) $8\sqrt{3}$ cm

8 Calculator

$$f(x) = x^2$$
$$g(x) = x - 9$$

The functions f and g are defined above. If $g(f(a - 2)) = 0$, which of the following could be the value of a ?

A) -2

B) -1

C) 3

D) 7

9 Calculator; Grid-in

A bag contains only blue marbles and green marbles. The ratio of blue marbles to green marbles in the bag is 8 to 7; there are 165 marbles in the bag. How many more blue marbles than green marbles are in the bag?

10 Calculator; Grid-in

If $(\sqrt{x}+9)(\sqrt{x}-9)=19$, what is the value of x ?

11 No Calculator

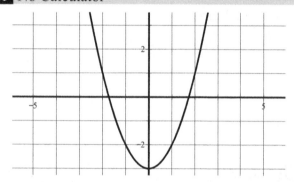

The figure above shows the graph of a parabola in the xy-plane. Which of the following could be the equation of the parabola?

A) $y=(x+\sqrt{3})(x-\sqrt{3})$

B) $y=(x+3)(x-3)$

C) $y=(x-\sqrt{3})^2$

D) $y=(x-3)^2$

12 Calculator

$$x + 4y = n$$
$$5x - y = 3$$

In the system of equations above, n is a constant. In terms of n, what is the x-value of the solution to the system.

A) $\dfrac{n+3}{6}$

B) $\dfrac{5n+7}{4}$

C) $\dfrac{4n+3}{9}$

D) $\dfrac{n+12}{21}$

13 Calculator; Grid-in

$$y=5x+17$$
$$y=\frac{a}{b}x+b$$

In the system of equations above, a and b are constants. If the system has an infinite number of solutions, what is the value of a ?

14 Calculator

Handedness	Grade	
	7th	8th
Right		
Left		
Total	322	356

The incomplete table above summarizes the number of right- and left-handed students by grade at Warren Junior High School. None of the students are both right- and left-handed. The ratio of right-handed 7th graders to left-handed 7th graders is 21 to 2. There are 4 more left-handed 8th graders than left-handed 7th graders. If an 8th grade student is chosen at random, what is the probability that the student is right-handed?

A) 9.0%

B) 52.4%

C) 91.0%

D) 92.1%

15 Calculator

Exam Results by Hours Spent on Homework

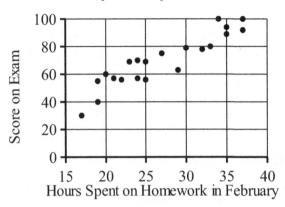

Because all the homework she assigns is online, a statistics professor is able to track how long her students spend on homework assignments. She plots that data for the month of February against the scores on an exam she gave at the end of February for one class of 21 students, as shown above. The professor calculates the line of best fit to be $s = 2.7t - 2.9$, where s equals score and t equals hours spent on homework. Which of the following best explains how the number 2.7 in the equation relates to the data in the scatterplot?

A) Students tended to score 10 points higher on the exam at the end of February when they who studied 2.7 additional hours each day during the month.

B) A student who did not spend any time on homework in February would have received a score of 2.7 on the exam at the end of the month.

C) Students' scores on the exam at the end of February were 2.7 times the number of hours they spent on homework in that month.

D) Students tended to score 2.7 points higher on the exam at the end of the February for every additional hour they spent on their homework throughout the month.

16 Calculator; Grid-in

$$\frac{x-8}{x+2}=\frac{x-5}{x-1}$$

In the equation above, $x \neq -2$ and $x \neq 1$. What is the value of x that satisfies the equation?

17 Calculator

Group	Adults	Children	Total Admission Fees
Group 1	3	5	$70.50
Group 2	2	6	$67.00
Group 3	1	2	

The Museum of Science charges different admission fees for adults and children. The incomplete table above shows total admission fees collected from three groups as they entered the museum and the composition of those groups. Which of the following equals the total admission fees that the museum would charge Group 3?

A) $23.50

B) $25.25

C) $26.00

D) $27.50

18 Calculator; Grid-in

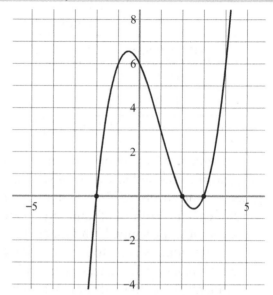

The graph of the cubic function f is shown in the xy-plane above. If $f(a) = 0$ and $f(-a) = 0$, where a is a positive constant, then what is the value of $f(a + 1) + 1$?

19 Calculator

$$y = -ax + b$$
$$y = -bx + a$$

In the equations above, a and b are constants. When the equations are graphed in the xy-plane, they intersect at the point $(-1, 9)$. What is the value of $a + b$?

A) 9

B) 7

C) 5

D) 3

20 Calculator

$$(3x + a)(4x + a) = 12x^2 + 28x + b$$

The equation above is true for all values of x, and a and b are constants. What is the value of b ?

A) 2

B) 4

C) 18

D) 16

21 Calculator

A wheel rolls along a straight path without slipping. After making 8 complete revolutions, it comes to a stop. If the wheel traveled a distance of m while it was rolling, what is the radius of the wheel, in terms of m ?

A) $\dfrac{\pi}{8m}$

B) $\dfrac{4\pi}{m}$

C) $\dfrac{m}{16\pi}$

D) $\dfrac{m}{8\pi}$

22 Calculator

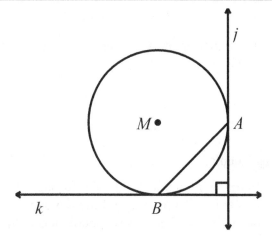

In the figure above, lines j and k are tangent to the circle with center M at points A and B, respectively. If the length of chord AB is $5\sqrt{2}$, which of the following is equal to the circumference of the circle?

A) 5π

B) 10π

C) $5\pi\sqrt{2}$

D) 25π

23 Calculator

$$f(x) = 2x^2 - 4x + 8$$

The function f is defined above. What is $f(x + 2)$?

A) $f(x + 2) = 2x^2 - 4x + 10$

B) $f(x + 2) = 2x^2 + 4x + 8$

C) $f(x + 2) = 4x^2 - 2x + 10$

D) $f(x + 2) = 2x^2 - 2x + 4$

24 Calculator; Grid-in

$$\left(x^{2y}\right)\left(x^{3y}\right)=\left(x^{y}\right)^{a}$$

The equation above is true for $x > y > 1$. What is the value of a ?

25 Calculator

In the xy-plane, line m passes through the points $(2, 9)$ and $(11, 3)$. Line n passes through $(12, 9)$ and is perpendicular to line m. What is the equation of line n ?

A) $y=\dfrac{3}{2}x-9$

B) $y=\dfrac{2}{3}x+8$

C) $y=\dfrac{2}{3}x-4$

D) $y=\dfrac{3}{2}x-2$

26 Calculator

Which of the following expressions is equivalent to $\dfrac{x^{4}-y^{4}}{x^{2}+y^{2}}$ for all nonzero values of x and y ?

A) $x^{2}-y^{2}$

B) $\left(\dfrac{x^{2}-y^{2}}{x+y}\right)^{2}$

C) $(x-y)^{2}$

D) $(x+y)^{2}$

27 Calculator

Calvin calculated that his investment account increased in value by roughly 8 percent last year. If the value of his account was $12,768 at the end of the year, which of the following could have been the value of his account at the beginning of the year?

A) $11,611

B) $11,747

C) $11,822

D) $11,968

28 Calculator

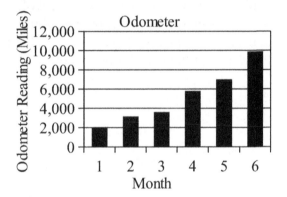

Six months ago, Gerald bought a new car. On the last day of each of the last six months, Gerald has written down the odometer reading (which shows the total number of miles the car has driven). That data is summarized in the graph above. During which of the last six months did Gerald drive the least number of miles?

A) Month 1

B) Month 2

C) Month 3

D) Month 5

29 No Calculator

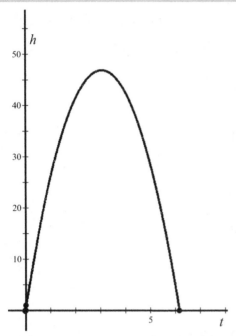

The graph above represents the height, h, in meters of a baseball as a function of time, t, in seconds. At time $t = 0$, the baseball is hit in the air. Which of the following equations best matches the flight of the baseball?

A) $h = -4.9t^2 - 30t - 1$

B) $h = 4.9t^2 - 30t - 1$

C) $h = 4.9t^2 + 30t + 1$

D) $h = -4.9t^2 + 30t + 1$

30 Calculator; Grid-in

$$0 = (x - 3)^2 - 6(x - 3) + 9$$

What value of x satisfies the equation above?

31 Calculator

$$10x^2 + ax - 36$$

The expression above is the product of $2x + b$ and $cx + 4$. If a, b, and c are unique integers, what is the value of a ?

A) -41

B) -37

C) 45

D) 53

32 No Calculator

In the xy-plane, a circle with center $(-5, 12)$ passes through the origin. What is the equation of this circle?

A) $(x - 5)^2 + (y - 12)^2 = 13$

B) $(x + 5)^2 + (y - 12)^2 = 169$

C) $(x - 5)^2 + (y + 12)^2 = 169$

D) $(x + 5)^2 + (y - 12)^2 = 13$

33 Calculator

The density, p, of an object can be calculated using the formula $p=\dfrac{m}{V}$, where m is the mass of the object and V is its volume. The volume of a sphere can be calculated using the formula $V=\dfrac{4}{3}\pi r^3$, where r is the radius of the sphere. Which of the following equations could be used to find the radius of a spherical object given its mass and density?

A) $r=\sqrt[3]{\dfrac{3m}{4\,p\pi}}$

B) $r=\sqrt[3]{\dfrac{4m}{3\,p\pi}}$

C) $r=\sqrt[3]{\dfrac{3m\pi}{4\,p}}$

D) $r=\sqrt[3]{\dfrac{4m\pi}{3\,p}}$

34 Calculator

In the xy-plane, line m has a slope of 4 and a y-intercept of 3. Line n is perpendicular to line m and has a y-intercept of -14. What are the coordinates of the intersection of lines m and n ?

A) $(-2,-5)$

B) $(-2.5,-5.25)$

C) $(-3,-12)$

D) $(-4,-13)$

35 Calculator

In triangle ABC, the measure of angle B is $90°$. If $\tan A=\dfrac{4}{3}$, what is the value of $\dfrac{\sin C}{\cos C}$?

A) $\dfrac{4}{3}$

B) $\dfrac{3}{4}$

C) $\dfrac{3}{5}$

D) $\dfrac{4}{5}$

36 No Calculator

$$\frac{18x^2+15x-12}{3x+2}=6x+1+\frac{a}{3x+2}$$

In the equation above, a is a constant. If the equation is true for all values of $x\neq-\dfrac{2}{3}$, what is the value of a ?

A) -30

B) -14

C) -12

D) -10

37 No Calculator; Grid-in

$$\frac{a^3+a^3+a^3}{6}=a^4$$

What positive value of a satisfies the equation above?

38 Calculator

$$3x + 2y = 18$$
$$4x + ay = 22$$

In the system of equations above, a is a constant. If the system has no solutions, what is the value of a ?

A) $\dfrac{8}{3}$

B) $-\dfrac{3}{2}$

C) $-\dfrac{8}{3}$

D) $\dfrac{4}{11}$

39 Calculator

$$4x + 3y = 18$$
$$ax + 4y = 10$$

For the system of equations above, where a is a constant, the value of $x - y$ is 8. What is the value of a ?

A) 1

B) 3

C) 4

D) 5

40 No Calculator

$$y = -(x - 5)^2 + k$$

In the parabola equation above, k is a constant. When the parabola is graphed in the xy-plane, its vertex is at (5, 16). If the parabola crosses the x-axis at $x = a$ and $x = b$, what is the value of $a + b$?

A) 5

B) 8

C) 10

D) 16

41 Calculator

Population Growth in Carterville

Year	2014	2015	2016
Population Growth	3.2%	2.8%	2.6%

The city of Carterville measures its population every year as of April 1st of that year. The table above shows the year-to-year percent growth of the population of Carterville from 2014 to 2016. If the population of Carterville was 1,059,382 on April 1, 2013, which of the following could have been the population on April 1, 2016 ?

A) 1,153,120

B) 1,145,489

C) 1,123,894

D) 1,086,296

42 Calculator

$$\frac{2^{(a-b)}}{2^{(b-a)}} = 4^c$$

In the equation above, a, b, and c are positive integers and $a > b$. Which of the following is equivalent to b ?

A) $-2c$

B) $a - c$

C) $a - \dfrac{c}{2}$

D) $c + a^2$

43 No Calculator; Grid-in

$$y = -x^2 + 3x + 1$$
$$y = 3x - 8$$

In the xy-plane, the graphs of the equations above intersect at two points. What is the sum of the x-coordinates of these two intersection points?

44 Calculator

In the xy-plane, the parabola with equation $y = -x^2 + 4$ has its vertex at point C and intersects the x-axis at two points, A and B. What is the area of triangle ABC?

A) 4

B) 8

C) 12

D) 16

45 Calculator; Grid-in

In the xy-plane, the point $(k, 5)$, where k is a constant, lies on the graph of the function f, which is defined as $f(x) = x^2 - 13x + 35$. What is one possible value of k ?

46 No Calculator

If $f(x) = (x - 5)(x + 4)$ and $g(x) = f(x) + 14$, what are the roots of $g(x)$?

A) -4 and 5

B) 10 and 19

C) -2 and 3

D) 2 and 6

47 Calculator; Grid-in

$$8x + 3y = 37$$
$$5y = 4x - 12$$

What value of y satisfies the system of equations above?

48 Calculator

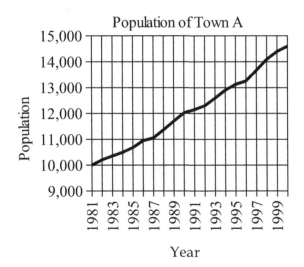

Population of Town A

The chart above shows the population of Town A over two decades, from 1981 to 2000. A demographer estimates that the town's population has increased by about 2% per year. If x is the number of years after 1981, which of the following functions P best models the data?

A) $P(x) = 0.02x + 10,000$

B) $P(x) = 10,000 \times 0.02^x$

C) $P(x) = 10,000 \times 1.02^x$

D) $P(x) = 10,000x^{1.02}$

49 Calculator; Grid-in

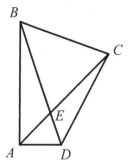

In the figure above, the area of triangle ABD is 8.8 cm^2, the area of triangle ACD is 6.5 cm^2, the area of triangle BCE is 12 cm^2, and the area of quadrilateral $ABCD$ is 25 cm^2. What is the area of triangle ADE, in cm^2 ?

50 No Calculator; Grid-in

a is greater than b.
The sum of a and b is 11.
The difference between a and b is 8.

For positive constants a and b, the above statements are true. What is the value of $a^2 - b^2$?

51 Calculator

In the xy-plane, the vertex of a certain parabola is at the point (–4, –8). The parabola contains the points (4, 0) and (a, 0). What is the value of a ?

A) –12

B) –8

C) 0

D) 8

52 Calculator; Grid-in

$$3x^2 + bx + 24 = (3x + 8)(x + a)$$

If the equation above is true for all values of *x*, what is the value of *b* ?

53 Calculator; Grid-in

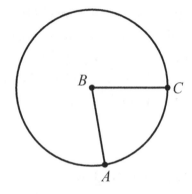

In the figure above, *B* is the center of the circle and points *A* and *C* are on the circle. If *AB* = 45 cm and the length of minor arc *AC* is 20π cm, what is the measure, in degrees, of angle *ABC* ? (Disregard the degree symbol when entering your answer.)

54 Calculator

Erik participates in a bowling league, and keeps careful track of his scores. Over his last 15 games, his mean score was 193. When Erik removes his lowest two scores from the list, his mean for the remaining 13 games increases to 203. What is the mean of Erik's lowest two scores?

A) 250

B) 133

C) 128

D) 112

55 Calculator

In the figure above, a circle is inscribed in a square. If the area of the circle is $x\pi$ square centimeters, what is the perimeter of the square, in centimeters?

A) $4x$

B) $8\sqrt{x}$

C) $8x$

D) $16\sqrt{x}$

56 Calculator

a is five more than half of *b*.
b minus *c* is three less than *a*.
c is two times *d*.

For constants *a*, *b*, *c* and *d*, the statements above are true. Which of the following must also be true?

A) $b - 2d = \frac{1}{2}b + 2$

B) $b - 2d - 3 = a$

C) $b - c - 8 = \frac{1}{2}b$

D) $b + c = a - 17$

57 No Calculator; Grid-in

$$3x - \frac{1}{3}y = a$$

$$ax - y = 27$$

In the system of equations above, a is a constant. For what value of a will the system have an infinite number of solutions?

58 Calculator

Scores and Review Sessions Attended

At the end of a semester, a chemistry professor created the scatterplot above to compare students' scores on the final exam to their attendance at non-mandatory review sessions hosted by her teaching assistant. The line of best fit is also shown. Which of the following could be the equation of the line of best fit?

A) $y = 0.6x + 27.3$

B) $y = 5.8x - 27.3$

C) $y = 27.3x + 0.6$

D) $y = 5.8x + 27.3$

59 Calculator

A certain polygon has n sides; each side has a length of 7 inches. Each interior angle in the polygon measures 162°. What is the perimeter of the polygon?

A) 98 inches

B) 119 inches

C) 128 inches

D) 140 inches

60 Calculator

$$f(x) = x^3$$
$$g(x) = x^{-2}$$
$$h(x) = x^5$$

The functions f, g, and h are defined above. If $a > 1$, which of the following expressions is NOT equal to a^6 ?

A) $f\left(a^2\right)$

B) $h\left(\sqrt[6]{a^5}\right)$

C) $\dfrac{1}{f\left(g\left(a\right)\right)}$

D) $f\left(a\right) \cdot g\left(a\right) \cdot h\left(a\right)$

61 No Calculator; Grid-in

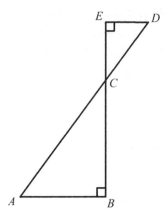

In the figure above, $ED = 3$, $AB = 6$, and $EB = 12$. What is the value of $\sin D$?

62 No Calculator

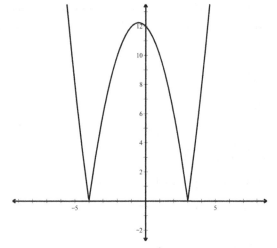

The figure above shows the graph of $y = |f(x)|$ in the xy-plane. Which of the following could be the definition of $f(x)$?

A) $f(x) = (-x - 4)(x - 3)$

B) $f(x) = (x - 4)(x - 3)$

C) $f(x) = (x - 4)(x + 3)$

D) $f(x) = (x - 4)(-x - 3)$

63 Calculator

Consecutive Hops on One Foot
In Mr. Hopkins' Kindergarten Class

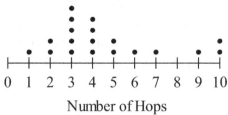

Number of Hops

Mr. Hopkins, a kindergarten teacher, asked each of his students to hop on one foot as many times as they could without their other foot touching the ground. He recorded the results in the dot plot above. Which of the following is true about the values of the mean, median, and mode of the data Mr. Hopkins recorded?

A) mean > median > mode

B) median > mode > mean

C) mode > mean > median

D) mean > mode > median

64 Calculator

Date	Distance	Time
Feb 2	2.04 miles	19 min, 21 sec
Feb 4	2.16 miles	18 min, 43 sec
Feb 5	1.72 miles	15 min, 46 sec
Feb 7	3.31 miles	27 min, 54 sec
Feb 9	2.23 miles	17 min, 03 sec

Marcel has an app on his phone that tracks his jogging workouts. The data above represents the total distance Marcel jogged and the time he was jogging on each of his last 5 workouts. During which of these workouts did Marcel have the greatest average speed, in miles per hour?

A) Feb 2

B) Feb 4

C) Feb 7

D) Feb 9

65 Calculator

$$y = 3x + 3a$$
$$y = ax + 9$$

In the system of equations above, a is a constant. If the equations are graphed in the xy-plane, they form perpendicular lines. At what point do the lines intersect?

A) $(3, 10)$

B) $(10, 3)$

C) $(3, 0)$

D) $(3, 8)$

66 No Calculator; Grid-in

What is the greater of the two x-intercepts of the parabola with the equation $y = -(x-7)^2 + 4$?

67 No Calculator

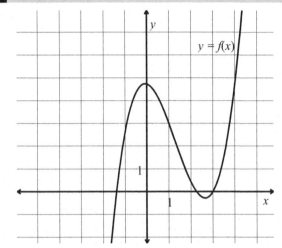

The figure above shows the graph of the function f. If the function g is defined such that $g(x) = 2f(x) - 1$, what is the value of $g(1)$?

A) 3

B) 4

C) 5

D) 6

68 No Calculator

$$\frac{2x+10}{x^2-x-6} = \frac{x+3}{x-3}$$

What is the solution set of the equation above?

A) $\{-4\}$

B) $\{-4, 1\}$

C) $\{-4, 2\}$

D) $\{2, 3\}$

69 Calculator

Final Exam Scores

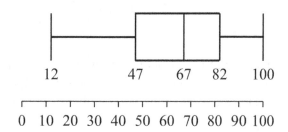

A chemistry professor created the box plot above to summarize the scores on her final exam. If 58 students took the exam, how many could have received a score greater than 82?

A) 29

B) 19

C) 18

D) 14

70 Grid-in

In the equation below, a is a positive integer constant.

$$y = -(x-a)^2 + 9$$

When the equation is graphed in the xy-plane, one of the graph's x-intercepts is at $x = 8$. What is the least possible value of a?

71 Calculator

Mr. Mehta's Math Classes	
Class	Enrollment
1	27
2	34
3	33

The table above shows the number of students in three 11th grade math classes taught by Mr. Mehta at South High School. The ratio of boys to girls in Class 1 is 5 to 4. The ratio of boys to girls in Class 2 is 1 to 1. The ratio of boys to girls in Class 3 is 4 to 7. How many more girls than boys does Mr. Mehta teach in his three 11th grade math classes?

72 Calculator

If $c^a c^b = c^{12}$ and $\dfrac{c^a}{c^b} = c^3$ for nonzero constants a, b, and c, which of the following is equivalent to $c^{(a^2-b^2)}$?

A) c^{36}

B) c^{15}

C) c^9

D) c^4

73 Calculator

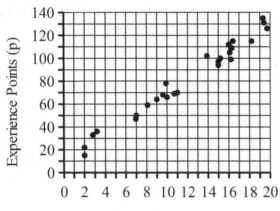

Hours Played (t)

The scatterplot above represents a sample of players of an online video game. The number of hours each player has played (t) is plotted on the horizontal axis and the number of experience points each player has collected (p) is plotted on the vertical axis. Which of the following could be the equation of the line of best fit for this data?

A) $p = 0.5t + 10$

B) $p = t + 12$

C) $p = 6t + 9$

D) $p = 10t + 5$

74 Calculator

Heather's math teacher gives her the equation of a line in the xy-plane, and then asks her to perform the following steps:

I.   Draw the given line.

II. Draw its reflection about the x-axis.

III. Draw a line that is perpendicular to the reflected line (drawn in step 2) and that intersects the reflected line at its y-intercept.

If the original line Heather is given is $y = 4x - 5$, what is the equation of the line she draws in step 3 ?

A) $y = -4x + 5$

B) $y = -4x - 5$

C) $y = -\dfrac{1}{4}x + \dfrac{1}{5}$

D) $y = \dfrac{1}{4}x + 5$

75 Calculator; Grid-in

The histogram above shows the results of a free throw contest held at the grand opening of a new sporting goods store. 81 people participated in the contest; each participant attempted 10 free throws. What was the median number of free throw attempts made?

76 No Calculator; Grid-in

In the function $f(x)=ab^x$, a and b are positive constants. If $f(0) = 8$ and $f(3) = 1$, what is the value of $f(4)$?

77 Calculator

$$\frac{1}{5}x - \frac{1}{15}y = 4$$
$$\frac{3}{7}x - ay = b$$

In the system of equations above, a and b are constants. If the system has an infinite number of solutions, what is the value of b ?

A) 60

B) 1

C) $\dfrac{4}{15}$

D) $\dfrac{60}{7}$

78 Calculator

Dana uses a wearable device that counts her footsteps. She turns the device on as she begins to walk on a paved path in the park near her home. The patch circles a pond, and Dana knows that the distance around the pond is exactly 0.29 miles. Her device tells her that after circling the pond four times, she has taken 2,940 steps. What is the average length covered by each of Dana's steps on this walk, to the nearest inch? (1 mile = 5,280 feet; 1 foot = 12 inches)

A) 2 feet, 10 inches

B) 2 feet, 5 inches

C) 2 feet, 1 inch

D) 1 foot, 8 inches

79 No Calculator; Grid-in

For constants a and b, $a^2 + b^2 = 19$ and $ab = 5$. What is the value of $(a - b)^2$?

80 Calculator

A parabola with equation $y = (x - p)(x - 5)$, where p is a constant, is graphed in the xy-plane. The x-coordinate of the vertex of the parabola is 9. What is the value of p ?

A) −18

B) −4

C) 4

D) 13

81 Calculator

A restaurant owner has determined that in her business selling hamburgers and french fries, she sells two thirds as many orders of french fries in a day as she does hamburgers. She charges $8 per hamburger and $5 per order of fries. According to this model, how many hamburgers would the restaurant owner have sold on a day when she collected $1,734 in revenue selling hamburgers and french fries?

A) 153

B) 144

C) 129

D) 102

82 Calculator; Grid-in

What value of x satisfies the equation $\dfrac{(3^x)^2}{3^{3x}} = \dfrac{1}{27}$?

83 Calculator

Traffic Accidents in Milwaukee, 2010–2019

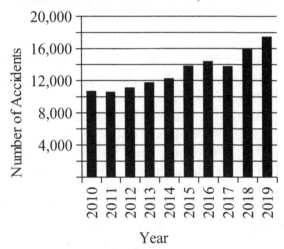

The bar graph above shows the number of reported automobile accidents in Milwaukee, Wisconsin from 2010 to 2019.[*] A traffic analyst calculates the percent change for each year, P_Y, using the following formula:

$$P_Y = \frac{[\text{Accidents in Year } Y] - [\text{Accidents in Year } (Y-1)]}{\text{Accidents in Year } (Y-1)} \times 100\%$$

For example, for she calculates the percent change for 2014 as follows:

$$P_Y = \frac{[\text{Accidents in 2014}] - [\text{Accidents in 2013}]}{\text{Accidents in 2013}} \times 100\%$$

Which of the following will have the *least* value?

A) P_{2012}

B) P_{2014}

C) P_{2017}

D) P_{2018}

---

* Data source: Milwaukee Open Data: Traffic Accident Data. Accessed 2020-01-26 at https://data.milwaukee.gov/dataset/trafficaccident

84 Calculator

Fiscal Year	2017-18	2018-19	2019-20
Budget Type	Adopted	Adopted	Planned
Total Operating Budget	$2.629 billion	$2.788 billion	$2.881 billion

The chart above shows the adopted operating budget for the City of Dallas, Texas over two fiscal years, and the City's planned operating budget for the next fiscal year.* A citizen notes that the percent increase from the 2017-18 to the 2018-19 adopted operating budgets is greater than the percent increase from the 2018-19 adopted to the 2019-20 planned operating budget. How much greater would the planned 2019-20 operating budget be if it increased by the same percent as the 2018-19 adopted operating budget increased?

A) $76 million

B) $61 million

C) $55 million

D) $52 million

85 Calculator

In the xy-plane, a certain parabola has the equation $y = ax^2 + bx + c$, where a, b, and c are constants. The parabola's vertex is at (19, 3), and the parabola passes through the point (16, –6). Which of the following points must the parabola also pass through?

A) (16, 6)

B) (16, 12)

C) (20, –1)

D) (22, –6)

86 Calculator

Day	Sales
Monday	$1,180
Tuesday	$1,331
Wednesday	$1,838
Thursday	$1,865
Friday	$1,574
Saturday	$2,454
Sunday	

The table above shows the total sales for the first six days of the week at a certain laundromat. The owner of the laundromat has calculated that, historically, about 25% of the laundromat's weekly sales are made on Sunday. Which of the following possible Sunday sales totals would best fit the historical pattern?

A) $2,561

B) $2,639

C) $3,401

D) $3,695

87 No Calculator; Grid-in

If $(a + b)(a^2 - b^2) = 18$ and $a^2 + 2ab + b^2 = 36$, what is the value of $a - b$?

88 Calculator; Grid-in

If the equation $x^2 + y^2 - 10x + 14y = -70$ is graphed in the xy-plane, it forms a circle. What is the radius of the circle?

---

* Data source: City of Dallas Fiscal Year 2018-19 Adopted Budget. Accessed 2019-05-05 at https://dallascityhall.com/departments/budget/financialtransparency/AnnualBudget/1819-0-Adopted-Budget.pdf

89 No Calculator

For some constants a and b, the equation $y = a(x - 3)^2 + 2$ forms a parabola in the xy-plane that passes through the points $(2, 0)$ and (a, b). What is the value of b ?

A) -6

B) -16

C) -30

D) -48

90 No Calculator

In triangle ABC, the measure of angle B is $90°$. If $AB = 5$ and $AC = 12$, what is the area of triangle ABC ?

A) $\dfrac{5\sqrt{119}}{2}$

B) 30

C) $\dfrac{65}{2}$

D) 60

91 No Calculator

If $i = \sqrt{-1}$, which of the following is equivalent to $\dfrac{14 - 5i}{3 - 2i}$?

A) $52 + 13i$

B) $4 + i$

C) $11 - 7i$

D) $9 - i$

92 No Calculator

What is the solution set of the equation $5 - x = \sqrt{x - 3}$?

A) $\{4\}$

B) $\{3, 5\}$

C) $\{4, 7\}$

D) $\{3, 7\}$

93 Calculator

Classroom	Number of Students	Average Age of Students (Years)
B1	16	9.6
B2	14	7.2
B3	p	5.5

On hallway B in a certain elementary school, there are three classrooms, B1, B2, and B3. The number and average age (rounded to one decimal point) of the students in each room are listed in the table above. If the average age of students on the hallway rounds to 7.7 years, which of the following could equal p ?

A) 14

B) 13

C) 11

D) 9

94 Calculator

City of Providence - Trash per Person

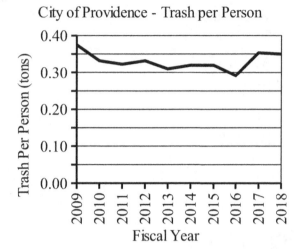

The City of Providence publishes data about trash generation by fiscal year.[*] The chart above represents the trash generated per person, in tons, over a 10-year period. Which of the following statements is NOT supported by the data?

A) The average person in Providence generated about one third of a ton of trash in fiscal year 2010.

B) The greatest year-over-year increase or decrease in trash per person in Providence occurred between 2016 and 2017.

C) The range of trash per person in Providence from fiscal year 2009 to fiscal year 2018 is greater than 0.1 tons.

D) From fiscal year 2009 to fiscal year 2018, trash per person in Providence decreased.

95 Calculator; Grid-in

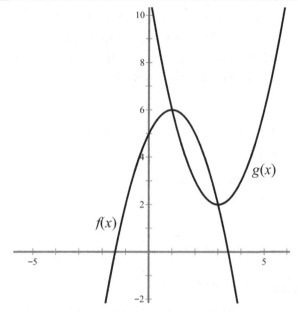

The figure above shows the graphs of $f(x)$ and $g(x)$, where $f(x) = -(x - 1)^2 + 6$ and $g(x) = (x - 3)^2 + 2$. If $h(x) = mx + b$, where m and b are constants, and $f(x) = g(x) = h(x)$ for exactly two values of x, what is the value of b ?

*   Data source: City of Providence, Fiscal Year Waste. Accessed 2019-05-04 at https://performance.providenceri.gov/Government/Fiscal-Year-Waste/yqq7-86b2

96 Calculator

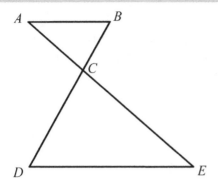

In the figure above, $\overline{AB} \parallel \overline{DE}$. If $AB = 5$, $DE = 10$, and $BC = \dfrac{10}{3}$, what is the length of $\overline{BD}$?

A) $\dfrac{20}{9}$

B) $\dfrac{20}{3}$

C) 10

D) 15

97 No Calculator; Grid-in

$$(x + a)(2x - b) = ax^2 + (2a - b)x - 32$$

If the equation above is true for all values of x, what is the value of b ?

98 No Calculator; Grid-in

If $f(x + 3) = 3x + 1$ for all values of x, what is the value of $f(10)$?

99 Calculator; Grid-in

The average age of all the people in a pre-kindergarten classroom, 17 children and two adults, is eight years. When one of the adults leaves the room temporarily, the average age in the room becomes six years. What is the age, in years, of the adult who left the room?

100 Calculator; Grid-in

Word Puzzle Results

The frequency graph above represents the time, in minutes, it took 39 people to complete a word puzzle. What is the median number of minutes it took for members of this group to complete the puzzle?

101 Calculator

Triangle ABC has a perimeter of 150 inches. The measure of angle A is 90°, and $\sin B = \dfrac{5}{13}$. What is the length of $\overline{AB}$, in inches?

A) 12

B) 23

C) 60

D) 65

102 Calculator

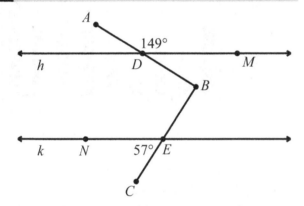

In the figure above, the measure of angle ADM is 149°, the measure of angle CEN is 57°, and lines DM and FN are parallel. What is the measure of angle ABC?

A) 98°

B) 92°

C) 88°

D) 82°

103 Calculator

In the xy-plane, the line $y = 8$ intersects a certain parabola exactly once. Which of the following could be the equation of the parabola?

A) $y = \dfrac{1}{8}(x-8)(x+8)$

B) $y = -\dfrac{1}{8}(x-8)(x+8)$

C) $y = (x+8)(8-x)$

D) $y = (x-8)(8-x)$

104 Calculator; Grid-in

$$(x + 11)(x + a) = x^2 - b$$

The equation above is true for all values of x; a and b are constants. What is the value of b?

105 No Calculator; Grid-in

$$\frac{1}{5}x + \frac{3}{4}y = 3$$
$$x - 15y = 5$$

What value of x satisfies the system of equations above?

106 Calculator

Which of the following is equivalent to $\dfrac{26-13i}{8+i}$? (Note: $i = \sqrt{-1}$)

A) $3 + 2i$

B) $2 + 3i$

C) $2 - 3i$

D) $3 - 2i$

107 Calculator

A company is forming a task force to brainstorm ways to improve its revenues. 30% of those invited to join the task force are sales people, 15% are marketing personnel, and 40% are product designers. The 3 remaining members of the task force are executives. If the task force were to be expanded to include 2 more product designers, then product designers would make up approximately what percent of the task force?

A) 42%

B) 44%

C) 45%

D) 50%

108 Calculator; Grid-in

The line with equation $y = 3x + b$, where b is a constant, passes through the point $(-5, -b)$. What is the y-intercept of the line?

109 Calculator; Grid-in

In the equation $ax^2 + 3x - b = (2x + 5)(3x - c)$, a, b, and c are constants. If the equation is true for all values of x, what is the value of abc ?

110 Calculator

Seth has some stock market investments that fluctuate in value. The value of one of his investments was $15,300 at the end of the day on Monday and $16,830 at the end of the day on Tuesday. The value of the investment decreased by the same percent on Wednesday that it increased on Tuesday. How much less was the investment worth at the end of the day Wednesday than it was at the end of the day on Monday?

A) $0

B) $153

C) $1,530

D) $1,683

111 Calculator; Grid-in

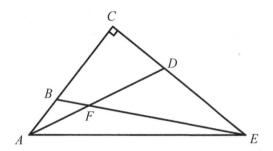

In the figure above, the measure of angle *CAD* is 26° and the measure of angle *BEC* is 28°. What is the measure of angle *BFD* in degrees? (Disregard the ° sign when gridding your answer.)

112 Calculator

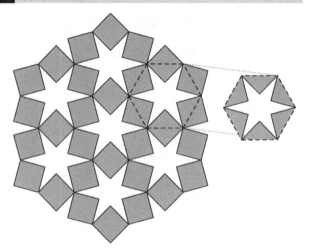

A homeowner is about to construct a large patio in her backyard. She designed the geometrical pattern above and plans to use white and gray paving stones to construct the patio in that pattern. The gray paving stones she needs are squares; gray squares are available for purchase in virtually any size. White paving stones are not available for purchase in the shape she needs. Therefore, the homeowner will purchase regular hexagonal white stones and have them cut to her specifications, as indicated by the dashed-line detail on the right side of the figure. The hexagonal white stones the homeowner can purchase are 6 feet in perimeter. What is the perimeter, in feet, of the gray square stones the homeowner should purchase?

A) $4\sqrt{2}$

B) 4

C) $2\sqrt{2}$

D) $\frac{1}{2}$

113 No Calculator

In the xy-plane, the graph of $f(x)$ is a parabola with a vertex of $(2, 3)$. What is the vertex of the graph of $f(x + 5) + 4$?

A) $(6, 8)$

B) $(7, 7)$

C) $(-2, 8)$

D) $(-3, 7)$

114 Calculator

$$(x - a)^2 + (y - b)^2 = c$$

In the equation above, a, b, and c are constants, and $c > 1$. The graph in the xy-plane of the equation is a circle. Which of the following expressions is equal to the area of the circle?

A) $2\pi\sqrt{c}$

B) πc

C) πc^2

D) $\pi(a - b)^2$

115 No Calculator; Grid-in

$$3x + y = 11$$
$$10x - 2y = 2$$

The system of equations shown above has solution (x, y). What is the value of xy ?

116 Calculator

A machine at a factory that makes phonograph records ensures that each disc produced has a mass between 198 and 212 grams, inclusive, by rejecting discs with masses outside that range. Which of the following inequalities represents the full range of disc masses, m, that the machine will not reject?

A) $|m - 205| \leq 7$

B) $|m - 205| \leq 14$

C) $|m - 198| \leq 14$

D) $|m - 212| \leq 14$

117 No Calculator; Grid-in

$$(2x - a)^2 = 4x^2 - bx + a + 12$$

In the equation above, a and b are positive constants. If the equation is true for all values of x, what is the value of a ?

118 Calculator; Grid-in

$$f(x) = \frac{3x^2 + 4x + 18}{x^2 - ax + 11}$$

In the rational function above, a is a constant. The function is defined for all but two values of x. If one of the values of x for which the function is undefined is 1, what is the value of a ?

119 Calculator

$$f(x) = (x + 2)(x - 1)$$
$$g(x) = -x + 6$$

The functions $y = f(x)$ and $y = g(x)$, defined above, are graphed in the xy-plane. They intersect twice, at the points (a, b) and (c, d), where a, b, c, and d are constants. If $a < c$, which of the following are true?

     I. $a < b$

     II. $b < d$

     III. $c < d$

A) I and II

B) I and III

C) III only

D) I, II, and III

120 No Calculator; Grid-in

In the equation below, a is a constant.

$$y = 3(x - a)(x + 6)$$

When the equation above is graphed in the xy-plane, it forms a parabola with a vertex at $(-2, -48)$. What is the value of a?

121 Calculator

Last week, Ms. Joseph gave the same test to two of her calculus classes, Class A and Class B. The box plots above summarize the scores received by students in the two classes. Each class has 29 students. Which of the following statements is supported by the box plots?

A) Class B had a higher median score than Class A.

B) Class B had a higher average score than Class A.

C) Class B had a larger range of scores than Class A

D) Class B had more students score 65 or higher than did Class A.

122 Calculator

The area of a certain regular hexagon is $216\sqrt{3}$. What is the length of one of the hexagon's sides?

A) 3

B) 6

C) 12

D) 18

123 Calculator

$$(x + 3)^2 + (y - 1)^2 = 25$$
$$(x - 3)^2 + (y - 1)^2 = 16$$

In the xy-plane, the two circles with the equations above intersect at points A and B. What is the equation of the line that contains both point A and point B?

A) $x = -1$

B) $x = 0.75$

C) $y = 1$

D) $y = 0.8x$

124 Calculator

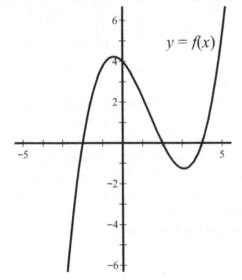

The figure above shows the graph of the polynomial function $y = f(x)$ in the xy-plane. Which of the following points is NOT on the graph of $y = -2f(x)$?

A) $(0, -8)$

B) $(-4, 0)$

C) $(2, 0)$

D) $(4, 0)$

125 No Calculator

If $2^a + 2^a = 2^{(b + 3)}$, what is the value of $a - b$?

A) 1

B) 2

C) 3

D) 5

126 Calculator; Grid-in

A fish tank at a pet store contains red and blue fish. The ratio of red fish to blue fish is 4 to 7. After a customer purchases 5 blue fish from the tank, the ratio of red fish to blue fish becomes 3 to 4. How many red fish are in the tank?

127 Calculator

Word Puzzle Results

The frequency graph above represents the time, in minutes, it took 39 people to complete a word puzzle. Which of the following box plots accurately represents the same data?

A)

B)

C)

D)

128 Calculator

In the xy-plane, perpendicular lines m and n intersect at the point (a, b), where $b > a > 0$. If line m passes through the origin, which of the following could be a point on line n?

A) $(b - a, a - b)$

B) $(a - b, a + b)$

C) $(a + b, a + b)$

D) $(b - a, b - a)$

129 Calculator; Grid-in

Team 1 Individual Scores		Team 2 Individual Scores	
Player 1	63	Player 6	47
Player 2	44	Player 7	66
Player 3	34	Player 8	47
Player 4	33	Player 9	31
Player 5	50	Player 10	

In a certain game, two teams with five members each compete for the highest team score. A team's score is determined by eliminating the team's greatest and least individual scores and then calculating the average (arithmetic mean) of the remaining three individual scores. The individual scores of nine of the ten players in a game are shown in the table above. What is the lowest integer score Player 10 can have so that Team 2 wins the game?

130 Calculator

Which of the following expressions is equivalent to $\dfrac{8x+4}{2x+8}$?

A) $x+\dfrac{2}{x}$

B) $4x+\dfrac{1}{2}$

C) $4-\dfrac{14}{x+4}$

D) $4+\dfrac{7}{x+4}$

131 No Calculator

$$f(x)=\frac{3x^2-5x+11}{7x^2-2x-5}$$

The values a and b are not included in the domain of the rational function above. What is the value of $a+b$?

A) $\dfrac{10}{3}$

B) $\dfrac{12}{7}$

C) $\dfrac{5}{3}$

D) $\dfrac{2}{7}$

132 Calculator

Free Throw Contest Results

The histogram above shows the results of a free throw contest held at the grand opening of a new sporting goods store. 81 people participated in the contest; each participant attempted 10 free throws. If 9 more people had entered the contest and each of them made 5 out of 10 free throws, how would the standard deviation of the data be different?

A) The standard deviation would be higher.

B) The standard deviation would be lower.

C) The standard deviation would not be different.

D) It cannot be determined from the information given.

Extra Practice

133 No Calculator

$$y = 5$$
$$y = a(x - b)^2 + c$$

In the system of equations above, a, b, and c are constants. For which of the following values of a, b, and c does the system have no solutions?

A) $a = -2, b = 1, c = 7$

B) $a = 3, b = 1, c = -3$

C) $a = 6, b = -3, c = 2$

D) $a = -5, b = 5, c = 4$

134 Calculator

What is the radius of the circle formed by the equation $x^2 + y^2 + 10x + 2y = 64$?

A) $\sqrt{38}$

B) 8

C) $3\sqrt{10}$

D) 90

135 Calculator; Grid-in

If $\sin x° = \cos y°$, $0 < x < y < 90$, and $xy = 800$, what is the value of $x^2 + y^2$?

136 No Calculator

A certain parabola has the equation $y = (x + a)(x + b)$, where a and b are constants. In terms of a and b, what is the x-value of the parabola's vertex?

A) $-\dfrac{a+b}{2}$

B) $\dfrac{a-b}{2}$

C) $\dfrac{a+b}{2}$

D) $-\dfrac{ab}{2}$

137 Calculator; Grid-in

In the xy-plane, a triangle is formed with vertices at $(5, 3)$, $(-2, -2)$, and $(0, -2)$. What is the area of the triangle?

138 Calculator

$$y = 3x + 4$$
$$ax - by = 11$$

In the system of equations above, a and b are constants. If the system has no solutions, what is the value of $\dfrac{b}{a}$?

A) $-\dfrac{1}{3}$

B) $\dfrac{1}{3}$

C) $\dfrac{11}{3}$

D) 3

139 No Calculator; Grid-in

A square is formed in the xy-plane by connecting four points: $(1, -2)$, $(2, 3)$, $(7, 2)$, and (a, b), where a and b are constants. What is the value of $a - b$?

140 No Calculator

Which of the following equations, when graphed in the xy-plane, does not contain any points in Quadrant IV?

A) $y = |3 - x| - 1$

B) $y = |x - 1| - 3$

C) $y = 1 - |3 - x|$

D) $y = |3 + x| - 1$

141 Calculator

Public Transportation Ridership Statistics[*]

Year	2006	2007	2008	2009	2010
Millions of Passengers	1,461	1,472	1,481	1,453	1,374
Millions of Passenger Kilometers	5,440	5,469	5,501	5,320	5,100

The table above shows ridership data over the course of five years for BKV Zrt., a public transportation provider in Budapest, Hungary. "Passenger kilometers" is a measure of the total distance traveled by all passengers throughout the year. Which of the following statements is supported by the data?

A) The average number of passengers per year was greater than the median number of passengers per year during the period from 2006 to 2010.

B) From 2009 to 2010, the number of passengers declined by a greater percentage than did the number of passenger kilometers.

C) The range of passenger kilometers per year over the period from 2006 to 2010 was about 61 million.

D) The average number of passenger kilometers over the period from 2006 to 2010 was closest to the passenger kilometers in 2006.

142 No Calculator; Grid-in

$$f(x) = (3x + 4)(4x + 1)(12x - 9)$$

The function $f(x)$, defined above, can be rewritten as $f(x) = ax^3 + bx^2 + cx + d$, where a, b, c, and d are constants. What is the value of $a - d$?

---

[*] Data source: BKV Zrt. Annual Report 2010. Accessed 2017-02-09 at https://static.bkv.hu/ftp/ftp/annual_report/annualreport2010.pdf

143 No Calculator

A parabola in the xy-plane has the equation $y = 3x^2 + 36x + 60$. Which of the following equations shows the parabola's minimum y-value as a constant or coefficient?

A) $y = 3((x + 6)^2 - 16)$

B) $y = 3(x^2 + 12x + 20)$

C) $y = 3(x + 2)(x + 10)$

D) $y = 3(x + 6)^2 - 48$

144 No Calculator

If $f(x + 3) = (x - 1)(x + 8)$, then which of the following is equal to zero?

A) $f(11)$

B) $f(2)$

C) $f(-4)$

D) $f(-5)$

145 Calculator

$$P = 5w + \frac{2}{3}t + \frac{3}{10}m$$

Speedy Courier Service delivers packages by car. The service uses the equation above to calculate P, the total fee in dollars to deliver a package. In the equation, w is the weight of the package in pounds, t is the amount of driving time in minutes required to deliver the package, and m is the number of miles the courier must drive to deliver the package. A customer has an 3-pound package that she needs delivered to a colleague 30 miles away. If the delivery fee is $54, what is the driver's average speed in miles per hour?

A) 30 miles per hour

B) 40 miles per hour

C) 45 miles per hour

D) 55 miles per hour

146 Calculator; Grid-in

Both Louis and Marcy work at jobs where they can collect overtime pay at a rate of 150% of their regular hourly wages for each hour they work beyond 40 hours in a week. Marcy's regular pay rate is $18 per hour, and Louis's regular pay rate is $16 per hour. Last week, Marcy worked for 48 hours and Louis made $64 more than Marcy. How many hours did Louis work last week?

147 No Calculator; Grid-in

In the equations below, *a* is a constant.

$$4x + 7y = 30$$
$$ax - 2y = 5$$

If the equations above are graphed in the *xy*-plane, they form perpendicular lines. What is the value of *a* ?

148 Calculator

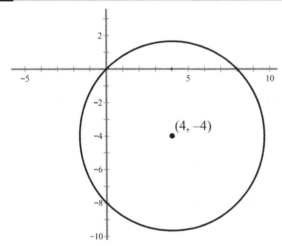

In the figure above, a circle with center (4, –4) passes through the origin. What is the equation of this circle?

A) $(x + 4)^2 + (y - 4)^2 = 16$

B) $(x - 4)^2 + (y + 4)^2 = 4\sqrt{2}$

C) $(x + 4)^2 + (y - 4)^2 = 4\sqrt{2}$

D) $(x - 4)^2 + (y + 4)^2 = 32$

149 Calculator

In the *xy*-plane, line *m* passes through the origin. Which of the following sets of ordered pairs could be on line *m* ?

A) (8, 5) and (13, 10)

B) $\left(-\dfrac{1}{3}, 3\right)$ and $\left(\dfrac{1}{9}, -1\right)$

C) $\left(2, \dfrac{1}{2}\right)$ and $\left(-\dfrac{1}{2}, -2\right)$

D) (5, 4) and (25, 16)

150 Calculator

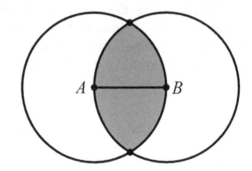

The figure above shows two circles with centers at points *A* and *B*. If the length of $\overline{AB}$ is 8 inches, what is the perimeter of the shaded region, in inches?

A) 8π

B) $\dfrac{24\pi}{5}$

C) $\dfrac{32\pi}{3}$

D) 16π

151 Calculator

Exam Results by Hours Spent on Homework

Hours Spent on Homework in February

Because all the homework she assigns is online, a statistics professor is able to track how long her students spend on homework assignments. She plots that data for the month of February against the scores on an exam she gave at the end of February for one class of 21 students, as shown above. Which of the following is closest to the median score on the exam?

A) 60

B) 63

C) 69

D) 75

152 Calculator; Grid-in

$$y \le \frac{2}{3}x + 2$$

$$y \ge \frac{1}{3}x + 5$$

If (a, b) is in the solution set for the system of inequalities above, what is the least possible value of $a + b$?

153 Calculator

$$2y + 3 > x - 2$$
$$y - 8 < 2x - 5$$

Which of the following ordered pairs (x, y) is in the solution set of the system of inequalities above?

A) $(-3, -1)$

B) $(-1, -4)$

C) $(4, -1)$

D) $(2, 5)$

154 Calculator

In the xy-plane, the graph of $y = f(x)$ is a line. If $f(3) = 8$ and $f(8) = 3$, which of the following is true?

A) $f(f(4)) = 4$

B) $f(0) = f(11)$

C) $f(-3) = -8$

D) $f(10) = -1$

155 No Calculator

The circle with equation $(x - 3)^2 + (y + 4)^2 = 9$ is plotted in the xy-plane. Which of the following ordered pairs (x, y) represents a point on the circle?

A) $(0, 4)$

B) $\left(-3 - \frac{3\sqrt{2}}{2}, 4 + \frac{3\sqrt{2}}{2}\right)$

C) $(6, -1)$

D) $\left(\frac{3}{2}, \frac{3\sqrt{3}}{2} - 4\right)$

156 Calculator; Grid-in

A musician recorded 15 songs with an average length of 215 seconds for potential inclusion on his new album. After discussion with the label that would release the album, it was decided that the final version of the album would include 13 songs and have a duration of 48 minutes and 15 seconds. No silence was added between songs. What is the average length, in seconds, of the recorded songs that were EXCLUDED from the final version of the album?

157 Calculator

If $f(x + 7) = 5x + 5$ for all values of x, which of the following is equal to $f(2x)$?

A) $10x + 19$

B) $10x + 14$

C) $10x - 30$

D) $10x - 60$

158 Calculator; Grid-in

The area of the figure above is 108 square inches. What is the value of m, in inches?

159 Calculator; Grid-in

$$\frac{\left(\dfrac{x^a x^2}{x^3}\right)^3}{x^a} = x^5$$

In the equation above, a is a constant. What is the value of a ?

160 Calculator; Grid-in

In the xy-plane, line k passes through the points $(-4, 0)$ and $(0, -7)$. Line j is parallel to line k and passes through the point $(8, 14)$. What is the value of the x-intercept of line j ?

161 Calculator; Grid-in

A cylindrical drinking glass with an inner diameter of 3 cm and a height of 22 cm is 61% full of water. To the nearest cubic centimeter, what is the volume of water in the glass?

162 Calculator; Grid-in

In an office break room, there is a large bowl that contains exactly three flavors of candy: strawberry, banana, and orange. Earlier today, there were five strawberry candies for every four orange candies, and two strawberry candies for every three banana candies. Then George, a banana candy enthusiast, removed 22 banana candies from the bowl and absconded back to his desk. Now the ratio of strawberry candies to banana candies is five to two. How many candies were in the bowl before George took the banana candies?

163 Calculator

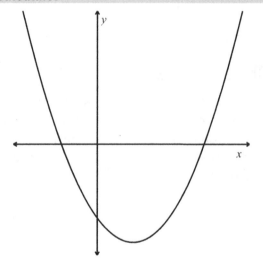

The figure above shows the graph of $y = a(x + b)(x + c)$, where a, b, and c are constants and $|c| > |b|$. Which of the following must be true?

     I. $a > 0$
     II. $c > b$
     III. $bc < 0$

A) I only

B) II only

C) I, II, and III

D) I and III only

164 Calculator; Grid-in

Christine is taking a timed math test with 30 questions. She is allowed to spend 50 minutes on the test. She spends an average of 50 seconds per question on the first 8 questions. She spends an average of 134 seconds per question on the next 15 questions. If she wants to have 5 minutes left after she completes all 30 questions so that she can check her work, what must be her average time, in seconds, for the final 7 questions? Round your answer to the nearest second.

165 Calculator; Grid-in

In triangle ABC, the measure of $\angle B$ is $90°$ and $\cos (\angle A) = \dfrac{5}{13}$. If $AB = 60$, what is the value of BC?

166 Calculator

$$(ax + b)(5x + 9) = (ax)^2 - b^2$$

The equation above is true for all values of x, and a and b are nonzero constants. What is the value of $a - b$?

A) −14

B) −4

C) 4

D) 14

167 Calculator

Which of the following inequalities has as its solution set all points that are a distance of 4 or less from −5 ?

A) $|x + 4| \leq -5$

B) $|x - 5| \leq 4$

C) $|x + 5| \leq 4$

D) $|x - 4| \geq -5$

168 Calculator; Grid-in

x	$f(x)$
0	24
6	22
15	19

Some values of the linear function f are given in the table above. If $g(x) = 3f(x)$, what is the value of $g(8)$?

169 Calculator; Grid-in

If $\sqrt[3]{x^{(2/5)} x^5} = x^m$ for $x > 1$, what is the value of m ?

170 Calculator; Grid-in

A jar contains candies in three different kinds of wrappers: red foil, red cellophane, and green foil. The total number of candies in the jar is 90. The ratio of candies in foil wrappers to candies in cellophane wrappers is 1:1. The ratio of red wrappers to green wrappers is 4:1. How many candies in the jar have red foil wrappers?

171 Calculator

Last week, the share price of a certain stock increased by $1.33, or approximately 1.76 percent, from Monday morning when the stock market opened to Friday evening when the stock market closed. What was the share price of the stock on Friday evening after the market closed?

A) $75.57

B) $76.12

C) $76.90

D) $78.28

172 Calculator; Grid-in

$$3x + 7y = 18$$
$$2x - 2y = 2$$

Given the system of equations above, if $ax + ay = 16$, what is the value of a ?

173 No Calculator; Grid-in

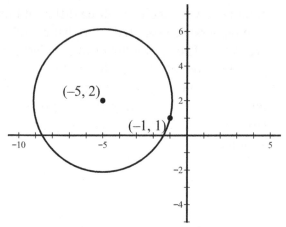

In the figure above, a circle with center (−5, 2) passes through the point (−1, 1). Line *l*, not shown, is tangent to the circle at (−1, 1). What is the *y*-intercept of line *l* ?

174 Calculator

Which of the following equations, when plotted in the *xy*-plane, will create a line that passes through the point (2, 5) and is parallel to the line formed by $3x − 4y = 12$?

A) $−6x + 8y = 28$

B) $3x − 4y = −12$

C) $−3x + 4y = −14$

D) $−6x − 8y = −52$

175 Calculator

In the equation below, the angle measures are in radians and *a* is a constant.

$$\sin\left(\frac{\pi}{8}\right) = \cos\left(\frac{\pi}{a}\right)$$

Which of the following could be the value of *a* ?

A) 8

B) $\dfrac{8}{3}$

C) $\dfrac{8}{7}$

D) $\dfrac{7}{8}$

176 Calculator

$$y = x^2 + x − 8$$
$$y = 2x − 2$$

If (x, y) is a solution to the system of equations above, what is the greatest possible value of $|x − y|$?

A) 1

B) 4

C) 7

D) 8

177 Calculator; Grid-in

Quiz Scores

A biology teacher surprised her class today with a quiz consisting of ten questions, each worth one point. The dot plot above represents the scores of the 15 students who were present to take the quiz. One additional student who was absent today will take the quiz tomorrow. If that student's score increases the range of scores, what will be the median quiz score for the 16 students in the class?

178 No Calculator; Grid-in

In the xy-plane, line m has the equation $y = -5x + a$, where a is a constant. Line n passes through the origin and is perpendicular to line m. If line m and line n intersect at the point $(15, b)$, where b is a constant, what is the value of a ?

179 No Calculator

In the complex number system, $(4 + 7i)(a + bi) = 130$ for some constants a and b. What is the value of $a + b$? (Note: $i = \sqrt{-1}$)

A) 22

B) 3

C) –3

D) –6

180 Calculator

Valentina is shopping for apartments. She sees one advertisement for an apartment on Maple Street that has a total area of 715 square feet and another advertisement for an apartment on Elm Street that has an area of 200 square meters. Which of the following statements is true? (Note: 1 foot = 0.3048 meters)

A) The area of the apartment on Maple Street is about 3 times that of the apartment on Elm Street.

B) The area of the apartment on Maple street is about 9 percent greater than that of the apartment on Elm Street.

C) The area of the apartment on Maple Street is about 8 percent less than that of the apartment on Elm Street.

D) The area of the apartment on Maple Street is about $\frac{1}{3}$ of that of the apartment on Elm Street.

181 Calculator; Grid-in

Distance (yards)		
Club A	Club B	Club C
227	113	178
221	111	178
239	107	183
237	106	181
232	107	182
236	105	179
254	102	183
259	111	179
261	100	183
236	105	178

A golfer went to the practice range with three clubs: Club A, Club B, and Club C. The golfer hit 30 balls in total—ten balls with each club. The table above shows the distance each ball traveled. What is the median distance, in yards, traveled by the 30 practice balls hit?

182 Calculator

Height of Water in Tank over Time

The graph above shows the height, in feet, of water in a tank over a particular ten minute period. At the beginning of the ten minutes, a hose at the top of the tank was turned on. Four minutes later, the hose was turned off. Three minutes after that, a drain at the bottom of the tank was opened.

On a different day, the same tank is filled with water to a height of four feet. Then, a student opens the drain, turns on the hose, and begins a timer simultaneously. How much time elapses before the tank is empty?

A) Three minutes

B) Four minutes

C) Six minutes

D) Eight minutes

183 Calculator

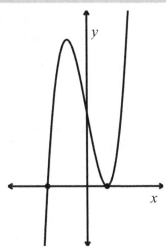

The figure above shows the graph of $y = (x + 4)(x + a)(x + b)$ in the xy-plane. Which of the following statements must be true?

    I. $a = b$

    II. $a > 0$

    III. $b < 4$

A) I only

B) II and III only

C) I and III only

D) I, II, and III

184 Calculator

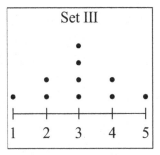

The dot plots above represent three different distributions of scores between one and five. If x equals the standard deviation of Set I, y equals the standard deviation of Set II, and z equals the standard deviation of Set III, which of the following inequalities is true?

A) $x < y < z$

B) $x < z < y$

C) $z < y < x$

D) $z < x < y$

185 Calculator; Grid-in

A certain bowl contains only red, blue, and yellow candies. The ratio of red candies to blue candies is 7:4, and the ratio of red candies to yellow candies is 2:3. There are 104 more yellow candies than blue candies. What is the total number of candies in the bowl?

186 No Calculator; Grid-in

$$3x + 4y = 8$$
$$2x + 8y = 4$$
$$10x - ay = a$$

If the three equations above are graphed in the xy-plane, they form three lines that intersect at one point. What is the value of the constant a?

187 Calculator

$$y > \frac{1}{3}x - 3$$
$$y > 2x + 1$$

If the system of inequalities above is graphed in the xy-plane and the ordered pair (a, b) is in the solution set, then which of the following statements cannot be disproven?

A) If $a > 0$, then $b > 0$.

B) If $a < 0$, then $b < 0$.

C) If $a < 0$, then $b > 0$.

D) If $a > 0$, then $b < 0$.

188 Calculator

Which of the following statements CANNOT be true about a set of 10 numbers?

   I.   The median of the 10 numbers is one of the 10 numbers.

   II. The sum of the 10 numbers is equal to the average (arithmetic mean) of the 10 numbers.

   III. The set of 10 numbers has 6 modes.

A) I and II

B) II and III

C) I, II, and III

D) III only

189 No Calculator

$$y = 6x - \frac{a}{2}$$
$$y - ax = 2a$$

In the system of equations above, a is a constant. When the equations are graphed in the xy-plane, they form parallel lines. What is the positive difference between the y-intercepts of the two lines?

A) 6

B) 9

C) 12

D) 15

190 Calculator; Grid-in

$$y \leq (x-3)^2$$
$$y \geq -x + 9$$

In the xy-plane, a point with coordinates (a, b) lies in the solution set of the system of inequalities above. If a and b are greater than zero, what is the least possible value of a ?

191 Calculator

x	$f(x)$
0	15
1	0
2	−7
3	0
4	27
5	80

The table above shows some values of the polynomial function f. Which of the following is a factor of $f(x + 3)$?

A) x

B) $x - 1$

C) $x - 2$

D) $x + 3$

192 Calculator; Grid-in

The expression $4(x - 5)(x + 6) + m$, where m is a constant, can be rewritten as a binomial square in the form of $(ax + b)^2$ where a and b are integer constants. What is the value of m ?

193 Calculator; Grid-in

The scoring in a certain game is based on the number of red tokens and blue tokens a player has. One player has red and blue tokens in a ratio of 7:10. Then she wins 10 more red tokens, changing her ratio of red to blue tokens to 4:5. How many total tokens does she have after winning the 10 red tokens?

194 Calculator

$$x^3 + bx^2 + cx + 90 = 0$$

The equation above has three unique roots at −5, 3, and k. If b, c, and k are constants, what is the value of k ?

A) −9

B) −6

C) 4

D) 6

195 No Calculator; Grid-in

If $ab = 19$ and $a - b = 7$, what is the value of $a^2 + b^2$?

196 Calculator; Grid-in

$$x^2 + y^2 + ax + by = c$$

In the equation above, a, b, and c are constants. If the equation represents a circle with center $(5, -2)$ and radius 7, what is the value of c ?

No Calculator; Grid-in

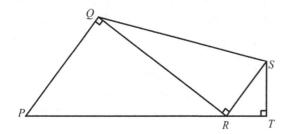

In the figure above, quadrilateral *PQST* is divided into three non-overlapping right triangles. the length of $\overline{QR}$ is 12, the length of $\overline{QS}$ is 13, and the length of $\overline{ST}$ is 4. What is the length of $\overline{PT}$?

198 No Calculator; Grid-in

In the *xy*-plane, line *n* passes through the origin and intersects line *m* at the point (10, 2). Line *m* is perpendicular to line *n*. What is the value of the *x*-intercept of line *m* ?

199 Calculator; Grid-in

The product of the complex numbers $5 - 7i$ and $a + bi$, where *a* and *b* are constants, is 148. What is the sum of *a* and *b*? (Note: $i = \sqrt{-1}$)

200 Calculator; Grid-in

A cube with edges of length $6\sqrt{3}$ is inscribed in a sphere with a volume of $a\pi$. What is the value of *a* ?

Note: The formula for the volume of a sphere is $V = \frac{4}{3}\pi r^3$.

Answers:

1	2	42	B	83	C	124	B	165	144
2	A	43	0	84	A	125	B	166	D
3	B	44	B	85	D	126	12	167	C
4	D	45	3, 10	86	C	127	B	168	64
5	.75, 3/4	46	C	87	.5, 1/2	128	B	169	1.8, 9/5
6	D	47	1	88	2	129	35	170	27
7	C	48	C	89	D	130	C	171	C
8	B	49	2.3	90	A	131	D	172	4
9	11	50	88	91	B	132	B	173	5
10	100	51	A	92	A	133	D	174	A
11	A	52	17	93	C	134	C	175	B
12	D	53	80	94	C	135	6500	176	B
13	85	54	C	95	8	136	A	177	6.5, 13/2
14	C	55	B	96	C	137	5	178	78
15	D	56	A	97	16	138	B	179	D
16	3	57	9	98	22	139	9	180	D
17	C	58	D	99	44	140	D	181	180
18	1	59	D	100	6	141	B	182	D
19	A	60	B	101	C	142	180	183	C
20	D	61	.8, 4/5	102	C	143	D	184	D
21	C	62	A	103	B	144	D	185	344
22	B	63	A	104	121	145	B	186	40
23	B	64	D	105	13	146	55	187	A
24	5	65	D	106	D	147	3.5, 7/2	188	D
25	A	66	9	107	C	148	D	189	D
26	A	67	C	108	7.5, 15/2	149	B	190	5
27	C	68	B	109	1080	150	C	191	A
28	C	69	D	110	B	151	C	192	121
29	D	70	5	111	144	152	17	193	180
30	6	71	6	112	C	153	D	194	D
31	B	72	A	113	D	154	A	195	87
32	B	73	C	114	B	155	D	196	20
33	A	74	D	115	9.75, 39/4	156	165	197	18
34	D	75	5	116	A	157	C	198	10.4, 52/5
35	B	76	.5, 1/2	117	4	158	12	199	24
36	B	77	D	118	12	159	4	200	972
37	.5, 1/2	78	C	119	B	160	16		
38	A	79	9	120	2	161	95		
39	B	80	D	121	D	162	66		
40	C	81	A	122	C	163	D		
41	A	82	3	123	B	164	41		

Solutions begin on page 403.

Solutions

On the following pages, you'll find solutions to all the drill questions in this book. In putting these together, I've tried to be concise and clear and show that even the hard problems don't have *too* many steps.

This is probably a good time to recommend that you get yourself a book owner's account on PWNTestPrep.com. There, you can view video solutions to some of these problems. You can also ask questions in the Q&A section of the site if any of these solutions leave you scratching your head.

Plug in

1. **Answer: C**

   Let's plug in for r, and let's be clever about it to avoid having to deal with negative numbers. Since there's an $r - 11$ in the problem, let's say $r = 12$.

   If $r = 12$, then $r + 9$ is 21. The question says 21 is 4 more than s, so s must be 17. Now, $12 - 11$ is how much less than 17? Well, that's easy! $12 - 11 = 1$, and 1 is 16 less than 17.

2. **Answer: A**

   The first thing you might think to do when plugging in here is to say that $x = 2$ and $y = 3$. That won't work, though, because $-3(2)$ isn't greater than 3.

   What's the only way something gets bigger when it's multiplied by a negative number? That only happens when the something being multiplied by a negative number is already negative! Let's try $x = -2$ and $y = 3$. There, x is definitely still less than y, like the question says it must be, but $-3(-2) = 6$ is greater than y.

   All the other choices can be eliminated by plugging in values, too. To eliminate B, try $x = -2$ and $y = -1$. The original statements still work, so y doesn't have to be greater than 0. To eliminate C, try the same values we used to find the right answer. When $x = -2$ and $y = 3$, the question works, but $|-2|$ is not greater than 3. To eliminate D, use $x = -1$ and $y = 2$. The conditions set out by the question still work, $-3(-1)$ is greater than 2, but $(-1)^2$ is not greater than 2.

3. **Answer: D**

   To solve percent questions like this, plug in 100 for your initial value. If Brunhilda begins her night with $100 and loses 40%, she loses $40. That means she has $60 left before she doubles it at the roulette table. She ends up with $120. $120 is what percent of $100? Easy —120%.

4. **Answer: A**

   Plug in a couple values here. First, because the question says that $x < 7$, plug in $x = 7$. That will tell you what y can almost but not quite be.

   $$2x + y = 8$$
   $$2(7) + y = 8$$
   $$14 + y = 8$$
   $$y = -6$$

   What you know from that, for sure, is that there should be a -6 in your answer. If you're not sure whether to go with choice A or choice B, though, plug in $x = 6$ to see which direction y moves in.

   $$2x + y = 8$$
   $$2(6) + y = 8$$
   $$12 + y = 8$$
   $$y = -4$$

   OK, now you know for sure that as x gets increasingly less than 7, y gets increasingly greater than -6. Choice A is the answer.

5. **Answer: A**

   Plug in the easiest right triangle you can think of with a leg of 3: the 3-4-5! That means $a = 4$, and the unmarked hypotenuse equals 5. (We'll discuss right triangles and trigonometry in great detail beginning on page 249.)

   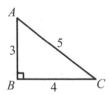

   The value of $\sin A$, then, is $\dfrac{4}{5}$. All you need to do is plug 4 in for a in each answer choice and look for $\dfrac{4}{5}$.

   A) $\dfrac{4}{\sqrt{9+4^2}} = \dfrac{4}{5}$ (Bingo!)

   B) $\dfrac{4}{\sqrt{9+6(4)+4^2}} \dfrac{4}{7}$

C) $\dfrac{4}{9+4^2}=\dfrac{4}{25}$

D) $\dfrac{4}{3}$

6. **Answer: C**

Plug in 2 for x. $2^3 = 8$, so $y = 8$. $2^6 = 64$. What is the difference between 64 and 8?

$64 - 8 = 56$

Which answer choice gives you 56 when you put 8 in for y?

A) $8^3 = 512$

B) $8^2 = 64$

C) $8(8 - 1) = 56$ (Ding ding ding!)

D) $2(8) - 8 = 8$

7. **Answer: B**

When the SAT gives you a geometrical figure with no information about angle measures or side lengths, you're being asked about something that is true for all such figures. In this case, that means we can plug in angle values for the easiest triangle to deal with, an equilateral triangle, where all the interior angles are 60°. Then you can use the fact that all straight lines are 180° angles to fill in the rest of the marked angles.

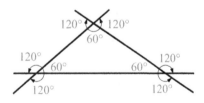

Remember: it doesn't matter that those angle measures are clearly wrong. We don't plug in to match reality; we plug in to make our calculations easy. Add all those angles up and you get a sum of 900°.

8. **Answer: B**

Here, all you need to do is plug in values for x and y that will make the simple linear equation true. This takes a little bit of mental figuring. Say $x = 4$ and $y = 1$ since $2(4) + 3(1) = 11$. (You could also use $x = 1$ and $y = 3$.)

Once you've got numbers that work, use your calculator to evaluate $4^x 8^y$.

$4^4 8^1 = 2048$

Which answer choice equals 2048? Again, use your calculator.

A) $2^{15} = 32{,}768$

B) $2^{11} = 2048$ (Yep!)

C) $2^9 = 512$

D) $2^8 = 256$

9. **Answer: A**

Wow, you can plug in on this? Yes! The question says $x > 4$, so plug in 5 for x and evaluate the original expression with your calculator.

$$\dfrac{x}{x-4}-\dfrac{2}{x+6}$$

$$=\dfrac{5}{5-4}-\dfrac{2}{5+6}$$

$$=5-\dfrac{2}{11}$$

$$=4.\overline{81}$$

Put 5 in for x in each answer choice and see which one gives you the same result!

A) $\dfrac{5^2+4(5)+8}{5^2+2(5)-24}=4.\overline{81}$ (Bangarang!)

B) $\dfrac{5^2+4(5)-8}{5^2-2(5)-24}=-4.\overline{1}$

C) $\dfrac{5+8}{5-6}=-13$

D) $\dfrac{5-4}{5+3}=\dfrac{1}{8}$

10. **Answer: D**

Yeah, so this one is pretty tough. My approach on a question like this is to start by plugging in the variable that contains the other two. In this case, desks have both chairs and employees at them, so let's say $d = 10$ and work from there.

If there are 10 desks, and 5 are not occupied, then 5 *are* occupied by employees. So there are 5 employees: $e = 5$.

If all but 2 employees have an extra chair, then 3 employees have extra chairs. So all 10 desks have one chair, and then 3 of those desks has an extra chair. Therefore, $c = 13$.

Which answer choice equals 13 when $d = 10$ and $e = 5$?

A) $2(10 - 5) + 5 = 15$

B) $2(10 - 5) = 10$

C) $2(10 - 2) = 16$

D) $2(5) + 3 = 13$ (We have a winner!)

Backsolve

1. **Answer: A**

To backsolve this, start by assuming C and see what happens. If Rajesh sold 5 hats on Monday, then the rest of the 15 items he sold were scarves. He made $5(13) + 10(7) = \$135$. That's too much! The question tells us he only made \$123, so that means fewer expensive hats.

So try B. 4 hats means 11 scarves, so Rajesh will make $4(13) + 11(7) = \$129$. Still too much, so we know A is going to be the answer. Here's how I'd do it in table form.

# H	$ H	# S	$ S	Total
5	$65	10	$70	$135
4	$52	11	$77	$129
3	**$39**	**12**	**$84**	**$123**

2. **Answer: D**

Start by assuming C. If a trip to Waconia is $7, then a trip to Chaska, which is $4 more, will be $11. He goes to Chaska 7 times and Waconia 8 times, so his total expense is $7(11) + 8(7) = \$133$. That's too much—the tickets need to be cheaper! Since only one choice offers cheaper tickets, you know the answer is D. Again, here's the table.

$ W	$ C	# W	# C	Total
$7	$11	8	7	$133
$5	**$9**	**8**	**7**	**$103**

3. **Answer: B**

(What the heck—imaginary numbers!? Yeah. We'll spend a whole chapter on them on page 292.) As always, start by assuming C. If $a = 2$, then we can simplify as follows.

$(9 + 2i)(1 - i) = 12 - 6i$
$9 - 9i + 2i - 2i^2 = 12 - 6i$
$9 - 7i + 2 = 12 - 6i$
$11 - 7i = 12 - 6i$

Obviously, that's incorrect, but it's *close*. So, try B, which is only one away from C, rather than D, which is five away. If $a = 3$, then everything is awesome!

$(9 + 3i)(1 - i) = 12 - 6i$
$9 - 9i + 3i - 3i^2 = 12 - 6i$
$9 - 6i + 3 = 12 - 6i$
$12 - 6i = 12 - 6i$

You may decide that you prefer to just solve questions like this algebraically—that's fine! But I think it's important that you also keep an open mind about these alternative solutions. Trust me when I say that the highest scorers on the SAT will, generally, be able to identify multiple approaches to tough questions.

4. **Answer: A**

This is a slightly different kind of backsolve than what we've seen so far, in that there's not really an order in which to try the choices— you just have to go until one works. You have to know yourself and whether you're more likely to be able to do the algebra more quickly than the backsolving.

To test choices, just plug them into the equations and make sure they're true. The right answer needs to work in both equations because we're talking about an intersection. Choice A, (3, 3), does the trick.

$3x + 2y = 15$
$3(3) + 2(3) = 15$ (Yes, this is true)

$5x - y = 12$

$5(3) - 3 = 12$ (Yes, this is also true.)

If you try the other choices, you'll find that choice B works in neither equation, choice C works in the second equation but not the first, and choice D works in the first equation but not the second.

5. **Answer: D**

Shortcut for inequality questions like this: try the biggest and smallest values first, as they're *far* more likely to be correct.

Does choice A work?

$$12 - 13(5) > \frac{5+1}{5-9}$$

$$-53 > -\frac{3}{2}$$

Nope, not true. What about choice D?

$$12 - 13(0) > \frac{0+1}{0-9}$$

$$12 > -\frac{1}{9}$$

Yep, that works!

6. **Answer: C**

Assume that 49.5% of the votes went to Brian. Calculate 49.5% of 3.4 million.

$$\frac{49.5}{100} \times 3,400,000 = 1,683,000$$

If that many votes went to Brian, then Susan must have received the rest.

$3,400,000 - 1,683,000 = 1,717,000$

Is the difference between those vote totals 34,000?

$1,717,000 - 1,683,000 = 34,000$

Nice! How great is it when the first choice you try works? I love that.

7. **Answer: B**

Start by trying C. If she took the car service 4 times, then she took the subway 6 times. That means she spent $4(18.50) + 6(2.75) = \$90.50$. Of course, the question tells us she spent less, so let's have her take fewer expensive car rides.

Try B. If she took the car service 3 times, then she took the subway 7 times. $3(18.50) + 7(2.75) = \$74.75$. Yep, that's what we're looking for!

# C	# S	$ C	$ S	Total
4	6	$74.00	$16.50	$90.50
3	**7**	**$55.50**	**$19.25**	**$74.75**

Bonus shortcut here: the total cost will only end in .75 when Marisol takes an odd number of car service rides. Only choice B is odd.

8. **Answer: D**

Questions like this are the best. Literally all you need to do is type the expression into your calculator and try exponents from the answer choices. Start with C.

$$V(3) = 8100 \left(\frac{7}{6}\right)^3 = \$12,862.50$$

That's too much. Which way do we go? To answer that, we need to recognize that the growth rate, $\frac{7}{6}$, in this question is greater than 1, so the higher the exponent, the greater the result. Three years was enough for this stock to surpass the $11,000 mark, so we need Andy to have held the stock for less time. D is the only answer that does that for us, but let's try it to be sure.

$$V(2) = 8100 \left(\frac{7}{6}\right)^2 = \$11,025$$

Yeah, that's good enough! (Note that the question says "roughly"! $25 is less than 1% of $11,000, so I'd say we're in the ballpark enough to say "roughly."

9. **Answer: D**

First, plug in values for the base and height of

triangle A (make them easy to work with!) so that you can evaluate. I'll say the base and height of triangle A are both 10.

$$A_A = \frac{1}{2}(10)(10) = 50$$

Now, Start by trying C. If $p = 23$, then $r = 18$. A 23% increase off of 10 is 12.3. An 18% decrease off of 10 is 8.2. Will we get an area of 50 for triangle B with those numbers?

$$A_B = \frac{1}{2}(12.3)(8.2) = 50.43$$

Ooh—that's *close*, but it's not quite there. Since we're so close, let's try the closest answer choice next. That's D.

If $p = 25$, then $r = 20$. Increasing 10 by 25% gives you 12.5, and decreasing 10 by 20% gives you 8. Now let's try the area of triangle B again.

$$A_B = \frac{1}{2}(12.5)(8) = 50$$

Yes! That worked! I love backsolving so much.

10. **Answer: B**
There's a little finesse and a little visualization involved in backsolving this one, but if you don't see the math route, then it's nice to have the backsolve escape route. First, take all four choices and, assuming they're a, write down the (a, a^3) they'd make.

A) $(-3, -27)$

B) $(-2, -8)$

C) $(3, 27)$

D) $(4, 64)$

Of those, which one connects to $(10, 40)$ and crosses through the origin? You should attempt to draw this, but here's a visualization from my calculator.

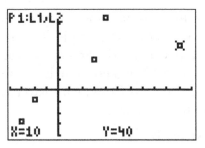

(That's using STAT PLOT and window dimensions of –4 to 11 for x and –40 to 70 for y. It's also way more calculator work than you need to do for this problem—I just did it to help you visualize and because I think calculators are so cool.) The point furthest right, with the marker on it, is $(10, 40)$. Drawing a line from that to which other point will hit the origin? Clearly only $(-2, -8)$.

Translating between Words and Math

1. **Answer: A**
Translate the original sentence.

$$xy = \frac{3}{2}ab$$

Of course, that's not an answer choice, so now you have to do some manipulating. Don't just move parts around willy-nilly, though! Look at the answer choices and let them guide you. Multiply everything by 2 and flip the sides of the equation and you land on choice A.

2. **Answer: C**
Translate the given relationships into a equations, using f for Francesca's gift card amount, g for Geraldine's, and h for Hilda's.

$$g = f + 20$$

$$h = \frac{1}{3}g$$

Now you'll have to do some substituting. Try substituting for g in the second equation.

$$h = \frac{1}{3}(f + 20)$$

Now just multiply both sides by 3 and you're on choice C!

Note that this question is also a pretty great one to practice plugging in. Try giving Geraldine a nice dollar amount that's divisible by 3, like 60, and go from there. If $g = 60$, then $h = 20$, and $f = 40$. Which answer choice works with those numbers?

3. **Answer: B**

Yeah, you can plug in on this one, too, but let's practice translating.

Day	Calls
Monday	x
Tuesday	$x + 13$
Wednesday	$x + 13 - 9 = x + 4$
Thursday	$x + 4 - 5 = x - 1$
Friday	118

Now just add up all those calls!

$x + (x + 13) + (x + 4) + (x - 1) + 118$
$= 4x + 134$

4. **Answer: 20**

Translate—it's what we're here to do!

$ab = a + 2b + 17$

Now substitute 3 in for a and solve.

$3b = 3 + 2b + 17$
$3b = 2b + 20$
$b = 20$

5. **Answer: 68**

You don't actually need to translate into equations here, but this question still belongs in this drill because if you're one of the many students who divides when you should multiply or vice versa when you're dealing with "half," "double," etc., then it's worth your time to sit down and *really* understand it if you want to do well on the SAT math section.

Kent has 68 marbles. That's half as many as Justine, so Justine has 136 marbles. Justine has twice as many as Eloise. 136 is twice what number?

$136 = 2x$
$68 = x$

6. **Answer: C**

I think the easiest way to go here is to plug in: say it's been 2 minutes. Then 14 rats should have been injected, meaning 105 are still waiting. Which answer choice works when $x = 2$ and $y = 105$?

But we're here to practice our translation, so let's write the equation. At zero minutes, there will be 119 rats waiting to be injected. Every minute after that, 7 rats will receive the hormone injection, so there will be 7 fewer awaiting injection. So we can write the following equation

$119 - 7x = y$

That's not an answer choice, but with only a tiny bit of manipulation, we get to answer choice C. Just add $7x$ to each side.

$119 = y + 7x$

7. **Answer: A**

The store was open for 8 hours on 29 days, and for 15 hours on the other day. So the open time is $8(29) + 15 = 247$ hours. That's what the manager needs to multiply by his open rate, r_1.

Pay attention to your answer choices. You don't need to calculate anything else—each choice has a 247 and a 473, and now we know for sure what the 247 is, so we can deduce that 473 must have been the hours that the store wasn't open.

From here, all you need to know is that the manager will *add* the costs from when the store was open and the costs from when the store was closed to come to his total monthly bill. Choice A does that.

8. **Answer: 3996**

Just follow the directions. First, we need to multiply the number of apartments, 6, by the average monthly rent, $740.

$6 \times \$740 = \$4440$

Now we need to subtract 10% from that. 10% of $4440 is $444, so Peter's conservative projection is $\$4440 - 444 = \$3996$.

9. **Answer: 621**

Between June 1, 2010 and June 1, 2015, the site gained 41,783 − 4,523 = 37,260 accounts. That's a 5-year period. Since we're modeling with months, though, it's more important to note that it's a 5 × 12 = 60 month period.

If the site gained 37,260 accounts in 60 months, then we can model the site's monthly growth by dividing.

$$\frac{37{,}260 \text{ accounts}}{60 \text{ months}} = 621 \text{ accounts per month}$$

Therefore, for every month after June 1, 2010, the model should say the site added 621 accounts. The model: $A(m) = 4{,}523 + 621m$.

10. **Answer: 23**

OK, so this question is certainly long-winded, but the actual math underneath it all is fairly straightforward. We know he has 50 shirts and we know he will sell them all. We know how much it cost him to make the shirts, and we know what he wants to make in profit. Let's start with that last bit.

It cost Gus $690 to make the shirts. He wants his profit to be at least 60% of that. Translation: he wants to make at least 60% more than he spent. So what's 60% more than $690?

$690 + 0.60(690) = $1104

Now all we need to do is figure out how much Gus needs to charge for each of his 50 shirts to make at least $1104. Let's call his price x.

$50x > 1104$
$x > 22.08$

Since Gus plans to sell his shirts at a whole dollar price, the lowest he can charge is $23.

Algebraic Manipulation

1. **Answer: C**

First, multiply by $(x - 3)$ to get it out of the denominator on the left.

$$\frac{x+3}{x-3} = 4$$

$x + 3 = 4(x - 3)$

Now solve away!

$x + 3 = 4x - 12$
$x + 15 = 4x$
$15 = 3x$
$5 = x$

2. **Answer: B**

The thing to be careful with here is the stuff outside the parentheses. Don't forget to distribute that negative and that 3!

$(5x + 1) − (3x + 2) + 3(x + 5)$
$5x + 1 − 3x − 2 + 3x + 15$
$5x + 14$

So when the expression is in $ax + b$ form, $a = 5$ and $b = 14$. $a < b$; the answer is B.

3. **Answer: A**

For all that text, all this question is asking you to do is solve the given equation for t. First thing you'll want to do is multiply by 10 so you can stop worrying about the fraction—just be careful to distribute it!

$$P = x + \frac{t - 70}{10}$$
$$10P = 10x + t - 70$$

There, that's better. Now manipulate to get t by itself.

$10P + 10x = t - 70$
$10P + 10x + 70 = t$

4. **Answer: 10**

There are a bunch of ways to go here, but the simplest is probably just to mess with the original equation until you get the left side to equal $\frac{m}{3n}$. First multiply by 2, then divide by 3.

$$\frac{m}{2n} = 15$$

$$\frac{m}{n} = 30$$

$$\frac{m}{3n} = 10$$

5. **Answer: .5 or 1/2**

Fractions are the worst. Multiply by the least common multiple of the denominators, 18, to make your life much easier.

$$\frac{1}{3}x + \frac{4}{9}x = \frac{5}{9} - \frac{1}{6}$$

$$18\left(\frac{1}{3}x + \frac{4}{9}x\right) = 18\left(\frac{5}{9} - \frac{1}{6}\right)$$

$$6x + 8x = 10 - 3$$
$$14x = 7$$
$$x = \frac{1}{2}$$

6. **Answer: C**

Add carefully! The sum of the expressions is as follows.

$$(9ax - 2ax) + (b + b) + (-3c + c)$$
$$= 7ax + 2b - 2c$$

That's not an answer choice! But look at choice C—it's equivalent. Distribute the 2 in choice C and you get $7ax + 2b - 2c$, same as above.

7. **Answer: A**

Two step problem: first subtract 6, then multiply by 31.

$$19 = 6 + \frac{x}{31}$$

$$13 = \frac{x}{31}$$

$$403 = x$$

8. **Answer: A**

Here's another question asking you to solve for a particular variable or constant. Easy enough, right? First subtract that wacky looking fraction—yep, all you need to do with it is subtract—then divide by 34.

$$\frac{pqr}{mn} + 34a = 374$$

$$34a = 374 - \frac{pqr}{mn}$$

$$a = \frac{374}{34} - \frac{pqr}{34mn}$$

$$a = 11 - \frac{pqr}{34mn}$$

9. **Answer: 260**

Note the shortcut here: you can just double everything and get pretty close.

$$11y + 6 = 139$$
$$2(11y + 6) = 2(139)$$
$$22y + 12 = 278$$

But wait—you're not all the way home yet. You need $22y - 6$, not $22y + 12$. So subtract 18 to get there.

$$22y + 12 - 18 = 278 - 18$$
$$22y - 6 = 260$$

10. **Answer: Any number between 0 and 1, not including 0 or 1.**

Combine like terms here—get the x terms on one side and the constant terms on the other. Then solve for x the same way you would in an equation. (The only thing you need to worry about with inequalities is that you flip the sign when you multiply or divide a negative number, but we don't end up doing that here.)

$$8x - 1 < 2x + 5$$
$$6x - 1 < 5$$
$$6x < 6$$
$$x < 1$$

Go ahead and grid in any value greater than zero and less than 1. Something like .5 will do just fine.

Solving Systems of Linear Equations

1. **Answer: B**

The *fastest* way to go here is probably backsolve. Only one choice even works in the first equation, so you don't even need to try the second one. Putting (1, 3) into the first equation goes thusly.

$$x + 2y = 7$$
$$1 + 2(3) = 7 \text{ (Yes, that's true, and none of the other choices work!)}$$

If you hate backsolving because you want your life to be difficult, here's the algebra with substitution.

$x + 2y = 7$
$x = 7 - 2y$

$2(7 - 2y) + 3y = 11$
$14 - 4y + 3y = 11$
$-y = -3$
$y = 3$

$x = 7 - 2(3)$
$x = 1$

2. **Answer: B**

Ooh! Ooh! Look! All you have to do is add these two equations and you're home free!

$$\begin{array}{r} -3x - 2y = 5 \\ +(8x + 2y = 0) \\ \hline 5x = 5 \end{array}$$

$x = 1$

Since only one answer choice has x equaling 1, you don't even need to calculate y—you're done!

3. **Answer: C**

If you've got a keen eye, you'll spot the opportunity to subtract here.

$$\begin{array}{r} 3x + 7y = 22 \\ -(2x + 6y = 12) \\ \hline x + y = 10 \end{array}$$

That's not $13x + 13y$, of course, but it's darn close! All we have to do now is multiply.

$13(x + y) = 13(10)$
$13x + 13y = 130$

4. **Answer: 9**

You have to *write* the system of equations here before you can solve it. The question uses n for lollipops, but doesn't give us a constant for campers, so we'll use x. Write the equations one at a time.

"She calculates that if she were to give each camper 7 lollipops, she would have 10 left over."

$n = 7x + 10$

"...if she eats one of the lollipops herself, she can give each camper 8 lollipops and have none left over."

$n - 1 = 8x$

Solve for x, which is all the question asks for, by substituting.

$(7x + 10) - 1 = 8x$
$7x + 9 = 8x$
$9 = x$

5. **Answer: 20**

OK, so this question might not actually be realistic for the SAT, but I think it's important to drive home the point that you should always be on the lookout for quick elimination opportunities. Here, all you have to do is add and you get rid of the y and z terms right away!

$$\begin{array}{r} x + 2y - 3z = 92 \\ +(2x - y + z = 36) \\ +(4x - y + 2z = 12) \\ \hline 7x = 140 \end{array}$$

$x = 20$

6. **Answer: D**

Ahh, now that we're into the questions where the calculator is allowed, let's use it! First, just get both equations into $y=$ form.

$3x - 2y = 16$
$-2y = -3x + 16$
$y = \dfrac{3}{2}x - 8$

$\dfrac{2}{5}x - 2y = 4$

$-2y = -\dfrac{2}{5}x + 4$

$y = \dfrac{2}{10}x - 2$

Graph those, and find their intersection.

Note the messy decimals. Without even putting the fractions in the answer choices into your calculator to see if they match, you should feel pretty good about choice D, with the 13s in the denominators.

Algebraically, you might also recognize the opportunity to eliminate here. (I'll convert the fraction in the second equation to a decimal to make it easier to deal with.)

$$3x - 2y = 16$$
$$\underline{-(0.4x - 2y = 4)}$$
$$2.6x = 12$$

$$x = \frac{12}{2.6} = \frac{60}{13}$$

From there, you should go right to the answer choices since only one choice has that as its x-value.

7. **Answer: A**
You could get these into $y=$ form and use your calculator to solve, but there's also a great elimination opportunity here that will probably be faster. Start by dividing the second equation by 5.

$$\frac{5x\sqrt{2}+20y}{5} = \frac{70}{5}$$

$$x\sqrt{2} + 4y = 14$$

Now subtract!

$$x\sqrt{2} + 4y = 14$$
$$\underline{-(x\sqrt{2} + 3y = 13)}$$
$$y = 1$$

Since only one choice has $y = 1$, you're done!

8. **Answer: 118**
First, calculate the tax on the $190 TV.

$$\frac{8}{100} \times 190 = 15.2$$

So you know the full price of the TV is $190 + 15.20 = $205.20.

Write the equations, using d for Dan's spend, and s for Seth's spend.

$$d + s = 205.20$$
$$d - s = 30.80$$

Add those together to solve quickly for d!

$$2d = 236$$
$$d = 118$$

9. **Answer: 1.11 or 10/9**
That first equation should have your spider sense tingling. You know $\sqrt{45}$ isn't simplified! That's $\sqrt{9}\sqrt{5} = 3\sqrt{5}$! Now look at that equation again.

$$2x\sqrt{5} - 9y\sqrt{5} = 12\sqrt{5}$$

That'll be a lot prettier if we just divide by $\sqrt{5}$.

$$2x - 9y = 12$$

You can do some easy elimination here.

$$5x - 9y = 18$$
$$\underline{-(2x - 9y = 12)}$$
$$3x = 6$$

$$x = 2$$

This question actually requires us to solve for both x and y, so for once we need to continue.

$$2x - 9y = 12$$
$$2(2) - 9y = 12$$
$$4 - 9y = 12$$
$$-9y = 8$$
$$y = -0.\overline{88}$$

The question says that (a, b) satisfies the system, and now we know that $(2, -0.\overline{88})$ satisfies the system. So $a = 2$ and $b = -0.\overline{88}$. Finally, we can evaluate the sum of a and b (i.e., $a + b$) and be done with this horrible problem.

$$2 + (-0.\overline{88}) = 1.\overline{11}$$

Of course, to grid that in, you can either convert to a fraction and grid "10/9", or you can just fill all four spaces with the repeating decimal: "1.11" is just as good.

10. **Answer: 2.33 or 7/3**

Inequalities can be graphed just like equations can—it's just that an inequality is satisfied not only by the line it makes, but by every point above or below that line, depending on the inequality sign. In this problem, we're given two $\geq$ signs, so we know any point on or above both lines will satisfy the system. Since we're asked for the smallest possible y-coordinate that'll satisfy this system, we're looking for the intersection of the lines.

I'm going to show you a cool calculator trick, but know that you needn't bother with the flashy shading when you do this yourself. You can find the intersection just the same without the shading.

If you move your cursor to the left of the equations and start hitting enter, you can cycle through some neat graph effects. In the graph below, I've got my calculator shading above each line. Any point in the overlapping, double-shaded area satisfies the system of inequalities.

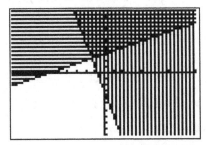

Cool, huh? Anyway, find the intersection to find the smallest possible y-coordinate.

So the answer to grid in is 2.33, or, converted to a fraction, 7/3.

Lines

1. **Answer: C**

The x-axis is where $y = 0$, so to find the x-intercept of a line, plug 0 in for y and solve for x.

$y = 5x - 20$
$0 = 5x - 20$
$20 = 5x$
$4 = x$

2. **Answer: C**

You can solve this algebraically if you plug the three things you know into the slope-intercept form: $x = -3$, $y = 2$, and $m = -2$.

$y = mx + b$
$2 = -2(-3) + b$
$2 = 6 + b$
$-4 = b$

You can also get this by simply drawing. Draw a coordinate plane and plot the point $(-3, 2)$. Then count down 2, right 1 until you reach the y-axis! You'll go through $(-2, 0)$, $(-1, -2)$, and finally $(0, -4)$.

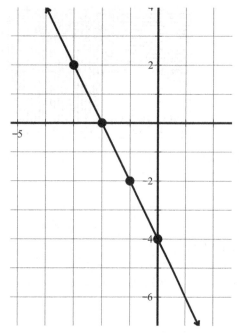

$$y = 3x + c$$
$$-2 = 3(-3) + c$$
$$-2 = -9 + c$$
$$7 = c$$

$$4y - 3x = 11 - d$$
$$4(-2) - 3(-3) = 11 - d$$
$$-8 + 9 = 11 - d$$
$$1 = 11 - d$$
$$10 = d$$

Therefore, the sum of c and d is $7 + 10 = 17$.

5. **Answer: .375 or 3/8**

When a line passes through the origin, all of its points other than $(0, 0)$ are in the same ratio. To see why, take the two points you know on this line: $(8, 3)$ and $(0, 0)$. What's the slope they make?

$$\frac{3-0}{8-0} = \frac{3}{8}$$

Any other point on the line must also simplify to the same slope with $(0, 0)$, so no matter what a and b are, if (a, b) is on that line, then $\frac{b-0}{a-0} = \frac{3}{8}$, so $\frac{b}{a} = \frac{3}{8}$.

6. **Answer: A**

Perpendicular lines have negative reciprocal slopes. The given line, in slope-intercept form, is $y = 3x - 11$. A line that's perpendicular to that will have a slope of $-\frac{1}{3}$.

So let's put all the answer choices into slope-intercept form!

A) $y = -\frac{1}{3}x + \frac{26}{3}$ (There it is!)

B) $y = \frac{2}{3}x + 2$ (Nuh-uh.)

C) $y = -3x + 9$ (Nyet.)

D) $y = 3x + 10$ (No.)

7. **Answer: D**

When a question says a system has no solutions, that's another way of saying that the lines in the system are parallel. So put both given equations into slope-intercept form.

3. **Answer: B**

Parallel lines have the same slope, so our first mission here is to put the given equation into slope-intercept form so we know what slope we're looking for.

$$3y = 2x + 11$$

$$y = \frac{2}{3}x + \frac{11}{3}$$

So the two points in the correct answer will give us a slope of $\frac{2}{3}$.

A) $\frac{-1-3}{3-(-1)} = -1$ (Nope.)

B) $\frac{-2-4}{3-12} = \frac{-6}{-9} = \frac{2}{3}$ (Yep, that's the one!)

C) $\frac{5-2}{8-6} = \frac{3}{2}$ (No.)

D) $\frac{7-4}{5-7} = -\frac{3}{2}$ (No.)

4. **Answer: D**

If the lines intersect at $(-3, -2)$, then you know that point exists on both lines. So you can plug it in to each equation to solve for c and d!

$7x + 12y = 31$

$$y = -\frac{7}{12}x + \frac{31}{12}$$

$ky = x + 19$

$$y = \frac{1}{k}x + \frac{19}{k}$$

What that tells us is that we want $\frac{1}{k} = -\frac{7}{12}$. To figure out k, just flip everything!

$$k = -\frac{12}{7}$$

8. **Answer: A**

If this equation is confusing you at all, then this is a great opportunity to practice using the calculator's table function.

See what's going on there? It takes 2 feet for Karen to lose 7% accuracy. That's what choice A says.

9. **Answer: D**

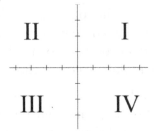

A line that contains only points in quadrants I and IV must be completely vertical.

A vertical line's slope is undefined. (Slope is rise over run, and a vertical line has a run of zero!)

10. **Answer: 14.3 or 43/3**

Well, easy part first. Since these lines are already in slope-intercept form, and we know they're perpendicular, we know that a must be $-\frac{1}{3}$.

To find b, all we need to do is plug the point we know into g.

$$g(x) = -\frac{1}{3}x + b$$

$$14 = -\frac{1}{3}(2) + b$$

$$14 + \frac{2}{3} = b$$

Throw that in your calculator to get a decimal or fraction value.

```
14+2/3
        14.66666667
Ans▶Frac
            44/3
```

You can check your work with your calculator, too. Graph to make sure the lines are perpendicular and intersect at (2, 14).

```
Plot1  Plot2  Plot3
\Y1◻3X+8
\Y2◻(-1/3)X+44/3
\Y3=
\Y4=
\Y5=
\Y6=
```

Yep—that worked!

So if $a=-\dfrac{1}{3}$ and $b=\dfrac{44}{3}$, then:

$$a+b=-\dfrac{1}{3}+\dfrac{44}{3}=\dfrac{43}{3}$$

Absolute Value

1. **Answer: C**

    Here's the thing to know about this one: The smallest anything inside absolute value brackets can ever be is 0. Since all the absolute value brackets in the answer choices in this question are linear expressions, all of them will equal 0 at some point, but none will ever be less than 0, because, well, that's how absolute values work.

    The key to this question, then, is what's *outside* the brackets. Any choice with subtraction outside the brackets will be negative, for a little while, but choice C, with a +3 outside the brackets, will never be 0. The smallest it will ever be is 3, when $x = 1$, and thus the part inside the brackets equals 0.

2. **Answer: D**

    This question is just another way of playing off the same concept tested in question 1. The smallest $|y-3|$ can ever be is 0. Since you have a +3 outside that, the smallest $|y-3|+3$ can ever be is 3. There is no value of y that would make that expression equal 2.

    Note that you can also backsolve this one easily. Put the three numerical choices in for y and see for yourself that the expression never equals 2.

3. **Answer: A**

    I'm so in love with this concept, apparently, that maybe I should marry it. The smallest $|3x|$ can be is when $x = 0$, which is allowed, since the question tells us that $x \le 0$.

    When $x = 0$, then $y \ge -7$. Therefore, since the part inside the absolute value brackets can't get any smaller than 0, we know that's the minimum value of y.

4. **Answer: 38.3**

    First, since you're asked for the answer in thousands of dollars, convert the numbers you're given into thousands. 24,800 becomes 24.8 thousand, and 13,500 becomes 13.5 thousand.

    From there, follow the process we discussed in the chapter to convert this inequality into something more intuitive.

    $$|x-24.8| \le 13.5$$
    $$-13.5 \le x-24.8 \le 13.5$$
    $$11.3 \le x \le 38.3$$

5. **Answer: 2.5**

    First, get the absolute value part of the equation by itself.

    $$|x-9|+1 = 7.5$$
    $$|x-9| = 6.5$$

    From there, recognize that you'll get the minimum value of x when the value inside the absolute value brackets is negative.

    $$x-9 = -6.5$$
    $$x = 2.5$$

6. **Answer: B**

    Useful to know: The only way two integers add to an odd integer like 7 is if one of them is odd and the other one is even. So you know either a is odd and b is even or vice versa. They will always sum to an odd number. 0 is an even number, so $a + b$ can never be 0.

7. **Answer: B**

    Try each of these until one doesn't work. You'll see that choice B is false.

$h(1) = |h(1)|$
$2(1) - 10 = |2(1) - 10|$
$-8 = |-8|$
$-8 = 8$ (Nope, not true!)

8. **Answer: D**
   To get this one, you can either use the formula to build an absolute value range discussed on page 86 (the average of 215 and 251 is 233, so that goes inside the absolute value with the s, and the distance from 233 to 251 is 18, so that goes across from the $<$ sign), or you can just convert the answer choices to regular, easy-to-read ranges and see which one lands on $215 < s < 251$. Here's how that looks with the correct choice.

   $|s - 233| < 18$
   $-18 < s - 233 < 18$
   $215 < s < 251$

9. **Answer: B**
   This kind of question exists just to make you think with two concepts at the same time—in this case, functions and absolute values.

   Anyway, to solve, just evaluate each choice until one is false.

   A) $|g(3)| = |-3| = 3$ (That's true.)

   B) $|g(5)| = |8| = 8$. (That's not greater than $g(5)$, which is also 8, so choice B is false.)

10. **Answer: 3 or 4**
    Since most of the graph of $g(x)$ is below the x-axis, most $g(x)$ will mostly *not* equal $|g(x)|$. However, when the graph is above the x-axis, it $g(x) = |g(x)|$. The only integer values for which that is true are $x = 3$ or $x = 4$, so pick one of those and bubble that bad boy in.

Functions

1. **Answer: B**
   First, you have to find out what k is. So see where the graph is when $x = -1$.

When $x = -1$, the graph is at $(-1, 3)$. So $k = 3$.

Now, what's $2f(k)$? Well, to figure that out, we find $f(k)$, and then multiply it by 2. We just figured out that $k = 3$, so what's $f(3)$?

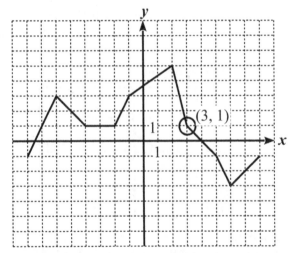

Using the same methodology, $f(3) = 1$. Since the question asked for 2 times that, the answer is 2.

2. **Answer: A**
   If $f(x - 1) = x + 1$, then we can figure out what $f(x)$ is. We can do that because we know that before it became a simple $x + 1$, $f(x - 1)$ must have had an $(x - 1)$ in it somewhere! In this case, it must have been $f(x - 1) = (x - 1) + 2$, which simplifies to $f(x - 1) = x + 1$. That tells us that plain old $f(x) = x + 2$. So to find $f(x + 1)$, all we need to do is put $x + 1$ through the function.

$f(x) = x + 2$

$f(x + 1) = (x + 1) + 2$

$f(x + 1) = x + 3$

Another way I like to think about this question is graphically. What is the shift that happens when you go from $f(x - 1)$ to $f(x + 1)$? The intermediate step is $f(x - 1 \pm 2) = f(x + 1)$; that's a shift of 2 to the left.

Here's the original graph of $y = x + 1$, with a slope of 1 and a y-intercept of 1.

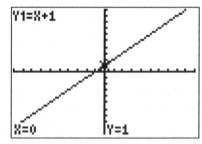

What happens when that shifts 2 to the left? $(0, 1)$ will become $(-2, 1)$, and since the slope is still 1, the new y-intercept will be 3. In other words, the graph will become $y = x + 3$.

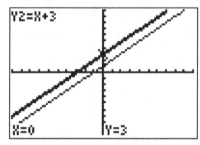

3. **Answer: A**

When you see $f(b) = g(b)$, you should be thinking intersection! That's telling you that when both functions have an x-value of b, their y-values are equal!

The only intersection on the graph is where x is negative, so the only answer choice that can work is -3.

4. **Answer: 10**

If $f(x) = 2x - 1$, then we can calculate f(10) and f(5) easily enough.

$f(10) = 2(10) - 1 = 19$

$f(5) = 2(5) - 1 = 9$

With those, it's just one easy subtraction to find the answer.

$f(10) - f(5) = 19 - 9 = 10$

5. **Answer: 54**

In this case, there's no need figure out $f(x)$ before answering the question. All we need to do is change $f(8)$ to $f(5 + 3)$ and then we can work with $f(x + 3)$ directly!

$f(x + 3) = 10x + 4$

$f(5 + 3) = 10(5) + 4$

$f(8) = 54$

6. **Answer: D**

The key to getting this one is recognizing that the graph labeled $h(x)$ is always exactly 3 lower than the graph labeled $g(x)$. When we want to shift something down in function notation, we subtract *outside* the parentheses. Since $h(x)$ is 3 lower than $g(x)$, we say $h(x) = g(x) - 3$.

7. **Answer: C**

Important: *everything* in the parentheses gets put in where the x was when you're changing the argument of a function. Of course, that includes negative signs.

$f(x) = 3x^2 + 8$

$f(-2x) = 3(-2x)^2 + 8$

$f(-2x) = 3(4x^2) + 8$

$f(-2x) = 12x^2 + 8$

8. **Answer: D**

Because $f(x) = |g(x)|$, you might find it helpful just to write the $f(x)$ values under the table.

x	1	3	5	7	9
$g(x)$	-2	15	6	-3	-10
$f(x)$	2	15	6	3	10

From there, it's easy enough to see that $f(7) = 3$, so $t = 3$. $f(t)$, then, becomes $f(3)$, which is 15.

9. **Answer: 118**

Just plop 11 down in there to find k.

$f(x) = 2x^2 - 14x + k$

$f(11) = 2(11)^2 - 14(11) + k$

$50 = 88 + k$

$-38 = k$

From there, all you need to do is evaluate $f(13)$.

$f(13) = 2(13)^2 - 14(13) - 38$

$f(13) = 118$

10. **Answer: 8**

The table tells you that $f(3) = k$ and $g(1) = m$, so you can't answer the question asked until you figure out what m and k are. So we'll have to use the rest of the table to find k and m.

x	$f(x)$	$g(x)$
1	11	m
2	18	-20
3	k	43
4	-29	88
5	-33	107

You're told that $f(4) = m + 9$. The table tells you that $f(4) = -29$, so you can solve for m.

$-29 = m + 9$

$-38 = m$

Likewise, you know that $g(4) = 2k - 4$, and the table tells you that $g(4) = 88$, so you can solve for k.

$88 = 2k - 4$

$92 = 2k$

$46 = k$

Now, finally, we can answer the question.

$f(3) + g(1) = k + m$

$f(3) + g(1) = 46 + (-38)$

$f(3) + g(1) = 8$

Exponents and Exponential Functions

1. **Answer: C**

It's easiest to see what's going on here if you break the expression into two parts.

First, how does knowing $x^6 = 60$ help you figure out x^{12}? Well, you need to multiply that exponent by 2. How do we multiply an exponent? We raise the expression it's in to a power!

$\left(x^6\right)^2 = 60^2$

$x^{12} = 3600$

OK, so that's settled. Now how does knowing that $w^{10} = 20$ help us figure out w^{-10}? Same basic idea—we need to multiply that exponent by something, and to do that we raise the whole expression to that power.

$\left(w^{10}\right)^{-1} = 20^{-1}$

$w^{-10} = \dfrac{1}{20}$

Now all we need to do is combine everything.

$x^{12} w^{-10} = (3600)\left(\dfrac{1}{20}\right)$

$x^{12} w^{-10} = 180$

2. **Answer: C**

You can plug in to get this one, but I actually find that doing so takes a fair amount of time on this particular question, so I'd encourage you to make sure you know the exponent rules well enough that you can get this one by sight. Simplify each choice as far as you can.

A) $z^{pq} - z^p$ (Can't be simplified.)

B) $\dfrac{z^{pq}}{z^p} = z^{pq-p} = z^{p(q-1)}$

C) $\dfrac{z^p}{z^{p-q}} = z^{p-(p-q)} = z^{p-p+q} = z^q$ YES!

D) $2z^{\frac{q}{2}} = 2\sqrt{z^q}$

3. **Answer: A**

So this one's trickier than it looks, and I bet it's going to fool a lot of people, even people who correctly identify the 10 percent increase year over year. The key is that the power in this table trails the year by 1. This is easier to see if you extend the table and write in the interest equation in each row.

Year	Value	Equation
1	$3,000	$3000(1.1)^0$
2	$3,300	$3000(1.1)^1$
3	$3,630	$3000(1.1)^2$
4	$3,993	$3000(1.1)^3$

See? The exponent in year 1 is 0, the exponent in year 2 is 1, etc. That tells you that the exponent in year 7 is going to be 6, and therefore the answer is A.

4. **Answer: .5 or 1/2**

Just simplify this one—carefully!

$$\sqrt[10]{x^2 x^3} = x^a$$

$$\left(x^2 x^3\right)^{\frac{1}{10}} = x^a$$

$$\left(x^{2+3}\right)^{\frac{1}{10}} = x^a$$

$$\left(x^5\right)^{\frac{1}{10}} = x^a$$

$$x^{\frac{5}{10}} = x^a$$

$$x^{\frac{1}{2}} = x^a$$

5. **Answer: 96**

This is a question that requires you to deal with the n in the standard interest equation since the interest compounds monthly but Chihiro wants to use years as her period unit. As a reminder, here's the standard formula.

$$A = P\left(1 + \frac{r}{n}\right)^{nt}$$

The P is Chihiro's initial deposit of $800. The r is 0.03, for the 3% interest rate. The n is the 12 times per period the interest compounds. The t is the 8 years Chihiro cares about. Plug all those values in and simplify.

$$A = 800\left(1 + \frac{0.03}{12}\right)^{(12)(8)}$$

$$A = 800\left(1 + 0.0025\right)^{96}$$

So there you have it—If Chihiro wants to use the equation provided, with the 0.0025 growth rate, then she needs to use $12 \times 8 = 96$ for the power.

6. **Answer: B**

This one's all about interpreting an exponential decay equation. Note that the base of the exponent in the equation is less than 1. That means that the equation one step before the step shown looked like below.

$$P(n) = 5,000,000(1 - 0.08)n$$

That's a negative 8% growth rate, just like choice A says. And if you know that you're dealing with exponential decay, then you are absolutely not dealing with 92% growth. Therefore, the biologist would disagree with choice B.

7. **Answer: C**

You don't need to write the equation to get this one right if you understand what the question is asking.

56° is 3° less than 59°, so the rate is going to decrease by 20% three times. So let's say the original rate was 100 reproduction rate units (note that in doing this, we're plugging in!).

Reduce 100 by 20% the first time and you're at 80. Reduce 80 by 20% and you're at 64. Reduce 64 by 20% and you're at 51.2. If you started at 100 and ended at 51.2, you'd be talking about a 48.8 percent reduction.

Solving with an exponential equation would look like this.

$$r_{56°} = r_{59°}\left(1 - 0.20\right)^{(59-56)}$$

$$r_{56°} = r_{59°}(0.8)^3$$

$$r_{56°} = 0.512\, r_{59°}$$

From there, you need to know that 0.512 is 51.2 percent, and that taking 51.2 percent of something is the same as reducing it by 48.8 percent.

8. **Answer: 330**

When the note goes up one octave, the string's frequency doubles. To go up two octaves, then, the frequency of the string must double twice!

$$82.41 \times 2^2 = 329.64$$

Round that to the nearest integer like the question asked, and you're at 330.

9. **Answer: 1**

First, recognize that $\left(3^m\right)^n$ is the same as 3^{mn}. That'll be important in a little bit.

Expand the binomial square and combine like terms.

$$(m+n)^2 = m^2 + n^2$$

$$m^2 + 2mn + n^2 = m^2 + n^2$$

$$2mn = 0$$

Of course, that means than $mn = 0$, which means that $3^{mn} = 3^0 = 1$.

10. **Answer: 30.6, 30.7, or 92/3**

This one is very much designed to trick you. Did you get got?

First, let's take care of those parentheses. When we raise an exponential expression to another power, we multiply the exponents.

$$\left(x^5\right)^6 x^{\frac{2}{3}} = x^a$$

$$x^{30}\, x^{\frac{2}{3}} = x^a$$

Now, be super careful. That does NOT equal x^{20}! When we multiply like bases with different exponents, we *add* the exponents.

$$x^{30+\frac{2}{3}} = x^a$$

So $a = 30 + \dfrac{2}{3}$. That's $\dfrac{92}{3}$ if you want to grid it exactly. You'd also be marked correct for gridding a truncated 30.6 or a rounded 30.7.

Quadratics

1. **Answer: D**

Don't be fooled by choice A! That expression isn't equal to zero, so you can't just say $x = -3$ or $x = 4$. To solve, first, you must FOIL.

$$(x+3)(x-4) = 8$$

$$x^2 - x - 12 = 8$$

$$x^2 - x - 20 = 0$$

Now you can factor and find the answer.

$$x^2 - x - 20 = 0$$

$$(x-5)(x+4) = 0$$

$$x = 5 \text{ or } x = -4$$

2. **Answer: B**

A leading coefficient that's not 1 and a *fraction*?! That calls for quadratic formula, big time.

$$x = \frac{-b \pm \sqrt{b^2 - 4ac}}{2a}$$

$$x = \frac{5 \pm \sqrt{(-5)^2 - 4(3)\left(-\frac{11}{12}\right)}}{2(3)}$$

$$x = \frac{5 \pm \sqrt{25 + 11}}{6}$$

$$x = \frac{5 \pm \sqrt{36}}{6}$$

The solution set there is $\left\{-\dfrac{1}{6}, \dfrac{11}{6}\right\}$. Since you know x must be positive, you only need to worry about $\dfrac{11}{6}$. That's just under 2, so you know the answer is that x is between 1 and 2.

3. **Answer: B**

It's good to be able to solve this, but the *fastest* way to go it probably just to backsolve. Between all the answer choices, the only numbers you need to check are –5, –1, 1, and 5. So check them! You'll see that only 5 works.

Now, the algebra.

$$\sqrt{2x-1}=x-2$$
$$2x - 1 = (x - 2)^2$$
$$2x - 1 = x^2 - 4x + 4$$
$$0 = x^2 - 6x + 5$$
$$0 = (x - 5)(x - 1)$$

Check $x = 5$ and $x = 1$ in the original equation to see if they're extraneous.

$$\sqrt{2(1)-1}=1-2$$

$1 = -1 \leftarrow$ Nope, extraneous.

$$\sqrt{2(5)-1}=5-2$$

$3 = 3 \leftarrow$ Yes, that works.

4. **Answer: 1**

Say, for the sake of argument, that $x + a$, where a is some constant, is the other factor. So you can say that $(x + 3)(x + a) = x^2 + bx - 6$.

From that, you know that $3a$ must equal –6, and that $3 + a$ must equal b.

If $3a = -6$, then $a = -2$.

If $a = -2$, then $3 + a = 1 = b$.

5. **Answer: 4**

This question is very similar to the last one because I think this is an important concept. Again, assume $x + a$ is the other factor, so you know $(x + 2)(x + a) = x^2 + px + p$.

From that, you know that $2a = p$ and $2 + a = p$. And from that, you can say that $2a = 2 + a$.

$$2a = 2 + a$$
$$a = 2$$

But wait—we're not solving for a. The question asked us for p. If $a = 2$, then $p = 4$ because $(x + 2)(x + 2) = x^2 + 4x + 4$.

6. **Answer: A**

Use the quadratic formula for this one—the leading coefficient isn't 1 and it's not easily factored out.

$$x = \frac{-b \pm \sqrt{b^2 - 4ac}}{2a}$$
$$x = \frac{10 \pm \sqrt{(-10)^2 - 4(4)(2)}}{2(4)}$$
$$x = \frac{10 \pm \sqrt{68}}{8}$$
$$x = \frac{10 \pm 2\sqrt{17}}{8}$$
$$x = \frac{5 \pm \sqrt{17}}{4}$$

7. **Answer: D**

This question isn't as gnarly as it looks if you remember that functions are undefined when the denominator equals zero. So all you need to do here is figure out when the denominator equals zero. This is a great job for your calculator. You don't even need to simplify—just graph the denominator as is!

Ignore that weird 7 in the 10 millionths place—this parabola's zero is at $x = 6$. So $x = 6$ is where $f(x)$ is undefined.

8. **Answer: C**

   You can solve this one with the same algebraic technique we used on question 3 in this drill, but since the calculator is allowed on this one you also have another option at your disposal: graphing! Graph to find the intersection.

   That tells you that the only solution will simplify to $x = 4.791...$

   You can eliminate choices A and D since they each have two solutions. So just put choices B and C into your calculator to see which equals 4.791...

   ```
   (5+√(29))/2
              5.192582404
   (5+√(21))/2
              4.791287847
   ```

   There you go—choice C it is!

9. **Answer: .664 or .665**

   The coin will land on the ground when its height equals zero. You can either set $h = 0$ and use the quadratic formula, or you can do like I *clearly* love to do and graph!

   That's it! Just make sure you grid to fill in all the bubbles. You can choose to round the answer up to .665 or leave it at .664, but if you just grid .66, you'll be wrong, and that'd be a bummer.

10. **Answer: 1.66 or 1.67 or 10/6**

    This one is straight up quadratic formula. First, get the equation into the $ax^2 + bx + c = 0$ form.

    $3x^2 - 5x - 30 = 0$

    Now put it into the quadratic formula and solve.

    $$x = \frac{-b \pm \sqrt{b^2 - 4ac}}{2a}$$

    $$x = \frac{5 \pm \sqrt{(-5)^2 - 4(3)(-30)}}{2(3)}$$

    $$x = \frac{5 \pm \sqrt{385}}{6}$$

    The possible values of x, then, are $\frac{5 + \sqrt{385}}{6}$ and $\frac{5 - \sqrt{385}}{6}$. Add those together and the radical bits cancel out, leaving you with only $\frac{10}{6}$.

Binomial Squares and Difference of Two Squares

1. **Answer: B**

   The key to getting this one, very simply, is factoring the numerator.

   $$\frac{x^2 - y^2}{x - y} = \frac{(x + y)(x - y)}{x - y}$$

   From there, of course, you can cancel out the $x - y$. You're left with just plain ol' $x + y$.

2. **Answer: A**

   You *could* plug in here, but without your calculator the numbers will get just big enough to be a pain to work with. Far better to recognize that you're looking at a binomial square.

   Note that the first and last terms of the expression are $25a^6$ and $16b^2$, so you should be looking right away for $5a^3$ and $4b$ in the answer choices. Choice A looks good right away, so FOIL it out and see if it's the same as the given expression.

   $$(5a^3 - 4b)(5a^3 - 4b)$$
   $$= 25a^6 - 20a^3b - 20a^3b + 16b^2$$
   $$= 25a^6 - 40a^3b + 16b^2$$

   Sure enough!

3. **Answer: D**

   You've got puzzle pieces here—how do they fit together? Well, if you square $a + b = -8$, then you'll have the $a^2 + b^2$ and ab components, so let's start there.

   $$(a + b)^2 = (-8)^2$$
   $$a^2 + 2ab + b^2 = 64$$
   $$a^2 + b^2 + 2ab = 64$$

   Now we can substitute. We know that $a^2 + b^2 = 50$.

   $$50 + 2ab = 64$$
   $$2ab = 14$$
   $$ab = 7$$

4. **Answer: 9**

   Easy one here, if you recognize the difference of two squares. Factor, substitute, and solve.

   $$p^2 - r^2 = 18$$
   $$(p + r)(p - r) = 18$$
   $$(p + r)(2) = 18$$
   $$p + r = 9$$

5. **Answer: 5.5 or 11/2**

   Start this one the same way we started the last one—factor and substitute.

   $$a^2 - b^2 = -24$$
   $$(a + b)(a - b) = -24$$
   $$(a + b)(-8) = -24$$
   $$a + b = 3$$

   Since the question asked for b, though, we're not quite done yet. We have to use the two simpler equation we have to solve.

   $$a - b = -8$$
   $$a + b = 3$$

   Subtract to eliminate the a terms.

   $$-2b = -11$$
   $$b = 5.5$$

6. **Answer: C**

   FOIL out the first equation and this one becomes much more clear.

   $$(x - y)2 = 71$$
   $$x^2 - 2xy + y^2 = 71$$
   $$x^2 + y^2 - 2xy = 71$$

   Now we can substitute 59 in for $x^2 + y^2$.

   $$59 - 2xy = 71$$
   $$-2xy = 12$$
   $$xy = -6$$

7. **Answer: B**

   I know this isn't the Plug In chapter, but I think plugging in is a really strong approach here. Say $x = 3$ and $y = 2$. That makes $m = 5$ and $n = 1$.

   $x^2 + y^2$ becomes $3^2 + 2^2 = 13$. So that's what we're looking for. Which answer choice gives it to us?

   A) $(5)(1) = 5$

   B) $\dfrac{5^2 + 1^2}{2} = 13$ (YASS!)

C) $(5-1)^2 = 16$

D) $\dfrac{5^2 - 1^2}{2} = 12$

The algebra is a little tricky.

$(x+y)^2 = m^2$

$x^2 + 2xy + y^2 = m^2$

$(x-y)^2 = n^2$

$x^2 - 2xy + y^2 = n^2$

Add those together and you're there.

$2x^2 + 2y^2 = m^2 + n^2$

$x^2 + y^2 = \dfrac{m^2 + n^2}{2}$

8. **Answer: 516**
If you FOIL out the expression you want the value of, you'll see pretty quickly what's going on here.

$(a+b)^2 + (a-b)^2$
$= (a^2 + 2ab + b^2) + (a^2 - 2ab + b^2)$
$= 2a^2 + 2b^2$
$= 2(a^2 + b^2)$

Of course, you know that $a^2 + b^2 = 258$, so the answer is $2(258) = 516$.

9. **Answer: 18**
You can factor the difference of two squares on the left of the given equation, and then you can factor it again.

$16x^4 - 81$
$= (4x^2 + 9)(4x^2 - 9)$
$= (4x^2 + 9)(2x + 3)(2x - 3)$

So, there you have it. You now know that $a = 4$, $b = 9$, $c = 2$, and $d = 3$. Their sum is $4 + 9 + 2 + 3 = 18$.

10. **Answer: 11**
Oh man, I so totally love this question. It combines some sweet sweet binomial squares action with the concept of corresponding coefficients, which is covered in the Polynomials chapter.

If you expand the binomial squared in the given equation, you get the following.

$x^2 + 2ax + a^2 + b = x^2 + 10x + 36$

Because that must be true for all values of x, you know that $2ax = 10x$, and $a^2 + b = 36$.

$2ax = 10x$
$a = 5$

$a^2 + b = 36$
$5^2 + b = 36$
$25 + b = 36$
$b = 11$

Parabolas

1. **Answer: D**
If you want the minimum value of the parabola as a constant or coefficient, then you want the parabola in vertex form. Since only one choice is in vertex form at all, you can probably choose it with confidence without even checking that it's equivalent, but just to be safe, we'll check.

$g(x) = (x+4)^2 - 25$
$g(x) = x^2 + 8x + 16 - 25$
$g(x) = x^2 + 8x - 9$

Yep, that checks out—they're equivalent.

2. **Answer: C**
Because parabolas are symmetrical, this parabola's zeros must be equidistant from the line of symmetry that goes through the vertex: $x = 2$. Also, the graph shows us that one zero must be negative, and closer to the y-axis than the positive zero.

The zeros in choice C are going to be 5 and –1. and that's perfect. Those are equidistant from 2 (check!) and one is negative and one is positive (check!).

3. **Answer: C**

A reflection across the *y*-axis will mean all the *x*-coordinates will be negated. The easiest way to make this happen is to negate the zeros, which we can do by flipping the signs. So instead of $y = (x + 3)(x - 5)$, we want $y = (x - 3)(x + 5)$. Since the answer choices are in standard form, let's FOIL that out and see where we land.

$$y = (x - 3)(x + 5)$$
$$y = x^2 + 5x - 3x - 15$$
$$y = x^2 + 2x - 15$$

4. **Answer: 4**

The *x*-coordinate of the minimum is where the vertical line of symmetry goes through. That's important here because the given points, (0, 3) and (8, 3) have the same *y*-coordinate, so they must be equidistant from that line of symmetry.

So, to find *p*, let's just take the average of the *x*-coordinates of the points we know. The average of 0 and 8 is 4, so *p* = 4.

5. **Answer: 19**

If *k* is a constant, then $y = k$ is a horizontal line. The only way a horizontal line intersects a parabola at exactly one point is if it goes through its vertex. And since the parabola is given to you in vertex form, all you need to do is take the *y*-coordinate of the vertex and grid that baby in.

6. **Answer: D**

Forget about the given equation that has no numbers in it. The only thing that matters here is that the parabola's minimum is at *g*(6). That tells you the parabola is symmetrical about $x = 6$, which is the key to this question. You're looking for one of two things: 1) two points equidistant from the line of symmetry with the same *y*-coordinate, or 2) two points where the higher *y*-coordinate is also farther from the line of symmetry. Choice D fits the first criterion: both points have the same *y*-coordinate of –5, and the *x*-coordinates of 2 and 10 are each 4 away from $x = 6$.

7. **Answer: C**

Thank goodness that this is a calculator allowed question! All we need to do is graph it to answer all three Roman numerals!

There it is in standard zoom on my calculator.

As you can see, Roman numeral I is true: it does go through the origin (although the equation also told us that—it's in standard form with a *c* of 0, so the *y*-intercept is 0).

Roman numeral II is false: that graph is definitely decreasing (i.e., going down as it goes left to right) from $x = 1$ to $x = 6$.

Roman numeral III is true, even though we don't see it at this zoom: *g*(–6) is definitely negative.

8. **Answer: D**

First, calculate the side lengths of the square given the area. If the square's area is 36, then its sides are 6 long.

Since the parabola goes through the origin and all parabolas are symmetrical, we know that *C* and *D*, which are on the parabola, must be equidistant from the *y*-axis, and that $CD = 6$. That means that their *x*-coordinates are 3 and –3, respectively. Since *A* and *B* are on the *x*-axis, the *y*-coordinates of *C* and *D* are each –6.

So *C* is (3, –6), and it's on the parabola. That means we can plug that point into the parabola equation and solve for *k*!

$$h(x) = kx^2$$
$$-6 = k(3)^2$$
$$-6 = 9k$$
$$-\frac{6}{9} = k$$
$$-\frac{2}{3} = k$$

9. **Answer: 49**

    Personally, I go straight to the calculator on this one.

    I had to zoom out once to see it, but using the maximum function I was able to see that the vertex is at (–4, 49) very quickly. The question asks for the *y*-value of the vertex, so 49 is all I need.

    The non-calculator way to get this, if you're curious, is to recognize that the zeros will be at 3 and –11, so the *x*-value of the vertex will be right between them at –4. From there, plug –4 into the equation for *x*, and you'll get 49 for *y*.

10. **Answer: 10 or 13**

    This one is a bit tricky! The quick-and-dirty way to go is to put it in your calculator, peek at the table, and hope that the answer is an integer (pretty likely on a grid-in question).

X	Y1	
7	25	
8	18	
9	13	
10	10	
11	9	
12	10	
13	13	

    X=10

    Woohoo!

The more elegant way to go is to recognize that this parabola is in vertex form, so you know its vertex is (11, 9). You also know it opens up, with a leading coefficient of 1. That means its first steps in either direction will be to go up 1 and over 1. So the next two points you know are (10, 10) (woohoo!) and (12, 10).

The final way to go here is to put *a* in for both *x* and *f*(*x*) and solve. This is not so bad, either.

$$a = (a - 11)^2 + 9$$
$$a = a^2 - 22a + 121 + 9$$
$$0 = a^2 - 23a + 130$$
$$0 = (a - 10)(a - 13)$$
$$a = 10 \text{ or } a = 13$$

Polynomials

1. **Answer: D**

    The rule about corresponding coefficients tells you that if $(a + b)x^3 = cx^3$, then $a + b = c$. That's not an answer choice, but if you move *a* to the other side of the equation, you get where you need to go.

    $$a + b = c$$
    $$b = c - a$$
    $$c - a = b$$

2. **Answer: A**

    Another corresponding coefficients question here. From the given equation, you know the following:

    - $a = r$
    - $-b = s$
    - $c = t$

    Since the question tells you those are all nonzero constants, you know that if $-b = s$, then $b \neq s$. Choice A is false.

3. Answer: C

The key to this one is that for the polynomial to be divisible by x, it must have no term that doesn't have an x in it. So if you look at the first part, $2(x^2 - 11x + 3)$, that simplifies to $2x^2 - 22x + 6$. The first two terms are fine—they have an x. The last term is trouble since it doesn't have an x. So what we need m to do in the second part of the polynomial is cancel that 6 out.

The second part of the polynomial is $7(x + m)$, or $7x + 7m$. We need $7m$ to equal –6 so that the constant term in the full polynomial goes away.

$$7m = -6$$
$$m = -\frac{6}{7}$$

Put all together, here's what the polynomial looks like when $m = -\frac{6}{7}$. Note how it simplifies down to something with no constant term.

$$r(x) = 2(x^2 - 11x + 3) + 7(x + m)$$
$$r(x) = 2x^2 - 22x + 6 + 7x + 7m$$
$$r(x) = 2x^2 - 15x + 6 + 7\left(-\frac{6}{7}\right)$$
$$r(x) = 2x^2 - 15x + 6 - 6$$
$$r(x) = 2x^2 - 15x$$

If the first part of this solution doesn't make intuitive sense, this is a great one to backsolve. Just put answers in for m and simplify the polynomial; you'll know you have the right answer when you're left with a polynomial with no constant term.

4. Answer: 9

That's an awful lot to look at, but the only parts you really need to pay attention to are the leading terms. The only way something that begins with $18x^2$ is divided by something that begins with ax and results in $2x$ in the first term of the quotient is if $a = 9$. If you like, you can do the division to be sure.

$$\begin{array}{r} 2x - 2 \\ 9x+1\overline{\smash{\big)}\,18x^2-16x+3} \\ \underline{-\left(18x^2+2x\right)} \\ -18x+3 \\ \underline{-\left(-18x-2\right)} \\ 5 \end{array}$$

Woohoo! $2x - 2$, remainder 5, just like we always wanted!

5. Answer: 27

Let's start this one by FOILing.

$$(x - 3)(x - d) = x^2 - 2dx + m$$
$$x^2 - dx - 3x + 3d = x^2 - 2dx + m$$

From there, we know from the corresponding coefficients rule that the x coefficients are equal, and the constant terms are equal.

- $-dx - 3x = -2dx$
- $3d = m$

We just need to solve the first equation for d, then use that to find m.

$$-dx - 3x = -2dx$$
$$-d - 3 = -2d$$
$$-3 = -d$$
$$3 = d$$

$$3d = m$$
$$3(3) = m$$
$$9 = m$$

Of course, the question asks us for dm, so our last step is to multiply.

$$dm = (3)(9) = 27$$

6. Answer: D

This is very similar to the last question—another one about corresponding coefficients!

$$(x - 5)(x - 7) = x^2 + mx + n$$
$$x^2 - 7x - 5x + 35 = x^2 + mx + n$$
$$x^2 - 12x + 35 = x^2 + mx + n$$

From there, we can see that $m = -12$ and $n = 35$. The question asks for $n - m$, so that's $35 - (-12) = 47$.

7. **Answer: D**

Note that the given graph has two zeros, one at $x = 3$ and one at $x = 5$. That tells you that $x - 3$ and $x - 5$ are factors of the polynomial that makes that graph. The latter is answer choice D.

8. **Answer: B**

We're in the calculator section, and some of these look like they'd be not very quick to test manually, so let's use the calculator like good little pwners to test the most easily calculator-testable choices first. To test choice B, throw $f(x)$ into your calculator and see where it has zeros.

(I'm getting cute with my window settings here, going from -10 to 10 on the x-axis, but -50 to 150 on the y-axis, so I can show the full curve. You don't need to do this; you can see the zeros at standard zoom.)

The zeros for that graph are at -5, 0, and 2, so you know that the polynomial has $x + 5$, x, and $x - 2$ as factors. It does *not* have $x - 5$ as a factor—that would mean a zero at 5, not -5. So the statement in choice B is false.

9. **Answer: 8**

You can probably factor that function into $(x + 10)(x - 2)$ pretty quickly to find the zeros at -10 and 2, but if you can't, your calculator is always a great option. They let you use these things (sometimes) for a reason!

Anyway, you don't know which is which, but you know that between a and b, one equals -10 and the other equals 2. So you can evaluate that absolute value expression.

$|a + b|$
$= |2 - 10|$
$= |{-8}|$
$= 8$

10. **Answer: 41**

We don't need to do the long division if all we care about is finding the remainder, a. All we need to do is plug -3 in for all the xs in $3x^2 - 4x + 2$ and see what gets spit out.

$3(-3)^2 - 4(-3) + 2$
$= 27 + 12 + 2$
$= 41$

This is *really* a shortcut worth remembering!

Working with Advanced Systems of Equations

1. **Answer: A**

The easiest way to see what's going on here, given that this is a no-calculator question, is to 1) know the shape of a basic x^3 graph, and 2) recognize that $(x + 1)^3$ and $(x - 1)^3$ are going to be left and right shifts of that graph.

In case you could use a calculator-assisted reminder, here's what $y = x^3$ looks like:

Shift that one right and one left, and you'll get no intersections.

2. **Answer: A**

    Set the expressions equal to each other and solve the quadratic.

    $$x^2 - 2x + 8 = -x^2 + 18x + 4$$

    $$2x^2 - 20x + 4 = 0$$

    $$x = \frac{20 \pm \sqrt{(-20)^2 - 4(2)(4)}}{2(2)}$$

    $$x = \frac{20 \pm \sqrt{368}}{4}$$

    $$x = \frac{20 \pm 4\sqrt{23}}{4}$$

    $$x = 5 \pm \sqrt{23}$$

3. **Answer: B**

    Since you're given the equation of $g(x)$, use it to find $g(0)$ and $g(5)$.

    $$g(0) = 0^2 + 3(0) - 10$$
    $$g(0) = -10$$

    $$g(5) = 5^2 + 3(5) - 10$$
    $$g(5) = 30$$

    From that work, you know the line in question must contain $(0, -10)$ and $(5, 30)$. Since you already know $(0, -10)$, you have the y-intercept of the line without any extra work. If you're being clever, you check the answer choices to see how many have -10 as the y-intercept. Choices A and B do. Oh well...you can't be done just yet, but it was worth a shot.

    Find the slope to finish this question off.

    $$\frac{30 - (-10)}{5 - 0} = \frac{40}{5} = 8$$

    So the equation of the line, in $y = mx + b$ form, must be $y = 8x - 10$. Choice B it is!

4. **Answer: 1**

    Recognize that those are two parabolas in vertex form, with their vertices on the same line: $x = 2$. The vertices are $(2, 4)$ and $(2, 6)$. The lower one opens up, and the higher one opens down. Everything inside the football-type shape the parabolas trace out, and the borders themselves, will satisfy the inequalities.

    From here, it's very helpful to know the general shape of a parabola with a leading coefficient of 1 or -1. From $(2, 4)$ opening up, and from $(2, 6)$ opening down, these two parabolas will go one unit step laterally and one unit step vertically before intersecting at $(1, 5)$ and $(3, 5)$. Since the question asks for the least possible x-value that satisfies the inequalities, the answer is 1.

    This was, of course, a no-calculator question, but if you're still scratching your head after the above explanation, the picture below might help.

5. **Answer: 4**

    To find the points of intersection, first solve for x by setting the expressions equal to each other.

    $$2(x - 4)^2 - 2 = (x - 3)^2$$

    $$2(x^2 - 8x + 16) - 2 = x^2 - 6x + 9$$

    $$2x^2 - 16x + 30 = x^2 - 6x + 9$$

    $$x^2 - 10x + 21 = 0$$

    $$(x - 3)(x - 7) = 0$$

    $$x = 3 \text{ or } x = 7$$

So the two intersection points have x-coordinates of 3 and 7. To find their y-coordinates, just substitute 3 and 7 into one of the equations. Since an intersection will be on both graphs, you should pick the easier one to substitute into.

$$y = (3-3)^2 = 0$$

$$y = (7-3)^2 = 16$$

OK! The points you care about are $(3, 0)$ and $(7, 16)$. What's the slope between them?

$$\frac{16-0}{7-3} = \frac{16}{4} = 4$$

6. **Answer: D**

You might not need your calculator for this one, but you get to use it, so why not have a look at the parabola just to be sure?

That's probably enough to see the right answer if you're paying attention to the form of the line equations. They're all in slope-intercept form, and they all have y-intercepts of 1. The one with the steepest positive slope will be the one that avoids intersecting the parabola.

7. **Answer: C**

In other words, how many times do those two graphs intersect? I have an idea that's so crazy it just might work!

Hmm. There's one obvious intersection, but to be sure you might want to play around with your window settings. *Or*, you might want to think about the fact that the skinnier parabola gets outside the fat one for a little bit at around $x = -3.5$. Since it's skinnier, it'll eventually have to get back inside the fat one. That means the graphs will intersect twice.

Below is a good view of the two intersections.

8. **Answer: C**

Note that you're given two parabola equations in vertex form, and that the vertices are $(5, 5)$ and $(5, 6)$. Because a and b are positive, both parabolas open up. That means they'll never intersect as long as they're either equally skinny, or the higher one (with leading coefficient a) is skinnier than the lower one (with leading coefficient b).

If $a = b$, the parabolas will have equal widths, and therefore never intersect, so Roman numeral II is true.

The greater the absolute value of the leading coefficient, the skinnier the parabola, so when $a > b$, the upper parabola with a as its leading coefficient will be skinnier than the lower parabola with b as its leading coefficient. Therefore, Roman numeral I is also true.

Roman numeral III is false. If $a < b$, the lower parabola will be skinnier than the upper parabola, so they'll eventually intersect.

Note that, if these rules are fuzzy at all in your head, all you need to do to get this right is play with each scenario by plugging in values for a and b and graphing.

9. **Answer: 7**
Easiest question in the world with a graphing calculator.

Of course, that's only one intersection, but since the parabolas have the same line of symmetry at $x = 4$ (and since the question tells you that both intersections are on the same horizontal line) you know the answer is 7.

This question isn't so tough without a calculator, either. It just involves knowing your parabola shapes. The parabola with the leading coefficient of 2 will rise twice as fast as the one with the leading coefficient of -1 will fall. Since the given equations tell you the vertices are at $(4, 8)$ and $(4, 5)$, you know the graphs should meet at $\frac{2}{3}$ of the distance between them, farther from the parabola with the higher leading coefficient. $\frac{2}{3}$ of the distance from 5 to 8 is 7.

10. **Answer: 16, 17.6, or 88/5**
You're told that the graphs intersect at a point where $y = 6$, so solve the first equation for x when $y = 6$.

$$6 = x^2 - 12x + 41$$
$$0 = x^2 - 12x + 35$$
$$0 = (x - 5)(x - 7)$$
$$x = 5 \text{ or } x = 7$$

OK, now use one of those values (and keep using 6 for y) to solve for b.

$$6 = -(5)^2 + 5b - 57$$
$$6 = -25 + 5b - 57$$
$$88 = 5b$$
$$\frac{88}{5} = b$$

Or...

$$6 = -(7)^2 + 7b - 57$$
$$6 = -49 + 7b - 57$$
$$112 = 7b$$
$$16 = b$$

Percents and Percent Change

1. **Answer: C**
A 25% raise on $75 per hour can be calculated thusly.

$\dfrac{25}{100} \times 75 = 18.75$

$75 + 18.75 = 93.75$

Or you could do the shortcut.

$1.25 \times 75 = 93.75$

Either way, once we know that Lucy now makes \$93.75 per hour, the last calculation we have to make is easy because Stephanie makes \$100 per hour. \$93.75 is what percent of \$100? 93.75%.

2. **Answer: B**
    Remember that calculating percent change is different than just calculating change! The biggest change is from June to July, but that big change is also coming from the biggest starting value.

    Calculate the percent change for each answer choice.

    A) $\dfrac{400}{2000} \times 100\% = 20.00\%$

    B) $\dfrac{600}{2400} \times 100\% = 25.00\%$

    C) $\dfrac{500}{3000} \times 100\% = 16.67\%$

    D) $\dfrac{800}{3500} \times 100\% = 22.86\%$

3. **Answer: B**
    Translate this into a pure math expression.

    $\dfrac{500}{100} \times \dfrac{45}{100} \times \dfrac{22}{100} \times n$

    $5 \times 0.45 \times 0.22n$

    $0.495n$

4. **Answer: A**
    Good for you if you thought to plug in here. Plug in 2 for p, 50 for q, and 4 for r and this question is a piece of cake. 2 is 50% of 4. The question asks for r, which is 4, so which answer choice works out to 4 when $p = 2$ and $q = 50$? Only choice A.

But of course, there's also an algebraic solution to this question. What tends to stymie students who struggle to solve this algebraically is the "q percent" part because they've trained themselves to make quick decimal conversions when presented with percents. That quick conversion doesn't work here; you can't just move the decimal point over on q.

Of course, when you make that quick decimal conversion in your mind, what you're really doing is dividing by 100. And that's why the little translation algorithm I outlined in the beginning of the Percents and Percent Change chapter is useful. Let's apply it: "p is q percent of r" translates to "p equals q divided by 100 times r," or $p = \dfrac{q}{100}r$. Now just solve for r in terms of p and q:

$p = \dfrac{q}{100}r$

$100p = qr$

$\dfrac{100p}{q} = r$

Unsurprisingly, plug in and algebra both lead us to answer choice A.

5. **Answer: B**
    Pro tip: make your first action here be to write in the value represented by each bar. That will make all the calculations you're going to have to do for this question (and the next two questions) much easier.

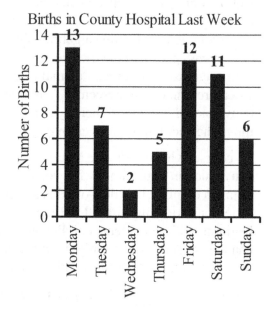

Births in County Hospital Last Week

Let's calculate the percent decrease for each choice. Remember, the formula here is change/original value.

A) $\dfrac{6}{13} \times 100\% = 46.15\%$

B) $\dfrac{5}{7} \times 100\% = 71.43\%$

C) $\dfrac{1}{12} \times 100\% = 8.33\%$

D) $\dfrac{5}{11} \times 100\% = 45.45\%$

What's the biggest percent decrease? Obviously choice B.

6. **Answer: D**
5 babies were born on Thursday, and 56 were born overall. 5 is what percent of 56?

$$5 = \dfrac{x}{100} \times 56$$

$$\dfrac{5}{56} = \dfrac{x}{100}$$

$$8.93 = x$$

7. **Answer: A**
We've already calculated that 56 children were born overall. What would be the change if 49 were born the next week? $56 - 49 = 7$, so there would be 7 fewer babies born. What's that as a percent change from 56?

$$\dfrac{7}{56} \times 100\% = 12.50\%$$

8. **Answer: C**
This is a great candidate for plugging in, especially if we're clever about the numbers we choose. Let's say $g = 35$. That way, there are 35 girls, and since there are 30 more boys than girls, there are 65 boys. That lands us at a total of 100 participants. How smart are we? *So* smart.

Of course, if there are 35 girls in 100 participants, then the league is 35% girls. Which answer choice gives you 35% when you plug in 35 for g? Only choice C does.

If you want to do this the "mathy" way, just set up the fraction: girls on top, all participants on bottom. Then multiply it by 100%.

$$\dfrac{g}{g + (g + 30)} \times 100\%$$

Do a little rearranging there, of course, and you get choice C.

$$\dfrac{100g}{2g + 30}\%$$

Note that although we don't typically throw the % around an expression, it's kosher to separate it from the 100. All the % sign means is "divided by 100." It can go anywhere in a multiplication expression.

9. **Answer: 25**
We can find x by calculating a 40% increase from 780.

$$1.40 \times 780 = 1092$$

So there were 1092 customers served in week 4.

Now, what's the percent increase from 1092 to 1365? That's a change of 1365 − 1092 = 273 and a starting value of 1092.

$$\frac{273}{1092}\times 100\%=25.00\%$$

10. **Answer: 86**

First, calculate how many strikes he had thrown in his first 16 games. What is 70% of 1550?

$$\frac{70}{100}\times 1550=1085\text{ strikes}$$

Now calculate how many total pitches he will have thrown after his 17th game.

1550 + 99 = 1649

We need more than 71% of those to be strikes, but we also want the least possible value of strikes thrown in the 17th game, so let's see what exactly 71% of 1649 is.

$$\frac{71}{100}\times 1649=1170.79\text{ strikes}$$

You can't throw 0.79 of a pitch, so let's round that up to 1171. If 1171 of his 1649 pitches were strikes, what's his strike percentage?

$$\frac{1171}{1649}\times 100\%=71.01\%$$

Yep, that's greater than 71%, but only barely, so it's what we're looking for.

The pitcher had thrown 1085 strikes before his 17th game, and then after the game he had thrown 1171 strikes.

1171 − 1085 = 86

Ratios and Proportionality

1. **Answer: C**

If the ratio of boys to girls is 7 to 5, then the ratio of boys to total students is 7 to 12. Now that we've converted from part:part to part:whole, we can solve.

$$\frac{7\text{ boys}}{12\text{ students}}=\frac{14\text{ boys}}{x\text{ students}}$$

$7x = 168$
$x = 24$

2. **Answer: B**

First, let's figure out how many pencils there are in the drawer. If there are 18 pens, and the ratio of pens to pencils is 3 to 1, then we can figure out the number of pencils easily enough.

$$\frac{3\text{ pens}}{1\text{ pencil}}=\frac{18\text{ pens}}{x\text{ pencils}}$$

$3x = 18$
$x = 6$

So there are 6 pencils. To figure out how many of them are sharpened, we have to convert from sharpened:unsharpened (a part:part ratio) to sharpened:total. If the ratio of sharpened to unsharpened is 2 to 1, then the ratio of sharpened to total is 2 to 3.

$$\frac{2\text{ sharpened}}{3\text{ total}}=\frac{y\text{ sharpened}}{6\text{ total}}$$

$y = 4$

3. **Answer: A**

For this question, it's useful to remember when x and y are in direct proportion, they will form a line that passes through the origin. So a shortcut here is to look for an equation with a y-intercept other than zero. Choice A gives that to you right away—it'll have a y-intercept of k.

4. **Answer: B**

Simple ratio question here—the only sneaky thing is that you're given some information (about eye of newt) that you just don't need.

$$\frac{1.5\text{ cups ww hair}}{2\text{ princesses}}=\frac{x\text{ cups ww hair}}{7\text{ princesses}}$$

$2x = 10.5$
$x = 5.25$

$x = 5\frac{1}{4}$

5. **Answer: C**

Note that if the pennies and quarters in Garrett's pocket are in a ratio of 4 to 1, then the amount of change he has must be a multiple of the 29 cents that 4 pennies and a quarter make. Which answer is a multiple of $0.29? Only $1.45 is: $1.45 is $0.29 times 5, so Garrett has 5 quarters and 20 pennies.

6. **Answer: B**

In a directly proportional relationship between x and $f(x)$, $\dfrac{x}{f(x)}$ will always equal the same fraction. Choice B does that for you: $\dfrac{3}{6}$, $\dfrac{5}{10}$, and $\dfrac{15}{30}$ are all equal to the same fraction: $\dfrac{1}{2}$.

Don't be fooled by choice C! You can see the relationship there fairly obviously: $f(x) = x^2$, but that's not a directly proportional relationship!

$$\frac{3}{9} \neq \frac{5}{25} \neq \frac{15}{225}$$

7. **Answer: B**

If Alistair runs at a constant pace, then the distance he covers is directly proportional to the time he spends running. So we're going to set up that proportion. But first! Don't forget to convert 45 seconds into minutes! 45 seconds is 0.75 minutes.

$$\frac{5000 \text{ meters}}{22 \text{ minutes}} = \frac{x \text{ meters}}{0.75 \text{ minutes}}$$

$170.\overline{45} = x$

That rounds to choice B.

8. **Answer: 24**

This is the classic proportion question setup. As long as you know how proportions work, you're golden.

$$\frac{r_1}{s_1} = \frac{r_2}{s_2}$$

$$\frac{18}{15} = \frac{r}{20}$$

$24 = r$

9. **Answer: 54**

First, figure out the Andy home runs (AHR) based on the Andy strike outs (ASO).

$$\frac{7 \text{ ASO}}{2 \text{ AHR}} = \frac{105 \text{ ASO}}{x \text{ AHR}}$$

$7x = 210$

$x = 30$

So Andy's team hit 30 home runs. Now we can figure out the number of Sean's team's home runs (SHR).

$$\frac{9 \text{ SHR}}{5 \text{ AHR}} = \frac{y \text{ SHR}}{30 \text{ AHR}}$$

$5y = 270$

$y = 54$

10. **Answer: 80**

Population density is measured in people per square mile, so we can figure out how many people live in this district.

$$\frac{x \text{ people}}{34 \text{ square miles}} = \frac{88 \text{ people}}{1 \text{ square mile}}$$

$x = 2992$

If the district is redrawn to lose 2 square miles and 432 people, then it will be 32 square miles and have $2992 - 432 = 2560$ people. We can use those numbers to calculate its new population density.

$$\frac{2560 \text{ people}}{32 \text{ square miles}} = 80 \text{ people per square mile}$$

Measures of Central Tendency and Variability

1. **Answer: B**

Remember: average questions are about sums! If 12 students have an average test score of 74, then they have a total score of $12 \times 74 = 888$.

The 4 students with an average of 96 have a total score of $4 \times 96 = 384$.

That means that when you take those kids out of the class, the total score for the 8 students that are left is $888 - 384 = 504$.

What's the new class average?

$$\frac{504}{8}=63$$

2. **Answer: D**

Same basic idea here—this is a question you can only solve by thinking about sums, not averages.

The average of the 5 numbers is f, so the sum of those numbers is $5f$.

3 of those numbers have a sum of g, so we need to subtract g from $5f$ to get the sum of the remaining two numbers.

Sum of last 2 numbers: $5f - g$

Average of last 2 numbers: $\dfrac{5f-g}{2}$

3. **Answer: D**

Tricky, but this is still about sums. The key is to recognize that there are two different expressions you can write for the same sum. So we can set those equal to each other and solve.

First, note that the sum of the temperatures after m days must be $87m$. So the sum after that next 93° day will become $87m + 93$.

Because you also know the average after that next day becomes 89°, you can also say that the sum of the temperatures after those $m + 1$ days is $89(m + 1)$. So let's solve.

$87m + 93 = 89(m + 1)$
$87m + 93 = 89m + 89$
$4 = 2m$
$2 = m$

4. **Answer: A**

For his 5-day average to be $100 per day, he Sam needs to make $500 over those 5 days. If his average over the first three days is $75, that means he's made a total of 3 × 75 = $225.

He needs to make a total of 500 − 225 = $275 on Thursday and Friday to meet his goal for the week.

5. **Answer: A**

The thing you're looking for here, visually, is whether there are outliers that will drag the mean away from the median. And sure enough, you do have those. The median of this set will fall between the 15th and 16th data point, which is somewhere around 20 mph. Because there are a few days in the 40-45 and 50-55 ranges, you know the average will be higher.

If you're curious, the actual median and mean (which you couldn't calculate from the graph, but which I can calculate from the raw data) are 20.05 and 22.51, respectively.

6. **Answer: B**

It should be fairly easy to see, given the shapes of the 2014 and 2015 histograms, that 2015 was a windier year overall, with higher mean and median daily average wind speeds. That eliminates Roman numerals I and II, which is actually enough to land you on the right answer since there's no "none of the above" choice.

2014 did in fact have a greater range of average daily wind speeds. You can see this on the graph because both years had a day with an average wind speed between 50 and 55 mph, but 2015 didn't have a day with an average wind speed between 5 and 10 mph.

If you're worried about boundary conditions and the fact that we don't have the data to calculate precise ranges here, then this is good time for me to remind you of the SAT's boundary conditions. In histograms on the SAT, left endpoints are included and right endpoints are not. So even if we maximize the 2015 range and minimize the 2014 range, the 2014 range is still bigger by a smidge.

Max 2015 range: 54.99 − 10 = 44.99
Min 2014 range: 50 − 9.99 = 45.01

7. **Answer: B**

The standard deviation is a measure of how close the data points are to the mean, so start by calculating the mean here. It won't take long—use your calculator!

Hopefully you're finding that the sum is 664, the number of data points is 40, and the mean is 16.6.

Now, what happens if 16, 17, 17, 17, and 18 are added to the data? Those are all *really close to the mean*! So when they're included, the data set will have more data very close to the mean than it used to. Its standard deviation will be lower than Olaf first calculated.

8. **Answer: C**
Maryanne currently has the slowest time. Changing it to match the 3rd slowest time will not change the median in a group of 10 times.

Changing Maryanne's time will change the mean because it will change the sum.

Changing Maryanne's time will change the range because it will change the greatest time.

9. **Answer: 20**
Find the average and the median of those 10 scores. The sum is 90 so the average is 9. In order, it's easy to see the median.

{3, 3, 6, 9, 10, 10, 11, 11, 12, 15}

The median goes between the middle two numbers. Those are both 10, so the median is 10.

Now the question becomes, simply, what score does Octavia need to bring the average from 9 to 10?

Remember that once she plays, there will be 11 scores, not 10, so the sum needs to be 110 to get an average score of 10. That means Octavia scored 20 points.

10. **Answer: 7**
If you want to minimize the average of these 5 numbers, you need to minimize their sum. You need to have three 11s to make 11 the median and the mode. Make the other two numbers 1s so keep the sum as low as possible while still using positive integers as the question demands. Here's your set.

{1, 1, 11, 11, 11}

$$\text{Average} = \frac{1+1+11+11+11}{5} = \frac{35}{5} = 7$$

Data Analysis 1

1. **Answer: A**
It'll be useful for answering this question and the next one to start by labeling the graph for quick reference.

Inches of Rainfall in Lorenville

To get this #1 right, you just have to remember the percent change formula. There were 14 inches of rainfall in April, and 9 inches of rainfall in May. That's a change of 5 inches, from a starting point of 14.

$$\frac{5}{14} \times 100\% = 35.7\%$$

2. **Answer: C**
Because we've already listed the rainfall totals, and they're already mostly in order, we can see that the median will be the average of 7 inches and 9 inches. That's 8 inches!

3. **Answer: A**
If you're good at mental math, you can probably eyeball this and get it—to have the biggest ratio you want a relatively large numerator and a relatively small denominator.

That said, it also won't take long to just calculate each ratio, and that's how you make *sure* you don't get a question like this wrong on test day.

A) $\dfrac{527.78}{325.85} = 1.62$

B) $\dfrac{464.46}{313.23} = 1.48$

C) $\dfrac{456.07}{342.59} = 1.33$

D) $\dfrac{359.11}{252.24} = 1.42$

Obviously, choice A is greatest.

4. **Answer: C**
Questions like this are really testing, at a very basic level, whether you can understand a graph with a lot of information in it. In this case, you can just follow the solid Aaron line and get the answer since Thursday is the only day on which Aaron graded the fewest papers. Once you spot that, you can see that the rest of what you need is also true: Betty graded the most papers on Thursday, too.

5. **Answer: D**
This one's easy to get if you label the relevant data points.

From that, it should be fairly obvious that Betty and Carla combined for the fewest papers graded on Friday with only 15 between them. On Tuesday, Wednesday, and Thursday, they combined for 18, 16, and 22, respectively.

6. **Answer: C**
Note how the table you're given here gives you information about three countries, but only asks you about one. That's not going to be uncommon—part of what you're being tested on is whether you can filter out unimportant data.

The key here is to be able to either write an equation given the data in the table and question, or backsolve by dividing each answer choice by 70,273 km^2.

Here's the equation.

$$\frac{x \text{ people}}{70{,}273 \text{ km}^2} = 65.25 \, \frac{\text{people}}{\text{km}^2}$$

$$x = 4{,}585{,}313$$

The other key, I suppose, is that you correctly count decimal places when you convert from the answer you get to scientific notation if you do the algebra. The result we got above rounds to 4.59 million, or 4.59×10^6. If you're uncomfortable with scientific notation, that's a great reason to backsolve since you can just enter the scientific notation into your calculator to convert.

7. **Answer: B**
This is a tricky set of questions! We're going to have to set up a system of equations to solve. I'm going to do it like this. Say x is the number of dogs without spots, and y is the number of cats without spots. Then we know that there are $3x$ dogs with spots and $4y$ cats with spots.

Species	Coat Pattern	
	Spots	No Spots
Dogs	$3x$	x
Cats	$4y$	y
Total	164	47

From there, you can see the two equations we need to write.

$3x + 4y = 164$
$x + y = 47$

I'm going to solve those by elimination, but you can, of course, solve them any way you like. To solve by elimination, multiply the second equation by 3.

$3x + 3y = 141$

Now subtract.

$$3x + 4y = 164$$
$$\underline{-(3x + 3y = 141)}$$
$$y = 23$$

From there, it's easy enough to find x using the original second equation.

$x + 23 = 47$
$x = 24$

And from *there*, we can fill in the table with real numbers.

Species	Coat Pattern	
	Spots	No Spots
Dogs	72	24
Cats	92	23
Total	164	47

Now, what were we doing again? Oh yeah—actually answering this question! If an animal with spots is chosen at random, what is the probability that it's a dog?

There are 72 dogs with spots, out of a total of 164 animals with spots.

$$\frac{72}{164} = 0.439$$

8. **Answer: A**

Because we did all the work above to solve question #7, this one is easy.

A) **False:** There are 72 dogs with spots, which is more than the 92 cats with spots.

B) **True:** there are 24 dogs without spots, which is more than the 23 cats without spots.

C) **True:** There are 92 + 23 = 115 cats, and only 72 + 24 = 96 dogs.

D) **True:** There are 23 cats without spots—that's the smallest group.

9. **Answer: 5**

If the author sold 4,443 books over the whole 12 months, then she sold an average of 370.25 books per month. Let's just draw that line onto the graph and then count how many points are above it!

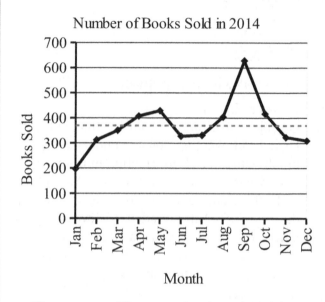

Number of Books Sold in 2014

There we go. There are 5 points above the average line.

10. **Answer: 80**

List the numbers you have in order to see where the median should fall.

27, 44, 47, 58, 61, 74, 81, 102, 168, 211, 259

So, of the 11 numbers you know, the median is 74. If the median becomes 77 once you add in x, then x must fall between 74 and 81.

So far so good? Now, the twist! When you are taking the median of 12 numbers, you have to find the mean of the middle two numbers. That means that the average of x and 74 must be 77.

$$\frac{74 + x}{2} = 77$$

$74 + x = 154$
$x = 80$

Data Analysis 2

1. **Answer: A**

   Remember, a box plot gives you the minimum, the maximum, the first and third quartiles, and the median. In this box plot, the minimum is 14, the maximum is 20, the first and third quartiles are 17 and 20, and the median is 19.

   Roman numeral I must be true—the minimum of a set must be part of the set.

   However, Roman numerals II and III don't have to be true!

   In a set of 20 numbers, the median doesn't need to actually be part of the set—it will be the average of the middle two numbers. So it's not the case that there MUST be a tomato plant with a height of 19 cm. Rather, the 10th and 11th tallest plants could be 18 cm tall and 20 cm tall, respectively.

   The same applies to the first quartile, which is the median of the 10 numbers below the median. In a set of 10 numbers, the median *also* doesn't need to be part of the set. It will be the average of the 5th and 6th highest numbers.

2. **Answer: D**

   You have to get this one by checking every choice against the graph until you come up against one that's true. Here are the reasons that the wrong answers aren't true and the right answer is.

   A) Nope. Most of the dots in the part of the graph to the right of the 30 minute tick mark are above the line of best fit. That means he usually made more in tips than the line predicted.

   B) Nope. Look at where the line of best fit crosses the $20 line. That's at like 30 minutes! So the line of best fit predicts that he makes less than a dollar per minute.

   C) Nope. The most time spend busking was about 40 minutes, but on that day, he made just over $20. He made more than $30 on a different day, when he only spent 37 or so minutes busking.

   D) Yes! If you look at the 20 minute tick mark, you'll see that there are only 10 dots to the left of it. You know he kept a month's worth of data, so you don't need to count the dots on the right to know that there are more than 10 of them. (Go ahead and count, though—there are more than 10 of them.)

3. **Answer: B**

   To find the median efficiently, first count how many students there are on the team in total.

   $$6 + 6 + 9 + 2 = 23$$

   That means there will be 11 students younger than the median-age student, and 11 students older than the median age student. There are exactly 11 students that have ages 16 or 17, so that means the median-age student is 15 years old.

4. **Answer: C**

   Look what happens when three 16-year-olds turn 17.

   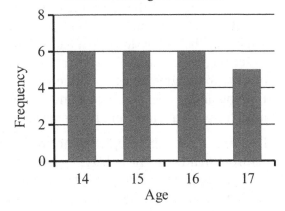

   Track Team Age Distribution

   Roman numeral I is not true—the range is still $17 - 14 = 3$, just like it was before.

   Roman numeral II is not true—the median isn't affected since all the changes happened to numbers that were already above the median. There are still 11 students of age 16 or 17.

   Roman numeral III is true—if any numbers in a set increase, the mean increases.

5. **Answer: C**

   If you draw a vertical line from the horizontal axis around where the distance equals 4, and then turn left when you hit the line of best fit, you should land between 80 and 100, closer to 100. No need to be super precise here—the answer choices are very far apart! Go with choice C, which says 95, and move on.

6. **Answer: B**

   You have to do some critical thinking here and not jump to broad conclusions from pretty limited data.

   A) This graph doesn't tell us who becomes customers, only how long people stay on the website. So while this choice *might* be true, it's a stretch to try to draw that conclusion from this graph.

   B) Yes, this is precisely what the graph says.

   C) No. This choice is drawing a very aggressive conclusion from limited data. We know about 40 site visits. We can't, from that, conclude that nobody from within 5 miles away *ever* stays on the site for less than a minute. In fact, if you think about the way you might use the web to look up a hair salon (e.g., to see its phone number or address) it should be easy to imagine that even someone who fully planned to become a customer wouldn't need to spend a whole minute on the site!

   D) Nope. Again, the people in our limited data set from that far away do leave quickly, but we don't know if that's always the case, and we certainly can't conclude with certainly *why* they leave quickly from only this data.

7. **Answer: B**

   Again, let's take these choices one at a time.

   A) No. We know that there are more children ages 6 to 11 in Town C than there are in Town B, but that doesn't necessarily mean there are more 7-year-olds. What if Town C just has tons of 10-year-olds?

   B) Yes, we can conclude this. If you compare Town B to Town A, you'll see that it is higher in all three age groups. Therefore, we can conclude that there are more children under the age of 12 (i.e., the first two categories) in Town B than in Town A.

   C) No, we can't conclude this. Because this histogram presents age ranges, we can't calculate medians with precision.

   D) Not necessarily. Town A has the smallest population of children, but that doesn't mean it isn't crawling with adults. Maybe it's a retirement community—you don't know.

8. **Answer: C**

   Here's the required insight: the $y = x$ line provided to you here represents the theoretical bear (no real bears in this scientist's study) that doesn't lose any weight over its hibernation. So if you're looking for the bear that lost the most weight, you need to find the point that's farthest from that line. Point C is farthest away from $y = x$, so that's our answer.

9. **Answer: D**

   What you should be able to see from the graph is that the number of cases more than doubled from 2012 to 2013: it's less than halfway to the 500 line in 2012, and it's above the 500 line in 2013. The only percent growth given to you that could possibly work is 155%.

10. **Answer: B**

    For this one, you'll want to use your calculator. Don't worry too much about precision with the number you choose for 2010 mumps cases—the numbers in the answer choices are so rounded that it doesn't matter if you go with 2,550 or 2,600. :)

    $$\frac{2,600}{309,300,000} = 8.41 \times 10^{-6}$$

    Now, be very careful of this dirty trick: the answer choices all have % signs in them! 5% is 0.05, right? That's because the % sign means divide by 100. So the answer we want, which will simplify to 8.41×10^{-6}, is $8.41 \times 10^{-4}\%$. That's choice B.

Designing and Interpreting Experiments

1. **Answer: D**

This is going to be a running theme in the solutions for this chapter: sample size matters! Especially when you're looking to learn something about a small percentage of the population like 10% left-handedness, you need to ask way more than 10 people to get a representative sample.

2. **Answer: D**

Because the students who received the extra help were not randomly selected, it is impossible to conclude that it was the extra help (and not, say, the fact that those students were motivated enough to seek extra help and maybe also studied harder on their own) that resulted in the improvement.

3. **Answer: A**

If you want to decrease your margin of error (i.e., the possible difference between your sample and the general population), increase your sample size!

Choices C and D are changing the group being studied. You will not be able to make firmer conclusions about American males ages 18–24 if you include females or start studying males who are 17 and 25, too.

4. **Answer: D**

A 95% confidence interval tells you that you can be 95% sure that the true average of the population you're studying is within your confidence interval. It does *not* tell you that 95% of the population falls into that interval!

5. **Answer: A**

The students in a dining hall are not necessarily a representative sample of the all the students at the college. For example, by conducting the survey there, this student's sample might under-represent students who study through dinner and who might be less likely to leave campus for the weekend, or students who go out to restaurants instead of eating at the dining hall and who might be more likely to leave campus for the weekend.

If the student truly wants to know the proportion of all students at the college who leave over the weekend, he needs to cast a wider net than just one location on one night.

6. **Answer: B**

This one's too easy, right? He only connected with 20 voters! That's not a big enough sample to conclude anything.

7. **Answer: B**

The key here is specificity. The study was conducted on people with insomnia, and the exercise prescribed to the randomized experimental group was intense cardiovascular exercise. Therefore, we can conclude that intense cardiovascular exercise (not necessarily *all* exercise) can help people with insomnia (not necessarily *all* people) sleep better.

8. **Answer: A**

Don't stretch outside of what the experiment tells you. Knock choices C and D right out— we don't know anything about fruit, and all the plants in this experiment got the same amount of water.

To decide between A and B, ask yourself which of those could be more easily disproved. A would be very hard to disprove: it doesn't pin itself to a specific weekly growth rate difference, which is good, since Courtney only measured the heights of the plants at the beginning of the experiment and then four weeks later. A is also very specific about the amount of light exposure, which matches the amount of light the faster-growing plants got in the experiment. B is not specific about the amount or kind of light.

9. **Answer: B**

Ooh, we finally get to do a little math! When the margin of error is given in percent form, it's a percent of the given mean. So in this case, what the question is saying is that the confidence interval is between 6% less than $197 and 6% greater than $197.

6% of $197 is $11.82, so let's add and subtract that.

$197 - 11.82 = $185.18
$197 + 11.82 = $208.82

Those round to $185 and $209, so that's our answer.

Note that a little estimation is fine here. $197 is awfully close to $200, and it's really easy to calculate 6% of $200—that's $12. Safe bet to assume that the right answer will round to $197 − 12 and $197 + 12.

10. **Answer: .018**

Yay, more actual calculations to do! The key to getting this is a good understanding of the relationship between margin of error and confidence interval. The margin of error is the difference between the sample mean and either end of the confidence interval. You can almost think of the margin of error as the radius of the confidence interval. Or maybe you hate me for just saying that.

Anyway, if we know the confidence interval goes from 1.782 to 1.818 gigabytes, then we can figure out the sample mean by taking the average of those points.

$$\frac{1.782 + 1.818}{2} = 1.800$$

If 1.8 is the mean, then how far from the mean are the endpoints of the confidence interval?

$$1.818 - 1.8 = 0.018$$

So that's the margin of error.

Angles, Triangles, and Polygons

1. **Answer: D**

Extend a line to create a transversal, and then you can use all the angle rules we talked about to solve.

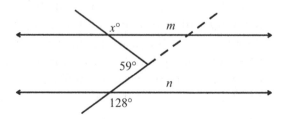

Fill in the corresponding angle the 128° angle, then calculate in the supplementary angles to 59° and the new 128° you just filled in. Lo and behold, you have 2 of the three angles in the triangle you created when you extended the transversal!

The third angle in that triangle must be $180° - 121° - 52° = 7°$. Because the angle we care about is supplemental to that, $x = 173$.

2. **Answer: B**

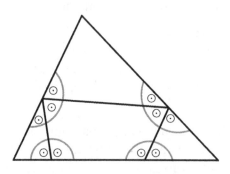

Note that all the marked angles are grouped around straight lines! There are four clusters of them, each representing 180°. $4 \times 180° = 720°$.

3. **Answer: A**

This question is testing you on the triangle inequality rule. Don't make a sadness gap! If 9 is one of the two congruent sides, then the perimeter must be greater than 18. If the congruent sides are the two unknown sides, then the perimeter *still* must be greater than 18, otherwise the shorter sides won't be able to reach each other. A triangle with sides 9, 3, and 3 can't exist, so the perimeter can't be 15.

4. **Answer: 360**

You can plug in 60° for every angle here and get where you need to go, but you can also note that the marked angles are all straight lines with an angle cut out of them. Since the angles cut out form a triangle, you can say that the marked angles add up thusly:

$$3 \times 180° - 180° = 360°$$

5. **Answer: 24**
A regular hexagon can be broken into 6 equilateral triangles.

So if we know we're starting with an area of $24\sqrt{3}$, we can divide by 6 to figure out that we're dealing with equilateral triangles with areas of $4\sqrt{3}$.

Because we know that the area of a triangle is calculated with the formula $\frac{1}{2}bh$, and because we know equilateral triangles have 60° angles in them and can therefore be broken into 30°-60°-90° right triangles, we can calculate the side length of an equilateral triangle with area $4\sqrt{3}$. (We'll do right triangles in more detail next chapter.)

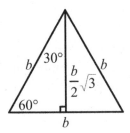

$$\left(\frac{1}{2}\right)(b)\left(\frac{b\sqrt{3}}{2}\right) = 4\sqrt{3}$$

$$\frac{b^2\sqrt{3}}{4} = 4\sqrt{3}$$

$$b^2\sqrt{3} = 16\sqrt{3}$$

$$b = 4$$

Anyway, now that we know the equilateral triangles' sides are all 4, we can multiply by 6 to get the hexagon's perimeter of 24.

6. **Answer: C**
More fun with equilaterals! This time, all you need to remember is that all their angles are 60°. If you fill in the 60° angles you know, you'll see that the middle triangle, the shaded one, also has two 60° angles, and therefore must have a third.

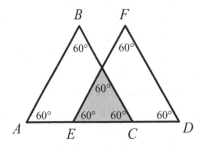

If $AB = 14$, then all the sides of the big equilateral triangles are 14. Since E is the midpoint of $\overline{AC}$, which is one of those sides, $EC = 7$. Therefore, the perimeter of the shaded equilateral triangle is 21.

7. **Answer: C**
Roman numeral I is another attempt to get you with the triangle inequality rule. I'm a jerk. :) If you move QR to the other side of that inequality, you get $PQ < PR + QR$. That will always be true for *any* triangle PQR—that's the rule!

Roman numeral II is also true. If $PQ > PR$, then the angle across from PQ, $\angle PRQ$, must be bigger than the angle across from PR, $\angle PQR$.

Roman numeral III doesn't have to be true. Imagine a triangle where $PQ = 8$, $QR = 7$, and $PR = 3$. $2PR$ still wouldn't be bigger and PQ.

8. **Answer: D**
If $y = 180 - x$, then the unmarked angle in the triangle is also x.

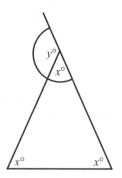

Therefore, all the angles in this triangle are the same—it's an equilateral triangle. Since the question tells you its side lengths are integers, the only possible perimeter is one that is a multiple of 3. Of the choices, only 24 is.

9. **Answer: 15**
Remember that the total degree measure of the interior angles of a polygon with n sides can be calculated with $(n - 2)180°$. To find the average angle measure, then, we divide that by $180°$. So we can solve for n if we know the average interior angle of the polygon is $156°$.

$$\frac{(n-2)\,180}{n} = 156$$
$$180n - 360 = 156n$$
$$24n = 360$$
$$n = 15$$

10. **Answer: 16**
The sum of the measures of the exterior angles on any polygon is $360°$. So all we need to do to find the number of vertices is divide!

$$22.5n = 360$$
$$n = 16$$

Right Triangles and Basic Trigonometry

1. **Answer: B**
If you draw a line straight down from point D, you break this figure into a rectangle and a right triangle. Sweet!

The key insight once you've drawn that line, of course, is recognizing that you can break $\overline{AB}$, which the question tells you is 11, into two segments of 8 and 3, based on the fact that the top of the rectangle you made has a length of 8. And that gives you a 3-4-5 triangle!

To find the perimeter of the quadrilateral, add.

$5 + 8 + 4 + 11 = 28$

2. **Answer: A**
In a 45°-45°-90° triangle like the one you're given, the sides are in the ratio $x : x : x\sqrt{2}$, with $x\sqrt{2}$ being your hypotenuse. Here, our hypotenuse is 10, so we need to do a little algebra.

$$x\sqrt{2} = 10$$
$$x = \frac{10}{\sqrt{2}}$$

That's not an answer choice, so we need to rationalize the denominator. Multiply by a clever form of 1!

$$x = \frac{10}{\sqrt{2}} \times \frac{\sqrt{2}}{\sqrt{2}}$$
$$x = \frac{10\sqrt{2}}{2}$$
$$x = 5\sqrt{2}$$

3. **Answer: C**
You'll really move more quickly through this one if you recognize the 5-12-13 triangles everywhere!

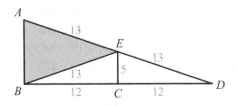

From there, you need to either recognize that △ABD is similar to △ECD by AA, which tells you that AB = 10, or recognize that ABD is a 10-24-26 triangle—the big brother of the 5-12-13!

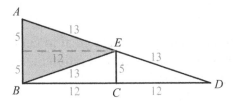

Last bit of insight needed: the height of △ABE is 12. Now you have everything you need to calculate the area of the shaded region.

$$A = \frac{1}{2}(10)(12)$$

$$A = 60$$

4.   **Answer: .4 or 2/5**
Remember your SOH-CAH-TOA! The fact that the sine of $n°$ is 0.4 tells you that you can plug in values that make that ratio for the opposite leg and hypotenuse.

Now you're looking for the cosine of $m°$. That's the ratio of the adjacent leg, 4 according to my plugged in numbers, and the hypotenuse, 10.

$$\cos(m°) = 0.4$$

This is mildly to fairly important, as trig questions you might see on the exam are likely to be this conceptual and SOH-CAH-TOA-based. Simple if you know it, but easy to go astray if you don't.

5.   **Answer: 90**
This one's a bit of a giveaway after the one we just worked through. The two acute angles in a right triangle will always have this relationship. For acute angles A and B in the same right triangle, $\sin A = \cos B$ and $\cos A = \sin B$. What else is true about the two acute angles in a right triangle? Their measures sum to 90°.

6.   **Answer: C**
This is another opportunity to exploit your knowledge of Pythagorean triples! Fill in what you're given, but make your life a little neater by noting that while BD is 24, we're told E is its midpoint, so fill in 12 for BE and 12 for DE.

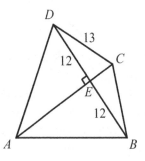

From there, you can see that EC must be 5 to complete the 5-12-13 triangle, which allows you to see that $CB = 13$ for the same reason. You can also calculate that $AE = 16$ since we know $AC = 21$ and $\overline{EC}$ takes up 5 of that 21.

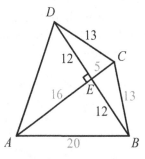

One more Pythagorean triple to go! △ABE, we now know, is a 12-16-20—big brother of the 3-4-5! Therefore, $AB = 20$.

7. **Answer: C**

You're given a tangent line, which means you have a right triangle. Since you're also told that $\angle RCS$ is a 135° angle, you know that this right triangle is *special*. It's a 45°-45°-90°. Because you know that the radius length, which is also the length of the legs of the triangle, is 3, you know that $SP = 3\sqrt{2}$.

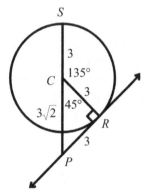

Note that even though this isn't impossible to solve with right triangle rules, it's *also* possible to get this one with your eyeballs alone. Obviously, $\overline{SP}$ must be longer than 6 because that's the diameter, but the part under the circle certainly isn't as long as a whole other radius, so it's not even close to 9. The only answer choice that feels right is the one that's approximately 7.24. Opportunities to solve by guesstimating are rare, but keep your eye out for them!

8. **Answer: D**

Man, what's up with all these circles in the right triangles drill? Connect the centers to reveal the triangle.

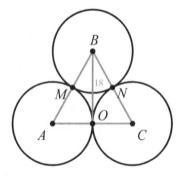

Do you see what's going on here? All those circles are congruent, so all their radii are congruent, so $\overline{BO}$ is a perpendicular bisector of an equilateral triangle. So $\triangle ABO$ and $\triangle CBO$ are two 30°-60°-90°s!

The sides in a 30°-60°-90° are in a $x : x\sqrt{3} : 2x$ ratio. The 18 we're given is the $x\sqrt{3}$ term, and the radius we want to find a circle area is the x term. So let's solve for x.

$$x\sqrt{3} = 18$$

$$x = \frac{18}{\sqrt{3}}$$

Since we need to square that to get to the circle area, we won't bother to rationalize the denominator.

$$A_{circle} = \pi \left(\frac{18}{\sqrt{3}} \right)^2$$

$$A_{circle} = 108\pi$$

9. **Answer: 9**

If the sine of an angle in a right triangle is $\frac{4}{5}$, then the triangle you're dealing with must be a 3-4-5 or similar to a 3-4-5. In this case, we're told the hypotenuse has a length of 15, so we know we're dealing with a big brother of the 3-4-5—the 9-12-15. Therefore, the shortest leg has a length of 9.

10. **Answer: .416, .417, or 5/12**

Again, this question uses trigonometry to thinly disguise a Pythagorean triple. If the ratio of a leg to the hypotenuse is 12 to 13, then this is a 5-12-13 triangle. Let's draw it to make sure we keep our sides and angles straight.

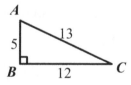

There we go: $\sin A = \dfrac{12}{13}$, just like the question says it should. So what's $\tan C$? Remember your SOH-CAH-TOA. The tangent is the ratio of the opposite leg to the adjacent leg, so $\tan C = \dfrac{5}{12}$.

Circles, Radians, and a Little More Trigonometry

1. **Answer: C**

   If the circle is divided into 12 arcs, each with length 3 centimeters, then its circumference must be $12 \times 3 = 36$ cm. To find the degree measure of an arc 8 cm long, then, we just set up a proportion:

   $$\frac{x}{360} = \frac{8}{36}$$
   $$x = 80$$

2. **Answer: A**

   Because the radius of the circle is 1, the arc length equals the radian measure of $\angle AOB$.

   So we know that $\angle AOB$ has a measure of $\dfrac{\pi}{3}$ radians. It's probably a good idea for you to have the basic trig ratios memorized (see the table on page 273), but if you don't have that, you *must* at least recognize that $\dfrac{\pi}{3}$ radians is 60°. In a 30°-60°-90° right triangle, the ratio of the sides is $x : x\sqrt{3} : 2x$. The cosine of 60° is the ratio of the short leg to the hypotenuse, or 1 to 2. Therefore, we know that $\cos\dfrac{\pi}{3} = \dfrac{1}{2}$.

3. **Answer: A**

   The fact that BC is tangent to the circle tells you that $\angle ABC$ is a right angle. Since $AB = BC$, you know two things. First, you know that you're dealing with an isosceles right triangle with hypotenuse AC. Second, you know that the shaded region is a sector with a central angle of 45°.

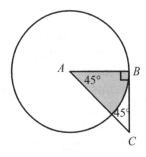

So we're going to use the isosceles right triangles to find the radius, use that to find the area of the circle, and then use the angle to get the sector area.

Isosceles right triangles have sides in the $x : x : x\sqrt{2}$ ratio. In this case, 8 is the $x\sqrt{2}$, and the radius is x. So solve for x.

$$x\sqrt{2} = 8$$
$$x = \frac{8}{\sqrt{2}}$$

Since you're going to be squaring that to find the circle's area, no need to rationalize the denominator. Just keep on truckin'.

$$A_{circle} = \pi\left(\frac{8}{\sqrt{2}}\right)^2$$
$$A_{circle} = 32\pi$$

The shaded region, as we said before, is a sector with a 45° central angle.

$$\frac{45}{360} = \frac{x}{32\pi}$$
$$4\pi = x$$

4. **Answer: B**

   A very common mistake on this one is to find the area of one of the circles, double it, and then subtract the area of the square. That doesn't work because, if not for the square cutout, the circles would overlap.

   The way to get this one is to recognize that the shaded region is made up of two 270° sectors; each is 3/4 of a circle. You're told that $AB = 2$, so you know that the area of each FULL circle is 4π. Since the shaded sectors are 3/4 of those circles, each is 3π. Since there are 2 shaded parts, the total area of the shaded regions is 6π.

5. **Answer: 2.5 or 5/2**

Draw OM since the question asks for it, but also draw another segment here: either OA or OB, whichever you like. I'm going to use OA, which is a radius. OM is a perpendicular bisector of AB. (Remember that a segment from a circle's center to the midpoint of a chord is always going to be perpendicular to the chord.)

Now you've got a right triangles with a hypotenuse of 5 and a long leg of $\frac{5\sqrt{3}}{2}$. You could use the Pythagorean theorem to solve for OM, but I hope that you just recognize that as a 30°-60°-90° triangle and save yourself the trouble! OM must be $\frac{5}{2}$, or 2.5.

6. **Answer: A**

A circle that is tangent to the y-axis with a center at $(3, -1)$ will have a radius of 3. So we can plug that center and that radius into the standard circle equation.

$$(x-3)^2 + (y+1)^2 = 3^2$$

FOIL that all out and see which answer choice you land on.

$$(x^2 - 6x + 9) + (y^2 + 2y + 1) = 9$$
$$x^2 - 6x + y^2 + 2y + 10 = 9$$
$$x^2 + y^2 - 6x + 2y = -1$$

7. **Answer: D**

We can use part to whole ratios here. The radius of that circle is 6, so its circumference is 12π. If arc QR has a length of π, then it's 1/12 of the circle. 2π radians make a full circle, so 1/12 of that will be the radian measure of $\angle RPQ$.

$$\frac{x}{2\pi} = \frac{\pi}{12\pi}$$

$$x = \frac{\pi}{6}$$

8. **Answer: B**

Complete the square (yuck!) to get the equation into standard form. (Note: I'm using underlines below to show what I'm adding to both sides as I complete the square.)

$$x^2 + 8x + y^2 = 36$$
$$x^2 + 8x \underline{+16} + y^2 = 36 \underline{+16}$$
$$(x+4)^2 + y^2 = 52$$

That tells you that the circle's center is at $(-4, 0)$, which does indeed put it on the x-axis, so Roman numeral I is true. It also shows you that the radius is *not* 6 units long: when the circle equation is in standard form, we see that its radius is actually $\sqrt{52}$, so Roman numeral II is false. To test Roman numeral III, plug the point into the equation and see if it's true.

$$(2+4)^2 + 4^2 = 52$$
$$6^2 + 4^2 = 52$$
$$36 + 16 = 52$$

Yes, that's true. So I and III are true; the answer is B.

9. **Answer: 8**

You can calculate that if the wheel rotates clockwise, then it will have to rotate 120° for the painted line to be perpendicular to the ground: 30° of rotation will make the line parallel to the ground; 90° more will make it perpendicular.

We know a wheel that rolls without slipping travels the distance of its circumference when it makes one complete turn, so to go any further we need the circle's circumference. Easy enough: the radius is 12, so the circumference is 24π. That's how far the wheel would travel if it made a full, 360° turn. Since it's only making a 120° turn, it's only going to go 1/3 of that distance. 1/3 of 24π is 8π.

10. **Answer: 4**

Don't be fooled! Yes, the figure shows that the radius of that circle is 3, but that equation isn't in standard form, so a is NOT 9. Put the equation in standard form. (Note: Again, I'm using underlines below to highlight the process of completing the square.)

$$x^2 + 4x + y^2 - 2y = a$$
$$x^2 + 4x \underline{+4} + y^2 - 2y \underline{+1} = a \underline{+5}$$
$$(x + 2)^2 + (y - 1)^2 = a + 5$$

Only now that you're in standard form can you use the fact that the radius is 3 to solve for a. You know that $a + 5$ is where 3^2 is supposed to live, so solve for a.

$$a + 5 = 3^2$$
$$a + 5 = 9$$
$$a = 4$$

Working in Three Dimensions

1. **Answer: A**

   A cube with a volume of 27 will have edges of length $\sqrt[3]{27} = 3$.

   That means that each face of the cube will have an area of $3^2 = 9$. There are 6 faces on a cube, so the surface area will be $6 \times 9 = 54$.

2. **Answer: B**

   This is a tricky one, huh? The thing you must recognize is that the formula you're given is derived from the formula for the volume of a sphere: $V = \frac{4}{3}\pi r^3$. First, since the bowls are semispherical, the formula is cut in half.

   $$\frac{1}{2}\left(\frac{4}{3}\pi r^3\right) = \frac{2}{3}\pi r^3$$

   Then, because Larry is looking for the volume of material he needs, he subtracts the volume of the semisphere with the inner radius b from the volume of the semisphere with the outer radius a.

   $$\frac{2}{3}\pi a^3 - \frac{2}{3}\pi b^3$$

   Finally, he factors.

   $$\frac{2}{3}\pi\left(a^3 - b^3\right)$$

All of this should hopefully give you the insight you need to solve, which is that the amount of liquid this bowl will be able to hold is equal to the volume of the semisphere with radius b! That's $\frac{2}{3}\pi b^3$.

If this still doesn't feel warm and fuzzy, I'll say it one more way: Imagine you have half a sphere. Then you carve another, smaller half sphere out of it, making a bowl. The amount of liquid that bowl can hold is equal to the volume of the small half of a sphere you carved out.

3. **Answer: C**

   The first insight you need to have for this one is that d must be the height. Why, you ask? Well, because of the four terms in the surface area expression, three of them have a d in them. That tells you that the three vertical faces of the prism have a height of d, and bases of a, b, and c.

   From there, you need to recognize that the ab term in the surface area expression must represent both the top *and* the bottom of the prism. Since this is a right prism and the top and bottom are congruent, that means each has an area of $\frac{1}{2}ab$.

   The only way a triangle has sides with lengths a and b and also an area of $\frac{1}{2}ab$ is if it's a right triangle with legs of length a and b. So c must be the length of the hypotenuse of the base, which is by definition the longest side.

4. **Answer: 61**

   The volume of cube A is $4^3 = 64$. The volume of cube B is $5^3 = 125$. $125 - 64 = 61$.

5. **Answer: 2**

   The volume of a right cone is found with this formula: $V = \frac{1}{3}\pi r^2 h$. If we know the radius is 6 and the volume is 24π, all we need to do is solve for h.

$$24\pi = \frac{1}{3}\pi 6^2 h$$
$$24 = 12h$$
$$2 = h$$

6. **Answer: C**

It's really helpful to draw this one because that can help us have the insight that for the bugs to be as far apart as possible, they need to be on each rim, and then on opposite sides of the rims.

Once you've done a proper drawing, this becomes a simple right triangle problem (as 3-D questions often do).

What is the hypotenuse of a right triangle with legs of length 5 and 12? That's a Pythagorean triple: 5-12-13!

7. **Answer: D**

A lot of people have trouble drawing this one, but a good picture is illustrative.

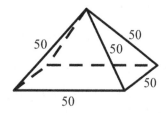

I'm not going overboard with the 50s there, but we know with a square base and equilateral triangle sides that *all* those edges have a length of 50.

At this point, it probably makes sense to consider the base in 2 dimensions. It's a square with sides of length 50. What's its diagonal? That's right, $50\sqrt{2}$. If we draw that onto our figure and draw in the height we care about, we make a right triangle that we can solve!

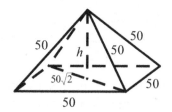

Let's just look at part of that figure in two dimensions. Note that the top vertex of the pyramid is directly above the center of the square, so the bottom leg of the right triangle below is half the square's diagonal: $25\sqrt{2}$.

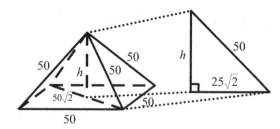

Do you recognize that as a 45°-45°-90°? If one leg is $25\sqrt{2}$ and the hypotenuse is 50, then the other leg is also $25\sqrt{2}$.

8. **Answer: A**

Calculate the volume of each ball! The volume of a sphere is calculated using this formula:
$$V = \frac{4}{3}\pi r^3.$$

$$V_{baseball} = \frac{4}{3}\pi (73.2 \text{ mm})^3$$

$$V_{baseball} = 1,642,940.6 \text{ mm}^3$$

$$V_{soccer ball} = \frac{4}{3}\pi (226.0 \text{ mm})^3$$

$$V_{soccer ball} = 48,351,942.6 \text{ mm}^3$$

Now divide!

$$\frac{48,351,942.6 \text{ mm}^3}{1,642,940.6 \text{ mm}^3} = 29.4$$

So there you have it—the volume of the soccer ball is roughly 29 times that of the baseball.

A notable shortcut exists here. Since the formula for volume for both shapes contains the $\frac{4}{3}\pi$ part, you can just ignore it! Fastest way to go is just to divide the only parts of the two volumes that are different!

$$\frac{226.0^3}{73.2^3} = 29.4$$

9. **Answer: B**

This one looks intimidating at first, but all we need to do to solve is subtract the volume of the cylindrical shape the drill will remove from the volume of the whole wood cube.

To do that, of course, we need to do some basic calculations about the cylindrical hole. Its diameter is 2, so its radius is 1. Its height is the full height of the cube, which is 3.

$$V_{cube} = (3 \text{ in})^3$$

$$V_{cube} = 27 \text{ in}^3$$

$$V_{cylindrical\ hole} = \pi r^2 h$$

$$V_{cylindrical\ hole} = \pi (1 \text{ in})^2 (3 \text{ in})$$

$$V_{cylindrical\ hole} = 3\pi \text{ in}^3$$

$$V_{cylindrical\ hole} = 9.4 \text{ in}^3$$

To find the volume of what's left of the block after the drilling, subtract.

$$V_{block\ with\ hole} = 27 \text{ in}^3 - 9.4 \text{ in}^3$$

$$V_{block\ with\ hole} = 17.6 \text{ in}^3$$

10. **Answer: .125 or 1/8**

The key to getting this one is recognizing that the stone will displace a volume of water equal to its own volume. The *other* key to getting this one is converting from inches to feet in the beginning. The stone's sides are 0.5 ft long, and the stone's volume, therefore, is $(0.5 \text{ ft})^3$, or 0.125 ft^3.

The volume of water in the tank is currently 3 ft × 4 ft × 1 ft = 12 ft^3. Once the stone is in there, it will be like the tank has 12.125 ft^3 of water. Given that the length and width of the tank can't change, we can calculate the new height.

$$3 \text{ ft} \times 4 \text{ ft} \times x \text{ ft} = 12.125 \text{ ft}^3$$

$$x \text{ ft} = \frac{12.125 \text{ ft}^3}{(3 \text{ ft})(4 \text{ ft})}$$

$$x \text{ ft} = \frac{12.125}{12} \text{ ft}$$

Now here's where we get clever. The question asks for the height the water rose *in inches*! There are 12 inches in a foot, so we have to multiply that height we just found by 12.

$$\left(\frac{12.125}{12} \text{ ft}\right)\left(12 \frac{\text{in}}{\text{ft}}\right) = 12.125 \text{ in}$$

So the new height of the water is 12.125 inches. The starting height was 1 foot, or 12 inches, so the water rose by 0.125 inches.

Complex Numbers

1. **Answer: A**

To multiply two complex numbers and come out with a real number, the complex numbers must be complex conjugates. The complex conjugate of $3 + 6i$ is $3 - 6i$, so you know b must equal –6. Just for kicks, let's FOIL to make sure we get 45, like the problem promised.

$(3 + 6i)(3 - 6i)$
$= 9 - 18i + 18i - 36i^2$
$= 9 - 36(-1)$
$= 45$

2. **Answer: B**

To get this one right, you need to remember (or derive) that $i^2 = -1$ and that $i^3 = -i$. From there, all you gotta do is substitute.

$$(5+8i)-(6i^2+3i^3)$$
$$=(5+8i)-(6(-1)+3(-i))$$
$$=(5+8i)-(-6-3i)$$
$$=5+8i+6+3i$$
$$=11+11i$$

3. **Answer: A**

To simplify a fraction with a complex number in its denominator, multiply top and bottom by a clever form of 1: the complex conjugate.

$$\left(\frac{5-i}{1-i}\right)\left(\frac{1+i}{1+i}\right)$$

$$=\frac{5+5i-i-i^2}{1+i-i-i^2}$$

$$=\frac{5+4i-(-1)}{1-(-1)}$$

$$=\frac{6+4i}{2}$$

$$=3+2i$$

4. **Answer: C**

Having a square root in the binomial adds a bit more complexity here (pun intended), but don't panic—you just need to FOIL.

$$\left(\sqrt{5}+2i\right)^2$$
$$=\left(\sqrt{5}+2i\right)\left(\sqrt{5}+2i\right)$$
$$=5+2i\sqrt{5}+2i\sqrt{5}+4i^2$$
$$=5+4i\sqrt{5}+(-4)$$
$$=1+4i\sqrt{5}$$

5. **Answer: B**

If you're savvy here, you might recognize a shortcut: the first and third complex numbers being multiplied here are conjugates! If you multiply those first, your final step is cake. So rearrange and get crackin'.

$$(3+2i)(3-2i)(2+3i)$$
$$=(9-6i+6i-4i^2)(2+3i)$$
$$=(9-4(-1))(2+3i)$$
$$=13(2+3i)$$
$$=26+39i$$

6. **Answer: 4**

You might recognize that, although the coefficients are different here, these would be complex conjugates if one of them was multiplied by a real factor. Also, since this is a grid-in, we can have faith that the correct answer will be griddable—it will be real!

$$(4+4i)\left(\frac{1}{2}-\frac{1}{2}i\right)$$
$$=2-2i+2i-2i^2$$
$$=2-2(-1)$$
$$=4$$

How come that worked? Well, here's another way the original expression could have been written: $8\left(\frac{1}{2}+\frac{1}{2}i\right)\left(\frac{1}{2}-\frac{1}{2}i\right)$.

7. **Answer: 3**

Similar deal here. We're getting a real number when we multiply, so we know that $6+bi$ and $4-2i$ must be conjugates after some factor is taken out. The super shortcut here is actually just to set up a ratio.

$$\frac{4}{2}=\frac{6}{b}$$

$$b=3$$

Put 3 in for b and do the multiplication just to be sure.

$$(4-2i)(6+3i)=30$$
$$24+12i-12i-6i^2=30$$
$$24-6(-1)=30$$
$$30=30$$

8. **Answer: 10**

This is just a creative way to ask a simple complex number multiplication question in the grid-in format. All you gotta do is multiply.

$$(3+8i)(5+9i)$$
$$=15+27i+40i+72i2$$
$$=15+67i+72(-1)$$
$$=-57+67i$$

If that's $m+ni$, then $m=-57$ and $n=67$. Therefore, $m+n=10$.

9. **Answer: 8**

This one isn't as bad as it looks! You don't need to do any division. Just multiply by the denominator and then do all your work on the right side of the equation.

$$\frac{9-bi}{1-2i}=5+2i$$
$$9 - bi = (5 + 2i)(1 - 2i)$$
$$9 - bi = 5 - 10i + 2i - 4i$$
$$9 - bi = 5 - 8i - 4(-1)$$
$$9 - bi = 9 - 8i$$
$$b = 8$$

10. **Answer: 0**

Yep, this one's sneaky. Do you see the setup, though? How about now?

$$\frac{3+8i}{6+16i}=\frac{3+8i}{2(3+8i)}$$

That's right—the whole business simplifies to $\frac{1}{2}$ right away! Since $\frac{1}{2}$ is a real number, when you put it in $a + bi$ form you get $\frac{1}{2}+0i$, so $a = \frac{1}{2}$ and $b = 0$. The product ab, therefore equals 0.

Extra Practice

---

1. **Answer: 2**

Topic(s): Data Analysis I (p. 195); Ratios and Proportionality (p. 171)

22% of the marbles landed in Bucket 3 and 18% landed in Bucket 5.

Since we know 50 marbles went through the run, we can calculate how many landed in those buckets.

Bucket 3: $50\times\frac{22}{100}=11$

Bucket 5: $50\times\frac{18}{100}=9$

Subtract for the answer: $11 - 9 = 2$, so 2 more marbles landed in Bucket 3 than in Bucket 5.

2. **Answer: A**

Topics: Angles, Triangles and Polygons (p. 236)

There are a couple ways to think about this. The one that may occur to you first is to use that trusty old formula: $(n - 2) \times 180°$ equals the sum of the interior angles in a polygon with n sides. In this case, you'd say $(9 - 2) \times 180° = 1260°$. But how do you get from there to the answer?

Well, because this is a *regular* 9-sided polygon, all those interior angles are the same: you can divide 1260° by 9 to get 140°. Then you can recognize that to draw triangle ABC, you need to cut those 140° angles in half, making isosceles triangles with base angles of 70° each. Remembering that each triangle has 180° in total, the last angle must measure 40°.

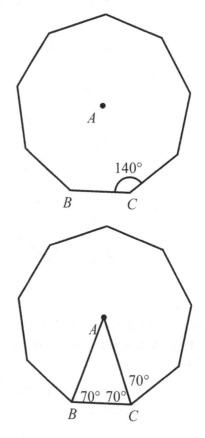

Here's another way to think about it, though. Recognize that the regular polygon we're dealing with here must be made up of triangle *ABC* and 8 others just like it—9 triangles in total. That means you need to be able to put 9 angles congruent with $\angle BAC$ next to each other to go all the way around a circle. There are 360° in a circle, so if we say the measure of $\angle BAC = x°$, then we can say $9x = 360$, which means $x = 40$ and the measure of $\angle BAC = 40°$.

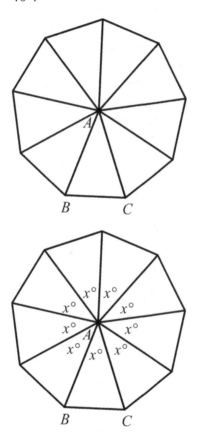

3. **Answer: B**
   Topic(s): Plugging in (p. 24); Functions (p. 92); Exponents and Exponential Functions (p. 104)

First of all, this is a great opportunity to plug in. Say $b = 2$, which means $a = 2^6 = 64$.

To find $f(g(64))$, just work from the inside out!

$$f(g(64))$$
$$= f(\sqrt{64})$$
$$= f(8)$$
$$= 8^3$$
$$= 512$$

Now just see which answer choice gives you 512 when you plug in 2 for *b*! Only choice B works.

The algebraic solution isn't much worse—it just requires you to know your exponent rules.

$$f(g(a))$$
$$= f(g(b^6))$$
$$= f(\sqrt{b^6})$$
$$= f(b^3)$$
$$= (b^3)^3$$
$$= b^9$$

Of course, both of the solutions above require you to be pretty comfortable with function notation!

4. **Answer: D**
   Topic(s): Plugging In (p. 24); Solving Systems of Linear Equations (p. 59)

We have a wealth of options here. First, we could plug in values for *a* and *b*. From there, we can graph or solve algebraically. For example, we could say $a = 2$ and $b = 17$; that would be consistent with the question's stipulation that $b = a + 15$. Then we could graph:

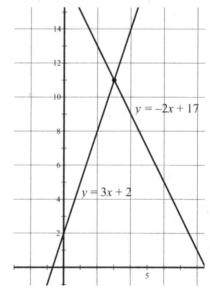

We don't even need to do any more to see that the answer must be $x = 3$.

A more algebraic way to go is to do some substitution. First, substitute $a + 15$ for b:

$y = 3x + a$
$y = -2x + a + 15$

Then, since both equations already have y isolated and we only care about x anyway, we can set the equations equal and solve:

$3x + a = -2x + a + 15$
$3x = -2x + 15$
$5x = 15$
$x = 3$

5. **Answer: .75 or 3/4**
Topic(s): Algebraic Manipulation (p. 52)

When a question gives us an equation with unknown constants and a point on its graph, *we should plug the point into the equation!* We know the graph contains $(8, 8)$, so:

$y = a(x - 6)^2 + 5$
$8 = a(8 - 6)^2 + 5$
$8 = a(2)^2 + 5$
$8 = 4a + 5$
$3 = 4a$
$\dfrac{3}{4} = a$

6. **Answer: D**
Topic(s): Backsolving (p. 32); Algebraic Manipulation (p. 52)

To solve this algebraically, just multiply the equation by $3x^2$ to eliminate all the denominators, and then solve.

$3x^2 \times \left(\dfrac{1}{x} + \dfrac{4}{2x}\right) = \left(\dfrac{27}{3x^2}\right) \times 3x^2$

$3x + 6x = 27$
$9x = 27$
$x = 3$

Since this is a multiple choice question, we also have the wonderful option of backsolving. Just try each choice until one gives you a

working equation. Here's how that looks with the right answer:

$\dfrac{1}{3} + \dfrac{4}{2(3)} = \dfrac{27}{3(3)^2}$

$\dfrac{1}{3} + \dfrac{4}{6} = \dfrac{27}{27}$

$\dfrac{1}{3} + \dfrac{2}{3} = 1$

Yup—that works!

7. **Answer: C**
Topic(s): Right Triangles and Basic Trigonometry (p. 249)

There are a few good routes on this one, but I'll give you what I think is the most intuitive.

You know that the area of triangle ABC is 2 square centimeters. Because the four small triangles that make up the square divide the square evenly, each of them must have the same area. Therefore, if one of them has an area of 2 square centimeters, the whole square must have an area four times that: 8 square centimeters.

You can use that to find the length of each side. For any rectangle, the area is the length times the width. Because we know we're dealing with a square, length and width are the same, so we can just say length = width = x and say:

$8 \text{ cm}^2 = (x \text{ cm})^2$
$\sqrt{8} \text{ cm} = x \text{ cm}$

The perimeter is just four times the length of one side, so we can simplify and solve:

$P = 4(\sqrt{8}) \text{ cm}$
$P = 4(\sqrt{2}\sqrt{4}) \text{ cm}$
$P = 8\sqrt{2} \text{ cm}$

8. **Answer: B**
Topic(s): Functions (p. 92)

I guess the first thing we should do is just figure out what $g(f(x))$ equals.

$$f(x)=x^2$$
$$g(f(x))=g(x^2)$$
$$g(f(x))=x^2-9$$
$$g(f(x))=(x+3)(x-3)$$

OK, so $g(f(x)) = 0$ when $x = \pm3$.

Which of the answer choices gives a value of a where $a - 2 = \pm3$? Choice B does! When $a = -1$, then $a - 2 = -3$!

9. **Answer: 11**
   Topic(s): Ratios and Proportionality (p. 171)

The ratio of blue marbles to green marbles is a part-to-part ratio, but we need to apply it to 165 total marbles, so we really need a part-to-whole ratio.

The trick here is simply to add the pars. If there are 8 blue marbles for every 7 green marbles, then there are 8 blue marbles for every $8 + 7 = 15$ total marbles. The ratio of blue marbles to all marbles is 8 to 15.

Now, let's solve.

$$\frac{8 \text{ blue marbles}}{15 \text{ total marbles}} = \frac{x \text{ blue marbles}}{165 \text{ total marbles}}$$

$$(8)(165) = 15x$$

$$88 = x$$

So there are 88 blue marbles. We know there are 165 marbles in total, so there are $165 - 88 = 77$ green marbles.

How many more blue marbles are there than green? $88 - 77 = 11$ more.

10. **Answer: 100**
    Topic(s): Binomial Squares and Difference of Two Squares (p. 123)

The fastest, most awesome way to get this question is to recognize that we've got difference-of-two-squares form here. Despite the presence of radicals, what we're given fits the $(a + b)(a - b) = a^2 - b^2$ form.

Which is to say that we can solve thusly:

$$(\sqrt{x}+9)(\sqrt{x}-9)=19$$
$$(\sqrt{x})^2-81^2=19$$
$$x-81=19$$
$$x=100$$

Easy, right?

11. **Answer: A**
    Topic(s): Quadratics (p. 114); Binomial Squares and Difference of Two Squares(p. 123)

There are a few ways to go here, but the most universal might be to plug in some obvious points you can get from the graph. For example, you can see from the graph the the the parabola goes through $(0, -3)$. Which of the given equations work with that?

Choice A does:

$$-3=(0+\sqrt{3})(0-\sqrt{3})$$
$$\text{A)} \quad -3=(\sqrt{3})(-\sqrt{3})$$
$$-3=-3$$

None of the other choices do:

$$\text{B)} \quad \begin{array}{l} -3=(0+3)(0-3) \\ -3\neq-9 \end{array}$$

$$\text{C)} \quad \begin{array}{l} -3=(0-\sqrt{3})^2 \\ -3\neq3 \end{array}$$

$$\text{D)} \quad \begin{array}{l} -3=(0-\sqrt{3})^2 \\ -3\neq9 \end{array}$$

12. **Answer: D**
    Topic(s): Solving Systems of Linear Equations (p. 59)

What we're being asked here, really, is to solve for x. We don't care about y, so let's try to eliminate that quickly. If we multiply the second equation by 4, we'll be able to eliminate the y terms by adding the equations together!

$$4(5x - y) = (3)4$$
$$20x - 4y = 12$$

Add that to the first equation now:

$$\begin{array}{r} x + 4y = n \\ +20x - 4y = +12 \\ \hline 21x \quad\quad = n + 12 \end{array}$$

From there, we can get x alone by dividing by 21:

$$21x = n + 12$$
$$x = \frac{n+12}{21}$$

13. **Answer: 85**
    Topic(s): Solving Systems of Linear Equations (p. 59)

When we know that a system of linear equations has an infinite number of solutions, what we really know is that both lines in the system are exactly the same. That is, they have the same y-intercept, and the same slope.

Both equations here are already in slope-intercept form, which is helpful. Because we know the lines must have the same slopes and intercepts, we can say that $\frac{a}{b} = 5$ and $17 = b$. And just like that, we're almost done! All we need to do is substitute.

$$\frac{a}{b} = 5$$

$$\frac{a}{17} = 5$$

$$a = 85$$

14. **Answer: C**
    Topic(s): Ratios and Proportionality (p. 171)

The first thing you'll want to do here is fill in the table with unknowns so that you can solve. Because you're told that left-handed to right-handed 7th grade students are in a 2 to 21 ratio, put a $2x$ and a $21x$ in the 7th grade column.

	Grade	
Handedness	7th	8th
Right	21x	
Left	2x	
Total	322	356

Now you can solve for x—just remember that you don't actually care about x except that it will help you find $2x$ and $21x$!

$$2x + 21x = 322$$
$$23x = 322$$
$$x = 14$$

If $x = 14$, then $2x = 28$ and $21x = 294$, so put those in the table.

	Grade	
Handedness	7th	8th
Right	294	
Left	28	
Total	322	356

Now remember that there are 4 more left-handed 8th graders than left-handed 7th graders. If there are 28 left-handed 7th graders, then there must be 32 lefty 8th graders. Since the table tells us there are 356 total 8th graders, we know there are $356 - 32 = 324$ right-handed 8th graders.

	Grade	
Handedness	7th	8th
Right	294	324
Left	28	32
Total	322	356

Now, let's choose an 8th grader at random. There are 356 8th graders to choose from, and 324 of them are right-handed. Therefore, the probability of our random 8th grader being right-handed is $\frac{324}{356} = 0.910112...$, or 91.0%.

15. **Answer: D**
    Topic(s): Data Analysis 2 (p. 203); Lines (p. 73)

The line of best fit is given in slope-intercept form, and that 2.7 represents the slope. Therefore, we're looking for the answer that most accurately describes how scores change for every additional hour of homework during the month.

Choice A and B miss the mark completely. Choice A mentions 10 points, which has no place in the equation given (nor does it make sense given the graph). Choice B mistakes 2.7 for the intercept.

Choice C is a little better, but it ignores the fact that there's an intercept, and it also uses language that's way too definite. Students scores showed a trend, but it's definitely not the case that scores were exactly 2.7 times the number of hours spent on homework.

Choice D is the best choice. That's really what slope is: the change in one variable given a change of one unit in the other variable. The line of best fit suggests that students who spent more time on homework scored higher on the exam at a rate of 2.7 points per hour. The inclusion of the word "tended" is good, too, because the actual data is scattered about—the dots aren't all right on any line.

16. **Answer: 3**
   Topic(s): Algebraic Manipulation (p. 52)

To get moving on this one, cross multiply to clear the fractions and FOIL.

$(x - 8)(x - 1) = (x - 5)(x + 2)$
$x^2 - 9x + 8 = x^2 - 3x - 10$

The x^2 terms conveniently cancel out, and we're left to solve a linear equation for x. How sweet is that?

$-9x + 8 = -3x - 10$
$18 = 6x$
$3 = x$

17. **Answer: C**
   Topic(s): Solving Systems of Linear Equations (p. 59)

To get this one, write and solve a system of linear equations. Say the fee for an adult is x and the fee for a child is y. Then you can say:

$3x + 5y = 70.5$
$2x + 6y = 67$

We can solve this system with multiple methods, but this time let's substitute after isolating x in the second equation.

$$\frac{2x + 6y}{2} = \frac{67}{2}$$
$x + 3y = 33.5$
$x = 33.5 - 3y$
$3(33.5 - 3y) + 5y = 70.5$
$100.5 - 9y + 5y = 70.5$
$30 - 4y = 0$
$30 = 4y$
$7.5 = y$

So it's $7.50 per child. To find the adult price, solve for x:

$2x + 6(7.5) = 67$
$2x + 45 = 67$
$2x = 22$
$x = 11$

Now that we know it's $11 per adult, we can finally calculate the cost for 2 children and 1 adult:

$2(7.5) + 11 = 26$

18. **Answer: 1**
   Topic(s): Functions (p. 92); Polynomials (p. 142)

We need to remember here that we can translate the function notation $f(a) = 0$ to an ordered pair. If we know that $f(a) = 0$, then we know that the point $(a, 0)$ is on the graph of the function f. That obviously also applies to $f(-a)=0$: we know the graph of function f also contains $(-a, 0)$.

Looking at the graph, we see there are only three points where $y = 0$: $(-2, 0)$, $(2, 0)$, and

(3, 0). Because we know a is a positive constant, we can conclude that $a = 2$.

So let's rewrite what we're asked to solve for.

$$f(a + 1) + 1$$
$$= f(2 + 1) + 1$$
$$= f(3) + 1$$

We've already noted that the graph contains the point (3, 0), so we know that $f(3) = 0$. So we can substitute more:

$$f(3) + 1$$
$$= 0 + 1$$
$$= 1$$

19. **Answer: A**
    Topic(s): Solving Systems of Linear Equations (p. 59)

To get started here, let's put the intersection point we know, (−1, 9), into both equations.

$$Y = -ax + b$$
$$y = -bx + a$$

$$9 = -a(-1) + b$$
$$9 = -b(-1) + a$$

When we distribute that negative, both equations resolve to...

$$9 = a + b$$
$$9 = b + a$$

Huh! Well. I guess we're done!

20. **Answer: D**
    Topic(s): Polynomials (p. 142)

Remember that when we have equivalent polynomials, the corresponding coefficients in each polynomial will be equivalent. In other words, if $ax^2 + bx + c = mx^2 + nx + p$ for all values of x, then $a = m$, $b = n$, and $c = p$.

The first thing to do to solve a question like this, then, is to get each side looking as similar

as possible. In this case, that means FOILing on the left.

$$(3x + a)(4x + a) = 12x^2 + 28x + b$$
$$12x^2 + 3ax + 4ax + a^2 = 12x^2 + 28x + b$$
$$12x^2 + 7ax + a^2 = 12x^2 + 28x + b$$

From that, we can conclude that $7a = 28$ and that $a^2 = b$. The first equation simplifies to $a = 4$, and if $a = 4$, then $a^2 = 16$, so $b = 16$.

21. **Answer: C**
    Topic(s): Circles, Radians, and a Little More Trigonometry (p. 258)

First, remember that when a wheel rolls one complete revolution (without slipping) it travels a distance of one circumference. I always remember this by thinking that for the wheel to roll one full revolution, every point on the edge of the wheel must touch the surface. Anyway, that's important here because we can say that 8 revolutions means the wheel traveled 8 circumferences. So we know that $m = 8C$.

We also know the circumference of a circle, $C = 2\pi r$. So we can say that $m = 8(2\pi r)$, or $m = 16\pi r$.

Now all we need to do is rearrange that equation to isolate r:

$$m = 16\pi r$$
$$\frac{m}{16\pi} = r$$

22. **Answer: B**
    Topic(s): Right Triangles and Basic Trigonometry (p. 249); Circles, Radians, and a Little More Trigonometry (p. 258)

The thing to remember to get this one right is that tangent lines are perpendicular to the radii they connect with, so if we draw in segments AM and BM, we end up making a square.

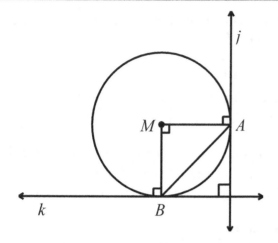

Chord AB is therefore the diagonal of a square, AKA the hypotenuse of a 45°-45°-90° triangle. If $AB = 5\sqrt{2}$, then AM and BM, the legs of the triangle, each equal 5. The radius of the circle is 5.

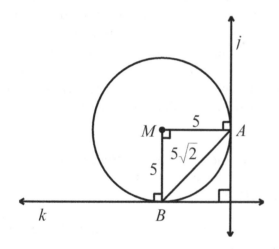

From there, it's easy to calculate the circumference:

$C = 2\pi r$
$C = 2\pi 5$
$C = 10\pi$

23. **Answer: B**
    Topic(s): Functions (p. 92)

For a question like this, make sure you remember to take the full argument, $(x + 2)$, and put it everywhere an x used to be. Here's the algebra:

$f(x) = 2x^2 - 4x + 8$
$f(x + 2) = 2(x + 2)^2 - 4(x + 2) + 8$
$f(x + 2) = 2(x^2 + 4x + 4) - 4x - 8 + 8$
$f(x + 2) = 2x^2 + 8x + 8 - 4x$
$f(x + 2) = 2x^2 + 4x + 8$

24. **Answer: 5**
    Topic(s): Exponents and Exponential Functions (p. 104)

Gotta know the exponent rules to get this one. First, remember that when we multiply two exponential expressions with the same base, we add the exponents. Thus, on the left side:

$(x^{2y})(x^{3y}) = (x^y)^a$
$x^{2y+3y} = (x^y)^a$
$x^{5y} = (x^y)^a$

From there, also remember that when we raise an exponential expression to a power, we multiply the exponents. Thus, on the right side:

$x^{5y} = (x^y)^a$
$x^{5y} = x^{ay}$

If, as the question stipulates, x and y are greater than 1, the only way that equation is true is if $a = 5$.

25. **Answer: A**
    Topic(s): Lines (p. 73)

If we remember that perpendicular lines have negative reciprocal slopes, we're in great shape on this one. First, calculate the slope of line m:

$$\text{slope}_m = \frac{y_2 - y_1}{x_2 - x_1} = \frac{3 - 9}{11 - 2} = -\frac{6}{9} = -\frac{2}{3}$$

If the slope of line m is $-\dfrac{2}{3}$, then a line perpendicular to line m will have a slope of $\dfrac{3}{2}$.

How do we go from knowing the slope and a point to knowing the equation of the line?

Well, my preferred method is to start with $y = mx + b$ form and use the slope and the point we know to solve for b. Like so:

$$y = mx + b$$
$$y = \frac{3}{2}x + b$$
$$9 = \frac{3}{2}(12) + b$$
$$9 = 18 + b$$
$$-9 = b$$

26. **Answer: A**
    Topic(s): Binomial Squares and Difference of Two Squares (p. 123)

Recognize the difference of two squares here: anytime we see something in the form $a^2 - b^2$, it should be at the front of our minds that we can factor it to $(a + b)(a - b)$!

In this case, we treat $x^4 - y^4$ as a difference of two squares. (Really, it's just the same as saying $(x^2)^2 - (y^2)^2$, which is obviously a difference of two squares.) The algebra:

$$\frac{x^4 - y^4}{x^2 + y^2}$$
$$= \frac{(x^2 + y^2)(x^2 - y^2)}{x^2 + y^2}$$
$$= x^2 - y^2$$

Of course, we could keep factoring: $x^2 - y^2 = (x + y)(x - y)$. However, the answer choices don't require us to take that step.

27. **Answer: C**
    Topic(s): Backsolving (p. 32); Percents and Percent Change (p. 161)

We can solve this algebraically, of course, but we can also backsolve super easily. Just pick B or C to start with, and if it doesn't give you 8 percent growth, choose a higher or lower choice accordingly!

Remember, we calculate percent change by dividing the amount of change by the starting value. Like so:

$$\text{percent change} = \frac{\text{end} - \text{start}}{\text{start}} \times 100\%$$

Let's see what happens if we try B:

$$\frac{12{,}768 - 11{,}747}{11{,}747} \times 100\% = 8.69\%$$

That's more like roughly 9 percent. So I guess his account value must have been a little higher at the beginning of the year.

Try C:

$$\frac{12{,}768 - 11{,}822}{11{,}822} \times 100\% = 8.00\%$$

Oh yeah, that's what we're looking for!

The algebra isn't bad either if that's how you like to roll.

$$\frac{12{,}768 - x}{x} \times 100\% = 8\%$$
$$(12{,}768 - x) \times 100\% = x(8\%)$$
$$12{,}768 - x = 0.08x$$
$$12{,}768 = 1.08x$$
$$11{,}822.22 = x$$

28. **Answer: C**
    Topic(s): Data Analysis 1 (p. 195)

Remember that the graph shows the *cumulative* miles driven by the car, so the month during which Gerald drove the least miles will be the month that shows the smallest increase in height from the month prior. Visually, it should be fairly obvious that the bar for Month 3 is only very slightly taller than the bar for Month 2. What that means is that on the last day of Month 3, the odometer increased from the last day of Month 2 by a relatively small amount. Since no other month-to-month increase is smaller, the answer is Month 3.

29. **Answer: D**
    Topic(s): Parabolas (p. 128)

    If you know the properties of the equation of a parabola in standard form, you can answer this easily without a calculator just by looking at the graph. This is a parabola equation in the form $y = ax^2 + bx + c$.

    We see that the parabola opens down, so we want a negative constant for the squared term, and we see the parabola has a positive y-intercept, so we want a positive constant term. Just knowing those two things eliminate all the wrong answers: Choices A and B have negative y-intercepts, and choices B and C are parabolas that open up.

30. **Answer: 6**
    Topic(s): Quadratics (p. 114); Binomial Squares and Difference of Two Squares (p. 123)

    We *could* expand this all the way out, simplify it, and then factor or use the quadratic formula to solve. But since we're here honing our skills to PWN the SAT, let's solve this one the fast way. We can factor the given equation without expanding it first. To make that easier to see, let's temporarily replace $(x - 3)$ with a:

    $$0 = a^2 - 6a + 9$$

    That's an obvious binomial square—easy to factor!

    $$0 = a^2 - 6a + 9$$
    $$0 = (a - 3)^2$$

    All we need to do now is remember that $a = x - 3$ and substitute back in:

    $$0 = (a - 3)^2$$
    $$0 = ((x - 3) - 3)^2$$
    $$0 = (x - 6)^2$$

    So there we have it—the value of x that satisfies the equation is 6.

31. **Answer: B**
    Topic(s): Polynomials (p. 142)

    The first thing we need to do here is translate the words into math:

    $$10x^2 + ax - 36 = (2x + b)(cx + 4)$$

    From there, we see that for FOILing to work, $2cx^2$ must equal $10x^2$, and $4b$ must equal -36. So we can conclude that $c = 5$ and $b = -9$.

    Of course, we need the value for a, so we still have to FOIL with those values in there.

    $$10x^2 + ax - 36 = (2x - 9)(5x + 4)$$
    $$10x^2 + ax - 36 = 10x^2 - 37x - 36$$

    And there we have it: $a = -37$.

32. **Answer: B**
    Topic(s): Circles, Radians, and a Little More Trigonometry (p. 258); Right Triangles and Basic Trigonometry (p. 249)

    Gotta know the circle formula cold to get this one right: $(x - h)^2 + (y - k)^2 = r^2$, where (h, k) is the center of the circle, and r is the circle's radius.

    We're given the circle's center, so step 1 is to plug those points into the formula:

    $$(x - h)^2 + (y - k)^2 = r^2$$
    $$(x - (-5))^2 + (y - 12)^2 = r^2$$
    $$(x + 5)^2 + (y - 12)^2 = r^2$$

    That eliminates two choices. Now we're only choosing between B and D.

    Because we remember that the circle equation requires r^2, at this point we just need to decide if the radius of this circle 13, or $\sqrt{13}$. We can probably just guesstimate that—$\sqrt{13}$ is less than 4, and the distance from $(0, 0)$ (a.k.a. the origin) to $(-5, 12)$ is obviously bigger than 4.

But for all the bonus points, recognize that the radius of this circle is the hypotenuse of a 5-12-13 right triangle! Because the radius of the circle is 13, and $13^2 = 169$, we want choice B.

33. **Answer: A**
Topic(s): Algebraic Manipulation (p. 52)

We have two jobs here. First, we need to combine the given equations to come up with one equation that has everything we need in it —a formula for the density of a sphere. Once we've got that, we need to solve that equation for r.

Combining the equations is easy enough: V appears in both, so we can substitute.

$$p = \frac{m}{V} \qquad V = \frac{4}{3}\pi r^3$$

$$p = \frac{m}{\left(\frac{4}{3}\pi r^3\right)}$$

Now, just solve that for r. Step 1 is to take care of that nasty fraction-in-a-fraction. Remember: when we divide by a fraction, that's the same as multiplying by its reciprocal.

$$p = \frac{m}{\left(\pi r^3\right)} \times \frac{1}{\left(\frac{4}{3}\right)}$$

$$p = \frac{m}{\left(\pi r^3\right)} \times \frac{3}{4}$$

$$p = \frac{3m}{4\pi r^3}$$

Now multiply everything by r^3 since we want to get r isolated so we might as well get it out of the denominator.

$$pr^3 = \frac{3m}{4\pi}$$

Keep isolating r: divide by p.

$$r^3 = \frac{3m}{4p\pi}$$

Now just take the cube root and we're there.

$$r = \sqrt[3]{\frac{3m}{4p\pi}}$$

34. **Answer: D**
Topic(s): Lines (p. 73)

There are a couple ways to go here, and all of them require remembering that perpendicular lines have negative reciprocal slopes. That means that if line m has a slope of 4, then line n must have a slope of $-\frac{1}{4}$.

First, a quick-and-dirty solution. Note that the answer choices are all in the same quadrant. That means it might be enough just to start from the y-intercepts we know and just count to more points on each line using the slopes.

That is, line m goes through $(0, 3)$. Slope is rise over run, so counting down 4 and left 1, we get to $(-1, -1)$, $(-2, -5)$, and so on.

Likewise, line n goes through $(0, -14)$. Counting up 1 and left 4, we land on $(-4, -13)$, $(-8, -12)$, and so on.

Can counting further on either line get us a solution? Yes! Count a few more points on line m, from $(-2, -5)$ to $(-3, -9)$ to $(-4, -13)$. Done!

And now for the solution your math teacher would want to see: Write the equations and solve.

$$m: y = 4x + 3$$
$$n: y = -\frac{1}{4}x - 14$$

Set them equal and solve:

$$4x + 3 = -\frac{1}{4}x - 14$$

$$\frac{17}{4}x = -17$$

$$x = -4$$

Given the answer choices, seeing $x = -4$ is enough, but might as well finish the job by plugging it back into one of the equations:

$$y = 4(-4) + 3$$
$$y = -13$$

Either way we solve it, choice D is the answer.

35. **Answer: B**
Topic(s): Right Triangles and Basic Trigonometry (p. 249)

Did you draw yourself a triangle? You really should—it makes it that much easier to SOH-CAH-TOA this question, and really, how long does it take you to draw a triangle?

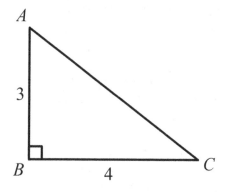

The tangent is the ratio of the opposite side to the adjacent leg, so we know that if $\tan A = \frac{4}{3}$, the sides I've labeled 3 and 4 are either exactly that, or some other values that still simplify to that. Let's make things easy on ourselves and just plug in 3 and 4.

From there, we have two paths. The first and more preferable is recognizing that $\frac{\sin C}{\cos C} = \tan C$ because we just know that iden-

tity. Then all we need to do is look at your diagram to see that $\tan C = \frac{3}{4}$.

The other, slightly longer path, is to recognize the 3-4-5 triangle, evaluate the sine and cosine separately, and then divide those values. That works just as well:

$$\frac{\sin C}{\cos C} = \frac{\left(\frac{3}{5}\right)}{\left(\frac{4}{5}\right)} = \frac{3}{5} \times \frac{5}{4} = \frac{3}{4}$$

36. **Answer: B**
Topic(s): Polynomials (p. 142), Algebraic Manipulation (p. 52)

While you *could* do this one with polynomial division, I'd recommend using multiplication instead. Multiply by the denominator to get rid of those ugly fractions!

$$\frac{18x^2 + 15x - 12}{3x + 2} = 6x + 1 + \frac{a}{3x + 2}$$

$$(3x + 2)\left(\frac{18x^2 + 15x - 12}{3x + 2}\right) =$$
$$\left(6x + 1 + \frac{a}{3x + 2}\right)(3x + 2)$$

$$18x^2 + 15x - 12 =$$
$$(6x + 1)(3x + 2) + \left(\frac{a}{3x + 2}\right)(3x + 2)$$

$$18x^2 + 15x - 12 = (6x + 1)(3x + 2) + a$$
$$18x^2 + 15x - 12 = 18x^2 + 15x + 2 + a$$

Now subtract out all the terms that match on both sides. You're left with simply $-12 = 2 + a$.

Solving that gives you $-14 = a$.

37. **Answer: .5 or 1/2**
Topic(s): Algebraic Manipulation (p. 52);

Exponents and Exponential Functions (p. 104)

This question involves exponents at a basic level, but it's really more of an algebraic manipulation question. To solve, clean up the left-hand side by adding up the numerator and then simplify the fraction.

$$\frac{a^3+a^3+a^3}{6}=a^4$$

$$\frac{3a^3}{6}=a^4$$

$$\frac{a^3}{2}=a^4$$

$$\frac{1}{2}a^3=a^4$$

$$\frac{1}{2}=\frac{a^4}{a^3}$$

$$\frac{1}{2}=a$$

38. **Answer: A**
   Topic(s): Lines (p. 73)

Remember: the *only* way a system of linear equations can have no solutions is if the lines are parallel. And lines are only parallel if they have equal slopes. Therefore, we can solve this one by putting both lines in slope-intercept form, setting the slopes equal, and solving for a.

Put the first equation into slope-intercept form:

$$3x + 2y = 18$$
$$2y = -3x + 18$$
$$y = -\frac{3}{2}x + 9$$

OK, so the first equation has a slope of $-\frac{3}{2}$.

Now put the second equation into slope-intercept form:

$$4x + ay = 22$$
$$ay = -4x + 22$$
$$y = -\frac{4}{a}x + \frac{22}{a}$$

The slope of the second line is $-\frac{4}{a}$.

The slopes have to be equal if the lines are parallel, so we can solve for a:

$$-\frac{4}{a} = -\frac{3}{2}$$
$$(4)(2) = 3a$$
$$8 = 3a$$
$$\frac{8}{3} = a$$

39. **Answer: B**
   Topic(s): Solving Systems of Linear Equations (p. 59)

The best clue we get here is that we're given a value for $x - y$, as opposed to, say, a value for x or y individually. That means we can probably get $x - y$ directly!

Once we're heading in that direction, we should notice that we're given $x - y = 8$ which matches up nicely with the fact that the equations in the system end in 18 and 10. Let's try subtracting!

$$\begin{array}{rcl} 4x + 3y & = & 18 \\ -(ax + 4y) & = & -10 \\ \hline (4-a)x - y & = & 8 \end{array}$$

Well, if $(4 - a)x - y = 8$, and $x - y = 8$, then $4 - a$ must equal 1. Therefore, $a = 3$.

40. **Answer: C**
   Topic(s): Parabolas (p. 128)

OK, first thing's first. If we recognize that the equation we're given is in vertex form (that is, $y = a(x - h)^2 + k$, where (h, k) is the vertex of the parabola), then we know right away that $k = 16$. So let's rewrite the equation and put it in standard form:

$$y = -(x-5)^2 + 16$$
$$y = -(x^2 - 10x + 25) + 16$$
$$y = -x^2 + 10x - 25 + 16$$
$$y = -x^2 + 10x - 9$$

Hmm...can we factor that? Remember, when a parabola is in factored form, it tells us the x-intercepts!

$$y = -x^2 + 10x - 9$$
$$y = -(x^2 - 10x + 9)$$
$$y = -(x-1)(x-9)$$

So the x-intercepts are 1 and 9, which means $a + b = 1 + 9 = 10$.

41. **Answer: A**
    Topic(s): Percents and Percent Change (p. 161)

The population grew by 3.2% from 2013 to 2014, then by 2.8% from 2014 to 2015, then by 2.6% from 2015 to 2016. To figure out what the 2016 population might be, we need to start with the population we know from 2013 and grow it incrementally by each of those percentages.

<u>2014:</u> 1,059,382 × 1.032 = 1,093,282.22
<u>2015:</u> 1,093,282.22 × 1.028 = 1,123,894.13
<u>2016:</u> 1,123,894.13 × 1.026 = 1,153,115.37

(I'm showing two decimal points above, but of course real population numbers will be whole numbers.)

Choice A is the closest to 1,153,115, so that's the answer.

Note this useful shortcut: you can just apply all those growth rates in one calculation:

1,059,382 × 1.032 × 1.028 × 1.026 = 1,153,115.37

42. **Answer: B**
    Topic(s): Exponents and Exponential Functions (p. 104)

Gotta work the exponent rules here. Remember, when we're dividing the same base with different exponents, we subtract the exponents. Like so:

$$\frac{2^{(a-b)}}{2^{(b-a)}} = 4^c$$
$$2^{(a-b)-(b-a)} = 4^c$$
$$2^{(a-b-b+a)} = 4^c$$
$$2^{(2a-2b)} = 4^c$$
$$2^{2(a-b)} = 4^c$$

Let's go a few more steps, this time remembering that $4 = 2^2$, and that a power raised to a power means we multiply the powers.

$$2^{2(a-b)} = \left(2^2\right)^c$$
$$2^{2(a-b)} = 2^{2c}$$

From there, we can conclude that $2(a - b) = 2c$ and solve for b:

$$2(a - b) = 2c$$
$$a - b = c$$
$$-b = c - a$$
$$b = a - c$$

43. **Answer: 0**
    Topic(s): Quadratics (p. 114); Binomial Squares and Difference of Two Squares (p. 123)

Because calculators aren't allowed here, we should approach this question with some basic confidence that the algebra won't be too tough! We need to solve for the x-coordinates of the intersections. Since both equations are already in $y=$ form, let's just set them equal and see what happens.

$$-x^2 + 3x + 1 = 3x - 8$$

Combine like terms (the $3x$ terms cancel!), and then factor (there's a difference of two squares!):

$-x^2 + 9 = 0$

$x^2 - 9 = 0$

$(x - 3)(x + 3) = 0$

Of course, that just leaves us with $x = 3$ and $x = -3$, so the x-coordinates of the intersections are 3 and -3. The sum of those is zero!

44. **Answer: B**
Topic(s): Parabolas (p. 128); Angles, Triangles, and Polygons (p. 236)

The vertex of that parabola will be at (0, 4). The x-intercepts (points A and B) are at (-2, 0) and (2, 0). Therefore, the height of triangle ABC will be 4, and its base will be 4. The area of the triangle will be equal to $\left(\dfrac{1}{2}\right)(4)(4) = 8$.

There are a number of ways to find the points we need in this question. One is just to be familiar enough with the structure of a parabola equation in standard form to recognize instantly that the parabola opens down from a vertex at (0, 4) and will only travel left or right 2 units before it travels down 4 units to the x-axis.

To calculate those points algebraically (if desired), set y equal to zero and solve for the x-intercepts:

$0 = x^2 - 4$

$0 = (x + 2)(x - 2)$

Finally, we could just graph!

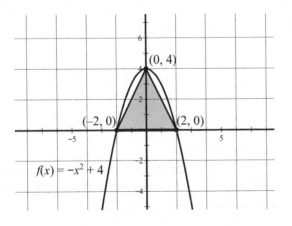

45. **Answer: 3 or 10**
Topic(s): Parabolas (p. 128); Quadratics (p. 128)

Remember: when given a point and a function, we're probably going to have to plug the point into the function.

$5 = k^2 - 13k + 35$

$0 = k^2 - 13k + 30$

From there, we can factor!

$0 = k^2 - 13k + 30$

$0 = (k - 3)(k - 10)$

Of course, that means the two acceptable answers are 3 and 10.

46. **Answer: C**
Topics: Quadratics (p. 128)

If calculators were allowed, I'd probably just be recommending a quick graph! But they're not, so let's do some algebra.

$g(x) = f(x) + 14$

$g(x) = (x - 5)(x + 4) + 14$

$g(x) = (x^2 - x - 20) + 14$

$g(x) = x^2 - x - 6$

$g(x) = (x - 3)(x + 2)$

Well, that wasn't so bad at all, actually. The roots of a function are the values of x that make the function equal zero, and from the factored binomial above we see that $g(x) = 0$ when x equals either -2 or 3.

47. **Answer: 1**
Topic(s): Solving Systems of Linear Equations (p. 59)

Because we're only asked to solve for y, let's see if we can eliminate x. In this case, we can do it in three steps: rearrange the second equation, double it, and then add it to the first equation. Steps 1 and 2:

$5y = 4x - 12$
$-4x + 5y = -12$
$-8x + 10y = -24$

Step 3:

$8x + 3y = 37$
$\underline{-8x + 10y = -24}$
$0x + 13y = 13$

Of course, from there, we're home free: $y = 1$, and we're done!

48. **Answer: C**
    Topic(s): Exponents and Exponential Functions (p. 104), Percents and Percent Change (p. 161)

    Generally speaking, it's good to just know the basic exponential growth formula: $y = ab^x$, where a is a starting value and b is a growth (or decay) factor. In the case of percentage growth, as we have in this problem, that can be modified. Say r is the percentage growth, then the formula we'd use is $y = a(1 + r)^x$.

    That's what we've got going on here. If population grows at 2% per year, then we know that the formula should have $(1+0.02)^x$ in it, which of course simplifies to 1.02^x. Just from that, we know the answer is choice C. The 10,000 in choice C also makes sense, because from the graph it looks like the population in 1981 in Town A was about 10,000.

    One final note: if you have any doubt about stuff like this and you come across it on a test, you backsolve by testing choices with your calculator. Pick a point on the graph that's easy to read (like about 12,000 in 1990, or about 14,000 in 1998) and see which answer choice lands you where you need to be. 1990 and 1998 are 9 and 17 years from 1981, respectively. Look what choice C spits out:

    $P(9) = 10,000 \times 1.02^9 \approx 11,951$
    $P(17) = 10,000 \times 1.02^{17} \approx 14,002$

Pretty good, right? None of the other choices will get close.

49. **Answer: 2.3**
    Topic(s): Angles, Triangles, and Polygons (p. 236)

    The most important thing here is recognizing that triangles ABD and ACD overlap, and that overlap is triangle ADE.

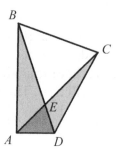

    The area of the quadrilateral will be the sum of the areas of the non-overlapping triangles, so need to come up with a way to deal with that overlap. Let's say that x is the area of triangle ADE. Then we can fill in non-overlapping areas in the figure thusly:

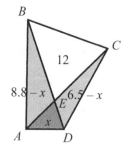

    Because we know the total area of the quadrilateral is 25, we can set up an equation to solve.

    $25 = 12 + (8.8 - x) + (6.5 - x) + x$
    $25 = 27.3 - x$
    $2.3 = x$

50. **Answer: 88**
    Topic(s): Translating between Words and Math (p. 44); Binomial Squares and Difference of Two Squares (p. 123)

Translate the given statements into math:

$a > b$
$a + b = 11$
$a - b = 8$

Recognize that the thing you're asked about, $a^2 - b^2$, is a difference of two squares and can therefore be easily factored into $(a + b)(a - b)$. Conveniently, you have values for both those factors!

$a^2 - b^2 = (a + b)(a - b) = (11)(8) = 88$

51. **Answer: A**
    Topic(s): Parabolas (p. 128)

This is a question about parabola symmetry—to get it, we need to remember that parabolas are symmetrical about the vertical line through their vertices. That means that the x-intercepts of the parabola will be equidistant from the $x = -4$ vertical line.

Since the point $(4, 0)$ is 8 units to the right of the $x = -4$ line, the other x-intercept is going to be 8 units to the left of the $x = -4$ line at $(-12, 0)$. Therefore, $a = -12$.

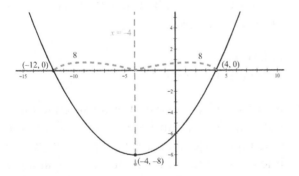

52. **Answer: 17**
    Topic(s): Polynomials (p. 142)

Remember: when we have equivalent polynomials, their corresponding coefficients are equal.

To use that fact to solve this, first let's FOIL out the right-hand side.

$3x^2 + bx + 24 = (3x + 8)(x + a)$
$3x^2 + bx + 24 = 3x^2 + 3ax + 8x + 8a$

From there you know that the constants, with no x-terms, are equal. In other words, $24 = 8a$, which of course means $3 = a$.

Use that to solve for the value of b. The x-coefficient terms must also be equal:
$bx = 3ax + 8x$.

If $a = 3$, then $bx = 3(3)x + 8x = 17x$. That means $b = 17$.

53. **Answer: 80**
    Topic(s): Circles, Radians, and a Little More Trigonometry (p. 258)

The thing we need to remember when we tackle questions like this is that circles are proportional.

We know an arc length, and we know a radius. From the radius, we can calculate a circumference, and then all we need to do is solve for the central angle. So let's go!

Circumference is $2\pi r$, so in this case it's $2\pi(45) = 90\pi$.

We can use that to find the proportion of the given arc length to the whole circumference, and then solve for the central angle's measure:

$$\frac{\text{measure of central angle}}{360°} = \frac{\text{arc length}}{\text{circumference}}$$
$$\frac{\text{measure of central angle}}{360°} = \frac{20\pi}{90\pi}$$
$$\frac{\text{measure of central angle}}{360°} = \frac{2}{9}$$
$$\text{measure of central angle} = \frac{2}{9} \times 360°$$
$$\text{measure of central angle} = 80°$$

54. **Answer: C**
    Topic(s): Measures of Central Tendency and Variability (p. 182)

Remember: mean (AKA average) questions are often really about sums. That's certainly the case here. If mean $= \dfrac{\text{sum of numbers}}{\text{count of numbers}}$, then we also know that

count of numbers × mean = sum of numbers. Let's use that to find the sums of all 15 scores and the 13 leftover scores:

$15 \times 193 = 2895$
$13 \times 203 = 2639$

See what's going on there? If all the scores add up to 2895, and the 13 highest scores add up to 2639, then the two lowest scores must add up to $2895 - 2639 = 256$. Because there are two scores adding up to 256, divide by two to get their mean: $\dfrac{256}{2} = 128$. That's the answer!

55. **Answer: B**
Topic(s): Circles, Radians, and a Little More Trigonometry (p. 258)

The area of a circle is πr^2. We know that the area of this circle is $x\pi$, so $r^2 = x$, and therefore we know $r = \sqrt{x}$.

Because the circle is inscribed in the square, we also know that the diameter (aka, $2\sqrt{x}$) is the same length as a side of the square. The perimeter is the sum of the lengths of the four sides, so it equals $4(2\sqrt{x}) = 8\sqrt{x}$.

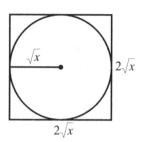

56. **Answer: A**
Topic(s): Translating between Words and Math (p. 44); Algebraic Manipulation (p. 52); Plugging In (p. 24)

Our first job here is to translate the statements into math sentences. Remember that "is" always means the equals sign!

a is five more than half of b.
$a = \dfrac{1}{2}b + 5$

b minus c is three less than a.
$b - c = a - 3$

c is two times d.
$c = 2d$

From there, see if you can spot obvious substitutions in the answer choices. Choice A is the right answer because it makes two "obvious" substitutions: into the second equation $(b - c = a - 3)$ $2d$ is substituted for c and $\dfrac{1}{2}b + 5$ is substituted for a.

We can actually also plug in here if we're careful. Starting with the first equation, pick values that work. For example, we might say that $a = 15$ and $b = 20$. The second equation then forces you to say that $c = 8$. From there, the third equation means that $d = 4$. Which answer choice will be true with those values? Only choice A will.

57. **Answer: 9**
Topic(s): Lines (p. 73)

Remember that a system of linear equations will only have an infinite number of solutions when both equations represent the exact same line—they must have the same slope and the same y-intercept. So our first step here should be to put both equations into slope-intercept form.

$3x - \dfrac{1}{3}y = a$

$-\dfrac{1}{3}y = -3x + a$

$y = 9x - 3a$

$$ax - y = 27$$
$$-y = -ax + 27$$
$$y = ax - 27$$

From there, the answer might already be clear, but if not we can set the slopes and y-intercepts equal to each other.

Setting the slopes equal to each other simply gives us $9 = a$, which is pretty great. Setting the y-intercepts equal gives us $-3a = -27$, which of course also simplifies to $9 = a$.

58. **Answer: D**
    Topic(s): Data Analysis 2 (p. 203); Lines (p. 73)

    How nice for us that the choices are all in $y = mx + b$ form! All we need to do is figure out what slope (m) and intercept (b) we're dealing with.

    We can eyeball the y-intercept of the graph easily enough: it's a little less than 30. Two answer choices use 27.3 as the intercept, A and D (careful—choice B uses negative 27.3!). So the answer must be A or D.

    From there, we can estimate the slope by picking two points on the graph. Looks to me like the line gets pretty close to (11, 90) and also pretty close to (4, 50), so let's use those. Slope is rise/run, or:

    $$\text{Slope} \approx \frac{90 - 50}{11 - 4}$$
    $$\text{Slope} \approx \frac{40}{7}$$
    $$\text{Slope} \approx 5.7$$

    That's an awful lot closer to 5.8 than 0.6, so we have our answer. Choice D it is.

59. **Answer: D**
    Topic(s): Angles, Triangles, and Polygons (p. 236)

    Remember: the sum of the interior angles in a polygon with n sides is equal to $(n - 2)180°$. If

it's a regular polygon with equal sides and equal angles like the one in this question, then the measure of each interior angle can be calculated by dividing by n: $\dfrac{(n-2)\,180°}{n}$.

Because the question gives the measure of the interior angles, all we need to do is solve:

$$162 = \frac{(n-2)\,180}{n}$$
$$162n = (n-2)\,180$$
$$162n = 180n - 360$$
$$-18n = 360$$
$$n = 20$$

So there are 20 sides in this polygon. Since each one has a length of 7 inches, the perimeter is $20 \times 7 = 140$ inches.

60. **Answer: B**
    Topic(s): Exponents and Exponential Functions (p. 104); Functions (p. 92)

    Gotta know your exponent rules and be comfortable with function notation to get this one!

    Choice A works. Remember, when you raise a power to a power, you multiply those powers.

    $$f\!\left(a^2\right)$$
    $$= \left(a^2\right)^3$$
    $$= a^6$$

    Choice B doesn't work. Remember, you can convert radical form to fractional exponent form—the root is the denominator and the power is the numerator.

    $$h\!\left(\sqrt[6]{a^5}\right)$$
    $$= h\!\left(a^{\frac{5}{6}}\right)$$
    $$= \left(a^{\frac{5}{6}}\right)^5$$
    $$= a^{\frac{25}{6}}$$

Choice C works. Remember that negative exponents flip fractions.

$$\frac{1}{f(g(a))}$$
$$=\frac{1}{f(a^{-2})}$$
$$=\frac{1}{(a^{-2})^3}$$
$$=\frac{1}{a^{-6}}$$
$$=a^6$$

Choice D works. Remember that when multiplying exponential expressions with the same base, you add the bases.

$$f(a)\cdot g(a)\cdot h(a)$$
$$=(a^3)\cdot(a^{-2})\cdot(a^5)$$
$$=a^{(3-2+5)}$$
$$=a^6$$

Since you're asked to find the expression that *doesn't* equal a^6, the answer is B.

61. **Answer: .8 or 4/5**
   Topic(s): Right Triangles and Basic Trigonometry (p. 249)

To get this one, we need to recognize that triangles ABC and DEC are similar. We know this because they have vertical angles at point C, and they each have right angles as well—that's enough for Angle-Angle similarity.

From there, knowing that $ED = 3$ and $AB = 6$ tells us that all the sides of triangle ABC are twice as long as their corresponding sides in triangle DEC.

We can use this fact to figure out the lengths of the other legs because we know their sum: $EB = 12$. If we say $EC = x$, then we must say $BC = 2x$. So we can solve:

$$12 = x + 2x$$
$$12 = 3x$$
$$4 = x$$

If $ED = 3$ and $EC = 4$, then triangle DEC is a 3-4-5 triangle: $CD=5$.

Remember SOH-CAH-TOA: the sine of an angle is equal to the length of its Opposite leg over the Hypotenuse. Therefore, $\sin D = \frac{4}{5}$.

62. **Answer: A**
   Topic(s): Absolute Value (p. 82); Parabolas (p. 128)

OK, so first of all, we need to remember that absolute values make graphs "bounce." This is because the absolute value of a positive number is just the number, while the absolute number of a negative number is the positive version of it. For a graph, that means the positive parts of the graph stay positive, while the negative parts become positive.

The answer choices in this question all make parabolas. So the task is to figure out which answer choice would make a parabola that, when bounced off the x-axis, would look like the given figure. Easy enough?

Because all the answer choices are in factored form, let's first look at what factored form gives us easily: x-intercepts. Absolute value should not impact x-intercepts at all: the absolute value of zero is zero! The given graph hits $(-4, 0)$ and $(3, 0)$. Which answer choices have the same intercepts?

Well, choice A does. What $x = -4$ or $x = 3$, the function defined in choice A equals zero. Any other choices?

Choice B has x-intercepts at 4 and 3.
Choice C has x-intercepts at 4 and -3.
Choice D also has x-intercepts at 4 and -3.

Well, that turned out to be easy enough!
Choice A it is!

63. Answer: A
Topic(s): Measures of Central Tendency and Variability (p. 182)

We're going to need calculate the values, but don't worry, it won't take long! Dot plots are actually perfect for this kind of thing.

Mode first—that's by far the easiest. The mode is the number that appears most, so just look for the tallest dot stack. That's at 3, so the mode is 3.

Now the mean. Add up the values and divide by the total number of values. The dot plot makes it easy to sum the values quickly because we can multiply the number of dots above each number by that number. Like so:

$1(1) + 2(2) + 5(3) + 4(4) + 2(5) + 1(6) + 1(7) + 1(9) + 2(10) = 88$.

To calculate the mean, just divide that sum by the total number of dots, 19.

$$\frac{88}{19} \approx 4.63$$

Finally, the median. That's the middle number when all the values are sorted, and the dot plot provides us with a sort! In a set of 19 numbers, there will be 9 values, then the median, then another 9 values. In other words, the median will be the 10th number. So just count dots!

Consecutive Hops on One Foot

In Mr. Hopkins' Kindergarten Class

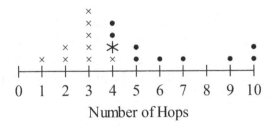

Number of Hops

So the median is 4. The mode was 3, and the mean was about 4.63. Therefore,
mean (4.63) > median (4) > mode (3).

64. Answer: D
Topic(s): Translating between Words and Math (p. 44)

A few notes to start this one. First, average speed is just total distance over total time, so all we're doing is dividing here. Second, even though the question asks about average speed in miles per hour, we don't need to convert to hours unless we really want to (which we shouldn't on a test where we're being timed). The fastest jog in miles per hour will still be the fastest jog in miles per minute! Finally, don't bother doing any calculations for the Feb 5 jog, since that's not an answer choice.

Let's have our first step be to take the given times and convert them, roughly to minutes in decimal form. Remember that 15 seconds is a quarter of a minute, 20 seconds is a 3rd of a minute, 30 seconds is half a minute, etc.

Feb 2: 19 min, 21 sec → 19.3 min
Feb 4: 18 min, 43 sec → 18.7 min
Feb 7: 27 min, 54 sec → 28 min
Feb 9: 17 min, 03 sec → 17 min

Now just divide!

Feb 2: 2.04 miles / 19.3 min ≈ 0.106 miles/min
Feb 4: 2.16 miles / 18.7 min ≈ 0.116 miles/min
Feb 7: 3.31 miles / 28 min ≈ 0.118 miles/min
Feb 9: 2.23 miles / 17 min ≈ 0.131 miles/min

One speed definitely stands out from the rest, and it stands our far enough that our little approximations won't have changed the outcome. Feb 9 was the fastest jog.

65. Answer: D
Topic(s): Lines (p. 73)

The first trick here is remembering that when lines are perpendicular, then their slopes are negative reciprocals. Because we know the slope of the first line is 3, we know the slope of the second line must be $-\frac{1}{3}$. We can solve from there.

The first equation simplifies:

$$y = 3x + 3\left(-\frac{1}{3}\right)$$
$$y = 3x - 1$$

The second equation just needs a little substitutin':

$$y = -\frac{1}{3}x + 9$$

From here, let's use the fact that both equations are already in $y=$ form to solve for x first:

$$3x - 1 = -\frac{1}{3}x + 9$$
$$\frac{9}{3}x - 1 = -\frac{1}{3}x + 9$$
$$\frac{10}{3}x = 10$$
$$10x = 30$$
$$x = 3$$

Great, now substitute to find y:

$$y = 3(3) - 1$$
$$y = 8$$

There—the intersection we seek is (3, 8)!

66. **Answer: 9**
Topic(s): Parabolas (p. 128)

This parabola is given in vertex form—we know from looking at the equation that it opens downwards from a vertex of (7, 4). If we know the normal shape of a parabola with a leading coefficient of 1 or –1, then we know it will travel 2 units left or right as it travels 4 units down to the x-axis. 2 units to the right of $x = 7$ will put us at the greater of the two x-intercepts at $x = 9$.

Another way to go is to solve algebraically: just FOIL, simplify, and factor:

$$y = -(x - 7)^2 + 4$$
$$y = -(x^2 - 14x + 49) + 4$$
$$y = -x^2 + 14x - 49 + 4$$
$$y = -x^2 + 14x - 45$$
$$y = -(x^2 - 14x + 45)$$
$$y = -(x - 5)(x - 9)$$

From that, we can see that the parabola will have zeros at 5 and 9, so again we see that the greater of the x-intercepts of the parabola is 9.

67. **Answer: C**
Topic(s): Functions (p. 92)

The thing to recognize here is that if $g(x) = 2f(x) - 1$, then $g(1) = 2f(1) - 1$. Since we can find the value of $f(1)$ from the graph, the rest is just simple arithmetic.

To find $f(1)$, just trace the x-axis to $x = 1$ and then trace straight up until you get to the graph. The intersection of the graph and the $x = 1$ line will give you the value of $f(1)$.

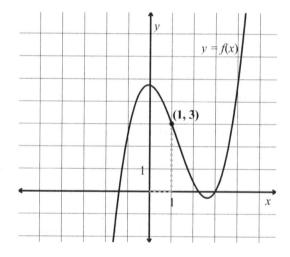

Since the graph touches the $x = 1$ line at (1, 3), we can say that $f(1) = 3$. (And of course, friendly reminder, generally we can say that if a point (a, b) lies on the graph of a function f, then $f(a)=b$.)

Anyway, now that we have the a value for $f(1)$, we can plug it into the expression we have for $g(1)$ to solve.

$g(1) = 2f(1) - 1$
$g(1) = 2(3) - 1$
$g(1) = 5$

68. **Answer: B**
Topic(s): Backsolving (p. 32); Quadratics (p. 114)

Pro-tip: we don't need to solve this equation! The answer choices present a total of four possible numbers to try, and they're all easy to plug back into the problem. Just see which ones work! (And be strategic about which ones you try first. For example, I'm going to try –4 first, because if –4 isn't a solution, I'll eliminate three choices.)

$$\frac{2x+10}{x^2-x-6} = \frac{x+3}{x-3}$$

$$\frac{2(-4)+10}{(-4)^2-(-4)-6} = \frac{-4+3}{-4-3}$$

$$\frac{-8+10}{16+4-6} = \frac{-1}{-7}$$

$$\frac{2}{14} = \frac{1}{7}$$

So –4 checks out as a solution. Guess we should try 1 next.

$$\frac{2x+10}{x^2-x-6} = \frac{x+3}{x-3}$$

$$\frac{2(1)+10}{(1)^2-(1)-6} = \frac{1+3}{1-3}$$

$$\frac{2+10}{1-1-6} = \frac{4}{-2}$$

$$\frac{12}{-6} = \frac{4}{-2}$$

$$-2 = -2$$

Welp, 1 worked, too. Choice B must be the answer!

People always wanna see the math, though, so here it is:

$$\frac{2x+10}{x^2-x-6} = \frac{x+3}{x-3}$$

$$\frac{2x+10}{(x-3)(x+2)} = \frac{x+3}{x-3}$$

$$\frac{2x+10}{(x+2)} = x+3$$

$$2x+10 = (x+3)(x+2)$$

$$2x+10 = x^2+5x+6$$

$$0 = x^2+3x-4$$

$$0 = (x+4)(x-1)$$

69. **Answer: D**
Topic(s): Data Analysis 2 (p. 203); Measures of Central Tendency and Variability (p. 206)

Remember: A box plot is a way to visualize a data set by highlighting 5 summary numbers: the minimum, the maximum, the median, and the first and third quartiles.

The way to think about the first and third quartile are that they're basically the medians of the lower and higher halves of the data. In this case, we have 58 scores, which means half of the scores (29 of them) will be above the median, and the other 29 scores will be below the median. The first quartile will be the median of the 29 scores below the true median, and the third quartile will be the median of the 29 scores above the true median.

The box plot tells you that 82 is the third quartile. That's the median of 29 scores. How many scores will be above the median of 29 scores? Well, the median will be the 15th highest score, and there will be 14 scores on either side of that. So there could be 14 scores higher than the 3rd quartile.

Note that the reason we say there *could be* 14 scores higher than 82 is that we don't know anything about repeat scores. The box plot wouldn't tell us if there were 6 students that all scored 82, for example, even though that's a possibility. We do know, however, that if more than 14 students scored higher than 82, then 82 wouldn't be the third quartile.

70. Answer: 5
Topic(s): Parabolas (p. 128)

The easiest way to go here might be to plug the point we know, (0, 8) into the given equation and solve for a:

$$0 = -(8 - a)^2 + 9$$
$$0 = -(64 - 16a + a^2) + 9$$
$$0 = -64 + 16a - a^2 + 9$$
$$0 = -a^2 + 16a - 55$$
$$0 = a^2 - 16a + 55$$
$$0 = (a - 5)(a - 11)$$

That tells us that $a = 5$ or $a = 11$. Since we want the least possible value, our answer is 5.

71. Answer: 6
Topic(s): Ratios and Proportionality (p. 171)

To solve this question, we need to convert between part:part ratios (boys:girls) to total numbers. So let's add the numbers in the original ratio to create a new ratio.

If there are 5 boys to 4 girls in Class 1, then there are 5 boys for every $5 + 4 = 9$ total students. In other words, $\frac{5}{9}$ of the 27 students in Class 1 are boys, and $\frac{4}{9}$ are girls. So there are 15 boys and 12 girls in Class 1.

Class 2 is easy: if the ratio is 1 to 1, then half of the class is boys and the other half is girls. There are 17 boys and 17 girls in Class 2.

In Class 3, $\frac{4}{11}$ of the students are boys and $\frac{7}{11}$ are girls. So there are 12 boys and 21 girls in Class 3.

In total, then, there are $15 + 17 + 12 = 44$ boys and $12 + 17 + 21 = 50$ girls. Therefore, there are $50 - 44 = 6$ more girls than boys in those three classes.

72. Answer: A
Topic(s): Exponents and Exponential Functions (p. 104); Binomial Squares and Difference of Two Squares (p. 123)

Remember, $c^a c^b$ simplifies to $c^{(a+b)}$ and $\frac{c^a}{c^b}$ simplifies to $c^{(a-b)}$. Once we've got those, we're off to the races.

If $c^{(a+b)} = c^{12}$, then $a + b = 12$.

If $c^{(a-b)} = c^3$, then $a - b = 3$.

Now recognize the difference of two squares in the expression we're trying to match: $c^{(a^2-b^2)}$ can be rewritten $c^{(a+b)(a-b)}$.

Once we see that, we're basically done. Just substitute!

$$c^{(a+b)(a-b)} = c^{(12)(3)} = c^{36}$$

73. Answer: C
Topic(s): Data Analysis 2 (p. 76); Lines (p. 73)

Note that all the answers are in slope-intercept form. The thing to zero in on as the big difference between the answer choices is slope—the possible intercepts are all plausible enough given the picture.

Pick two points (they don't actually have to be points on the scatterplot!) that you think should be on or near the line of best fit, and figure out the slope between them. I'm thinking let's use (10, 70) and (18, 120):

The slope between those two points is $\frac{120-70}{18-10} = 6.25$. The only answer choice with a slope even close to that is choice C.

74. Answer: D
Topic(s): Lines (p. 73)

Take this one step at a time. The original line is $y = 4x - 5$.

When a line reflects across the x-axis, its slope and its y-intercept are negated. So the equation of the reflection is going to be $y = -4x + 5$.

The next step calls for drawing a line perpendicular to the reflection (in other words, perpendicular to $y = -4x + 5$) that crosses it at its y-intercept. We know its slope will be $\frac{1}{4}$ because it's perpendicular to a line with a slope of -4 (and actually looking at the answer choices that's all we need) and we know its y-intercept will be 5 because that's where it meets the other line whose y-intercept we know is 5.

75. **Answer: 5**
    Topic(s): Data Analysis 2 (p. 203); Measures of Central Tendency and Variability (p. 182)

Note that if the total number of participants in the contest was 81, there will be 40 participants who did the same or worse than the median, and 40 participants who did the same or better. Then there's the median participant, #41, right there in the middle.

Because we know the median score will be the 41st score in the list when the list is in order, all we need to do is start counting up from either side until we get past 41. The bar that pushes us past 41, from either side, will contain the median.

Counting from the left we have $3 + 0 + 6 + 15 + 11 = 35$ people in the bars before 5 free throws made. Adding the 9 from the bar for 5 shots made gets us up to 44, past the 41st score, so the median is 5.

Counting from the right we have $1 + 7 + 3 + 11 + 15 = 37$ in the bars to the right of 5 free throws made. Adding the 9 from the bar for 5 shots made gets us up to 46, past the 41st score, so again, the median is 5.

76. **Answer: .5 or 1/2**
    Topic(s): Exponents and Exponential Functions (p. 104)

To get this one, we first must remember that anything to the 0 power equals 1, so when we're told that $f(0) = 8$, that helps us solve for a:

$$f(0) = 8$$
$$ab^0 = 8$$
$$a(1) = 8$$
$$a = 8$$

From there, we can use $f(3) = 1$ to solve for b:

$$f(3) = 1$$
$$8b^3 = 1$$
$$b^3 = \frac{1}{8}$$
$$b = \sqrt[3]{\frac{1}{8}}$$
$$b = \frac{1}{2}$$

Now that we have values for a and b, we can find $f(4)$:

$$f(4) = 8\left(\frac{1}{2}\right)^4$$
$$f(4) = 8\left(\frac{1^4}{2^4}\right)$$
$$f(4) = 8\left(\frac{1}{16}\right)$$
$$f(4) = \frac{1}{2}$$

77. **Answer: D**
    Topic(s): Solving Systems of Linear Equations (p. 59); Lines (p. 73)

For a system of linear equations to have an infinite number of solutions, both equations must end up making the same line. In other words, both equations must have the same slope and the same y-intercept. So let's get the first equation into $y = mx + b$ form. First, let's multiply everything by 15 to make life easier:

$$15 \times \left(\frac{1}{5} x + \frac{1}{15} y \right) = (4) \times 15$$
$$3x - y = 60$$
$$-y = -3x + 60$$
$$y = 3x - 60$$

Now, let's get the second equation into the same slope-intercept form:

$$\frac{3}{7} x - ay = b$$

$$-ay = -\frac{3}{7} x + b$$

$$y = \frac{3}{7a} x - \frac{b}{a}$$

For the system to have an infinite number of solutions, then, $\frac{3}{7a}$ must equal 3, and $-\frac{b}{a}$ must equal –60.

Solve for a:

$$\frac{3}{7a} = 3$$
$$3 = 21a$$
$$\frac{1}{7} = a$$

Then solve for b:

$$-\frac{b}{\left(\frac{1}{7} \right)} = -60$$

$$b = 60 \left(\frac{1}{7} \right)$$

$$b = \frac{60}{7}$$

78. **Answer: C**
Topic(s): Ratios and Proportionality (p. 171)

Just gotta be really careful with units here. First, we know Dana circled the pond four times, so she traveled

4×0.29 miles = 1.16 miles. Convert that to inches:

$$1.16 \text{ mi} \times \frac{5{,}280 \text{ ft}}{1 \text{ mi}} \times \frac{12 \text{ in}}{1 \text{ ft}} = 73{,}497.6 \text{ in}$$

If Dana took 2,940 steps to cover 73,497.6 inches, then we can calculate the average distance she covered with each step:

$$\frac{73{,}497.6 \text{ in}}{2{,}940 \text{ steps}} = 25.0 \text{ inches per step}$$

Now, the answer choices are in feet and inches, so we need to do one more conversion. There are 12 inches in a foot, so in 25 inches there are 2 feet (24 inches) and then one more inch left over. 25 inches = 2 feet, 1 inch.

79. **Answer: 9**
Topic(s): Binomial Squares and Difference of Two Squares (p. 123)

We'd get into trouble pretty quickly if we tried to solve for a and b directly here—they aren't integers. Good thing we don't need to solve for them!

Note that the two equations we're given provide values for the pieces of the binomial square we're meant to find the value of! FOILing out $(a - b)^2$ gives us $a^2 - 2ab + b^2$, which of course can be rearranged to $a^2 + b^2 - 2ab$. We can substitute the given values right into there.

$$(a - b)^2 = a^2 + b^2 - 2ab$$
$$(a - b)^2 = 19 - 2(5)$$
$$(a - b)^2 = 9$$

80. **Answer: D**
Topic(s): Parabolas (p. 128)

The best way to get this one is to remember that when we get a parabola in factored form (like the one given), we know the parabola's zeros. In this case, the parabola will have zeros at $x = 5$ and $x = p$. Because parabolas are symmetrical about their vertex, the x-coordinate of the vertex will always be the average of the x-coordinates of the parabolas zeros (or any other two points on the parabola with the same y-coordinate).

In other words, we know that 9 will be the average of 5 and p.

$$9 = \frac{5+p}{2}$$
$$13 = p$$

81. **Answer: A**
Topic(s): Backsolving (p. 32); Translating between Words and Math (p. 44)

This is a great question to backsolve. Start by assuming choice C is correct and she sold 129 hamburgers. At $8 per hamburger, she'll have made $1,032 in burgers. She sells two thirds as many orders of fries, so she will have sold 86 orders of fries. At $5 per order, that's $430 for fries. Total sales: $1,032 + 430 = \$1,462$. That's not enough money, so she needs to sell more burgers.

Try choice B, which says she sold 144 burgers. Two thirds of that is 96, so she will have sold 96 orders of fries. Total sales: $144(8) + 96(5) = \$1,632$. That's warmer, but we're still not there. At this point, if we're in a real rush, we can just pick A, but if we have the time it shouldn't take long to confirm.

If she sold 153 burgers, then she sold 102 orders of fries. $153(8) + 102(5) = \$1,734$. Done.

The algebra:

$$1734 = 8x + 5\left(\frac{2}{3}x\right)$$
$$1734 = 8x + \frac{10}{3}x$$
$$1734 = \frac{34}{3}x$$
$$154 = x$$

82. **Answer: 3**
Topic(s): Exponents and Exponential Functions (p. 104)

Start by simplifying the numerator on the left. When we raise an exponential expression to another power, we multiply the exponents.

$$\frac{\left(3^x\right)^2}{3^{3x}} = \frac{1}{27}$$
$$\frac{3^{2x}}{3^{3x}} = \frac{1}{27}$$

Now we're ready to simplify the fraction. When we divide two exponential expressions with the same base, we subtract the exponents.

$$\frac{3^{2x}}{3^{3x}} = \frac{1}{27}$$
$$3^{2x-3x} = \frac{1}{27}$$
$$3^{-x} = \frac{1}{27}$$

Finally, remember that a negative exponent is the same as the inverse of the positive exponent. In other words...

$$3^{-x} = \frac{1}{27}$$
$$\frac{1}{3^x} = \frac{1}{27}$$
$$3^x = 27$$
$$x = 3$$

83. **Answer: C**
Topic(s): Percents and Percent Change (p. 161); Data Analysis 1 (p. 195)

The big shortcut here is recognizing right away that percent change will be negative in a year that the number of accidents declines. Just scanning the bar graph, we've got a very minimal decrease from 2010 to 2011, and then the big decrease from 2016 to 2017. Of the answer choices, only P_{2017} represents a decrease, so C is the answer.

84. Answer: A
Topic(s): Percents and Percent Change (p. 161); Data Analysis 1 (p. 195)

Forget about the very big numbers and the confusing fiscal years. All we need to do here is calculate percent growth!

We can calculate the percent growth from 2017-18 to 2018-19 like so:

$$\text{percent growth} = \frac{2.788 - 2.629}{2.629} \times 100\%$$

$$\text{percent growth} \approx 6.05\%$$

Now just increase that 2018-19 budget of $2.788 billion by 6.05% and see how much higher it is than the City's planned budget.

$$2.788 + (0.0605)(2.788) \approx 2.957$$

So if the budget increased by the same percent in 2019-20 that it did in 2018-19, it would be $2.957 billion. The table says that the planned budget is actually $2.881 billion. What's the difference?

$$2.957 - 2.881 = 0.076$$

Of course, $0.076 billion is $76 million.

85. Answer: D
Topic(s): Parabolas (p. 128)

Remember that parabolas are symmetrical, and that their lines of symmetry pass through their vertex. This is a vertical parabola (i.e., it has an x^2 term) so the line of symmetry for this parabola is $x = 19$.

That means that the other given point we have, $(16, -6)$ must have a mirror image on the other side of the $x = 19$ line. 16 is 3 away from 19, so we can go 3 away from 19 in the other direction, to $(22, -6)$ and be sure we're at another point on the parabola.

86. Answer: C
Topic(s): Backsolving (p. 32); Percents and Percent Change (p. 161)

It would be test prep malpractice not to recommend backsolving on this one. Start with choice C, and just see if that choice does what the question says we want.

If Sunday sales are $3,401, then total sales for the week will be:

$1,180 + 1,331 + 1,838 + 1,865 + 1,574 + 2,454 + 3,401 = $13,643

Is $3,401 25% of that total?

$$\frac{3,401}{13,643} = 0.2493$$

That's 24.93%, which certainly rounds to 25%. C's the answer!

But of course, we can solve algebraically. Say Sunday's sales are x. The total weekly sales will be:

$1,180 + 1,331 + 1,838 + 1,865 + 1,574 + 2,454 + x = $10,242 + x$

So we can set up and solve the following equation:

$$\frac{x}{10,242 + x} = 0.25$$
$$x = 0.25(10,242 + x)$$
$$x = 2560.5 + 0.25x$$
$$0.75x = 2560.5$$
$$x = 3,414$$

No answer choice matches that exactly, but choice C is by far the closest!

87. Answer: .5 or 1/2
Topic(s): Binomial Squares and Difference of Two Squares (p. 123)

The trick here is factoring—recognizing a difference of two squares and a binomial square. Here, let's write the question again, only factored:

If $(a + b)[(a + b)(a - b)] = 18$ and $(a + b)^2 = 36$, what is the value of $a - b$?

Or...

If $(a + b)^2(a - b) = 18$ and $(a + b)^2 = 36$, what is the value of $a - b$?

Now isn't that better?

Just plug 36 in for $(a + b)^2$ and solve:

$(a + b)^2(a - b) = 18$
$36(a - b) = 18$
$a - b = 0.5$

88. **Answer: 2**
   Topic(s): Circles, Radians, and a little more Trigonometry (p. 258)

For circle equation questions, you'll often be in the position of having to complete some squares. That's certainly the case here.

$x^2 + y^2 - 10x + 14y = -70$
$(x^2 - 10x) + (y^2 + 14y) = -70$
$(x^2 - 10x + 25) + (y^2 + 14y + 49) = -70 + 25 + 49$
$(x^2 - 10x + 25) + (y^2 + 14y + 49) = 4$
$(x - 5)^2 + (y + 7)^2 = 4$

Now, remember that the standard circle equation is $(x - h)^2 + (y - k)^2 = r^2$, where the center of the circle is (h, k) and the radius is r.

Therefore, the circle in this question has a center at $(5, -7)$ and, more importantly, a radius of 2.

89. **Answer: D**
   Topic(s): Parabolas (p. 128)

When we're given a point on a graph, we should always try to plug the point into the graph's equation! In this case, that's how we'll solve for a

$y = a(x - 3)^2 + 2$
$0 = a(2 - 3)^2 + 2$
$0 = a(-1)^2 + 2$
$0 = a + 2$
$-2 = a$

So that tells that that the parabola equation is really $y = -2(x - 3)^2 + 2$ and the point we're trying to solve for, (a, b), is really $(-2, b)$.

Now we just need to plug a point into an equation one more time!

$y = -2(x - 3)^2 + 2$
$b = -2((-2) - 3)^2 + 2$
$b = -2(-5)^2 + 2$
$b = -2(25) + 2$
$b = -48$

90. **Answer: A**
   Topic(s): Right Triangles and Basic Trigonometry (p. 249)

When you're not given a figure for a geometry question like this, you should always do a quick sketch. In this case, doing so might be the difference between assuming this is a simple 5-12-13 triangle and recognizing that, oh no wait, 12 is the *hypotenuse* and this triangle isn't really special at all!

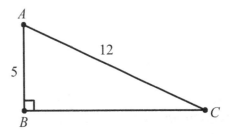

The area of a triangle is equal to $\frac{1}{2}bh$, so we need to calculate BC, the base. Let's Pythagorize:

$5^2 + BC^2 = 12^2$
$25 + BC^2 = 144$

$BC^2 = 119$

$BC = \sqrt{119}$

With that, we're basically done. The base of this triangle is $\sqrt{119}$ and the height is 5. The area is $\frac{1}{2}\left(5\sqrt{119}\right)$, choice A.

91. **Answer: B**
    Topic(s): Complex Numbers (p. 292)

The only way to divide complex numbers like this is to multiply by the complex conjugate of the denominator divided by itself. In other words, our first step is this:

$$\frac{14-5i}{3-2i} \times \frac{3+2i}{3+2i}$$

This will make the denominator a real number, which will let us divide. Just remember to substitute -1 whenever FOILing produces an i^2.

$$\frac{14-5i}{3-2i} \times \frac{3+2i}{3+2i}$$
$$= \frac{(14-5i)(3+2i)}{(3-2i)(3+2i)}$$
$$= \frac{42+28i-15i-10i^2}{9+6i-6i-4i^2}$$
$$= \frac{42+13i-10(-1)}{9-4(-1)}$$
$$= \frac{52+13i}{13}$$
$$= 4+i$$

92. **Answer: A**
    Topic(s): Quadratics (p. 114)

This is an excellent backsolving question. There are only a few possible numbers in the answer choices (3, 4, 5, and 7), and substituting them into the given equation won't take long at all. Further, even if we do this question the math way, we end up having to substitute back into the original equation, doing exactly what backsolving would have had us doing from the beginning!

Start by trying $x = 4$:

$$5-x=\sqrt{x-3}$$
$$5-4=\sqrt{4-3}$$
$$1=\sqrt{1}$$

OK, that worked, so we already know the answer must be A or C, the only choices that contain 4. So let's try 7, to see whether the answer is A or C.

$$5-x=\sqrt{x-3}$$
$$5-7=\sqrt{7-3}$$
$$-2\neq\sqrt{4}$$

That one does *not* work. If 4 is in the solution set but 7 is not, the answer must be A.

93. **Answer: C**
    Topic(s): Backsolving (p. 32); Measures of Central Tendency and Variability (p. 182)

Remember that when we have the average of a set of numbers, and the number of numbers, we can calculate the sum of those numbers by multiplying. So, for example, the sum of ages in classroom B1 will be $16 \times 9.6 = 153.6$.

Because the average age of all the students on the hallway will just be the sum of the ages of all the students on the hallway divided by the number of students, we can set up an equation:

$$7.7 \approx \frac{16\times9.6+14\times7.2+5.5\,p}{16+14+p}$$

At this point, we could do the algebra to solve, or we could simply try answer choices. And I'm feeling the backsolve pull here. Let's try C.

$$7.7 \approx \frac{16\times9.6+14\times7.2+5.5\times11}{16+14+11}$$
$$7.7 \approx \frac{314.9}{41}$$
$$7.7 \approx 7.68\ldots$$

Looks like that's our answer!

94. **Answer: C**
Topic(s): Data Analysis 1 (p. 195); Measures of Central Tendency and Variability (p. 182)

The range of a set of data is simply the greatest value minus the least value. We don't need to be very precise to test choice C and see that it isn't true: The greatest value is about 0.37 tons in fiscal year 2009, and the least value is about 0.29 tons in fiscal year 2016. $0.37 - 0.29 = 0.08$, which is less than 0.1. Choice C says the range is greater than 0.1 tons, so that choice isn't supported by the data.

95. **Answer: 8**
Topic(s): Parabolas (p. 128); Lines (p. 73); Working with Advanced Systems of Equations (p. 152)

The first thing to see here is that $f(x) = g(x) = h(x)$ means all three functions intersect. Because we're told that this happens exactly twice, and we can see from the graph that $f(x)$ and $g(x)$ intersect only twice, we know that $h(x)$ must go through both of those intersection points. So we need to figure out those intersection points. Let's set the functions equal to do that.

$$f(x) = g(x)$$
$$-(x - 1)^2 + 6 = (x - 3)^2 + 2$$
$$-(x^2 - 2x + 1) + 6 = (x^2 - 6x + 9) + 2$$
$$-x^2 + 2x + 5 = x^2 - 6x + 11$$
$$0 = 2x^2 - 8x + 6$$
$$0 = x^2 - 4x + 3$$
$$0 = (x - 3)(x - 1)$$

We could kinda have seen that from the graph, to be honest, but now we know the x-values of the intersections are 3 and 1. To find the y-values, just plug them back into either equation. I'm thinking $g(x)$ just to avoid the negative.

$$g(x) = (x - 3)^2 + 2$$

$$g(1) = (1 - 3)^2 + 2$$
$$g(1) = 6$$

$$g(3) = (3 - 3)^2 + 2$$
$$g(3) = 2$$

OK, so the $h(x)$ line goes through $(1, 6)$ and $(3, 2)$. That's going to have a slope of $\frac{2-6}{3-1} = -2$. Counting back from $(1, 6)$, that'll result in a y-intercept of $(0, 8)$. So $b = 8$.

96. **Answer: C**
Topic(s): Angles, Triangles, and Polygons (p. 236)

We're dealing with similar triangles here. Angles ACB and ECD are vertical angles, so they're congruent. Because of the parallel segments $\overline{AB}$ and $\overline{DE}$, angles A and E are congruent and angles B and D are congruent. So, yeah. Similar triangles.

We're told that $AB = 5$ and $DE = 10$, so we know that the sides of the small triangle are half the length of the sides of the large triangle. Therefore, if $BC = \frac{10}{3}$, then the corresponding side in the larger triangle must be twice as long: $DC = \frac{20}{3}$.

To find the length of $\overline{BD}$, just add BC and DC.

$$\frac{10}{3} + \frac{20}{3} = \frac{30}{3} = 10$$

97. **Answer: 16**
Topic(s): Polynomials (p. 142)

As long as we remember that corresponding coefficients of equivalent polynomials are equal, we'll be fine here.

Let's get started by FOILing the left hand side.

$$(x + a)(2x - b) = ax^2 + (2a - b)x - 32$$
$$2x^2 - bx + 2ax - ab = ax^2 + (2a - b)x - 32$$

What we know from there, right away without even messing with the x-terms, is that $2 = a$ (those are the x^2 coefficients) and $-ab = -32$ (those are the constants).

Substituting for a, we find that $-2b = -32$ and therefore $b = 16$.

98. **Answer: 22**
   Topic(s): Functions (p. 92)

The quick and dirty way to solve this one is to set $x + 3 = 10$ and solve. If $x + 3 = 10$ then $x = 7$, so:

$f(10)$
$= f(7+3)$
$= 3(7)+1$
$= 22$

99. **Answer: 44**
   Topic(s): Measures of Central Tendency and Variability (p. 182)

Most average questions like this are really questions about sums, and this one definitely is. Start by figuring out the sum of the ages in the room when all 19 people are in there. If the average age is 8, then the sum of the ages will be $8 \times 19 = 152$.

Now figure out the sum of the ages once the one adult we care about leaves. The new average in the room becomes 6, and there are now 18 people in the room, so the new sum is $6 \times 18 = 108$.

How old must the person who left be if the sum of the ages in the room went from 152 to 108? $152 - 108 = 44$.

100. **Answer: 6**
    Topic(s): Measures of Central Tendency and Variability (p. 182); Data Analysis 2 (p. 203)

The trick here is recognizing that the median of 39 data points will be the 20th point once the points are in order. Once we know that, all we need to do is count to 20!

Start from the right since the numbers are bigger there. There are 8 9's, 5 8's, and 6 7's. $8 + 5 + 6 = 19$, so the next number, a 6, will be the 20th point from the top: the median!

We can also count from the left, and of course we'll get the same result. There are 5 1's, 2 2's, 3 3's, 2 4's, and 3 5's. $5 + 2 + 3 + 2 + 3 = 15$. Now add the 6's: there are 5 of them, so the last 6 counting from the left will be the 20th number.

101. **Answer: C**
    Topic(s): Right Triangles and Basic Trigonometry (p. 249)

Because we know that $\sin B = \dfrac{5}{13}$, we know that $\dfrac{AC}{BC} = \dfrac{5}{13}$. That's a clue that we're dealing with a 5-12-13 triangle, and $\overline{AB}$ will have to be the 12 side. Since $5 + 12 + 13 \neq 150$, though, we have to do a little algebra.

$5x + 12x + 13x = 150$
$30x = 150$
$x = 5$

If $x = 5$, then $AB = 12x = 12(5) = 60$.

102. **Answer: C**
    Topic(s): Angles, Triangles, and Polygons (p. 236)

Let's tackle this one in a few steps. First, use vertical and supplemental angle rules to fill in all the angles we can based on the measures we're given.

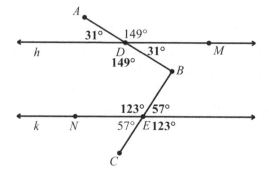

Now take either $\overline{AB}$ or $\overline{CB}$ (either one will do) and extend it to create a transversal. I'm going to extend $\overline{CB}$. Because we have parallel lines, we know all the angles we've filled in at point E will translate to the new intersection we create.

Now we have a triangle with angles measuring 31° and 57°. Every triangle's angles add up to 180°, so the third angle in that triangle must measure $180° - 57° - 31° = 92°$.

Angle ABC is the supplement of that 92° angle (i.e., it makes a straight line with that angle) so its measure must be $180° - 92° = 88°$.

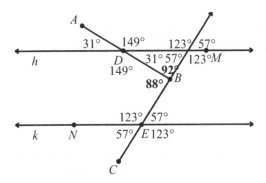

103. **Answer: B**
Topic(s): Parabolas (p. 128)

Since this is a calculator allowed question, the fastest way to go might just be to graph each parabola. For a parabola to intersect a horizontal line like $y = 8$ exactly once, its vertex must be on that horizontal line. Just graph each equation and look for the one with its vertex at $y = 8$.

If you don't want to or can't do that, the other way to go is to manipulate each choice until you find one with its vertex at $y = 8$.

Look at choice B:

$$y = -\frac{1}{8}(x - 8)(x + 8)$$
$$y = -\frac{1}{8}(x^2 - 64)$$
$$y = -\frac{1}{8}x^2 + 8$$

That works! It's a parabola that opens down with its vertex (and y-intercept) at $y = 8$. None of the other choices will give you a vertex in the right place.

104. **Answer: 121**
Topic(s): Polynomials (p. 142); Binomial Squares and Difference of Two Squares (p. 123)

When we're told that the equation is true for all values of x, we can assume we're dealing with equivalent polynomials, and therefore that all corresponding coefficients are equal.

That means we can take the equation, expand the left hand side, and then set up some smaller equations.

$$(x + 11)(x + a) = x^2 - b$$
$$x^2 + ax + 11x + 11a = x^2 - b$$

The corresponding coefficient equations we can write, then:

For the x^2 terms: $x^2 = x^2$. That doesn't help us at all.

For the x terms: $ax + 11x = 0$. There aren't any x terms on the right hand side. That must mean that $a = -11$.

For the constant terms: $11a = -b$. Because we just solved for a above, we can substitute and solve for b:

$11(-11) = -b$

$-121 = -b$

$121 = b$

105. Answer: 13

Topic(s): Solving Systems of Linear Equations (p. 59)

Let's get this one by elimination. To do that, multiply the first equation by the lowest common denominator: 20.

$$20\left(\frac{1}{5}x + \frac{3}{4}y\right) = (3)20$$

$$\frac{20}{5}x + \frac{60}{4}y = 60$$

$$4x + 15y = 60$$

Now eliminate the y terms simply by adding the equations, and solve for x!

$$
\begin{array}{r}
4x + 15y = 60 \\
+\ x - 15y = \ \ 5 \\
\hline
5x + 0y = 65 \\
5x = 65 \\
x = 13
\end{array}
$$

106. Answer: D

Topic(s): Complex Numbers (p. 292)

To divide complex numbers, we must multiply by a clever form of one made up of the complex conjugate of the denominator. This makes the denominator a real number, and then we can just do normal division. In this case, that means we multiply our fraction by $\frac{8-i}{8-i}$.

$$\frac{26-13i}{8+i} \times \frac{8-i}{8-i}$$

$$= \frac{208 - 26i - 104i + 13i^2}{64 - i^2}$$

$$= \frac{208 - 130i + 13(-1)}{64 - (-1)}$$

$$= \frac{195 - 130i}{65}$$

$$= 3 - 2i$$

107. Answer: C

Topic(s): Percents and Percent Change (p. 161)

The first thing we need to do here is figure out how many people are on this task force to start with. We know that $30\% + 15\% + 40\% = 85\%$ of the task force is sales, marketing, or product design, so that means the 3 executives must comprise 15% of the task force. 3 is 15% of what?

$$3 = \frac{15}{100}x$$

$$20 = x$$

Now, to figure out how many product designers we're starting with. What is 40% of 20?

$$\frac{40}{100} \times 20 = 8$$

If we're starting with 8 product designers and we add 2 more, we'll have 10. But be careful! We're also increasing the total size of the task force from 20 to 22! So the question we need to ask is: 10 is what percent of 22?

$$10 = \frac{y}{100} \times 22$$

$$\frac{1000}{22} = y$$

$$45.\overline{45} = y$$

If the task force were expanded to include 2 more product designers, product designers would make up about 45% of the task force.

108. Answer: 7.5 or 15/2
   Topic(s): Lines (p. 73)

When presented with a point that an equation passes through, we should always plug that point into the equation, even if that point is partially unknown!

So let's plug $(-5, -b)$ into the line:

$y = 3x + b$
$-b = 3(-5) + b$
$-b = -15 + b$
$-2b = -15$
$b = 7.5$

The question asked for the line's y-intercept, and the given line is in slope-intercept form, so b is the y-intercept. The answer is 7.5 (or 15/2).

109. Answer: 1080
   Topic(s): Polynomials (p. 142)

This is a corresponding coefficients question, so get right to work FOILing to get both sides of the equation into standard form.

$ax^2 + 3x - b = (2x + 5)(3x - c)$
$ax^2 + 3x - b = 6x^2 - 2cx + 15x - 5c$
$ax^2 + 3x - b = 6x^2 + (15 - 2c)x - 5c$

From that we know three things: $a = 6$, $3 = 15 - 2c$, and $-b = -5c$.

Solve the second equation for c to get $c = 6$. Once we know $c = 6$ we know $-b = -5(6)$, which means $b = 30$.

The question asks for the value of abc, which is $(6)(30)(6) = 1080$.

110. Answer: B
   Topic(s): Percents and Percent Change (p. 161)

The first task here is to figure out what the percent increase was from Monday to Tuesday. The increase was $16,830 - 15,300 = 1,530$, and

the starting value was 15,300, so the percent change is $\frac{1,530}{15,300} \times 100\% = 10\%$.

Now all we need to do is figure out what the value of the investment would be on Wednesday if it was a 10% decrease from Tuesday's value. To do that, we simply subtract 10% of 16,830 from 16,830:

$16,830 - \frac{10}{100} \times 16,830 = 15,147$.

If the value of the investment at the end of the day Wednesday was $15,147, then it's easy enough to calculate how much less that is than the 15,300 on Monday:
$15,300 - 15,147 = 153$. Therefore, the answer is B.

Shortcut for the percent wizards:
$15,300 - 15,300 \times 1.1 \times 0.9 = 153$.

111. Answer: 144
   Topic(s): Angles, Triangles, and Polygons (p. 236)

If the measure of angle CAD is 26° and angle ACE is a right angle with a measure of 90°, then we can solve for the measure of angle CDA. Each triangle's angles add up 180°, so the last angle in triangle CAD must measure:

$180° - 90° - 26° = 64°$

Because angle ADE is supplementary, we know it must therefore measure:

$180° - 64° = 116°$

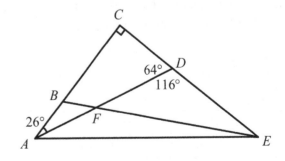

Now we're almost home. Because we know the measures of angles *ADE* and *BEC*, we can solve for the measure of angle *DFE*:

$$180° - 116° - 28° = 36°$$

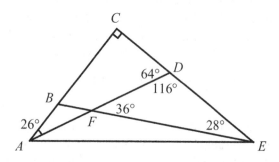

The angle we want, angle *BFD*, is supplementary to angle *DFE*, so we just need to subtract from 180° one last time:

$$180° - 36° = 144°$$

112. **Answer: C**
Topic(s): Angles, Triangles, and Polygons (p. 236); Right Triangles and Basic Trigonometry (p. 249)

The white hexagons she can buy have a perimeter of 6 feet, which means each side is 1 foot long. That means the diagonal of each gray square is 1 foot.

Now let's use what we know about squares and their diagonals: if a square has a side of length *x*, then its diagonal is $x\sqrt{2}$. (A good way to remember this is to remember that a square's diagonal cuts the square into two 45°-45°-90° triangles.)

So if the diagonal of this square is 1, we can solve for the side of the square:

$$1 = x\sqrt{2}$$
$$\frac{1}{\sqrt{2}} = x$$
$$\frac{\sqrt{2}}{2} = x$$

That's the length of one side, and a square has four sides, so the perimeter of the squares the homeowner should buy is $4\left(\dfrac{\sqrt{2}}{2}\right) = 2\sqrt{2}$.

113. **Answer: D**
Topic(s): Functions (p. 92); Parabolas (p. 128)

All about function translation here. Remember, if we know the position of *f*(*x*), then we can figure out the position of *f*(*x* + *a*) + *b*, where *a* and *b* are constants.

In this case, *f*(*x* + 5) + 4 means the graph moves 5 units to the left and 4 units up. So starting from the vertex of *f*(*x*), (2, 3), we can move 5 units left (to *x* = –3) and 4 units up (to *y* = 7).

So the answer we're looking for is (–3, 7).

114. **Answer: B**
Topic(s): Circles, Radians, and a Little More Trigonometry (p. 258)

Remember the general circle formula: $(x - h)^2 + (y - k)^2 = r^2$, where (*h*, *k*) are the coordinates of the circle's center, and *r* is the circle's radius. It's particularly important to remember that last part for this question, which hinges on us remembering that the constant on the right side of the equal sign is the radius *squared*.

We know the area of a circle can be calculated using $A = \pi r^2$, and now we know that the square of the radius of this circle is *c*. So we can substitute!

$$A = \pi r^2$$
$$r^2 = c$$
$$A = \pi c$$

115. **Answer: 9.75 or 39/4**
Topic(s): Solving Systems of Linear Equations (p. 59)

Let's solve this one by elimination. Multiply the first equation by 2 so that we can cancel out the y-terms, then add the equations:

$$
\begin{array}{r}
6x + 2y = 22 \\
+10x - 2y = 2 \\
\hline
16x + 0y = 24
\end{array}
$$

Of course, that means $x = \dfrac{24}{16} = \dfrac{3}{2}$.

Now just solve for y, using whichever equation looks easier to work with.

$$10\left(\frac{3}{2}\right) - 2y = 2$$
$$\frac{30}{2} - 2y = 2$$
$$15 - 2y = 2$$
$$-2y = -13$$
$$y = \frac{13}{2}$$

Now that we have values for x and y, multiply to get the answer we seek.

$$xy = \left(\frac{3}{2}\right)\left(\frac{13}{2}\right) = \frac{39}{4}$$

116. **Answer: A**
Topic(s): Absolute Value (p. 82)

Remember that we can convert absolute value inequalities thusly: $|x - y| < z$ can be rewritten as $-z < x - y < z$.

Let's use that fact to convert answer choices until we get what we want—the answer choice that can be manipulated to be equivalent to $198 \leq m \leq 212$.

Here's how that works with A, which happens to be the right answer:

$$|m - 205| \leq 7$$
$$-7 \leq m - 205 \leq 7$$
$$198 \leq m \leq 212$$

A useful way to think about the initially-less-intuitive absolute value range is this: $|m - 205| \leq 7$ is really just saying that m can't be farther than 7 away from 205. That makes sense! 205 is the middle of the range we care about, and 7 is the distance from 205 to 198.

117. **Answer: 4**
Topic(s): Polynomials (p. 142)

Remember the corresponding coefficients rule to get this one.

FOIL out the left hand side and see where things line up:

$$(2x - a)^2 = 4x^2 - bx + a + 12$$
$$4x^2 - 4ax + a^2 = 4x^2 - bx + a + 12$$

Obviously the $4x^2$ terms are equal. We also know that $-4ax = -bx$ and, most importantly, that $a^2 = a + 12$. Since that last equation has only a terms in it and that's what we're looking for, solve it!

$$a^2 = a + 12$$
$$a^2 - a - 12 = 0$$
$$(a + 3)(a - 4) = 0$$

So $a = -3$ or $a = 4$. Since the question says that a is positive, the answer is 4.

118. **Answer: 12**
Topic(s): Quadratics (p. 114)

The function will be undefined when its denominator equals zero. Given that we know the function is undefined when $x = 1$, we can substitute into the denominator and solve for a without much fuss:

$$0 = 1^2 - a(1) + 11$$
$$0 = 12 - a$$
$$a = 12$$

And...that's it! Man, that was fast.

119. **Answer: B**
   Topic(s): Working with Advanced Systems of Equations (p. 152)

   Although it's not necessary, a graph makes this one much easier to work through, so...

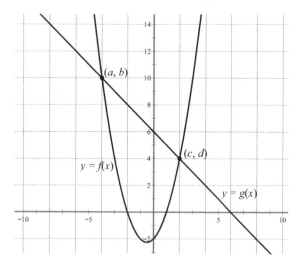

   Once the system is graphed out, it's easy to check each Roman numeral.

   I. $a < b \leftarrow$ This is true: $a = -4$ and $b = 10$.

   II. $b < d \leftarrow$ This is false: $b = 10$ and $d = 4$.

   III. $c < d \leftarrow$ This is true: $c = 2$ and $d = 4$.

   Therefore, the answer is B.

   The reason you don't need a calculator to get this quickly, though, is that you know $g(x)$ is a linear function with a negative slope! So as soon as we know (a, b) and (c, d) are both on a line with a negative slope, and that a is to the left of c, we know b must be higher than d! So we can eliminate Roman numeral II, which means we're really only choosing between choices B and C.

   Roman numeral III appears in both of those choices, so we don't need to test it. We only need to test Roman numeral I, which we can do without a precise graph if we recognize that the parabola will have one positive and one negative root, which means the (a, b) intersection will be in Quadrant II, which means a must be negative and b must be positive.

   Therefore, Roman numeral I checks out, and the answer is B.

120. **Answer: 2**
   Topic(s): Parabolas (p. 128)

   There are a couple ways to go here, but to my mind the easiest way is to remember that parabolas are symmetrical about their vertex.

   Since this parabola is in factored form, we know its zeros are at -6 and a. The vertex is on the $x = -2$ line, which means the root we know, $x = -6$, is a distance of 4 away. That means the other root, a must also be a distance of 4 from the $x = -2$ line. Count 4 steps to the right and you land on $x = 2$, so $a = 2$.

   Of course, we can also substitute and solve algebraically:

   $$-48 = 3(-2 - a)(-2 + 6)$$
   $$-48 = 3(-2 - a)(4)$$
   $$-48 = 12(-2 - a)$$
   $$-4 = -2 - a$$
   $$2 = a$$

121. **Answer: D**
   Topic(s): Data Analysis 2 (p. 203); Measures of Central Tendency and Variability (p. 182)

   Let's get this one by elimination. Looking at the box plots for Classes A and B, we see that they have the same median at 70, so choice A is right out.

   Box plots don't actually tell us anything about average, so we can't choose choice B.

   The range of a set of data is just the difference between the highest value and the lowest value, so we actually can calculate the ranges for these classes. However, they're equal. Class A's range is $95 - 45 = 50$, and Class B's range is $100 - 50 = 50$. Same range, so choice C is wrong.

   That leaves D. We can pick it without much thought if we're very confident about our reasons for eliminating A, B, and C—and we should be.

But of course, for prep purposes, we should also talk through why choice D works. It works because quartiles, like the median (btw, the median is the same as the 2nd quartile) are calculated by counting how many numbers are greater or less than them. Because the question tells us that Class A and Class B each have 29 students, we know that the same number of students must be represented by each section of the box plots. That is, both Class A and Class B have the same number of students above and below the median; both Class A and Class B have the same number of people in the "middle 50%" between the quartiles. That also means that each class will have the same number of people who scored greater than the 1st quartile.

In a set of 29 numbers, the median will be the 15th greatest (or 15th least) number in the set. Then the 1st and 3rd quartiles will be 8th greatest and 8th least numbers, respectively.

What that means is that Class A's 8th lowest score is 60, while Class B's 8th lowest score is 65. That means Class B will have at least one more score greater than or equal to 65 than Class A does.

122. **Answer: C**
   Topic(s): Angles, Triangles, and Polygons (p. 236); Right Triangles and Basic Trigonometry (p. 249)

   You can derive this using $(n - 2)180°$ if you don't just know it by heart, but regular hexagons are made up of 6 equilateral triangles. Like so:

So another way to ask this question is: what is the length of one side of an equilateral triangle with an area of $\dfrac{216\sqrt{3}}{6} = 36\sqrt{3}$?

We can get this by breaking an equilateral triangle into two 30°-60°-90° triangles. (Huge clue that we'd need to do this is the $\sqrt{3}$ in the question!) If a side of an equilateral triangle has a length of x, then its height will be $\dfrac{x\sqrt{3}}{2}$.

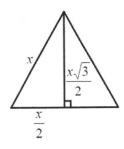

We can now use the triangle area formula to solve for x.

$$\frac{1}{2}bh = 36\sqrt{3}$$

$$\frac{1}{2}x\left(\frac{x\sqrt{3}}{2}\right) = 36\sqrt{3}$$

$$\frac{x^2\sqrt{3}}{4} = 36\sqrt{3}$$

$$\frac{x^2}{4} = 36$$

$$x^2 = 144$$

$$x = 12$$

123. **Answer: B**
   Topic(s): Circles, Radians, and a Little More Trigonometry (p. 258)

We must resist, if we possibly can, the urge to solve this algebraically.

We know our circle equation, so we know we're dealing with: a circle of radius 5 centered at (–3, 1), and a circle of radius 4 centered at (3, 1)

We can draw that easily enough, but even before drawing we might see that the centers of both circles are on the $y = 1$ line, so their intersection should be on an $x =$ something line. Cross a couple choices (C and D) off.

Helpfully, the x-coordinates of the circles' centers are –3 and 3, so if they each had the same radius, you'd expect them to intersect right on the y-axis. But because the circle centered at (3, 1) has a shorter radius, the intersections should be closer to that circle. That means all we need to do is pick the choice with a $x=$ that's to the right of the y-axis. That's choice B.

The picture:

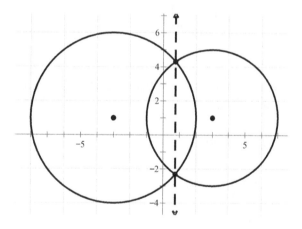

124. **Answer: B**

Topic(s): Functions (p. 92); Polynomials (p. 142)

Think about this one in two steps. First, remember that the graph of $-f(x)$ will be the reflection of the graph of $f(x)$ about the x-axis. Like so:

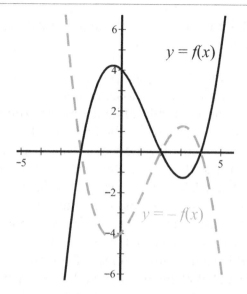

Now remember that multiplying by 2 outside the function will make all y-values twice as big. That won't change the x-intercepts, but it will make every other point on the graph twice as far away from the x-axis.

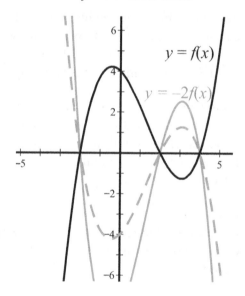

Since (0, 4) is on the graph of $y = f(x)$, (0, –8) is on the graph of $y = -2f(x)$; we can cross off choice A.

The x-intercepts of the graph don't change, so we can eliminate choices C and D: (2, 0) and (4, 0) will be on both $y = f(x)$ and $y = -2f(x)$.

That leaves us with B. (–4, 0) would be a y-intercept if it appeared on the original $y = f(x)$

graph, but it doesn't. Therefore, it won't appear on the graph of $y = -2f(x)$ either.

125. Answer: B

Topic(s): Exponents and Exponential Functions (p. 104)

To crack this one open, rewrite the left side of the equation thusly:

$$2^a + 2^a = 2^{(b+3)}$$
$$2(2^a) = 2^{(b+3)}$$

Now, noting that $2 = 2^1$, apply the exponent rule that says when we multiply two exponential expressions with the same base, we add the exponents:

$$2^1 \times 2^a = 2^{(b+3)}$$
$$2^{(a+1)} = 2^{(b+3)}$$

From there, we can just say that $a + 1 = b + 3$.

$$a + 1 = b + 3$$
$$a - b = 3 - 1$$
$$a - b = 2$$

126. Answer: 12

Topic(s): Ratios and Proportionality (p. 171); Translating between Words and Math (p. 44); Solving Systems of Linear Equations (p. 59)

An algebraic solution to this one is probably most expedient. Using r for red fish and b for blue fish before any were sold, we can write the following equations from the given ratios:

$$\frac{r}{b} = \frac{4}{7}$$
$$\frac{r}{b-5} = \frac{3}{4}$$

Even though we want r, I can't resist the urge to solve for b first given the setup. Let's use substitution:

$$\frac{r}{b} = \frac{4}{7}$$
$$r = \frac{4}{7}b$$

$$\frac{r}{b-5} = \frac{3}{4}$$
$$r = \frac{3}{4}(b-5)$$

$$\frac{4}{7}b = \frac{3}{4}(b-5)$$
$$28\left(\frac{4}{7}b\right) = 28\left(\frac{3}{4}(b-5)\right)$$
$$16b = 21(b-5)$$
$$16b = 21b - 105$$
$$-5b = -105$$
$$b = 21$$

Remember though: we're not looking for b, we're looking for r!

If $b = 21$, then we can use one of the original ratios to solve for r.

$$\frac{r}{b} = \frac{4}{7}$$
$$\frac{r}{21} = \frac{4}{7}$$
$$r = \left(\frac{4}{7}\right)21$$
$$r = 12$$

127. Answer: B

Topic(s): Data Analysis 2 (p. 203); Measures of Central Tendency and Variability (p. 182)

As a reminder, a box plot shows 5 data points to summarize a set of data: the minimum, the first quartile, the median, the third quartile, and the maximum. The whiskers reach out to the minimum and maximum; the box reaches out to the first and third quartiles.

Reading the minimum and maximum from the frequency graph is easy: 1 and 9.

Reading the median is a little trickier. The median of 39 data points will be the 20th point once the points are in order. (There will be 19 numbers smaller than the median and 19 numbers bigger than the median. That 20th number, counting from either end, is the median.)

Anyway, once we recognize that, all we need to do is count to 20! Start from either side. From the left, there are 5 1's, 2 2's, 3 3's, 2 4's, and 3 5's. $5 + 2 + 3 + 2 + 3 = 15$. Now add the 6's: there are 5 of them, so the last 6 counting from the left will be the 20th number. That means the median is 6.

Now finally, the first and third quartiles. These are basically the medians of the subsets of data above and below the median. So the first quartile is the median of the first 19 numbers in the set, and the third quartile is the median of the last 19 numbers in the set. In a set of 19 numbers, the 10th one will be the median.

As we just did for the main median, we can find the 10th number in the first half for the first quartile. There are 5 1's, 2 2's, and 3 3's, so the final 3 is the 10th number. That means the first quartile is 3.

For the third quartile, we can find the 10th number from the right. There are 8 9's and 5 8's, which means the 10th number from the top is one of those 8's. Therefore, the third quartile is 8.

Which box plot captures all the points?

minimum: 1
first quartile: 3
median: 6
third quartile: 8
maximum: 9

Choice B it is!

128. **Answer: B**
   Topic(s): Plugging In (p. 24); Lines (p. 73)

If you thought to plug in here, congratulations! You've been well trained. Say $a = 2$ and $b = 3$. So lines m and n contain the point $(2, 3)$. We also know, of course, that line m contains the origin: $(0, 0)$. That means the slope of line m is $\frac{3-0}{2-0} = \frac{3}{2}$. Because line n is perpendicular, we can say that line n has a slope of $-\frac{2}{3}$.

From there, just plug 2 for a and 3 for b into each answer choice, then test it in the slope formula against the one point we know we have on line n: $(2, 3)$.

A) $\dfrac{(2-3)-3}{(3-2)-2} = \dfrac{-4}{-1} = 4$

B) $\dfrac{(2+3)-3}{(2-3)-2} = -\dfrac{2}{3}$

C) $\dfrac{(2+3)-3}{(2+3)-2} = \dfrac{2}{3}$

D) $\dfrac{(3-2)-3}{(3-2)-2} = \dfrac{-2}{-1} = 2$

Only choice B lands on $-\frac{2}{3}$, so B is the answer.

129. **Answer: 35**
   Topic(s): Measures of Central Tendency and Variability (p. 182); Data Analysis 1 (p. 195)

The first step to solving this is calculating the Team 1's score. Cross out the highest and lowest scores (Players 1 and 4, respectively) and then find the average of the remaining three scores.

$$\text{Team 1 Score} = \frac{44 + 34 + 50}{3} = 42.\overline{6}$$

To deal with Team 2, first eliminate the highest score (Player 7).

Now calculate Team 2's score if Player 10's ended up being the lowest and thus inconsequential. Can Team 2 win without Player 10?

Team 2 Score (no Player 10) $= \dfrac{47+47+31}{3} = 41.\overline{6}$

Nope, Team 2 can't win without Player 10! So that means Player 9's score will have to end up being the lowest on Team 2. Player 10's score must be combined with two 47 scores to beat Team 1. So let's call Player 10's score x and solve.

$$\dfrac{44+34+50}{3} < \dfrac{47+47+x}{3}$$
$$44+34+50 < 47+47+x$$
$$128 < 94+x$$
$$34 < x$$

Since x must be an integer, the lowest it can be is 35.

130. **Answer: C**
    Topic(s): Plugging In (p. 24); Polynomials (p. 142)

Questions like this, where the task is to figure out equivalent expressions—and those expressions only have one variable—are an incredible opportunity to PLUG IN!

The only math I want to do first is factor out a 2, since that'll make plugging in even easier.

$$\dfrac{8x+4}{2x+8} = \dfrac{4x+2}{x+4}$$

There, that's better. Now, pick a simple value for x, like $x = 2$. If $x = 2$, then $\dfrac{4x+2}{x+4} = \dfrac{10}{6}$.

Which answer choice also equals $\dfrac{10}{6}$ when $x = 2$?

Because we picked an easy number like 2 to work with, we can check answer choices very quickly.

A) $x + \dfrac{2}{x} = 2 + \dfrac{2}{2} = 3 \leftarrow$ NOPE

B) $4x + \dfrac{1}{2} = 4(2) + \dfrac{1}{2} = 8.5 \leftarrow$ NOPE

C) $4 - \dfrac{14}{x+4} = 4 - \dfrac{14}{2+4} = \dfrac{24-14}{6} = \dfrac{10}{6} \leftarrow$ YES!

D) $4 + \dfrac{7}{x+4} = 4 + \dfrac{7}{2+4} = \dfrac{24+7}{6} = \dfrac{31}{6} \leftarrow$ NOPE

Important: when plugging in, we must check every choice even after we find one that works, just to make sure we didn't inadvertently pick a number to plug in that would make more than one choice work.

Who in the world would want to do polynomial division instead?

131. **Answer: D**
    Topic(s): Quadratics (p. 114); Polynomials (p. 142)

The domain of the function will exclude the zeros of the polynomial in the denominator—you needn't pay any attention at all to the numerator to solve this question. Just solve $0 = 7x^2 - 2x - 5$.

Since the polynomial isn't easy to factor, let's throw it into the quadratic formula.

$$x = \dfrac{-(-2) \pm \sqrt{(-2)^2 + 4(7)(-5)}}{2(7)}$$
$$x = \dfrac{2 \pm \sqrt{144}}{14}$$
$$x = \dfrac{2 \pm 12}{14}$$
$$x = \dfrac{1}{7} \pm \dfrac{6}{7}$$

In other words, the values of a and b are 1 and $-\dfrac{5}{7}$. Since we're asked for the value of $a + b$, the correct answer is $1 + \left(-\dfrac{5}{7}\right) = \dfrac{2}{7}$.

132. Answer: B
Topic(s): Measures of Central Tendency and Variability (p. 206); Data Analysis 2 (p. 203)

The more the data is spread out away from the mean, the larger its standard deviation. The more concentrated the data is around its mean, the smaller its standard deviation.

In this case, 9 more scores of 5 (or any more scores of 5) would decrease the standard deviation because 5 is very close to the mean. (The actual mean, not that you need to calculate it, is 5.06.) The more 5s you add, the more the data in this set is concentrated near the mean, and the smaller the standard deviation becomes.

133. Answer: D
Topic(s): Parabolas (p. 128)

To get this one, it's helpful to recognize that the second equation in the system is that of a parabola in vertex form!

For the system to have no solutions, the graphs of the two equations must not intersect: the parabola must either have a vertex above the horizontal $y = 5$ line and open upwards, or have a vertex below the $y = 5$ line and open downwards. The x-coordinate of the vertex, therefore, doesn't matter at all. We're really only looking at the a and c values here.

In choice A, the vertex is at (1, 7), higher than the $y = 5$ line, and $a < 0$ so it opens down. That will have intersections.

In choice B, the vertex is at (1, –3), lower than the $y = 5$ line, and $a > 0$ so it opens up. That will have intersections.

In choice C, the vertex is at (–3, 2), lower than the $y = 5$ line, and $a > 0$ so it opens up. That will have intersections.

In choice D, the vertex is at (5, 4), lower than the $y = 5$ line, and $a < 0$ so it opens down. That

will NOT have intersections, so D is the answer.

134. Answer: C
Topic(s): Circles, Radians, and a Little More Trigonometry (p. 258)

Before we can determine the radius of this circle, we need to complete two squares to get into standard form.

$$x^2 + y^2 + 10x + 2y = 64$$
$$(x^2 + 10x) + (y^2 + 2y) = 64$$
$$(x^2 + 10x + 25) + (y^2 + 2y + 1) = 64 + 25 + 1$$
$$(x + 5)^2 + (y + 1)^2 = 90$$

From that, we see that the value of r^2 in the standard equation is 90. Take the square root to find r.

$$r^2 = 90$$
$$r = \sqrt{90}$$
$$r = (\sqrt{9})(\sqrt{10})$$
$$r = 3\sqrt{10}$$

135. Answer: 6500
Topic(s): Right Triangles and Basic Trigonometry (p. 249)

To get this, we need to remember the complementary angle rule, which tells us that if $\sin x° = \cos y°$, then $x + y = 90$. If we remember that, the rest of this question is pretty straightforward. Just to think for a minute about what numbers add up to 90 and multiply to 800. 80 and 10 do, so x and y must be 80 and 10 (or vice versa). What's the value of $80^2 + 10^2$? Easy, that's $6400 + 100 = 6500$.

There's also algebra:

$$x + y = 90$$
$$(x + y)^2 = 90^2$$
$$x^2 + 2xy + y^2 = 8100$$
$$x^2 + 2(800) + y^2 = 8100$$
$$x^2 + 1600 + y^2 = 8100$$
$$x^2 + y^2 = 6500$$

136. **Answer: A**
     Topic(s): Plugging In (p. 24); Parabolas (p. 37)

This is a great opportunity to plug in. Wouldn't it be easier to work with $y = (x + 2)(x + 3)$? Make it so! Now we just need to remember that parabolas are symmetrical, so a parabola's vertex will be equidistant from its x-intercepts. $y = (x + 2)(x + 3)$ will have x-intercepts at -2 and -3, so its vertex will have an x-value of -2.5. Which answer choice gives you -2.5 for $a = 2$ and $b = 3$?

A) $-\dfrac{a+b}{2} = -\dfrac{2+3}{2} = -2.5 \leftarrow$ YES!

B) $\dfrac{a-b}{2} = \dfrac{2-3}{2} = -0.5 \leftarrow$ Nope.

C) $\dfrac{a+b}{2} = \dfrac{2+3}{2} = 2.5 \leftarrow$ Wrong sign.

D) $-\dfrac{ab}{2} = -\dfrac{(2)(3)}{2} = -3 \leftarrow$ No again.

Well there we go, answer must be A!

Algebraically, this isn't much different. We just need to recognize that the x-intercepts will be at $-a$ and $-b$. Therefore, the x-coordinate of the vertex will be the average of those:

$$\frac{-a+(-b)}{2} = \frac{-a-b}{2} = -\frac{a+b}{2}$$

137. **Answer: 5**
     Topic(s): Angles, Triangles, and Polygons (p. 236)

Draw the triangle!

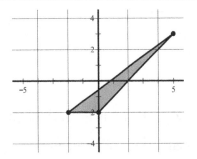

From that, we can see that the base of the triangle, from $(-2, -2)$ to $(0, -2)$ has a length of 2. We can also count up from the base to the point $(5, 3)$ to see that it's a vertical distance of 5 from the base, so the triangle's height is 5.

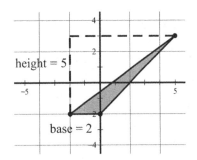

The area of the triangle can be calculated using the formula $A = \dfrac{1}{2}bh$:

$$A = \frac{1}{2}bh = \frac{1}{2}(2)(5) = 5$$

138. **Answer: B**
     Topic(s): Lines (p. 73)

If a system of equations has no solutions, that means the graphs of those equations will never intersect. In the case of a system of linear equations, the only way that happens is if the two lines are parallel.

Parallel lines have the same slope, and the first line is given already in slope-intercept form— its slope is 3. Therefore, we need to figure out how to get the second equation to have a slope of 3, too. Let's put it into slope-intercept form:

$$ax - by = 11$$
$$-by = -ax + 11$$
$$y = \frac{a}{b} - \frac{11}{b}$$

That tells us that the first line has a slope of $\frac{a}{b}$, which must equal 3 if the lines are to be parallel.

Be careful! I'm sneaky, so the question asks you for the reciprocal, $\frac{b}{a}$. If $\frac{a}{b} = 3$, then $\frac{b}{a} = \frac{1}{3}$.

139. **Answer: 9**
    Topic(s): Lines (p. 73)

The best way to get this one is to draw the given points:

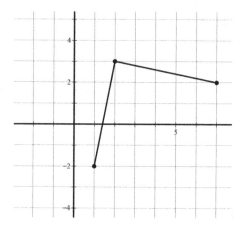

This isn't very mathematical, but count the up-and-over steps from the first point to the second, and from the second to the third. You'll see that the first side goes up 5 and right 1, and the second side goes right 5 and down 1. To figure out where the fourth vertex is, simply follow the same pattern: either move down 5 and left 1 from the third point or go right 5 and down 1 from the first. (This works because we're essentially calculating slopes, and the sides in a square will be parallel—they'll have the same slopes!)

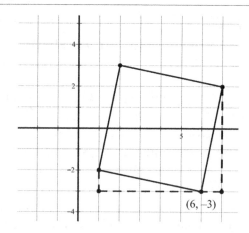

So the final point $(a, b) = (6, -3)$, which means $a = 6$ and $b = -3$.

Therefore, $a - b = 6 - (-3) = 6 + 3 = 9$.

140. **Answer: D**
    Topic(s): Absolute Value (p. 82); Lines (p. 73)

Without a calculator to help graph this, we'll need to either use finely honed knowledge of how graph translations and reflections work with $y = |x|$ (which makes a V-shape at the origin) or do a little trial and error to see which choices won't produce any negative y-values when $x > 0$. This works, of course, because $y < 0$ and $x > 0$ in Quadrant IV.

Let's just make a chart showing y-values for $x = 1$ through $x = 3$.

		x equals...	
	1	2	3
A) $y = |3 - x| - 1$	1	0	−1
B) $y = |x - 1| - 3$	−3	−2	−1
C) $y = 1 - |3 - x|$	−1	0	1
D) $y = |3 + x| - 1$	3	4	5

We don't need to try many positive values of x before we can eliminate all the wrong answer choices. Only choice D remains after trying only 3 values of x!

141. Answer: B

Topic(s): Percents and Percent Change (p. 182); Measures of Central Tendency and Variability (p. 182)

Only one of the choices will be true, so we just need to start working through choices until we find it. Pro tip: start with the fastest ones to check.

For example, C is easy to check—the range of passenger kilometers will be just the difference between the highest number and the lowest number: $5501 - 5100 = 401$, not 61, so C is not the answer.

D is pretty easy to check, too. The average passenger kilometers will be

$$\frac{5440 + 5469 + 5501 + 5320 + 5100}{5} = 5366.$$

That's closer to the 2009 number than it is the 2006 number, so D isn't true.

From there, B is probably easier to check than A. To calculate the percent decrease from 2009 to 2010, do the following:

Passengers: $\dfrac{1374 - 1453}{1453} \times 100\% = -5.3\%$

Passenger km: $\dfrac{5100 - 5320}{5320} \times 100\% = -4.1\%$

So choice B is true: the percent decrease in passengers was greater than the percent decrease in passenger kilometers from 2009 to 2010.

(Just for good measure, choice A doesn't work. The median number of passengers per year is 1461 and the average is 1448. The average is less than the median.)

142. Answer: 180

Topic(s): Polynomials (p. 142)

If we only care about the first and last coefficient, there's a shortcut we can take! We don't need to do all the polynomial multiplying—we just need to find the products of the first and last numbers in the binomials. Think about it this way: you only get ax^3 by multiplying all the x terms, and you only get d (a constant) by multiplying all the constant terms.

Therefore, given $f(x) = (3x + 4)(4x + 1)(12x - 9)$, we know $a = (3)(4)(12) = 144$, and $d = (4)(1)(-9) = -36$.

The value of $a - d$ is $144 - (-36) = 180$.

143. Answer: D

Topic(s): Parabolas (p. 128)

A parabola's minimum value is at its vertex, so you're looking for an equation in vertex form!

Of course, you could complete the square to wrestle the given equation into vertex form, but the beauty of this question being multiple choice is that the only choice in vertex form must be correct! Go with choice D.

I won't leave you hanging on the algebra, though. Here's how you go from the given equation to the version in choice D: you complete the square.

$y = 3x^2 + 36x + 60$
$y = 3(x^2 + 12x + 20)$
$y = 3((x^2 + 12x + 36) - 16)$
$y = 3((x + 6)^2 - 16)$
$y = 3(x + 6)^2 - 48$

The parabola's vertex is at $(-6, -48)$, and -48 is a constant or coefficient in the equation in choice D.

144. Answer: D

Topic(s): Functions (p. 92); Parabolas (p. 128)

Because we're given the definition of $f(x + 3)$ in factored form, we know that $f(x + 3)$ has zeros at -8 and 1. Because we know our function translation rules, we also know that

$f(x + 3)$ represents a shift of 3 units left from $f(x)$.

Armed with that knowledge, all we need to do here is undo the shift!

If $f(x + 3)$ has zeros at –8 and 1, and $f(x + 3)$ represents a shift 3 units left from $f(x)$, then all we need to do is move 3 units back to the right to have the zeros of $f(x)$.

In other words, if $f(x + 3)$ has zeros at –8 and 1, then $f(x)$ has zeros at –5 and 4. Of those, only one corresponds to an answer choice, so $f(-5)$ is the answer.

145. Answer: B
Topic(s): Algebraic Manipulation (p. 52); Translating between Words and Math (p. 44)

The math on this one isn't that hard, but it's still pretty easy to get fooled! Start by plugging all the numbers you know into the equation and solve for t:

$$P = 5w + \frac{2}{3}t + \frac{3}{10}m$$
$$54 = 5(3) + \frac{2}{3}t + \frac{3}{10}(30)$$
$$54 = 15 + \frac{2}{3}t + 9$$
$$54 = 24 + \frac{2}{3}t$$
$$30 = \frac{2}{3}t$$
$$45 = t$$

Careful! Don't stop here and pick C! 45 is t, the number of minutes spent driving, and we need the driver's average speed in miles per hour!

Average speed is calculated by dividing distance traveled by time spent traveling. In other words,

$$\text{Average speed (mph)} = \frac{\text{miles traveled}}{\text{hours spent traveling}}.$$

We know the distance is 30 miles, and we know 45 minutes is $\frac{3}{4}$ of an hour. So we can calculate the average speed:

$$\text{Average speed (mph)} = \frac{30 \text{ miles}}{\frac{3}{4} \text{ hours}} = 40 \text{ mph}$$

146. Answer: 55
Topic(s): Translating between Words and Math (p. 44)

To solve this, first calculate how much money Marcy makes by working 48 hours. For the first 40 hours, she makes her normal rate of $18 per hour. For the next 8 hours, she makes 150% of her normal rate (AKA time-and-a-half).

Marcy makes:

$$40(18) + 8\left(18 \times \frac{150}{100}\right) = 936$$

If Louis makes $64 more than Marcy, then he makes $1000. We know that he must work more than 40 hours to make that much (he makes less than Marcy does per hour and she had to work more than 40 hours to make $936) so we can solve the following equation to figure out the number of hours Louis worked beyond 40.

$$40(16) + x\left(16 \times \frac{150}{100}\right) = 1000$$
$$640 + 24x = 1000$$
$$24x = 360$$
$$x = 15$$

Be careful! The answer isn't 15! That's how many hours Louis worked beyond 40 hours. The total number of hours he worked includes the first 40, so the answer we want is 40 + 15 = 55 hours.

147. **Answer: 3.5 or 7/2**
Topic(s): Lines (p. 73)

The slopes of perpendicular lines are negative reciprocals. So the first thing we'll want to do (as usual for line questions) is put both equations into $y = mx + b$ form.

$$4x + 7y = 30$$
$$7y = -4x + 30$$
$$y = -\frac{4}{7}x + \frac{30}{7}$$

$$ax - 2y = 5$$
$$-2y = -ax + 5$$
$$y = \frac{a}{2}x + \frac{5}{2}$$

The slope of the first line is $-\frac{4}{7}$, so the slope of the second line must be $\frac{7}{4}$ for the lines to be perpendicular. That means $\frac{a}{2} = \frac{7}{4}$, which means $a = \frac{7}{2}$.

148. **Answer: D**
Topic(s): Circles, Radians, and a Little More Trigonometry (p. 258); Right Triangles and Basic Trigonometry (p. 261)

We know the center is (4, –4), so we know that the left hand side of the equation should be $(x - 4)^2 + (y + 4)^2$. That eliminates choices A and C, but we still need to know the radius to decide between B and D.

To find the radius, consider the right triangle formed when you count over and down from the origin (which we know is a point on the circle) and the center.

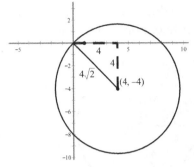

That's a right triangle with two legs of length 4, AKA a 45°-45°-90° triangle! The hypotenuse is the radius, so we know the radius equals $4\sqrt{2}$.

Careful—don't pick B! Remember, the circle equation calls for r^2 on the right hand side, so we need $(4\sqrt{2})^2 = 32$ on the right hand side. The answer is D.

149. **Answer: B**
Topic(s): Lines (p. 73)

The thing to remember about lines that pass through the origin is that you can tell their slope from any non-origin point. For both points in a choice to be on a line that goes through the origin, they both must indicate the same slope. Only choice B accomplishes that:

$$\frac{3 - 0}{\left(-\frac{1}{3} - 0\right)} = -9$$

$$\frac{-1 - 0}{\left(\frac{1}{9} - 0\right)} = -9$$

150. **Answer: C**
Topic(s): Circles, Radians, and a Little More Trigonometry (p. 258); Angles, Triangles, and Polygons (p. 236)

To get this one, we need to recognize that $\overline{AB}$ is a radius of both circles, so each circle has a radius of 8 inches and therefore a circumference of 16π inches. From there, we also need to see that, if we draw in a couple more radii, like so, we create equilateral triangles:

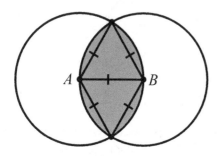

All the angles in an equilateral triangle measure 60°, so the central angles that correspond to the arcs that make up the shaded region measure 120°.

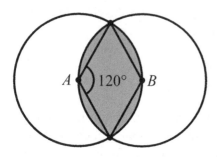

120° is $\frac{1}{3}$ of 360°, so each of the two arcs is $\frac{1}{3}$ of the full circumference of 16π.

$$\frac{16\pi}{3} + \frac{16\pi}{3} = \frac{32\pi}{3}$$

151. **Answer: C**
Topic(s): Measures of Central Tendency and Variability (p. 182); Data Analysis 2 (p. 203)

Even though a scatterplot isn't really made to highlight medians, one like this without too much data in it makes finding the median of one series really easy! The median of a set of 21 numbers will be the 11th highest/lowest number in the set (in other words, there will be 10 values higher than it and 10 values lower than it. We can completely ignore the time spent studying axis to answer this question and just cross off the 10 highest scores.

Exam Results by Hours Spent on Homework

There, how's that? Top 10 scores are crossed out, median is a big star. (Actually, there's another dot that looks about the same as the median—I could have just as easily starred that one.) Looks like it's just under smack in the middle of 60 and 80 on the vertical axis, so 69 is the best answer.

152. **Answer: 17**
Topic(s): Solving Systems of Linear Equations (p. 59)

Look, I know those are inequalities, but we can work this problem just like any system of linear equations problem. Because those are the __-or-equal-to kinds of inequalities, the intersection of the lines will be in the solution set. And when a question like this asks for a least or greatest kind of answer, it's pretty much gotta be talking about that intersection.

So let's just solve for the intersection.

$$\frac{2}{3}x + 2 = \frac{1}{3}x + 5$$

$$\frac{1}{3}x = 3$$

$$x = 9$$

$$y = \frac{2}{3}x + 2$$

$$y = \frac{2}{3}(9) + 2$$

$$y = 8$$

There we have it, the intersection is (9,8).

It's also possible to get this quickly (and more intuitively for those who hate inequalities) by graphing.

153. **Answer: D**
Topic(s): Backsolving (p. 32); Lines (p. 73)

Totally fine to just graph both lines and check the points, but this one is also easy to backsolve. Just try each choice in both inequalities. The first one that satisfies both is the right answer. Here's what that looks like with choice D:

$2(5) + 3 > (2) - 2$
$13 > 0$

$(5) - 8 < 2(2) - 5$
$-3 < -1$

Since both of those inequalities work out true, choice D is in the solution set of the system of inequalities.

154. **Answer: A**
Topic(s): Functions (p. 92); Lines (p. 73)

Recall that when this question tells us that $f(3) = 8$ and $f(8) = 3$, we know the line we care about contains the points (3, 8) and (8, 3).

Think about those two points and what the line connecting them looks like. (In fact, draw it!) Calculate the slope: $\frac{8-3}{3-8} = -1$.

From there, we can derive the equation of the line in $y = mx + b$ form. A line going through (3, 8) with a slope of -1 will have a y-intercept of 11—just count up and back 3 steps! Therefore, the equation of the line is $y = f(x) = -x + 11$. Use the equation to test answer choices:

Choice A:

$f(f(4)) = 4$
$f(-4 + 11) = 4$
$f(7) = 4$
$-7 + 11 = 4$
$4 = 4$

Welp, I guess we're done—choice A worked!

I started with A because that's what I usually do unless the choices are in numerical order, but it's worth noting that a couple choices can probably be eliminated without doing the math based on the fact that you have a line with a negative slope and a positive y-intercept.

For example, C can be knocked right out. Based on the two points you're given, you should be able to see easily that $(-3, -8)$ is nowhere near the line.

B should also be a pretty quick elimination. The only time $f(0) = f(11)$ will be true about a linear function is when the line is horizontal.

So if A didn't work, I'd probably jump right to trying D. But A *did* work, yay!

155. **Answer: D**
Topic(s): Circles, Radians, and a Little More Trignometry (p. 258)

Get this one the fast way by drawing the circle. We know the standard form of a circle so we know that the equation we're given is a circle centered at (3, −4) with radius 3. So draw that.

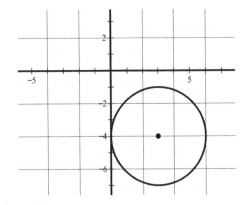

We don't have to draw it very accurately at all to be able to eliminate choices A, B, and C.

(Choices A and B aren't even in the right quadrant!) Therefore, without having to do much math, we can conclude that since choices A, B, and C are not correct, choice D must be correct!

156. **Answer: 165**

   Topic(s): Measures of Central Tendency and Variability (p. 182)

   Let's figure out how many seconds of music, in total, the musician recorded. If he has 15 songs with an average length of 215 seconds, then in total he has $15 \times 215 = 3{,}225$ seconds of music.

   Now we can figure out how many seconds of music the final version of the album will have, based on the given number of minutes and seconds. 48 minutes is $48 \times 60 = 2{,}880$ seconds. Add the last 15 seconds on there and you get 2,895 seconds.

   The musician originally recorded 15 songs, and only 13 go on the album, so 2 songs were excluded. To figure out how many seconds of music were excluded, subtract! $3{,}225 - 2{,}895 = 330$ seconds, so there are 330 seconds of music excluded from the final version of the album.

   Therefore, the average length of the excluded songs is $\dfrac{330}{2} = 165$ seconds.

157. **Answer: C**

   Topic(s): Functions (p. 92)

   What has to happen to $x + 7$ to turn it into $5x + 5$? Whatever it is that has to happen, that's what the function will do to anything that's put into it.

   The first thing that needs to happen to $x + 7$ to turn it into $5x + 5$ is multiplication by 5. There's no way to turn x into $5x$ without doing that! However, multiplying by 5 alone gives us $5(x + 7) = 5x + 35$. We're not there yet.

The next thing we have to do is subtract! If we take away 30, then we'll be where we want to be: $(5x + 35) - 30 = 5x + 5$.

So, let's recap. We figured out that to turn $x + 7$ into $5x + 5$, we first need to multiply by 5, and then we need to subtract 30. Therefore, we can define the f function like so: $f(x) = 5x - 30$.

We can check our work here, of course, and we should! If $f(x) = 5x - 30$, then

$f(x + 7) = 5(x + 7) - 30$
$f(x + 7) = 5x + 35 - 30$
$f(x + 7) = 5x + 5$

Nice.

Now that we know $f(x) = 5x - 30$, it's easy to calculate $f(2x)$.

$f(2x) = 5(2x) - 30$
$f(2x) = 10x - 30$

158. **Answer: 12**

   Topic(s): Angles, Triangles, and Polygons (p. 236)

   The easiest way to get this one is to recognize that the figure is a square with one quarter of it missing:

   square_with_quarter_missing_gsp 2

   From there, we just need to do a little algebra. We know that the area of the square we now see is m^2. We also know that $\dfrac{3}{4}$ of the area of the square is 108!

   $\dfrac{3}{4}m^2 = 108$
   $m^2 = 144$
   $m = 12$

159. **Answer: 4**

   Topic(s): Exponents and Exponential Functions (p. 104)

Let's break the left side of the equation into pieces to simplify. First, the numerator of the numerator. When we multiply like bases, we add the exponents.

$$x^a x^2 = x^{a+2}$$

Now let's take care of that whole fraction inside the parentheses on top. When we divide like bases, we subtract the exponents.

$$\frac{x^{a+2}}{x^3} = x^{a+2-3} = x^{a-1}$$

Now we're ready to apply the outer exponent. When we raise a power to a power, we multiply the powers.

$$\left(x^{a-1}\right)^3 = x^{3a-3}$$

Finally, we can incorporate the big denominator.

$$\frac{x^{3a-3}}{x^a} = x^{3a-3-a} = x^{2a-3}$$

That's what we can set equal to x^5 to solve for a.

$$x^{2a-3} = x^5$$
$$2a - 3 = 5$$
$$2a = 8$$
$$a = 4$$

160. **Answer: 16**
Topic(s): Lines (p. 73)

Parallel lines have the same slope. Therefore, our first step here should be to calculate the slope of line k.

$$\text{slope}_k = \frac{0 - (-7)}{-4 - 0} = -\frac{7}{4}$$

From there, noting that this is a grid-in where the numbers are almost always simple, the boss move is just to calculate the x-intercept of line j from the one point we know.

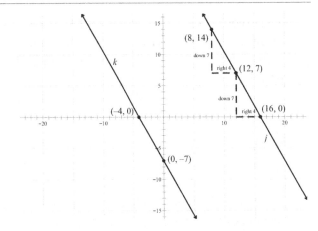

There we have it: the x-intercept of line j is 16.

161. **Answer: 95**
Topic(s): Working in Three Dimensions (p. 279)

The formula for the volume of a cylinder is $V = \pi r^2 h$, so we know a few things up front. First, we need to convert the given 3 cm diameter into a 1.5 cm radius. Second, in this case, we don't want the volume of the whole cylindrical glass—we only want the volume of the water inside! So instead of using 22 cm for h, let's figure out the height of the water when the glass is 61% full.

$$h = \frac{61}{100} \times 22 \text{ cm} = 13.42 \text{ cm}$$

Now we can calculate the volume of water in the glass.

$$V = \pi (1.5 \text{ cm})^2 (13.42 \text{ cm})$$
$$V \approx 94.86 \text{ cm}^3$$

Because the question asks for the volume to the nearest cubic centimeter, the answer is 95.

162. **Answer: 66**
Topic(s): Ratios and Proportionality (p. 171); Translating between Words and Math (p. 44)

Come on, George. That's not cool.

To solve this one, first write out the ratios we know were in the bowl before George came, using s for strawberry, b for banana, and o for orange.

$$\frac{s}{o}=\frac{5}{4}$$

$$\frac{s}{b}=\frac{2}{3}$$

Now, what happened when George took out 22 banana candies? The ratio became 5 to 2!

$$\frac{s}{b-22}=\frac{5}{2}$$

Now we have two equations for the variables s and b, so we can solve for them.

First, cross multiply each.

$3s = 2b$

$2s = 5(b-22)$
$2s = 5b - 110$

Now substitute and solve.

$$\frac{3}{2}s=b$$

$$2s=5\left(\frac{3}{2}s\right)-110$$
$$2s=7.5s-110$$
$$-5.5s=-110$$
$$s=20$$

Now that we have s, all we need to do is work back through our original ratios to get b and o.

$$\frac{20}{o}=\frac{5}{4}$$
$$16=o$$

$$\frac{20}{b}=\frac{2}{3}$$
$$30=b$$

So if the bowl started with 20 strawberry, 16 orange, and 30 banana candies, then there

were $20 + 16 + 30 = 66$ candies in the bowl before George raided it.

163. **Answer: D**
   Topic(s): Parabolas (p. 128)

First, note that the parabola in the graph opens upwards. That tells us that the leading coefficient, which is a in this case, must be positive. So Roman numeral I must be true.

Since the parabola is in factored form, we know that the zeros of the parabola must therefore be at $x = -b$ and $x = -c$. Because we're told that the absolute value of c is greater than the absolute value of b, we know that the zero corresponding to c must be the one that's farther away from the origin.

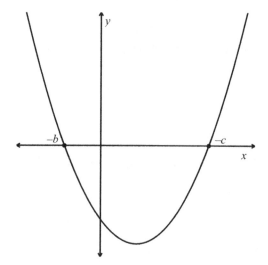

Because $-c$ represents a positive value, c must be negative. Likewise, because $-b$ represents a negative value, b must be positive. If c is negative and b is positive, Roman numeral II cannot be true, and Roman numeral III must be true.

Therefore, the answer is choice D.

164. **Answer: 41**
   Topic(s): Measures of Central Tendency and Variability (p. 182)

Let's start by converting everything to seconds. If the test is 50 minutes long, then it's

50 minutes $\times 60 \dfrac{\text{seconds}}{\text{minute}} = 3000$ seconds long.

However, Christine's goal is to leave 5 minutes to check her work, so she really has

5 minutes $\times 60 \dfrac{\text{seconds}}{\text{minute}} = 300$ seconds less than

that: Christine has $3000 - 300 = 2700$ seconds to work with.

We can use number of values × average = sum to figure out how much time Christine spends on the first 8 and the next 15 questions.

She averages 50 seconds per question on the first 8 questions, so she spends a total of $8 \times 50 = 400$ seconds on the first 8 questions.

She averages 134 seconds per question on the next 15 questions, so she spends a total of $15 \times 134 = 2010$ seconds on the next 15 questions.

So far, she's done $8 + 15 = 23$ questions and spent $400 + 2010 = 2410$ seconds. Therefore, Christine has $2700 - 2410 = 290$ seconds left to do the last 7 questions.

She must average $\dfrac{290}{7} = 41.42...$ seconds per question to finish when she wants to.

Since the question says to round to the nearest second, the answer is 41.

165. **Answer: 144**
Topic(s): Right Triangles and Basic Trigonometry (p. 249)

The question tells us that we have a right triangle (the measure of $\angle B = 90°$) and that two of its sides are in a 5 to 13 ratio. That's enough for us to know that all three sides will be in a 5:12:13 ratio!

From there, we must remember what cos ($\angle A$) means. Cosine is the ratio of the lengths of the angle's adjacent leg to the hypotenuse (remember your SOH-CAH-TOA!) so

$\cos (\angle A) = \dfrac{5}{13}$ means the leg next to $\angle A$ is the short one.

We can draw this now, right?

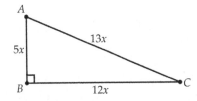

If $AB = 5x = 60$, then $x = 12$. That means $BC = 12x = 12(12) = 144$.

166. **Answer: D**
Topic(s): Polynomials (p.); Binomial Squares and Difference of Two Squares (p.)

To get this one, we need to recognize that we're dealing with a difference of two squares. We can factor the right-hand side of the given equation:

$(ax + b)(5x + 9) = (ax)^2 - b^2$
$(ax + b)(5x + 9) = (ax + b)(ax - b)$

Now divide both sides by $(ax + b)$ and you're left with:

$5x + 9 = ax - b$

Here's where the mistake is likely to happen. Look closely. We know the equation is true for all x and y, so we know the corresponding coefficients are equal. That means that $a = 5$ and $b = -9$. Therefore, $a - b = 5 - (-9) = 14$.

167. **Answer: C**
Topic(s): Absolute Value (p. 82)

Remember that the distance between a and b can be expressed using absolute value brackets thusly: $|a - b|$. Since this question involves distances from -5, we want to see an absolute value expression that either contains $|-5 - x|$ or $|x - (-5)| = |x + 5|$. Choice C contains the latter.

Since no other choice has an absolute value expression that represents the distance between x and -5, we're basically done!

168. Answer: 64
Topic(s): Lines (p. 73); Functions (p. 92)

Use the given points to figure out the slope and y-intercept of f.

The intercept is easy—it's the first row in the table! The point $(0, 24)$ is on the graph, so the y-intercept is 24.

To find the slope, use the slope formula:

$$\text{slope} = \frac{22-24}{6-0} = \frac{-2}{6} = -\frac{1}{3}$$

Therefore, we can say that $f(x) = -\frac{1}{3}x + 24$.

Now, let's calculate $g(8)$:

$$g(8) = 3f(8)$$
$$g(8) = 3\left(-\frac{1}{3}(8) + 24\right)$$
$$g(8) = -8 + 72$$
$$g(8) = 64$$

169. Answer: 1.8 or 9/5
Topic(s): Exponents and Exponential Functions (p. 104)

Remember that when we multiply the same base with different exponents, we add the exponents. So $x^{(2/5)}x^5 = x^{(2/5+5)}$, which simplifies to $x^{(27/5)}$.

From there, remember that the cube root is the same as raising the expression to the $\frac{1}{3}$ power, and when we raise an exponential expression to a power we multiply the exponents.

$$\sqrt[3]{x^{(27/5)}} = \left(x^{(27/5)}\right)^{(1/3)} = x^{(27/15)} = x^{(9/5)}$$

And we're done: $m = \frac{9}{5}$, or 1.8.

170. Answer: 27
Topic(s): Ratios and Proportionality (p. 171)

It's easy to get turned around on this one, because we're given two different breakdowns of the same 90 candies.

Start with the last bit of information we're given: red wrappers to green wrappers is 4 to 1. We can convert that part-part ratio to a part-whole ratio: red wrappers to all wrappers is 4 to 5. That means of the 90 candies, $\frac{4}{5}$ of them, or 72, have red wrappers.

Now consider the other bit of information you have: foil wrappers to cellophane wrappers is 1 to 1. In other words, of the 90 candies, 45 are wrapped in foil, and 45 are wrapped in cellophane.

Now, we know that the only color of cellophane wrapper is red. Therefore, all 45 of the cellophane wrappers are red. We also know that there are, in total, 72 red wrappers. The number of red foil wrappers must therefore be the total number of red wrappers minus the number of red cellophane wrappers. $72 - 45 = 27$, so there are 27 candies with red foil wrappers.

171. Answer: C
Topic(s): Backsolving (p. 32); Percents and Percent Change (p. 161)

This is a word problem, with numbers in the answer choices, in order. That means it's a prime candidate for backsolving!

If we assume B is the answer, for example, then the ending price was $76.12, which means the beginning price was $76.12 - 1.33 = \$74.79$. Is a price increase of $1.33 from $74.79 equal to a 1.76 percent increase?

$$\frac{1.33}{74.79} \times 100\% \approx 1.78\%$$

That's close, but not close enough for me to be comfortable. The percent should decrease a little bit if the opening price increases a little bit, so let's try C. If C is the answer, then the ending price is $76.90, which means the beginning price was $79.90 − 1.33 = $75.57. Is a price increase of $1.33 from $75.57 equal to a 1.76 percent increase?

$$\frac{1.33}{75.57} \times 100\% \approx 1.76\%$$

On yeah, that's much better! C is the answer.

172. **Answer: 4**
Topic(s): Solving Systems of Linear Equations (p. 59)

We *could* try to solve this by finding values for x and y individually, but we very much don't need to. Instead, note that we're asked about a different combination of x and y. Can we combine the equations to get there directly?

Of course we can! Try adding the equations:

$$\begin{array}{r} 3x + 7y = 18 \\ + \ 2x - 2y = \ 2 \\ \hline 5x + 5y = 20 \end{array}$$

Of course, if $5x + 5y = 20$, then we can divide by 5 to see that $x + y = 4$.

And if $x + y = 4$, and $ax + ay = a(x + y) = 16$, we can conclude that $a = 4$.

173. **Answer: 5**
Topic(s): Circles, Radians, and a Little More Trigonometry (p. 258); Lines (p. 73)

We'll need two important facts to get this one: 1) tangent lines are perpendicular to the radius at the point they meet the circle, and 2) perpendicular lines have negative reciprocal slopes.

We can calculate the slope of the radius from the center of $(-5, 2)$ to $(-1, 1)$:

$$\text{slope} = \frac{1-2}{-1-(-5)} = -\frac{1}{4}$$

Because perpendicular lines have negative reciprocal slopes and tangent lines are perpendicular, we know the slope of line l must be 4.

Now all that's left is to figure out the y-intercept of a line with a slope of 4 that passes through $(-1, 1)$. Just count up 4 units and right 1 unit and you're at the y-axis: the y-intercept is 5.

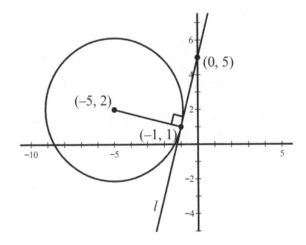

174. **Answer: A**
Topic(s): Lines (p. 73)

If you ask me, it's faster to test the answer choices here than to derive the right one. There are two things we must test them for: whether they go through $(2, 5)$ and whether they're parallel to $3x - 4y = 12$. Since all we need to do to test whether they pass through the point is plug the point into each equation, let's do that first and see if it eliminates any answers.

A) $-6(2) + 8(5) = 28 \leftarrow$ Yes, that's true!
B) $3(2) - 4(5) = -12 \leftarrow$ Not true!
C) $-3(2) + 4(5) = -14 \leftarrow$ Not true!
D) $-6(2) - 8(5) = -52 \leftarrow$ Yes, that's true!

Now that we're down to only A and D, see which one is parallel to the given line. To do that, put each into slope-intercept form. First, the given line:

$$3x - 4y = 12$$
$$-4y = -3x + 12$$
$$y = \frac{3}{4}x - 3$$

Now try choice A:

$$6x + 8y = 28$$
$$8y = 6x + 28$$
$$y = \frac{6}{8}x + \frac{28}{8}$$
$$y = \frac{3}{4}x + \frac{7}{2}$$

Yep...that's the $\frac{3}{4}$ slope we're looking for. Choice A works!

Just for good measure, try choice D even though we already know choice A works:

$$-6x - 8y = -52$$
$$-8y = 6x - 52$$
$$y = -\frac{6}{8}x + \frac{52}{8}$$
$$y = -\frac{3}{4}x + \frac{13}{2}$$

Sure enough, that's the wrong slope!

175. **Answer: B**
Topic(s): Circles, Radians, and a Little More Trigonometry (p. 258)

The thing we must remember to get this one right is that if $\sin A = \cos B$, then A and B will be complementary (their sum will be 90° or $\frac{\pi}{2}$ radians). Knowing that, all we need to do is see which choice will give us a sum of $\frac{\pi}{2}$ when we add the angle measures together.

Choice A doesn't work: $\frac{\pi}{8} + \frac{\pi}{8} = \frac{\pi}{4}$. That's not $\frac{\pi}{2}$, so we move on.

Choice B works, though:
$\frac{\pi}{8} + \frac{\pi}{8/3} = \frac{\pi}{8} + \frac{3\pi}{8} = \frac{4\pi}{8} = \frac{\pi}{2}$. Wahoo!

176. **Answer: B**
Topic(s): Working with Advanced Systems of Equations (p. 152)

First, solve for x by substituting:

$$x^2 + x - 8 = 2x - 2$$
$$x^2 - x - 6 = 0$$
$$(x - 3)(x + 2) = 0$$

Now that we know x can equal 3 or –2, find the corresponding y-values by plugging back into the simpler equation:

$$y = 2(3) - 2 = 4$$
$$y = 2(-2) - 2 = -6$$

So the two possible ordered pairs are (3, 4) and (–2, –6). The values of $|x - y|$, then, are:

$$|3 - 4| = 1$$
$$|-2 - (-6)| = 4$$

Obviously the greater of those values is 4, so that's the answer.

177. **Answer: 6.5 or 13/2**
Topic(s): Measures of Central Tendency and Variability (p. 182)

The range of a set of data is simply the difference between the largest value and the smallest value, so the range of scores currently is $10 - 4 = 6$. Because there are only 10 questions on this quiz and someone has already achieved a score of 10, we know that the last student must score 3 or below to increase the range. (If the last student scores 2, for example, $10 - 2 = 8$, so the range increases from 6 to 8.)

Once we know that the final student's score will be the new minimum, we have enough information to calculate the median.

In a set of 16 numbers, the median will be the average of the middle two numbers. The dot plot already sorts the scores for us, so all we need to do is draw one more dot and count. Let's say the last student gets a score of 2.

0 1 2 3 4 5 6 7 8 9 10
Quiz Scores

If you count the dots, you'll see that once the new gray dot is added, there are 8 dots less than or equal to 6 and dots greater than or equal to 7. The median will be the average of 6 and 7, or 6.5.

178. **Answer: 78**
Topic(s): Lines (p. 73)

First, figure out the equation of line n. We can do this because we know it's perpendicular to line m, which means its slope must be $\frac{1}{5}$, and we know it goes through the origin, which means its y-intercept is 0. So the equation of line n is $y = \frac{1}{5}x$.

From there, we can solve for b:

$$y = \frac{1}{5}x$$
$$b = \frac{1}{5}(15)$$
$$b = 3$$

Once we have the value of b, it's smooth sailing to solve for a. Since we know the intersection point (15, 3) is on line m, we can use that point to solve for a:

$$y = -5x + a$$
$$3 = -5(15) + a$$
$$3 = -75 + a$$
$$78 = a$$

179. **Answer: D**
Topic(s): Complex Numbers (p. 292)

The only way you get a real number (which 130 is) by multiplying complex numbers is if the complex numbers being multiplied contain conjugates—if they contain something in the form of $(a + bi)(a - bi)$.

Of course, because I'm mean, that's not the only thing going on here. It's just our starting point. What if we assume that $a + bi$ is the conjugate of $4 + 7i$, so $a = 4$ and $b = -7$?

$$(4 + 7i)(4 - 7i)$$
$$= 16 - 28i + 28i - 49i^2$$
$$= 16 - 49i^2$$
$$= 16 - 49(-1)$$
$$= 65$$

Wait a minute—that's not 130! It is, however, half of 130, so we're still in business. What that tells us is that we're really dealing with conjugates and a real number multiplied in, too. Like so:

$$(4 + 7i)(4 - 7i)(2)$$
$$= (65)(2)$$
$$= 130$$

The original equation we have doesn't contain a real number multiplied in separately, though, so we need to incorporate it into $a + bi$. Like so:

$$(4 + 7i)(a + bi) = (4 + 7i)(4 - 7i)(2)$$
$$a + bi = (4 - 7i)(2)$$
$$a + bi = 8 - 14i$$

Therefore, $a = 8$, $b = -14$, and $a + b = 8 + (-14) = -6$. There's the answer!

180. **Answer: D**
Topic(s): Ratios and Proportionality (p. 171)

Obviously, we're going to have to convert square meters to square feet (or vice versa) to solve this, but we have to be careful! We're given that 1 foot is 0.3048 meters, but that doesn't mean that 1 square foot is 0.3048 square meters! To get that conversion, we must square both values!

$$1 \text{ foot} = 0.3048 \text{ meters}$$
$$(1 \text{ foot})^2 = (0.3048 \text{ meters})^2$$
$$1 \text{ square foot} = 0.09290304 \text{ square meters}$$

NOW we're ready to convert. The apartment on Maple Street that's 715 square feet? Well...

$$715 \text{ square feet} \times 0.9290304 \frac{\text{square meters}}{\text{square foot}}$$
$$\approx 66.43 \text{ square meters}$$

So the apartment on Maple Street is way smaller than the Apartment on Elm Street: $\frac{66.43}{200} \approx \frac{1}{3}$. Therefore, the answer is D.

181. **Answer: 180**
Topic(s): Measures of Central Tendency and Variability (p. 182)

We can really cut down on the work we have to do here by recognizing that the swings on Club A and Club B don't matter. Club A hit the ball farthest and Club B hit the ball the least distance, and there is no overlap in distances between the clubs. Therefore the 10 balls from Club A will be at the top of the list and the 10 balls from Club B will be at the bottom of the list—neither will affect the median. All we need to do is find the median of the ten swings for Club C.

Because there are ten balls hit by Club C, the median will be the average of the 5th and 6th distances once they're put in order. So let's list the distances in order:

178, 178, 178, 179, 179, 181, 182, 183, 183, 183

179 and 181 are the 5th and 6th values, so the median will be the average of those:

$$\frac{179+181}{2} = 180$$

182. **Answer: D**
Topic(s): Data Analysis 1 (p. 195); Lines (p. 73)

The key to getting this one is comparing the speed at which the hose fills up the tank (6 feet in 4 minutes, so $\frac{6}{4} = 1.5$ feet per minute) and the speed at which the drain empties the tank (6 feet in 3 minutes, so $\frac{6}{3} = 2$ feet per minute).

Note: these are the slopes of the two relevant sections of the graph.

Because the drain works faster than the hose, if the hose is turned on and the drain is open at the same time, the tank will end up slowly losing water at a rate of $2 - 1.5 = 0.5$ feet per minute.

If the water is four feet high when the timer starts, and it drains at a rate of 0.5 feet per minute, then the tank will be empty in

$$\frac{4 \text{ feet}}{0.5 \text{ feet per minute}} = 8 \text{ minutes.}$$

183. **Answer: C**
Topic(s): Polynomials (p. 142)

Let's take these one at a time. For I, note that the graph only has two zeros despite the fact that $(x + 4)(x + a)(x + b)$ would appear to have 3 factors. If a and b were different numbers, then there would be x-intercepts at $x = -a$ and $x = -b$ in addition to the intercept at $x = -4$. Because there aren't, we know that $a = b$.

As for II, that's going to be false. The factor we know, $x + 4$, results in a zero at $x = -4$. The fact that the other zero has a positive x-value indicates that a and b are negative.

Finally, III. If we got I and II nailed down right, we don't need to do much additional thinking about III. We know $a = b$ and we know a is negative, so therefore b is negative. Of course, if b is negative, it's definitely less than 4.

So the answer we want is C: I and III are true, but II is false.

184. **Answer: D**

   Topic(s): Measures of Central Tendency and Variability (p. 182)

   While we don't need to know much about standard deviation for the SAT, we do need to know that it's a measure of variability. The more spread out the data in a set is from its mean, the higher the standard deviation. The closer most of the data is to the mean, the lower the standard deviation.

   All three of the data sets we're given here have the same mean: 3. The data in Set I is spread out evenly. Comparatively, the data in Set II is spread farther from 3 (imagine moving dots from 2 and 4 in Set I to 1 and 5 in Set II, actually spreading the data further away). Meanwhile, the data in Set III is concentrated at 3 (again, imagine moving dots from 1 and 5 in Set I to 3 in Set III, actually packing the data in on the mean).

   Therefore, we can say that Set III has the lowest standard deviation, while Set II has the highest. Since the standard deviations of Sets I, II, and III are represented by x, y, and z, respectively, we can say that $z < x < y$.

185. **Answer: 344**

   Topic(s): Ratios and Proportionality (p. 171)

   We're given ratios for red:blue and red:yellow, but what we really want to be able to solve this is blue:yellow. How do we get that? Well, we could divide!

   $$\frac{\text{red}}{\text{yellow}} \div \frac{\text{red}}{\text{blue}} = \frac{\text{red}}{\text{yellow}} \times \frac{\text{blue}}{\text{red}} = \frac{\text{blue}}{\text{yellow}}$$

Now plug numbers into that!

$$\frac{2 \text{ red}}{3 \text{ yellow}} \div \frac{7 \text{ red}}{4 \text{ blue}} = \frac{2 \text{ red}}{3 \text{ yellow}} \times \frac{4 \text{ blue}}{7 \text{ red}}$$

$$= \frac{8 \text{ blue}}{21 \text{ yellow}}$$

Now we can set up system of equations!

$$\frac{b}{y} = \frac{8}{21}$$
$$y - b = 104$$

Let's do a little substituting and solve. If $y - b = 104$, then $y = 104 + b$.

$$\frac{b}{104 + b} = \frac{8}{21}$$
$$21b = 8(104 + b)$$
$$21b = 832 + 8b$$
$$13b = 832$$
$$b = 64$$

From there, we know there were 64 blue candies. We can use the original ratios to find how many other kinds there were. Red:blue was 7:4, so:

$$\frac{7 \text{ red}}{4 \text{ blue}} \times 64 \text{ blue} = 112 \text{ red}$$

If there are 112 red, and red:yellow is 2:3, then:

$$\frac{3 \text{ yellow}}{2 \text{ red}} \times 112 \text{ red} = 168 \text{ yellow}$$

Altogether, that's 112 red, 64 blue, and 168 yellow—a total of 344 candies.

186. **Answer: 40**

   Topic(s): Solving Systems of Linear Equations (p. 59)

   Let's first find the intersection point of the two lines without unknowns. Since this is a no-calculator question, it's a great opportunity to practice the elimination method of solving systems of linear equations.

$3x + 4y = 8$
$2x + 8y = 4$

Divide the second equation by 2 to get $4y$ in both equations, so that we can subtract and eliminate.

$$\begin{array}{r} 3x + 4y = 8 \\ -(x + 4y = 2) \\ \hline 2x = 6 \end{array}$$

That tells us that $x = 3$. Easy enough to solve for y now:

$3x + 4y = 8$
$3(3) + 4y = 8$
$9 + 4y = 8$
$4y = -1$
$y = -\dfrac{1}{4}$

All that's left now is to plug the point $\left(3, -\dfrac{1}{4}\right)$ into the third equation to solve for a.

$10x - ay = a$
$10(3) - a\left(-\dfrac{1}{4}\right) = a$
$30 + \dfrac{1}{4}a = a$
$30 = \dfrac{3}{4}a$
$40 = a$

187. **Answer: A**
Topic(s): Lines (p. 73)

A graph is helpful here, but this question was written to be solvable without a calculator—simple line drawings based only on slope and intercept should be enough to arrive at the right conclusions.

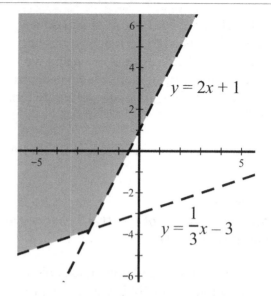

From the graph above, we see the solution set, shaded in gray. That's every point that is above both lines. Each quadrant has some shaded area except quadrant IV, where $x > 0$ and $y < 0$. Therefore, we can conclude that, if the x-value of the solution is positive, the y-value must also be positive. In other words, if $a > 0$, then $b > 0$.

188. **Answer: D**
Topic(s): Measures of Central Tendency and Variability (p. 182)

Let's get this by elimination—if we can come up with an example that supports one of these statements, that's good enough to say that it can be true.

For Roman numeral I, the median of the set is a member of the set—While it's possible for the median of an even-numbered set to not be in the set, the median can be in the set when the middle two numbers are equal. For example, the median of $\{1, 2, 3, 4, 5, 5, 6, 7, 8, 9\}$ is 5.

For Roman numeral II, the sum of the 10 numbers is equal to the average (arithmetic mean) of the 10 numbers—This is possible when the sum of the numbers is zero. The average and the sum of $\{-5, -4, -3, -2, -1, 1, 2, 3, 4, 5\}$ is zero.

For Roman numeral III, the set has 6 modes—This one can't be true. While a set can have multiple modes, to have 6 modes, we'd need 6 different elements of the set to appear more frequently than the rest of the set. Even if those 6 elements only appeared twice, we're already up to 12 elements without even counting the elements that appear less frequently than twice.

Note that once we come up with examples for I and II, we've logically eliminated every answer choice besides D, so we don't actually need to think about III at all.

189. **Answer: D**
    Topic(s): Lines (p. 73)

First, get both equations into $y = mx + b$ form. The first equation already is, so we just need to add ax to both sides of the second equation. Now we've got:

$$y = 6x - \frac{a}{2}$$
$$y = ax + 2a$$

We know that parallel lines have the same slope, so now that the equations are lined up this way we can see that $a = 6$. Substituting in, we can see both y-intercepts more clearly:

$$y = 6x - 3$$
$$y = 6x + 12$$

The y-intercepts are -3 and 12. The positive difference between those values is $12 - (-3) = 15$.

190. **Answer: 5**
    Topic(s): Working with Advanced Systems of Equations (p. 152)

The easiest way to see what's going on in this one is to graph the parabola and the line with a calculator. Here's what they look like on mine after a little window adjustment:

The inequalities tell you that the solution set will be all points below or on the parabola and above or on the line. In other words, the overlapping shaded area below:

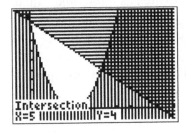

Because a and b are greater than zero, the least possible x-value in that solution set will be the x-value where the parabola and line intersect there in quadrant I. The calculator shows us that the intersection is at $(5, 4)$. Therefore, the answer we seek is 5.

191. **Answer: A**
    Topic(s): Functions (p. 92); Polynomials (p. 142)

Remember that $f(x + 3)$ will be $f(x)$ shifted 3 units to the left. Also, remember that zeros in polynomial functions indicate factors: if, as is the case here, a polynomial has a zero at $f(3)$, then $x - 3$ is a factor of that polynomial.

So what we're really doing here is figuring out where the zeros of $f(x + 3)$ will be.

Since $f(x)$ has zeros at $x = 1$ and $x = 3$, a graph shifted 3 units to the left will have zeros at $x = -2$ and $x = 0$.

Therefore, you know that $x + 2$ and x are factors of $f(x + 3)$. The latter is an answer choice, so the answer is A.

192. Answer: 121

Topic(s): Binomial Squares and Difference of Two Squares (p. 123)

To get this one, start by FOILing.

$4(x-5)(x+6)+m$
$4(x^2+6x-5x-30)+m$
$4(x^2+x-30)+m$
$4x^2+4x-120+m$

If that can be rewritten as a binomial square, then you can use the first two terms, $4x^2+4x$ to determine what that square must be.

If the first term of the FOILed out square is $4x^2$, then the factored square must look like this: $(2x+b)(2x+b)$.

From there, we can set up an equation.

$4x^2+4x-120+m=(2x+b)(2x+b)$
$4x^2+4x-120+m=4x^2+2bx+2bx+b^2$
$4x^2+4x-120+m=4x^2+4bx+b^2$

Because we know that corresponding coefficients of equivalent polynomials are equal, we know that $4=4b$, which means that $b=1$. Corresponding coefficients rules also tell us that $-120+m=b^2$. If $b=1$, then $-120+m=1$, which means $m=121$. That's our answer.

The binomial square at work here is $(2x+1)^2$. FOILed out, that's $4x^2+4x+1$.

193. Answer: 180

Topic(s): Ratios and Proportionality (p. 171)

Let's solve this one by setting up two equations based on the ratios we know. First, the player starts with red and blue tokens in the ratio 7:10, so we can say $\dfrac{r}{b}=\dfrac{7}{10}$.

Then we can say that adding 10 red tokens changes the ratio to 4:5. In other words, $\dfrac{r+10}{b}=\dfrac{4}{5}$.

We can substitute and solve. From the first equation, we can rearrange to get $b=\dfrac{10r}{7}$.

Then we can drop that into the second equation:

$$\frac{r+10}{b}=\frac{4}{5}$$
$$\frac{r+10}{\left(\dfrac{10r}{7}\right)}=\frac{4}{5}$$
$$5(r+10)=4\left(\frac{10r}{7}\right)$$
$$5r+50=\frac{40r}{7}$$
$$35r+350=40r$$
$$350=5r$$
$$70=r$$

Now, be careful! That's the original number of red tokens, and we want the TOTAL tokens AFTER 10 more were won. So let's remember that the ratio after the 10 tokens were won was 4:5.

$$\frac{r+10}{b}=\frac{4}{5}$$
$$\frac{70+10}{b}=\frac{4}{5}$$
$$(80)(5)=4b$$
$$400=4b$$
$$100=b$$

If there are 80 red and 100 blue tokens, then the player has a total of 180 tokens. That's the answer!

194. Answer: D

Topic(s): Polynomials (p. 142)

What do we know? We know a lot! We know that we have a 3rd degree polynomial with a leading coefficient of 1 and a constant term of 90. We know the polynomial has factors including $(x + 5)$, $(x - 3)$, and $(x - k)$.

The fact that the leading coefficient is 1 and we have a 3rd degree polynomial tells us that there are no other factors at play here. If there were other constants being multiplied through, the leading coefficient would tell us so. If there were more binomial factors, the polynomial would have a higher degree.

Once we realize all that, we're actually almost done. We've done enough FOILing in our lives to know that the constant, 90, will be the product of the constants in the factors we've listed. That is, we know that $(5)(-3)(-k) = 90$. Simplify and solve that and you see that $k = 6$.

195. **Answer: 87**
    Topic(s): Binomial Squares and Difference of Two Squares (p. 123)

The way to get this one is to recognize that we're given a bunch of components of a binomial square: $(a - b)^2 = a^2 - 2ab + b^2$. We can use that to arrive at the answer quickly.

$$a - b = 7$$
$$(a - b)^2 = 7^2$$
$$a^2 - 2ab + b^2 = 49$$

Now substitute! We know that $ab = 19$, which will allow us to solve for $a^2 + b^2$:

$$a^2 - 2ab + b^2 = 49$$
$$a^2 - 2(19) + b^2 = 49$$
$$a^2 + b^2 - 38 = 49$$
$$a^2 + b^2 = 87$$

196. **Answer: 20**
    Topic(s): Circles, Radians, and a Little More Trigonometry (p. 258)

We know our circle equation (*right?!?*) so all we need to do is insert the center and radius we're given and then manipulate the resulting

equation until it resembles the one in the question. Here's what that looks like:

$$(x - 5)^2 + (y + 2)^2 = 7^2$$
$$(x^2 - 10x + 25) + (y^2 + 4y + 4) = 49$$
$$x^2 + y^2 - 10x + 4y + 29 = 49$$
$$x^2 + y^2 - 10x + 4y = 20$$

The answer is 20.

197. **Answer: 18**
    Topic(s): Right Triangles and Basic Trigonometry (p. 249)

First task, as is often the case with geometry questions, is just to label what we know. We're given a few side lengths:

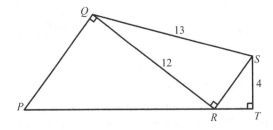

From there, we can use the Pythagorean theorem to fill in the remaining lengths in triangles QRS and RST. (Or, if we're next-level, which we ARE, we can recognize the 5-12-13 Pythagorean triple at work in triangle QRS, and then the 3-4-5 that reveals in triangle RST).

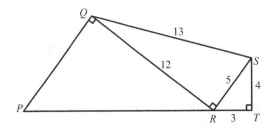

OK, now what? Well, now we should note that triangles PQR and RTS are similar. There are a few ways to see this, but I think the easiest is to note that $\overline{PQ}$ and $\overline{RS}$ are parallel:

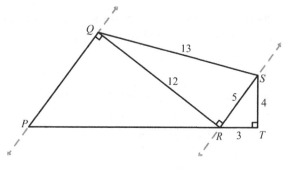

$\overline{RT}$ is a transversal of those parallel lines, so angles QPR and TRS are corresponding congruent angles. Of course, that means that angles QRP and RST are also congruent.

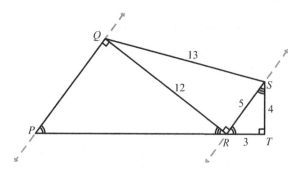

So, triangle PQR must also be a 3-4-5. We know that the length of $\overline{QR}$ is 12, and we know that $\overline{QR}$ is across from angle QPR, which corresponds to angle TRS, which is across from the 4 side in the smaller triangle. Therefore, we know that the other two side lengths in triangle QPS are 9 and 15: 9-12-15 is just a bigger 3-4-5.

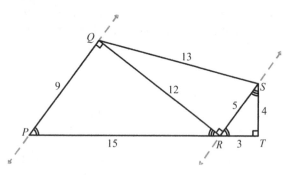

Phew! Finally, we know the length of $\overline{PT}$ is $15 + 3 = 18$.

198. **Answer: 10.4 or 52/5**
    Topic(s): Lines (p. 73)

We know line n passes through the origin—aka, (0, 0)—and (10, 2), so we can calculate its slope:

$$\text{slope}_n = \frac{2-0}{10-0} = \frac{1}{5}$$

Because lines n and m are perpendicular, the slope of line m must be the negative reciprocal, or –5. Now we know the slope of line m and a single point. How do we find the rest?

Just plug what we know into a simple $y = mx + b$ equation! We have a slope of –5 and the point (10, 2), so:

$$2 = -5(10) + b$$
$$2 = -50 + b$$
$$52 = b$$

But wait! 52 is the y-intercept, not the x-intercept, so we're not done yet! At the x-intercept, the value of y is zero, so let's plug that into the equation we just derived to solve for x:

$$y = -5x + 52$$
$$0 = -5x + 52$$
$$5x = 52$$
$$x = \frac{52}{5}$$

199. **Answer: 24**
    Topic(s): Complex Numbers (p. 292)

The only way we can multiply two complex numbers and get a real number result is if we multiply complex conjugates. Since we know one of the complex numbers is $5 - 7i$, we should naturally see what happens when we multiply by its complex conjugate, $5 + 7i$.

$$(5 - 7i)(5 + 7i)$$
$$= 25 + 35i - 35i - 49i^2$$
$$= 25 - 49i^2$$
$$= 25 - 49(-1)$$
$$= 25 + 49$$
$$= 74$$

Huh...that's not 148. However, it is HALF of 148! So if we had, for example, $(5 - 7i)(5 + 7i)(2)$, that would indeed equal 148:

$(5 - 7i)(5 + 7i)(2)$
$= (74)(2)$
$= 148$

So all we need to do is take $(5 - 7i)(5 + 7i)(2)$ and express it in $(5 - 7i)(a + bi)$ form. To do that, just distribute that 2:

$(5 - 7i)(5 + 7i)(2)$
$= (5 - 7i)(10 + 14i)$

That tells us that $a = 10$ and $b = 14$, so $a + b = 24$.

200. **Answer: 972**

Topic(s): Working in Three Dimensions (p. 279); Circles, Radians, and a Little More Trigonometry (p. 258); Right Triangles and Basic Trigonometry (p. 249)

Yikes, right? But really, this isn't so bad, provided we know a few useful shortcuts for the occasional 3-D problem we might come across.

First, when a cube is inscribed in a sphere, its long diagonal is the same as the sphere's diameter.

Second, the long diagonal of a cube has a length of $\sqrt{3}$ times the length of one of the cube's edges.

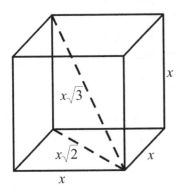

If we know those, then all we have to do here is calculate the long diagonal/diameter length, divide it by 2 to get the radius, and plug that radius into the formula for the volume of a sphere.

$d = \left(6\sqrt{3}\right)\sqrt{3}$
$d = 6(3)$
$d = 18$
$r = 9$

$V = \dfrac{4}{3}\pi\left(9^3\right)$

$V = \dfrac{4}{3}729\pi$

$V = 972\pi$

Therefore, the value of a is 972.

Official Test Breakdown

What follows is a listing of every question in the free downloads/Official SAT Study Guide and which techniques or concepts in this guide apply. This section is meant to be used as an after-test reference, not as a during-test road map. Work through the tests on your own, and then use this section to keep track of the history of your mistakes by highlighting the questions you missed, guessed on, or struggled with before getting right. Later in your prep process, use this section to revisit the questions that used to give you trouble, to make sure that the lessons you learned from them stuck.

Please note that when I say that a question is a plug in question, that's because it *could* be solved that way. It might just be a solve-it-in-your-head algebra question for you. *That's fine.* But even if you're not going to use techniques on the easiest questions, it's good for you to recognize opportunities to apply them. This is how it becomes easier for you to recognize the same opportunities on harder questions. This is part of becoming nimble.

Finally, note that I keep a running database of Official Test questions that I've solved thoroughly on my website, PWNTestPrep.com. Chances are very good that if you find a math problem you can't solve in the Official Tests, I've explained it in detail on the Q&A page. If I haven't, all you need to do is ask!

Test 1

Date taken: _____   # correct: _____   Score: _____

Calculator allowed?	Grid-in?	Question #	Techniques and concepts
N	N	1	Algebraic Manipulation (p. 52)
N	N	2	Complex Numbers (p. 292)
N	N	3	Translating between Words and Math (p. 44)
N	N	4	Translating between Words and Math (p. 44)
N	N	5	Algebraic Manipulation (p. 52)
N	N	6	Translating between Words and Math (p. 44)
N	N	7	Algebraic Manipulation (p. 52)
N	N	8	Plugging In (p. 24), Algebraic Manipulation (p. 52)
N	N	9	Backsolving (p. 32), Solving Systems of Linear Equations (p. 59)
N	N	10	Functions (p. 92)
N	N	11	Solving Systems of Linear Equations (p. 59)
N	N	12	Lines (p. 73)
N	N	13	Plugging In (p. 24), Algebraic Manipulation (p. 52)
N	N	14	Plugging In (p. 24), Exponents and Exponential Functions (p. 104)
N	N	15	Polynomials (p. 142)
N	Y	16	Algebraic Manipulation (p. 52)
N	Y	17	Angles, Triangles, and Polygons (p. 236)
N	Y	18	Solving Systems of Linear Equations (p. 59)
N	Y	19	Right Triangles and Basic Trigonometry (p. 249)
N	Y	20	Exponents and Exponential Functions (p. 104)
Y	N	1	Data Analysis 1 (p. 195)
Y	N	2	Ratios and Proportionality (p. 171)
Y	N	3	Angles, Triangles, and Polygons (p. 236)
Y	N	4	Translating between Words and Math (p. 44)
Y	N	5	Data Analysis 2 (p. 203)
Y	N	6	Ratios and Proportionality (p. 171)
Y	N	7	Data Analysis 1 (p. 195)
Y	N	8	Backsolving (p. 32), Absolute Value (p. 82)
Y	N	9	Algebraic Manipulation (p. 52)
Y	N	10	Backsolving (p. 32), Algebraic Manipulation (p. 52)
Y	N	11	Backsolving (p. 32), Algebraic Manipulation (p. 52)
Y	N	12	Data Analysis 2 (p. 203), Measures of Central Tendency and Variability (p. 182)
Y	N	13	Data Analysis 1 (p. 195), Percents and Percent Change (p. 161)
Y	N	14	Data Analysis 1 (p. 195), Measures of Central Tendency and Variability (p. 182)
Y	N	15	Data Analysis 1 (p. 195), Lines (p. 73)
Y	N	16	Data Analysis 1 (p. 195), Lines (p. 73)
Y	N	17	Functions (p. 92)
Y	N	18	Solving Systems of Linear Equations (p. 59)
Y	N	19	Backsolving (p. 32), Translating between Words and Math (p. 44), Solving Systems of Linear Equations (p. 59)
Y	N	20	Backsolving (p. 32), Translating between Words and Math (p. 44), Percents and Percent Change (p. 161)
Y	N	21	Data Analysis 1 (p. 195)
Y	N	22	Data Analysis 1 (p. 195)
Y	N	23	Data Analysis 1 (p. 195), Ratios and Proportionality (p. 171)
Y	N	24	Circles, Radians, and a Little More Trigonometry (p. 258)
Y	N	25	Backsolving (p. 32), Quadratics (p. 114)
Y	N	26	Backsolving (p. 32), Percents and Percent Change (p. 161)
Y	N	27	Data Analysis 1 (p. 195)
Y	N	28	Solving Systems of Linear Equations (p. 59)
Y	N	29	Polynomials (p. 142)
Y	N	30	Parabolas (p. 128)
Y	Y	31	Plugging In (p. 24), Translating between Words and Math (p. 44)
Y	Y	32	Translating between Words and Math (p. 44), Percents and Percent Change (p. 161)
Y	Y	33	Data Analysis 1 (p. 195)
Y	Y	34	Ratios and Proportionality (p. 171)
Y	Y	35	Working in Three Dimensions (p. 279)
Y	Y	36	Quadratics (p. 114)
Y	Y	37	Exponents and Exponential Functions (p. 104)
Y	Y	38	Exponents and Exponential Functions (p. 104)

Test 2

Date taken: _____   # correct: _____   Score: _____

Calculator allowed?	Grid-in?	Question #	Techniques and concepts
N	N	1	Algebraic Manipulation (p. 52)
N	N	2	Backsolving (p. 32), Solving Systems of Linear Equations (p. 59)
N	N	3	Translating between Words and Math (p. 44)
N	N	4	Plugging In (p. 24), Binomial Squares and Difference of Two Squares (p. 123)
N	N	5	Backsolving (p. 32), Algebraic Manipulation (p. 52), Quadratics (p. 114)
N	N	6	Backsolving (p. 32), Angles, Triangles, and Polygons (p. 236), Lines (p. 73)
N	N	7	Exponents and Exponential Functions (p. 104)
N	N	8	Backsolving (p. 32), Angles, Triangles, and Polygons (p. 236)
N	N	9	Lines (p. 73), Solving Systems of Linear Equations (p. 59)
N	N	10	Functions (p. 92)
N	N	11	Complex Numbers (p. 292)
N	N	12	Algebraic Manipulation (p. 52)
N	N	13	Quadratics (p. 114)
N	N	14	Translating between Words and Math (p. 44), Exponents and Exponential Functions (p. 104)
N	N	15	Plugging In (p. 24), Polynomials (p. 142)
N	Y	16	Translating between Words and Math (p. 44)
N	Y	17	Algebraic Manipulation (p. 52), Polynomials (p. 142)
N	Y	18	Angles, Triangles, and Polygons (p. 236)
N	Y	19	Circles, Radians, and a Little More Trigonometry (p. 258), Right Triangles and Basic Trigonometry (p. 249)
N	Y	20	Lines (p. 73), Solving Systems of Linear Equations (p. 59)
Y	N	1	Plugging In (p. 24), Translating between Words and Math (p. 44)
Y	N	2	Ratios and Proportionality (p. 171)
Y	N	3	Backsolving (p. 32), Algebraic Manipulation (p. 52)
Y	N	4	Ratios and Proportionality (p. 171)
Y	N	5	Percents and Percent Change (p. 161)
Y	N	6	Translating between Words and Math (p. 44)
Y	N	7	Parabolas (p. 128)
Y	N	8	Backsolving (p. 32), Translating between Words and Math (p. 44)
Y	N	9	Translating between Words and Math (p. 44)
Y	N	10	Functions (p. 92)
Y	N	11	Data Analysis 1 (p. 195)
Y	N	12	Translating between Words and Math (p. 44)
Y	N	13	Designing and Interpreting Experiments and Studies (p. 224)
Y	N	14	Data Analysis 2 (p. 203)
Y	N	15	Ratios and Proportionality (p. 171)
Y	N	16	Data Analysis 1 (p. 195)
Y	N	17	Percents and Percent Change (p. 161)
Y	N	18	Measures of Central Tendency and Variability (p. 182)
Y	N	19	Data Analysis 1 (p. 195), Measures of Central Tendency and Variability (p. 182)
Y	N	20	Data Analysis 1 (p. 195), Ratios and Proportionality (p. 171)
Y	N	21	Translating between Words and Math (p. 44)
Y	N	22	Algebraic Manipulation (p. 52)
Y	N	23	Plugging In (p. 24), Translating between Words and Math (p. 44)
Y	N	24	Circles, Radians, and a Little More Trigonometry (p. 258)
Y	N	25	Plugging In (p. 24), Lines (p. 73)
Y	N	26	Functions (p. 92)
Y	N	27	Data Analysis 2 (p. 203)
Y	N	28	Lines (p. 73)
Y	N	29	Backsolving (p. 32), Parabolas (p. 128)
Y	N	30	Angles, Triangles, and Polygons (p. 236)
Y	Y	31	Ratios and Proportionality (p. 171)
Y	Y	32	Ratios and Proportionality (p. 171)
Y	Y	33	Functions (p. 92)
Y	Y	34	Translating between Words and Math (p. 44), Solving Systems of Linear Equations (p. 59)
Y	Y	35	Translating between Words and Math (p. 44)
Y	Y	36	Circles, Radians, and a Little More Trigonometry (p. 258), Angles, Triangles, and Polygons (p. 236)
Y	Y	37	Translating between Words and Math (p. 44)
Y	Y	38	Translating between Words and Math (p. 44)

Test 3

Date taken: _____ # correct: _____ Score: _____

Calculator allowed?	Grid-in?	Question #	Techniques and concepts
N	N	1	Translating between Words and Math (p. 44)
N	N	2	Algebraic Manipulation (p. 52)
N	N	3	Exponents and Exponential Functions (p. 104)
N	N	4	Translating between Words and Math (p. 44)
N	N	5	Algebraic Manipulation (p. 52)
N	N	6	Solving Systems of Linear Equations (p. 59)
N	N	7	Functions (p. 92), Polynomials (p. 142)
N	N	8	Lines (p. 73)
N	N	9	Lines (p. 73)
N	N	10	Parabolas (p. 128)
N	N	11	Plugging In (p. 24), Angles, Triangles, and Polygons (p. 236)
N	N	12	Parabolas (p. 128)
N	N	13	Backsolving (p. 32), Polynomials (p. 142)
N	N	14	Quadratics (p. 114)
N	N	15	Translating between Words and Math (p. 44)
N	Y	16	Algebraic Manipulation (p. 52), Polynomials (p. 142)
N	Y	17	Algebraic Manipulation (p. 52)
N	Y	18	Angles, Triangles, and Polygons (p. 236)
N	Y	19	Translating between Words and Math (p. 44), Solving Systems of Linear Equations (p. 59)
N	Y	20	Right Triangles and Basic Trigonometry (p. 249)
Y	N	1	Data Analysis 1 (p. 195)
Y	N	2	Data Analysis 1 (p. 195)
Y	N	3	Data Analysis 1 (p. 195)
Y	N	4	Functions (p. 92), Lines (p. 73)
Y	N	5	Percents and Percent Change (p. 161)
Y	N	6	Algebraic Manipulation (p. 52)
Y	N	7	Algebraic Manipulation (p. 52)
Y	N	8	Translating between Words and Math (p. 44)
Y	N	9	Ratios and Proportionality (p. 171)
Y	N	10	Data Analysis 1 (p. 195)
Y	N	11	Data Analysis 1 (p. 195)
Y	N	12	Polynomials (p. 142)
Y	N	13	Plugging In (p. 24), Algebraic Manipulation (p. 52)
Y	N	14	Plugging In (p. 24), Translating between Words and Math (p. 44), Ratios and Proportionality (p. 171)
Y	N	15	Designing and Interpreting Experiments and Studies (p. 224)
Y	N	16	Backsolving (p. 32), Functions (p. 92), Parabolas (p. 128)
Y	N	17	Translating between Words and Math (p. 44)
Y	N	18	Solving Systems of Linear Equations (p. 59)
Y	N	19	Ratios and Proportionality (p. 171)
Y	N	20	Data Analysis 2 (p. 203)
Y	N	21	Exponents and Exponential Functions (p. 104)
Y	N	22	Backsolving (p. 32), Translating between Words and Math (p. 44)
Y	N	23	Right Triangles and Basic Trigonometry (p. 249)
Y	N	24	Backsolving (p. 32), Translating between Words and Math (p. 44), Solving Systems of Linear Equations (p. 59)
Y	N	25	Working in Three Dimensions (p. 279)
Y	N	26	Backsolving (p. 32), Lines (p. 73)
Y	N	27	Backsolving (p. 32), Percents and Percent Change (p. 161)
Y	N	28	Exponents and Exponential Functions (p. 104)
Y	N	29	Data Analysis 1 (p. 195), Solving Systems of Linear Equations (p. 59)
Y	N	30	Algebraic Manipulation (p. 52)
Y	Y	31	Translating between Words and Math (p. 44)
Y	Y	32	Data Analysis 1 (p. 195), Measures of Central Tendency and Variability (p. 182)
Y	Y	33	Algebraic Manipulation (p. 52)
Y	Y	34	Circles, Radians, and a Little More Trigonometry (p. 258)
Y	Y	35	Translating between Words and Math (p. 44), Measures of Central Tendency and Variability (p. 182)
Y	Y	36	Solving Systems of Linear Equations (p. 59)
Y	Y	37	Translating between Words and Math (p. 44)
Y	Y	38	Translating between Words and Math (p. 44), Ratios and Proportionality (p. 171)

Test 4

Date taken: _____   # correct: _____   Score: _____

Calculator allowed?	Grid-in?	Question #	Techniques and concepts
N	N	1	Absolute Value (p. 82)
N	N	2	Functions (p. 92)
N	N	3	Solving Systems of Linear Equations (p. 59)
N	N	4	Functions (p. 92)
N	N	5	Plugging In (p. 24), Algebraic Manipulation (p. 52)
N	N	6	Plugging In (p. 24), Algebraic Manipulation (p. 52)
N	N	7	Translating between Words and Math (p. 44)
N	N	8	Lines (p. 73)
N	N	9	Backsolving (p. 32), Algebraic Manipulation (p. 52), Quadratics (p. 114)
N	N	10	Algebraic Manipulation (p. 52)
N	N	11	Working with Advanced Systems of Equations (p. 152), Parabolas (p. 128)
N	N	12	Plugging In (p. 24), Translating between Words and Math (p. 44)
N	N	13	Backsolving (p. 32), Parabolas (p. 128), Algebraic Manipulation (p. 52), Quadratics (p. 114), Working with Advanced Systems of Equations (p. 152)
N	N	14	Complex Numbers (p. 292), Algebraic Manipulation (p. 52)
N	N	15	Quadratics (p. 114)
N	Y	16	Angles, Triangles, and Polygons (p. 236), Ratios and Proportionality (p. 171)
N	Y	17	Right Triangles and Basic Trigonometry (p. 249)
N	Y	18	Polynomials (p. 142)
N	Y	19	Solving Systems of Linear Equations (p. 59)
N	Y	20	Translating between Words and Math (p. 44)
Y	N	1	Backsolving (p. 32), Translating between Words and Math (p. 44)
Y	N	2	Translating between Words and Math (p. 44)
Y	N	3	Translating between Words and Math (p. 44), Ratios and Proportionality (p. 171)
Y	N	4	Ratios and Proportionality (p. 171)
Y	N	5	Translating between Words and Math (p. 44)
Y	N	6	Backsolving (p. 32), Translating between Words and Math (p. 44), Solving Systems of Linear Equations (p. 59)
Y	N	7	Data Analysis 1 (p. 195), Ratios and Proportionality (p. 171)
Y	N	8	Lines (p. 73)
Y	N	9	Data Analysis 1 (p. 195), Ratios and Proportionality (p. 171)
Y	N	10	Data Analysis 2 (p. 203)
Y	N	11	Data Analysis 2 (p. 203)
Y	N	12	Functions (p. 92)
Y	N	13	Exponents and Exponential Functions (p. 104)
Y	N	14	Exponents and Exponential Functions (p. 104)
Y	N	15	Data Analysis 2 (p. 203), Exponents and Exponential Functions (p. 104)
Y	N	16	Data Analysis 1 (p. 195), Translating between Words and Math (p. 44), Solving Systems of Linear Equations (p. 59)
Y	N	17	Data Analysis 1 (p. 195), Translating between Words and Math (p. 44), Lines (p. 73)
Y	N	18	Working in Three Dimensions (p. 279)
Y	N	19	Algebraic Manipulation (p. 52)
Y	N	20	Data Analysis 2 (p. 203), Exponents and Exponential Functions (p. 104)
Y	N	21	Data Analysis 2 (p. 203)
Y	N	22	Data Analysis 1 (p. 195), Percents and Percent Change (p. 161)
Y	N	23	Data Analysis 1 (p. 195), Measures of Central Tendency and Variability (p. 182)
Y	N	24	Circles, Radians, and a Little More Trigonometry (p. 258)
Y	N	25	Polynomials (p. 142)
Y	N	26	Plugging In (p. 24), Absolute Value (p. 82)
Y	N	27	Data Analysis 2 (p. 203)
Y	N	28	Parabolas (p. 128)
Y	N	29	Plugging In (p. 24), Measures of Central Tendency and Variability (p. 182)
Y	N	30	Functions (p. 92), Polynomials (p. 142)
Y	Y	31	Translating between Words and Math (p. 44)
Y	Y	32	Translating between Words and Math (p. 44)
Y	Y	33	Ratios and Proportionality (p. 171)
Y	Y	34	Translating between Words and Math (p. 44)
Y	Y	35	Translating between Words and Math (p. 44)
Y	Y	36	Circles, Radians, and a Little More Trigonometry (p. 258)
Y	Y	37	Translating between Words and Math (p. 44), Exponents and Exponential Functions (p. 104)
Y	Y	38	Translating between Words and Math (p. 44), Exponents and Exponential Functions (p. 104)

Test 5

Date taken: _____   # correct: _____   Score: _____

Calculator allowed?	Grid-in?	Question #	Techniques and concepts
N	N	1	Lines (p. 73)
N	N	2	Circles, Radians, and a Little More Trigonometry (p. 258)
N	N	3	Backsolving (p. 32), Quadratics (p. 114)
N	N	4	Parabolas (p. 128)
N	N	5	Backsolving (p. 32), Algebraic Manipulation (p. 52)
N	N	6	Algebraic Manipulation (p. 52)
N	N	7	Translating between Words and Math (p. 44)
N	N	8	Translating between Words and Math (p. 44)
N	N	9	Working with Advanced Systems of Equations (p. 152)
N	N	10	Binomial Squares and Difference of Two Squares (p. 123)
N	N	11	Working in Three Dimensions (p. 279)
N	N	12	Exponents and Exponential Functions (p. 104)
N	N	13	Plugging In (p. 24), Translating between Words and Math (p. 44)
N	N	14	Functions (p. 92), Exponents and Exponential Functions (p. 104)
N	N	15	Translating between Words and Math (p. 44), Algebraic Manipulation (p. 52)
N	Y	16	Translating between Words and Math (p. 44), Algebraic Manipulation (p. 52)
N	Y	17	Algebraic Manipulation (p. 52)
N	Y	18	Solving Systems of Linear Equations (p. 59)
N	Y	19	Algebraic Manipulation (p. 52)
N	Y	20	Angles, Triangles, and Polygons (p. 236)
Y	N	1	Data Analysis 1 (p. 195)
Y	N	2	Functions (p. 92)
Y	N	3	Ratios and Proportionality (p. 171)
Y	N	4	Algebraic Manipulation (p. 52)
Y	N	5	Ratios and Proportionality (p. 171)
Y	N	6	Backsolving (p. 32), Translating between Words and Math (p. 44), Solving Systems of Linear Equations (p. 59)
Y	N	7	Translating between Words and Math (p. 44)
Y	N	8	Algebraic Manipulation (p. 52)
Y	N	9	Ratios and Proportionality (p. 171)
Y	N	10	Algebraic Manipulation (p. 52)
Y	N	11	Lines (p. 73)
Y	N	12	Solving Systems of Linear Equations (p. 59)
Y	N	13	Lines (p. 73), Solving Systems of Linear Equations (p. 59)
Y	N	14	Data Analysis 1 (p. 195)
Y	N	15	Designing and Interpreting Experiments and Studies (p. 224)
Y	N	16	Ratios and Proportionality (p. 171)
Y	N	17	Data Analysis 2 (p. 203), Ratios and Proportionality (p. 171)
Y	N	18	Ratios and Proportionality (p. 171)
Y	N	19	Right Triangles and Basic Trigonometry (p. 249)
Y	N	20	Circles, Radians, and a Little More Trigonometry (p. 258)
Y	N	21	Plugging In (p. 24), Algebraic Manipulation (p. 52)
Y	N	22	Ratios and Proportionality (p. 171), Designing and Interpreting Experiments and Studies (p. 224)
Y	N	23	Functions (p. 92)
Y	N	24	Backsolving (p. 32), Percents and Percent Change (p. 161)
Y	N	25	Translating between Words and Math (p. 44), Percents and Percent Change (p. 161)
Y	N	26	Working in Three Dimensions (p. 279), Algebraic Manipulation (p. 52)
Y	N	27	Measures of Central Tendency and Variability (p. 182)
Y	N	28	Lines (p. 73), Functions (p. 92)
Y	N	29	Circles, Radians, and a Little More Trigonometry (p. 258)
Y	N	30	Binomial Squares and Difference of Two Squares (p. 123)
Y	Y	31	Ratios and Proportionality (p. 171)
Y	Y	32	Ratios and Proportionality (p. 171)
Y	Y	33	Algebraic Manipulation (p. 52)
Y	Y	34	Functions (p. 92)
Y	Y	35	Translating between Words and Math (p. 44), Quadratics (p. 114)
Y	Y	36	Circles, Radians, and a Little More Trigonometry (p. 258), Angles, Triangles, and Polygons (p. 236)
Y	Y	37	Ratios and Proportionality (p. 171)
Y	Y	38	Ratios and Proportionality (p. 171), Percents and Percent Change (p. 161)

Test 6

Date taken: _____   # correct: _____   Score: _____

Calculator allowed?	Grid-in?	Question #	Techniques and concepts
N	N	1	Translating between Words and Math (p. 44)
N	N	2	Translating between Words and Math (p. 44)
N	N	3	Complex Numbers (p. 292)
N	N	4	Backsolving (p. 32), Binomial Squares and Difference of Two Squares (p. 123)
N	N	5	Lines (p. 73)
N	N	6	Algebraic Manipulation (p. 52)
N	N	7	Plugging In (p. 24), Algebraic Manipulation (p. 52)
N	N	8	Functions (p. 92)
N	N	9	Exponents and Exponential Functions (p. 104)
N	N	10	Measures of Central Tendency and Variability (p. 182)
N	N	11	Parabolas (p. 128)
N	N	12	Plugging In (p. 24), Polynomials (p. 142)
N	N	13	Backsolving (p. 32), Quadratics (p. 114)
N	N	14	Translating between Words and Math (p. 44)
N	N	15	Binomial Squares and Difference of Two Squares (p. 123)
N	Y	16	Exponents and Exponential Functions (p. 104)
N	Y	17	Algebraic Manipulation (p. 52)
N	Y	18	Angles, Triangles, and Polygons (p. 236), Right Triangles and Basic Trigonometry (p. 249)
N	Y	19	Translating between Words and Math (p. 44), Percents and Percent Change (p. 161)
N	Y	20	Circles, Radians, and a Little More Trigonometry (p. 258)
Y	N	1	Algebraic Manipulation (p. 52)
Y	N	2	Translating between Words and Math (p. 44), Lines (p. 73)
Y	N	3	Translating between Words and Math (p. 44)
Y	N	4	Backsolving (p. 32), Translating between Words and Math (p. 44)
Y	N	5	Algebraic Manipulation (p. 52)
Y	N	6	Data Analysis 1 (p. 195)
Y	N	7	Designing and Interpreting Experiments and Studies (p. 224)
Y	N	8	Data Analysis 1 (p. 195)
Y	N	9	Translating between Words and Math (p. 44)
Y	N	10	Backsolving (p. 32), Translating between Words and Math (p. 44)
Y	N	11	Solving Systems of Linear Equations (p. 59)
Y	N	12	Data Analysis 1 (p. 195)
Y	N	13	Data Analysis 1 (p. 195)
Y	N	14	Lines (p. 73)
Y	N	15	Functions (p. 92)
Y	N	16	Angles, Triangles, and Polygons (p. 236)
Y	N	17	Algebraic Manipulation (p. 52)
Y	N	18	Translating between Words and Math (p. 44)
Y	N	19	Translating between Words and Math (p. 44)
Y	N	20	Quadratics (p. 114)
Y	N	21	Designing and Interpreting Experiments and Studies (p. 224)
Y	N	22	Data Analysis 1 (p. 195), Measures of Central Tendency and Variability (p. 182)
Y	N	23	Translating between Words and Math (p. 44), Data Analysis 1 (p. 195)
Y	N	24	Percents and Percent Change (p. 161)
Y	N	25	Functions (p. 92), Lines (p. 73)
Y	N	26	Ratios and Proportionality (p. 171)
Y	N	27	Circles, Radians, and a Little More Trigonometry (p. 258)
Y	N	28	Plugging In (p. 24), Absolute Value (p. 82)
Y	N	29	Translating between Words and Math (p. 44), Algebraic Manipulation (p. 52)
Y	N	30	Data Analysis 2 (p. 203), Parabolas (p. 128)
Y	Y	31	Translating between Words and Math (p. 44), Algebraic Manipulation (p. 52)
Y	Y	32	Algebraic Manipulation (p. 52)
Y	Y	33	Translating between Words and Math (p. 44), Working in Three Dimensions (p. 279)
Y	Y	34	Working with Advanced Systems of Equations (p. 152)
Y	Y	35	Lines (p. 73)
Y	Y	36	Data Analysis 1 (p. 195), Measures of Central Tendency and Variability (p. 182)
Y	Y	37	Translating between Words and Math (p. 44), Exponents and Exponential Functions (p. 104)
Y	Y	38	Translating between Words and Math (p. 44), Percents and Percent Change (p. 161)

Test 7

Date taken: _____ # correct: _____ Score: _____

Calculator allowed?	Grid-in?	Question #	Techniques and concepts
N	N	1	Translating between Words and Math (p. 44)
N	N	2	Algebraic Manipulation (p. 52)
N	N	3	Backsolving (p. 32), Solving Systems of Linear Equations (p. 59)
N	N	4	Complex Numbers (p. 292)
N	N	5	Functions (p. 92)
N	N	6	Translating between Words and Math (p. 44), Lines (p. 73)
N	N	7	Plugging In (p. 24), Backsolving (p. 32), Parabolas (p. 128)
N	N	8	Backsolving (p. 32), Translating between Words and Math (p. 44)
N	N	9	Translating between Words and Math (p. 44)
N	N	10	Polynomials (p. 142)
N	N	11	Exponents and Exponential Functions (p. 104)
N	N	12	Parabolas (p. 128)
N	N	13	Plugging In (p. 24), Polynomials (p. 142)
N	N	14	Translating between Words and Math (p. 44)
N	N	15	Backsolving (p. 32), Binomial Squares and Difference of Two Squares (p. 123)
N	Y	16	Algebraic Manipulation (p. 52)
N	Y	17	Angles, Triangles, and Polygons (p. 236)
N	Y	18	Circles, Radians, and a Little More Trigonometry (p. 258)
N	Y	19	Lines (p. 73)
N	Y	20	Algebraic Manipulation (p. 52)
Y	N	1	Data Analysis 1 (p. 195)
Y	N	2	Plugging In (p. 24), Algebraic Manipulation (p. 52)
Y	N	3	Ratios and Proportionality (p. 171)
Y	N	4	Designing and Interpreting Experiments and Studies (p. 224)
Y	N	5	Backsolving (p. 32), Lines (p. 73)
Y	N	6	Backsolving (p. 32), Algebraic Manipulation (p. 52)
Y	N	7	Data Analysis 2 (p. 203)
Y	N	8	Data Analysis 2 (p. 203)
Y	N	9	Algebraic Manipulation (p. 52)
Y	N	10	Ratios and Proportionality (p. 171)
Y	N	11	Translating between Words and Math (p. 44)
Y	N	12	Percents and Percent Change (p. 161)
Y	N	13	Data Analysis 1 (p. 195)
Y	N	14	Backsolving (p. 32), Angles, Triangles, and Polygons (p. 236)
Y	N	15	Ratios and Proportionality (p. 171)
Y	N	16	Solving Systems of Linear Equations (p. 59)
Y	N	17	Translating between Words and Math (p. 44), Lines (p. 73)
Y	N	18	Data Analysis 2 (p. 203)
Y	N	19	Algebraic Manipulation (p. 52)
Y	N	20	Algebraic Manipulation (p. 52)
Y	N	21	Data Analysis 2 (p. 203), Lines (p. 73)
Y	N	22	Data Analysis 1 (p. 195), Measures of Central Tendency and Variability (p. 182)
Y	N	23	Working in Three Dimensions (p. 279)
Y	N	24	Parabolas (p. 128)
Y	N	25	Backsolving (p. 32), Data Analysis 1 (p. 195), Ratios and Proportionality (p. 171)
Y	N	26	Data Analysis 1 (p. 195), Translating between Words and Math (p. 44), Algebraic Manipulation (p. 52)
Y	N	27	Exponents and Exponential Functions (p. 104)
Y	N	28	Lines (p. 73)
Y	N	29	Circles, Radians, and a Little More Trigonometry (p. 258)
Y	N	30	Percents and Percent Change (p. 161)
Y	Y	31	Ratios and Proportionality (p. 171)
Y	Y	32	Lines (p. 73)
Y	Y	33	Translating between Words and Math (p. 44), Solving Systems of Linear Equations (p. 59)
Y	Y	34	Circles, Radians, and a Little More Trigonometry (p. 258)
Y	Y	35	Quadratics (p. 114), Working with Advanced Systems of Equations (p. 152)
Y	Y	36	Right Triangles and Basic Trigonometry (p. 249)
Y	Y	37	Data Analysis 1 (p. 195), Measures of Central Tendency and Variability (p. 182)
Y	Y	38	Data Analysis 1 (p. 195)

Test 8

Date taken: _____   # correct: _____   Score: _____

Calculator allowed?	Grid-in?	Question #	Techniques and concepts
N	N	1	Backsolving (p. 32), Algebraic Manipulation (p. 52)
N	N	2	Lines (p. 73)
N	N	3	Algebraic Manipulation (p. 52)
N	N	4	Angles, Triangles, and Polygons (p. 236)
N	N	5	Plugging In (p. 24), Translating between Words and Math (p. 44)
N	N	6	Plugging In (p. 24), Solving Systems of Linear Equations (p. 59)
N	N	7	Backsolving (p. 32), Quadratics (p. 114)
N	N	8	Plugging In (p. 24), Binomial Squares and Difference of Two Squares (p. 123), Quadratics (p. 114)
N	N	9	Circles, Radians, and a Little More Trigonometry (p. 258)
N	N	10	Backsolving (p. 32), Translating between Words and Math (p. 44), Lines (p. 73)
N	N	11	Polynomials (p. 142)
N	N	12	Algebraic Manipulation (p. 52)
N	N	13	Backsolving (p. 32), Translating between Words and Math (p. 44), Lines (p. 73)
N	N	14	Quadratics (p. 114)
N	N	15	Functions (p. 92)
N	Y	16	Quadratics (p. 114)
N	Y	17	Polynomials (p. 142)
N	Y	18	Solving Systems of Linear Equations (p. 59)
N	Y	19	Translating between Words and Math (p. 44), Lines (p. 73)
N	Y	20	Circles, Radians, and a Little More Trigonometry (p. 258)
Y	N	1	Plugging In (p. 24), Translating between Words and Math (p. 44)
Y	N	2	Data Analysis 1 (p. 195)
Y	N	3	Ratios and Proportionality (p. 171)
Y	N	4	Data Analysis 2 (p. 203)
Y	N	5	Angles, Triangles, and Polygons (p. 236)
Y	N	6	Translating between Words and Math (p. 44)
Y	N	7	Translating between Words and Math (p. 44), Lines (p. 73)
Y	N	8	Backsolving (p. 32), Algebraic Manipulation (p. 52), Quadratics (p. 114)
Y	N	9	Backsolving (p. 32), Algebraic Manipulation (p. 52)
Y	N	10	Data Analysis 1 (p. 195)
Y	N	11	Ratios and Proportionality (p. 171)
Y	N	12	Translating between Words and Math (p. 44)
Y	N	13	Plugging In (p. 24), Exponents and Exponential Functions (p. 104)
Y	N	14	Backsolving (p. 32), Quadratics (p. 114)
Y	N	15	Translating between Words and Math (p. 44), Working in Three Dimensions (p. 279)
Y	N	16	Data Analysis 1 (p. 195)
Y	N	17	Data Analysis 2 (p. 203), Measures of Central Tendency and Variability (p. 182)
Y	N	18	Data Analysis 2 (p. 203)
Y	N	19	Polynomials (p. 142), Quadratics (p. 114)
Y	N	20	Translating between Words and Math (p. 44)
Y	N	21	Translating between Words and Math (p. 44), Lines (p. 73)
Y	N	22	Percents and Percent Change (p. 161)
Y	N	23	Plugging In (p. 24), Exponents and Exponential Functions (p. 104)
Y	N	24	Designing and Interpreting Experiments and Studies (p. 224)
Y	N	25	Plugging In (p. 24), Lines (p. 73)
Y	N	26	Designing and Interpreting Experiments and Studies (p. 224)
Y	N	27	Solving Systems of Linear Equations (p. 59), Algebraic Manipulation (p. 52)
Y	N	28	Measures of Central Tendency and Variability (p. 182)
Y	N	29	Translating between Words and Math (p. 44), Lines (p. 73), Percents and Percent Change (p. 161)
Y	N	30	Functions (p. 92)
Y	Y	31	Ratios and Proportionality (p. 171)
Y	Y	32	Algebraic Manipulation (p. 52)
Y	Y	33	Lines (p. 73)
Y	Y	34	Ratios and Proportionality (p. 171)
Y	Y	35	Lines (p. 73), Working with Advanced Systems of Equations (p. 152), Functions (p. 92)
Y	Y	36	Plugging In (p. 24), Right Triangles and Basic Trigonometry (p. 249)
Y	Y	37	Data Analysis 1 (p. 195), Translating between Words and Math (p. 44)
Y	Y	38	Data Analysis 1 (p. 195), Exponents and Exponential Functions (p. 104), Functions (p. 92)

Test 9

Date taken: _____   # correct: _____   Score: _____

Calculator allowed?	Grid-in?	Question #	Techniques and concepts
N	N	1	Solving Systems of Linear Equations (p. 59)
N	N	2	Algebraic Manipulation (p. 52)
N	N	3	Lines (p. 73)
N	N	4	Translating between Words and Math (p. 44)
N	N	5	Translating between Words and Math (p. 44)
N	N	6	Circles, Radians, and a Little More Trigonometry (p. 258)
N	N	7	Backsolving (p. 32), Algebraic Manipulation (p. 52)
N	N	8	Lines (p. 73), Algebraic Manipulation (p. 52)
N	N	9	Working with Advanced Systems of Equations (p. 152)
N	N	10	Polynomials (p. 142)
N	N	11	Backsolving (p. 32), Quadratics (p. 114), Algebraic Manipulation (p. 52)
N	N	12	Plugging In (p. 24), Algebraic Manipulation (p. 52)
N	N	13	Parabolas (p. 128)
N	N	14	Lines (p. 73)
N	N	15	Backsolving (p. 32), Quadratics (p. 114)
N	Y	16	Working in Three Dimensions (p. 279)
N	Y	17	Algebraic Manipulation (p. 52)
N	Y	18	Functions (p. 92)
N	Y	19	Right Triangles and Basic Trigonometry (p. 249)
N	Y	20	Lines (p. 73), Functions (p. 92)
Y	N	1	Backsolving (p. 32), Algebraic Manipulation (p. 52)
Y	N	2	Ratios and Proportionality (p. 171)
Y	N	3	Algebraic Manipulation (p. 52)
Y	N	4	Exponents and Exponential Functions (p. 104)
Y	N	5	Data Analysis 1 (p. 195)
Y	N	6	Data Analysis 1 (p. 195)
Y	N	7	Angles, Triangles, and Polygons (p. 236)
Y	N	8	Data Analysis 1 (p. 195), Lines (p. 73)
Y	N	9	Data Analysis 1 (p. 195)
Y	N	10	Translating between Words and Math (p. 44)
Y	N	11	Ratios and Proportionality (p. 171)
Y	N	12	Ratios and Proportionality (p. 171)
Y	N	13	Backsolving (p. 32), Translating between Words and Math (p. 44), Solving Systems of Linear Equations (p. 59)
Y	N	14	Plugging In (p. 24), Translating between Words and Math (p. 44), Lines (p. 73)
Y	N	15	Backsolving (p. 32), Lines (p. 73)
Y	N	16	Algebraic Manipulation (p. 52)
Y	N	17	Solving Systems of Linear Equations (p. 59)
Y	N	18	Plugging In (p. 24), Translating between Words and Math (p. 44)
Y	N	19	Backsolving (p. 32), Translating between Words and Math (p. 44), Solving Systems of Linear Equations (p. 59)
Y	N	20	Data Analysis 1 (p. 195), Lines (p. 73)
Y	N	21	Plugging In (p. 24), Exponents and Exponential Functions (p. 104)
Y	N	22	Measures of Central Tendency and Variability (p. 182)
Y	N	23	Designing and Interpreting Experiments and Studies (p. 224)
Y	N	24	Backsolving (p. 32), Functions (p. 92)
Y	N	25	Plugging In (p. 24), Right Triangles and Basic Trigonometry (p. 249)
Y	N	26	Parabolas (p. 128)
Y	N	27	Parabolas (p. 128), Polynomials (p. 142)
Y	N	28	Parabolas (p. 128)
Y	N	29	Data Analysis 2 (p. 203), Lines (p. 73)
Y	N	30	Data Analysis 2 (p. 203), Lines (p. 73)
Y	Y	31	Circles, Radians, and a Little More Trigonometry (p. 258), Right Triangles and Basic Trigonometry (p. 249)
Y	Y	32	Lines (p. 73)
Y	Y	33	Data Analysis 1 (p. 195)
Y	Y	34	Data Analysis 2 (p. 203), Measures of Central Tendency and Variability (p. 182)
Y	Y	35	Percents and Percent Change (p. 161)
Y	Y	36	Lines (p. 73), Solving Systems of Linear Equations (p. 59)
Y	Y	37	Data Analysis 1 (p. 195), Measures of Central Tendency and Variability (p. 182)
Y	Y	38	Data Analysis 1 (p. 195), Percents and Percent Change (p. 161)

Test 10

Date taken: _____   # correct: _____   Score: _____

Calculator allowed?	Grid-in?	Question #	Techniques and concepts
N	N	1	Backsolving (p. 32), Algebraic Manipulation (p. 52)
N	N	2	Translating between Words and Math (p. 44)
N	N	3	Functions (p. 92), Translating between Words and Math (p. 44)
N	N	4	Lines (p. 73), Functions (p. 92)
N	N	5	Plugging In (p. 24), Exponents and Exponential Functions (p. 104)
N	N	6	Backsolving (p. 32), Binomial Squares and Difference of Two Squares (p. 123)
N	N	7	Functions (p. 92)
N	N	8	Angles, Triangles, and Polygons (p. 236), Algebraic Manipulation (p. 52)
N	N	9	Lines (p. 73)
N	N	10	Parabolas (p. 128)
N	N	11	Circles, Radians, and a Little More Trigonometry (p. 258)
N	N	12	Angles, Triangles, and Polygons (p. 236), Right Triangles and Basic Trigonometry (p. 249)
N	N	13	Quadratics (p. 114), Parabolas (p. 128)
N	N	14	Backsolving (p. 32), Quadratics (p. 114)
N	N	15	Lines (p. 73)
N	Y	16	Translating between Words and Math (p. 44)
N	Y	17	Absolute Value (p. 82)
N	Y	18	Percents and Percent Change (p. 161)
N	Y	19	Solving Systems of Linear Equations (p. 59)
N	Y	20	Binomial Squares and Difference of Two Squares (p. 123)
Y	N	1	Plugging In (p. 24), Translating between Words and Math (p. 44), Lines (p. 73)
Y	N	2	Translating between Words and Math (p. 44), Data Analysis 1 (p. 195)
Y	N	3	Translating between Words and Math (p. 44), Data Analysis 1 (p. 195)
Y	N	4	Algebraic Manipulation (p. 52)
Y	N	5	Functions (p. 92)
Y	N	6	Algebraic Manipulation (p. 52)
Y	N	7	Designing and Interpreting Experiments and Studies (p. 224)
Y	N	8	Data Analysis 1 (p. 195)
Y	N	9	Functions (p. 92), Exponents and Exponential Functions (p. 104)
Y	N	10	Designing and Interpreting Experiments and Studies (p. 224)
Y	N	11	Measures of Central Tendency and Variability (p. 182)
Y	N	12	Percents and Percent Change (p. 161)
Y	N	13	Data Analysis 1 (p. 195)
Y	N	14	Ratios and Proportionality (p. 171), Data Analysis 1 (p. 195)
Y	N	15	Backsolving (p. 32), Working in Three Dimensions (p. 279)
Y	N	16	Backsolving (p. 32), Percents and Percent Change (p. 161)
Y	N	17	Algebraic Manipulation (p. 52)
Y	N	18	Data Analysis 1 (p. 195), Percents and Percent Change (p. 161)
Y	N	19	Parabolas (p. 128)
Y	N	20	Measures of Central Tendency and Variability (p. 182)
Y	N	21	Algebraic Manipulation (p. 52), Translating between Words and Math (p. 44)
Y	N	22	Exponents and Exponential Functions (p. 104), Translating between Words and Math (p. 44)
Y	N	23	Backsolving (p. 32), Lines (p. 73)
Y	N	24	Data Analysis 2 (p. 203)
Y	N	25	Solving Systems of Linear Equations (p. 59)
Y	N	26	Exponents and Exponential Functions (p. 104)
Y	N	27	Algebraic Manipulation (p. 52)
Y	N	28	Parabolas (p. 128)
Y	N	29	Translating between Words and Math (p. 44)
Y	N	30	Right Triangles and Basic Trigonometry (p. 249)
Y	Y	31	Translating between Words and Math (p. 44)
Y	Y	32	Angles, Triangles, and Polygons (p. 236)
Y	Y	33	Measures of Central Tendency and Variability (p. 182)
Y	Y	34	Plugging In (p. 24), Ratios and Proportionality (p. 171)
Y	Y	35	Polynomials (p. 142)
Y	Y	36	Parabolas (p. 128)
Y	Y	37	Ratios and Proportionality (p. 171)
Y	Y	38	Ratios and Proportionality (p. 171)

PSAT/NMSQT Test 1

Date taken: _____   # correct: _____   Score: _____

Calculator allowed?	Grid-in?	Question #	Techniques and concepts
N	N	1	Plugging In (p. 24), Translating between Words and Math (p. 44)
N	N	2	Algebraic Manipulation (p. 52)
N	N	3	Solving Systems of Linear Equations (p. 59)
N	N	4	Angles, Triangles, and Polygons (p. 236)
N	N	5	Backsolving (p. 32), Translating between Words and Math (p. 44)
N	N	6	Quadratics (p. 114)
N	N	7	Translating between Words and Math (p. 44), Algebraic Manipulation (p. 52)
N	N	8	Translating between Words and Math (p. 44)
N	N	9	Translating between Words and Math (p. 44)
N	N	10	Functions (p. 92)
N	N	11	Plugging In (p. 24), Algebraic Manipulation (p. 52)
N	N	12	Polynomials (p. 142)
N	N	13	Parabolas (p. 128)
N	Y	14	Algebraic Manipulation (p. 52)
N	Y	15	Algebraic Manipulation (p. 52)
N	Y	16	Algebraic Manipulation (p. 52)
N	Y	17	Quadratics (p. 114)
Y	N	1	Translating between Words and Math (p. 44)
Y	N	2	Translating between Words and Math (p. 44)
Y	N	3	Data Analysis 1 (p. 195)
Y	N	4	Algebraic Manipulation (p. 52)
Y	N	5	Solving Systems of Linear Equations (p. 59)
Y	N	6	Ratios and Proportionality (p. 171)
Y	N	7	Translating between Words and Math (p. 44), Ratios and Proportionality (p. 171)
Y	N	8	Lines (p. 73)
Y	N	9	Data Analysis 2 (p. 203)
Y	N	10	Percents and Percent Change (p. 161)
Y	N	11	Translating between Words and Math (p. 44)
Y	N	12	Data Analysis 2 (p. 203)
Y	N	13	Data Analysis 2 (p. 203), Measures of Central Tendency and Variability (p. 182)
Y	N	14	Data Analysis 1 (p. 195), Percents and Percent Change (p. 161)
Y	N	15	Data Analysis 1 (p. 195), Ratios and Proportionality (p. 171)
Y	N	16	Data Analysis 1 (p. 195), Ratios and Proportionality (p. 171)
Y	N	17	Data Analysis 1 (p. 195)
Y	N	18	Plugging In (p. 24), Angles, Triangles, and Polygons (p. 236), Percents and Percent Change (p. 161)
Y	N	19	Percents and Percent Change (p. 161)
Y	N	20	Data Analysis 2 (p. 203), Measures of Central Tendency and Variability (p. 182)
Y	N	21	Functions (p. 92)
Y	N	22	Data Analysis 2 (p. 203)
Y	N	23	Data Analysis 2 (p. 203), Measures of Central Tendency and Variability (p. 182)
Y	N	24	Translating between Words and Math (p. 44)
Y	N	25	Translating between Words and Math (p. 44), Solving Systems of Linear Equations (p. 59)
Y	N	26	Right Triangles and Basic Trigonometry (p. 249)
Y	N	27	Solving Systems of Linear Equations (p. 59), Lines (p. 73)
Y	Y	28	Parabolas (p. 128), Lines (p. 73), Working with Advanced Systems of Equations (p. 152)
Y	Y	29	Translating between Words and Math (p. 44), Solving Systems of Linear Equations (p. 59)
Y	Y	30	Translating between Words and Math (p. 44), Parabolas (p. 128)
Y	Y	31	Translating between Words and Math (p. 44), Parabolas (p. 128)

PSAT/NMSQT Test 2

Date taken: _____ # correct: _____ Score: _____

Calculator allowed?	Grid-in?	Question #	Techniques and concepts
N	N	1	Plugging In (p. 24), Algebraic Manipulation (p. 52)
N	N	2	Plugging In (p. 24), Algebraic Manipulation (p. 52)
N	N	3	Backsolving (p. 32), Working with Advanced Systems of Equations (p. 152)
N	N	4	Backsolving (p. 32), Quadratics (p. 114)
N	N	5	Solving Systems of Linear Equations (p. 59)
N	N	6	Lines (p. 73), Translating between Words and Math (p. 44)
N	N	7	Translating between Words and Math (p. 44), Percents and Percent Change (p. 161)
N	N	8	Lines (p. 73)
N	N	9	Translating between Words and Math (p. 44)
N	N	10	Translating between Words and Math (p. 44)
N	N	11	Angles, Triangles, and Polygons (p. 236)
N	N	12	Exponents and Exponential Functions (p. 104)
N	N	13	Parabolas (p. 128)
N	Y	14	Polynomials (p. 142)
N	Y	15	Translating between Words and Math (p. 44)
N	Y	16	Quadratics (p. 114), Polynomials (p. 142)
N	Y	17	Algebraic Manipulation (p. 52), Polynomials (p. 142), Binomial Squares and Difference of Two Squares (p. 123)
Y	N	1	Data Analysis 1 (p. 195)
Y	N	2	Translating between Words and Math (p. 44)
Y	N	3	Ratios and Proportionality (p. 171)
Y	N	4	Lines (p. 73)
Y	N	5	Data Analysis 2 (p. 203)
Y	N	6	Data Analysis 2 (p. 203)
Y	N	7	Ratios and Proportionality (p. 171)
Y	N	8	Data Analysis 1 (p. 195)
Y	N	9	Algebraic Manipulation (p. 52)
Y	N	10	Algebraic Manipulation (p. 52)
Y	N	11	Measures of Central Tendency and Variability (p. 182)
Y	N	12	Data Analysis 1 (p. 195), Percents and Percent Change (p. 161)
Y	N	13	Ratios and Proportionality (p. 171)
Y	N	14	Measures of Central Tendency and Variability (p. 182)
Y	N	15	Circles, Radians, and a Little More Trigonometry (p. 258)
Y	N	16	Data Analysis 1 (p. 195), Percents and Percent Change (p. 161)
Y	N	17	Data Analysis 1 (p. 195), Percents and Percent Change (p. 161)
Y	N	18	Data Analysis 1 (p. 195), Ratios and Proportionality (p. 171)
Y	N	19	Translating between Words and Math (p. 44)
Y	N	20	Polynomials (p. 142), Quadratics (p. 114)
Y	N	21	Plugging In (p. 24), Algebraic Manipulation (p. 52)
Y	N	22	Parabolas (p. 128)
Y	N	23	Translating between Words and Math (p. 44)
Y	N	24	Plugging In (p. 24), Working in Three Dimensions (p. 279)
Y	N	25	Exponents and Exponential Functions (p. 104)
Y	N	26	Functions (p. 92)
Y	N	27	Solving Systems of Linear Equations (p. 59)
Y	Y	28	Translating between Words and Math (p. 44)
Y	Y	29	Working with Advanced Systems of Equations (p. 152)
Y	Y	30	Translating between Words and Math (p. 44)
Y	Y	31	Translating between Words and Math (p. 44)

Thanks for reading!

I hope you've enjoyed working through this book as much as I enjoyed putting it together. If you have questions, or would just like to say hello, please reach out to me online. You can find me at PWNTestPrep.com or as username PWNTestPrep on Facebook or Twitter. I'd love to hear from you.

Cheers,

Mike

Made in United States
Orlando, FL
23 April 2024

46107262R00265